VEDIC INDIA

THE CONQUEST OF LANKA (ISLE OF CEYLON), BY THE HINDUS:—FINAL BATTLE BETWEEN RAMA WITH HIS ALLIES THE APES, AND RAVANA, THE DEMON-KING OF LANKA, WITH HIS ARMY OF BLACK RAKSHASAS (FIENDS).—*FROM THE RAMAYANA.*

THE STORY OF THE NATIONS

VEDIC INDIA

AS EMBODIED PRINCIPALLY IN THE RIG-VEDA

By

ZENAIDE A. RAGOZIN

GYAN

Published by

Gyan Publishing House
5, Ansari Road
Daryaganj, New Delhi-110002
Phone: 011-47034999, 9811692060
E-mail: books@gyanbooks.com

Distribution Network
gyanbooks.com
India, USA, Canada, UK, Australia, France

ISBN : 978-81-212-6701-4 (PB)
First Published, 1895

2nd Impression 2022

Printed at: Gyan Press, Delhi.

VEDIC INDIA
Author: ZENAIDE A. RAGOZIN

THE STORY OF THE NATIONS

VEDIC INDIA

AS EMBODIED PRINCIPALLY IN THE RIG-VEDA

BY

ZÉNAÏDE A. RAGOZIN

MEMBER OF THE "ROYAL ASIATIC SOCIETY OF GREAT BRITAIN AND IRELAND"; OF THE "AMERICAN ORIENTAL SOCIETY"; OF THE "SOCIÉTÉ ETHNOLOGIQUE" OF PARIS, ETC.

AUTHOR OF "THE STORY OF CHALDEA," "THE STORY OF ASSYRIA" "THE STORY OF MEDIA, BABYLON, AND PERSIA," ETC.

"He [Carlyle] says it is part of his creed that history is poetry, could we tell it right."—EMERSON.

"Da mihi, Domine, scire quod sciendum est."—"IMITATION OF CHRIST."
("*Grant that the knowledge I get may be the knowledge worth having.*"—
Matthew Arnold's version)

1899

PREFACE.

THE present volume, as originally planned, was to have included the post-vedic or Brahmanic period, and to have borne the title of *Story of Vedic and Brahmanic India.* The overwhelming mass of material, however, made it impossible to keep to the original plan, except at the cost of lucidity, completeness, interesting detail, and all the qualities that go to make a book with any claim to popularity. Nothing remained but to divide the subject-matter into the two halves into which it naturally separates, and leave the *Story of Brahmanic India* to the immediately following volume, which will embrace the results attained by the study of the Atharva-Veda, the Brâhmanas, the Upanishads, the Laws, and a synopsis at least of the great epics.

Z. A. R.

CLASSIFIED CONTENTS.

X.

XI.

ILLUSTRATIONS.

[1] From Hooker's *Himalayan Journals.*

[2] From Heber's *Indian Journal.* John Murray: London.

[3] From Lefmann's *Geschichte des alten Indiens.* Muller, Grote, & Baumgärtel: Berlin.

[1] From Lefmann's *Geschichte des alten Indiens.* Muller, Grote, & Baumgärtel: Berlin.

[2] From Rousselet's *India.* J. S. Virtue & Co.: London.

[3] From Hooker's *Himalayan Journals.*

[4] From Fergusson's *Tree and Serpent Worship.*

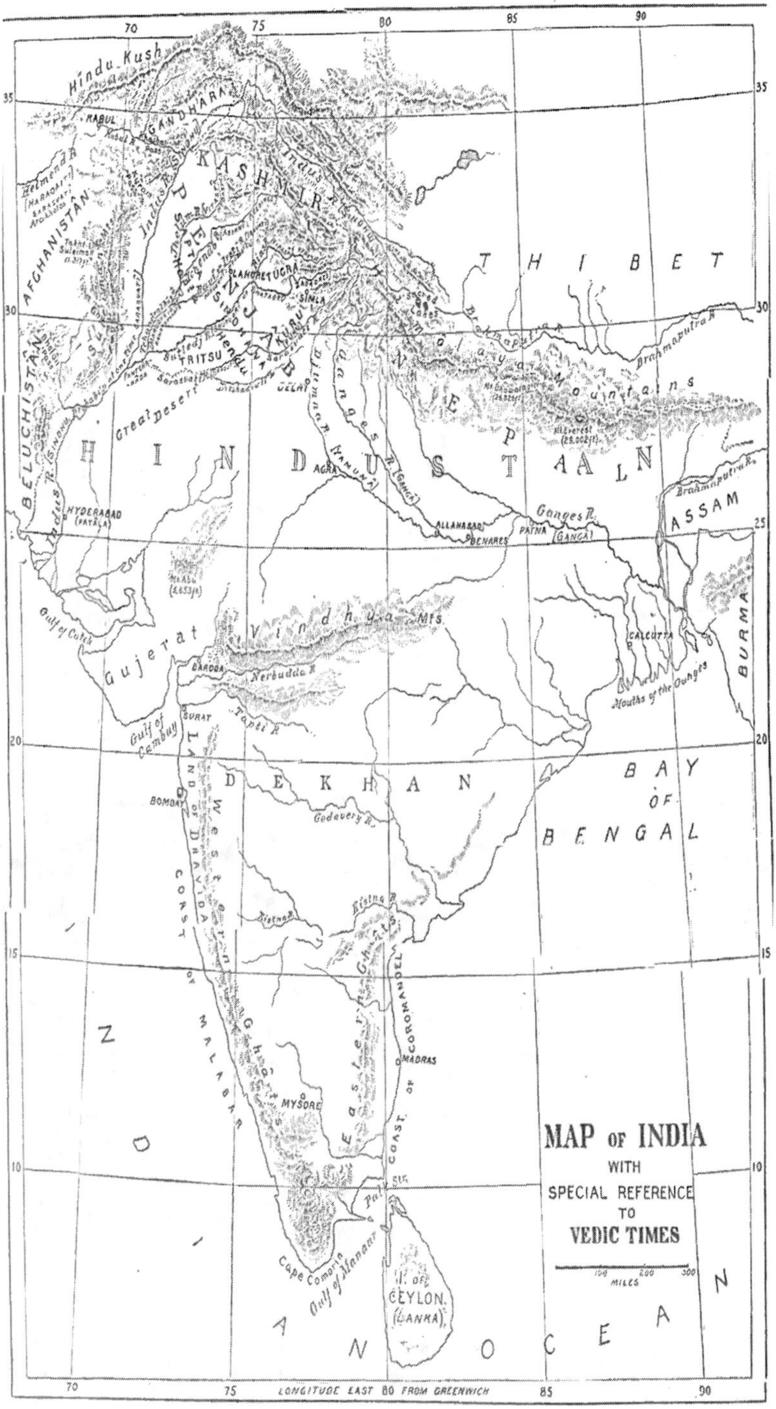

MAP OF INDIA WITH SPECIAL REFERENCE TO VEDIC TIMES

VEDIC INDIA.

CHAPTER I.

THE WONDERLAND OF THE EAST.

1. ". . . And I saw the blue, holy Ganges, the eternally radiant Himâlaya, the gigantic banyan-forests, with their wide leafy avenues, in which the clever elephants and the white-robed pilgrims peacefully wander ; strangely dreamy flowers gazed at me, with mysterious meaning ; golden, wondrous birds burst into glad, wild song ; glittering sunbeams and the sweetly silly laugh of apes teased me playfully ; and from distant pagodas came the pious strains of praying priests. . . ."[1]

ONLY a poet's day-dream ; but how telling each feature of the fanciful picture ; and how each quaintly worded sentence lifts you out of the screechy, glary reality of steam whistle and electric light, till the few perfect lines, like the richly patterned flying-rug of Oriental story, land you in the very midst of that world of mystery and enchantment, of gorgeousness and twilight, restful at once and exciting, which the name INDIA has always represented to the Western mind.

---

[1] Heine (prose works).

2. Another world; a world in itself. That is what India pre-eminently is, and therein lies the charm. The word has been said and repeated times out of number, yet seldom with a full realization of the literalness and extent of its truth. Not even an attentive survey of the map is sufficient to impress it on the mind anything but vaguely. Comparison and a few figures are needed to create a clear and definite perception. Nothing less will convince us that we have to do not with a country, but with a continent, and that we can no more speak of the climate, the people, the language of India, in the singular, than of those of Europe—which it very nearly equals in size. For a line drawn from the mouths of the Indus to those of the Ganges gives the distance between Bayonne (on the Atlantic coast by the Pyrenees) and Constantinople; while another, stretched from the northernmost angle, just where the Indus turns southwards, to Cape Comorin, equals in length that from Arkhangelsk on the White Sea to Naples. Nor would the latter line take in, by a great deal, the entire length of the Isle of Ceylon, which is itself not very much smaller than Ireland. Were we to include the extreme Northeast (Assam) and the Indian lands east of the mouths of the Ganges and the Indian Ocean —(Burma, Siam, etc.)—we should obtain even more imposing parallels; but we are not concerned in the present work with more than the great western peninsula,—nor, strictly speaking, with the whole of that; since the beginnings of political and social life and the spiritual development in religion and philosophy, that are to be our theme, were perfected almost en-

tirely within the northern half of it. This at various periods received divers expressive and significant native names, but it is found convenient, in our own time, to gather it under the general appellation of HINDUSTÂN, roughly bordered in the south by the VINDHYA MOUNTAINS, a chain of several ridges, which stretches across the continent and divides it into two pretty even halves. All that lies south of the Vindhyas is no less sweepingly designated as DEKHAN.[1] For general purposes this simple division, though somewhat arbitrary, does excellently well. Even after a careful survey of these proportions, it comes home to us with something of a shock when we are told that the population of India (the western peninsula alone) amounted in 1872, on the showing of the census taken that year, to over 250,000,000 (not including Burma), or about one sixth of the entire human race.

3. But extent and numbers do not alone, nor even chiefly, go to produce the imposing impression we associate with the name of India. It is the various features of its physical geography, and especially its mountain scenery, that make of it a vision of glory and majesty. Some countries, like Babylonia and Egypt, are what their rivers make them. India—physically and intellectually—is the creation of her HIMÂLAYA. Never was wall of separation more towering, more impassable, raised by nature. Scarcely an opening along the immense extent of this, the most compact and highest range in the world, yields a passage to either the rude winds or ruder peoples

[1] "South Country," corrupted from "Dakshinapâti."

of the North. For ages Erân and Turân might roam and fight, and settle and migrate, across and athwart that vast table-land of Central Asia, itself the loftiest terrace on the face of the earth—and all their random waves broke against the stupendous, impervious barrier.[1] Whatever conquering or civilizing swarms made their way at various times into the land of the Indus, reached it through a few gaps in the lesser chains of the Northwest, the HINDU-KUSH and the SULEÏMAN MOUNTAINS, the passes that became celebrated in history under the names of KHAÏBAR, KURAM, and BHOLÂN. The ruggedness and small number of even these breaks made such occurrences difficult and far between, while the waters which surrounded the lower half of the continent, being those of an ocean rather than of inland seas, for many centuries served purposes of isolation far more than of intercourse. So the great North beyond the mountains remained a region of mystery and awe, from which the oldest native peoples vaguely fancied their ancestors to have come down at some time, so that some of their descendant tribes were wont, even till very lately, to bury their dead with the feet turned northwards, ready for the journey to the old home, where they were to find their final rest.

4. Travellers agree that no mountain scenery—not that of the Alps, nor any in the Caucasus, the Andes, or other famed highlands of the world—is

[1] The level of this table-land is itself, on a rough average, 10,000 feet above the sea, and the Himâlaya wall rises 10,000 feet above that, not including such exceptional giants as Mt. Everest, Dhawalagiri and some others, whose peaks tower up to nearly as many feet more. (Mt. Everest–29,002 ft.)

I.—A RIDGE OF HIMÂLAYA.

remotely comparable in splendor and sublimity to what the Himâlaya offers in almost any of its valleys. A continuous ridge nearly double the height and five times the length of the Swiss-Italian Alps, with a mountain region depending on it, the size of Spain, Italy, and Greece put together in a row, and of which one small portion, Kashmir, looking like a nook nestled in the northwest corner, is as large as all Switzerland,—surely such a ridge gives scope to variety of scenery. We are told that it is not uncommon to stand on some point, from which the eye takes in a semicircular sweep of undulating or jagged snow-line with an iridescent, opal-like glory ever playing along it, and with peaks rising from it at intervals,—" heaven-kissing hills " indeed !—the least of which is several thousand feet higher than Mont Blanc, like pillars of ice supporting a dome of a blue so intense as to seem solid; while at your feet, forest-clothed and cut by valleys, stretch down the lower ridges, which descend, tier below tier, in four great terraces, into the hot plains of Lower Hindustân. If the spectator had taken his station on a summit of the northernmost—and highest — ridge, somewhere on the northwest boundary of Nepâl, the grandeur of the physical surroundings would be helped by that of memories and associations. He would there be at the very core and centre of the divine HIMÂVAT—to use the fine ancient name, which means " Abode of Winter," —the region to which the Aryan Hindu has, for ages well-nigh untold, looked with longing and reverence; for there, on the fairest and loftiest heights

2.—VIEW FROM AN ELEVATION OF 18,000 FEET OF THE EAST TOP OF KANCHANJANGA (S. E. BOUNDARY OF THIBET).

he knew, he placed the dwellings of his gods. There they were enthroned in serene and unattainable majesty; there they guarded the hidden storehouses of their choicest gifts to men: for there lay the mysterious caves of KUVERA, the god of wealth, the keeper of gold and silver and other precious ore, and of sparkling gems: there, snow-fed and pure, at a height of about 15,000 feet, slumber the sacred lakes, eternally mirroring in their still waters only the heavens and the mountain wilderness that cradles them; and there, too, cluster the springs of the great rivers, holiest of things,—the INDUS, and the SUTLEJ, and the GANGES, and the BRAHMAPUTRA with the most glorious name—"Son of God,"—that river ever had. To such regions, all wildness and mystery, all peace and silence, but for the rush of torrents and the music of winds and leaves, world-weary men and women, longing for the rest and beauty of passionless, eternal things, have come age after age, and still come, on long pilgrimages, frequently stretching into years of self-exile in rude forest-hermitages, to drink deep of solitude and meditation, and return, heart-healed and renovated, to the plains below; unless—and thrice blessed those to whom this is given,—they can stay among the mountains and woods, as in the vestibule to a higher world, stripped of all earthly clingings, desires and repinings, patiently and happily waiting for the final release. Thus the Himâlayas have ever been woven into the deepest spiritual life of the people whose physical destinies they helped to shape. They literally bounded their view in every sense, and what lay beyond was the great unknown North, where dwelt the UTTARA-KURA, the "remotest of men" —whether the spirits of the happy dead or a fabulous race enjoying a perpetual golden age of sinlessness and bliss, cannot be made out with absolute clearness—perhaps both.

5. A review of all the conditions and manifestations of India's physical life were needed to appreciate the entire range of the influence exercised by that stupendous chain, which, as it is the main feature of India's geography, is also the main agent of her prosperity. Its eternally renewed, inexhaustible treasury of snows is drawn on by the whole of Hindustân through the channels of its noble and numerous rivers, its true wealth-givers, which a thousand branching smaller ridges, dwindling down to mere slopes, direct into as many valleys, breaking the mass into a perfect, nicely graded and distributed network. Indeed, the privileged land gets more than its share of the great store; for some of its largest rivers—the Indus with its companion and later feeder, the Sutlej, and also the Brahmaputra—have their springs and a certain length of course on the northern side of the watershed, thus bringing to their own side much of the rainfall which should by rights go to the far thirstier plains of Tibet and Bokharia. Nor is it only by storing the moisture in its snowdrifts and glaciers, by nursing and feeding India's infant rivers, that the Himâlaya benefits the land it overshadows and protects: it also secures to it the largest rainfall in the world, as far as measured to this day, and regulates the "rainy

season," without which even such rivers would be insufficient to ensure the productiveness of a soil exposed to torrid heat during most of the year. Shut off from the cooling gales of the north, India depends entirely on that peculiar form of trade-winds known as the MONSOONS, or rather on the southwestern monsoon which sets in in June, laden with the accumulated vapors exhaled through many months by the vast expanse of the Indian Ocean, and condensed in mid-air into huge solid banks of clouds. These clouds travel with great swiftness northward across the atmosphere or hang over the land obscuring the light of day, according as the violence of the wind rages or abates, until they are dashed against the stony breast of the Himâlaya, whose elevation infinitely overtops the region of drifting vapors. Shattered with the shock, they discharge their torrents of rain as would a water-filled skin cut open by a rock against which it was hurled. The monsoon, being abruptly stopped as well as the clouds by the double Himâlayan wall, besides getting involved in the countless narrow valleys and winding passes of the intricate highlands which lead up to it, combined with the tremendous accumulation of electricity, produces the most terrific thunderstorms of the world—and thus the Himâlayas detain and confiscate for the exclusive benefit of their privileged land the supply of waters which cannot sail over their lofty heads, and for want of which the great Central Tableland is doomed to thirst and comparative barrenness. The consequence is that the average yearly rainfalls

3.—TAMBUR RIVER AT LOWEST LIMIT OF FIRS (HIMÂLAYA).

recorded for Hindustân, according to the most exact scientific calculations, give well-nigh incredible figures: 125 inches in that part of the Penjâb highlands which faces the southwest and is exposed to the full force of the monsoon; 220 inches in similarly situated parts of Bengal; while Assam, raised on a higher tier of the Himâlayan platforms, and backed more closely by the main ridge, claims the honor of owning the largest rainfall in the whole world: 481 inches.[1] Even this tremendous figure is surpassed in exceptional years; indeed it was all but doubled in the year 1861, for which 805 inches were shown, 366 inches having fallen in the single month of July. But this, again, is a visitation nothing short of a public calamity, as disastrous in its way as the opposite extreme.

6. It would seem that failing crops and dearth should be evils unknown in a country blessed with rivers so many and so noble, and so bountiful a sky. Unfortunately, the contrary is frequently the case, owing to the extremely uneven distribution of the rainfall, excessive in places and insufficient in others. Meteorological observations are carried on at 435 stations in British India. With such a number the distances between the stations cannot be very great; yet the figures returned vary as much as though they belonged to different climes. Thus in Penjâb, not a very extensive province, the average fall dwin-

[1] At the station of Cherra-Poonjee. All the figures and scientific data which, it is hoped, will lend this chapter an authority beyond that of a mere general description, are taken from that mine of precise knowledge, W. W. Hunter's *Indian Empire—Its People, History, and Products* (second edition, 1886).

dles from 125 inches to 7 and even 5, at the stations along the Indus, because they are protected by the Suleïman range, which breaks the force and direction of the monsoon, being attacked by it not in front, but sideways, and, so to speak, indirectly. The same causes—*i. e.*, the disposition of the various mountain ridges and spurs—interferes with the even distribution of rain all over Dekhan no less than Hindustân. Thus it is that the same year not infrequently brings both floods and drought, crops and whole villages being swept away in one province, while in another nothing has come up at all, with the uniform result—famine and frightful mortality—not to speak of such seasons when the southwestern monsoon itself, for some unknown reason, totally fails at the appointed time, or comes along feeble and unsteady. And as everything in India seems to affect an extravagant scale, so a year of famine, even local, is attended with horrors well-nigh indescribable, for with a population so dense, and, as a rule, so poor and improvident, the ravages of actual starvation are doubled by its attendant diseases, and deaths are numbered by hundreds of thousands. With truly Oriental resignation and apathy, the people look to the Government for relief, and, when the calamity gets beyond the possibility of help, die without a word, as they stand, or sit, or lie. The annals of India from the time it came under British rule show a string of famines, separated by intervals of no more than from three to eight years, seldom ten, and lasting quite frequently over a year, even as long as three years. Some are limited to particular provinces, but only too many are recorded as general.

7. Of these, the most widely spread and most prolonged that India ever experienced, was that of 1876–78. The southwest monsoon failed in 1875, and again in 1876; and in this latter year the north-east monsoon,—which sets in in October, and is at best a poor resource, coming, as it does, not across an ocean but an inland waste, and being, moreover, intercepted by the Himâlaya,—proved even less efficient than usual. The main crops had perished in the drought of 1875, and this disappointment finished the rest. Nor did the summer of 1877 bring relief, for the southwest monsoon failed for the third time, and though the autumn monsoon, for a wonder, did arrive laden with some goodly showers, the curse was not removed from the land until a normal rainfall once more visited it in June, 1878. All these years the people died—of starvation, of cholera, of hunger-fevers; mortality rose to forty per cent. above the usual rates, and as the number of births greatly diminished at the same time, and the normal proportions were not restored until 1880, the total of the population was found in this year to have actually decreased during the last four years, instead of increasing at a moderate but steady rate, as is the case wherever the normal law of life-statistics is undisturbed and the number of births exceeds that of deaths. To give one palpable illustration of the ghastly phenomenon, we will borrow the record for the single province of Madras from a contemporary work of the highest authority and reliability[1]:

[1] W. W. Hunter's, *The Indian Empire*, etc.

"In 1876, when famine, with its companion, cholera, was already beginning to be felt, the births registered in Madras numbered 632,113, and the deaths 680,381. In 1877, the year of famine, the births fell to 477,447, while the deaths rose to 1,556,312. In 1878 the results of the famine showed themselves by a still further reduction of the births to 348,346, and by the still high number of 810,921 deaths. In 1879 the births recovered to 476,307, still below the average, and the deaths diminished to 548,158. These figures are only approximate, but they serve to show how long the results of famine are to be traced in the vital statistics of a people."

To complete this appalling picture, it may be mentioned that the British Government spent, in famine relief, during the three tragic years, 1876–78, 11,000,000 pounds sterling = 55,000,000 dollars, in actual cash out of pocket, not including the negative expense in loss of revenue. In September, 1877, 2,600,000 persons were supported by the Government in Madras alone; of these, a few over 600,000 were nominally employed on works, and nearly two millions were gratuitously fed. It is asserted that this last tremendous visitation has been a lesson to the British Government that will not fail to bear beneficent fruits, in the shape of more numerous and better means of communication, an increase in the acreage under cultivation, for which there is, fortunately, still a large margin, and various lesser local measures,—a combination which is to make up for the unequal distribution of the rainfall by a prompter and more even exchange and distribution of the earth's products between the different provinces.

8. The Himâlayas, with their immense sweep and elevation—reaching, in the higher edges, an average of 19,000 feet, a height equal to the lower half of the atmosphere, are apt to monopolize one's powers

of attention, and to fire the imagination to the exclusion of the many other chains of mountains that cut up the Indian continent into numerous larger and smaller divisions. Yet some of them are very considerable, and, on a lesser scale, influence the climate and conditions of life of their respective regions much in the same way that the giant-ridge of the north does those of the entire continent. After the fourth and lowest of the Himâlayan terraces has sloped down into the low, hot riverland which, with only a slight swelling to serve as watershed between the systems of the Indus and the Ganges, stretches across from sea to sea, from the mouth of one of these royal rivers to that of the other, forming a wide belt of plain, the ground slopes up again, southward, into the VINDHYA range, which, broken up into a number of confused chains and spurs, interposes its broad wild mountain belt between the more properly continental Hindustân and the tapering, peninsular Dekhan. Although of a more—or rather less—than moderate elevation (averaging from 1500 to 4000 feet, with no peak to surpass or even equal the 5650 feet of MT. ABU at its western end), this intricate system of "hills," with its exuberant growth of forest and jungle, was very difficult of access until pierced with roads and railways by European engineering, forming almost as effective a barrier between the northern and southern halves of the continent, as the Himâlayas themselves between the whole of India and the rest of the world, and during long ages kept the two separate in race, language, and culture.

4.—A VIEW IN DEKHAN; THE GHÂTS.

9. A bird's-eye view, embracing the whole of Dekhan, would show it to be a roughly outlined triangular table-land, raised from one to three thousand feet above the sea on three massive buttresses of which the broad Vindhya ridge is one, covering the base of the reversed triangle, while the sides are represented by two chains of unequal height, respectively named WESTERN and EASTERN GHÂTS. This name, meaning "landing stairs," is particularly appropriate to the western chain, which rises in serrated and precipitous rocky steeps almost from the very sea, only in places receding from the shore sufficiently to leave a narrow strip of cultivable and habitable land. On such a strip the wealthy and magnificent city of Bombay is built, very much like the Phœnician cities of yore, the Ghâts stretching their protecting wall behind them just as the Lebanon did behind Tyre and Sidon, the sea-queens of Canaan. Like the Lebanon, too, they slope inland, directing the course of all the rivers of Dekhan from west to east. In scenery they are much sterner and grander than the Vindhya range, which they, moreover, surpass in elevation, their average height being uniformly about 3000 feet along the coast, with abrupt peaks reaching 4700 feet, and nearly the double of that in the considerably upheaved southern angle of the peninsula, where they form a sort of knot, joining the southern extremity of the Eastern Ghâts. This latter range is really not a continuous mountain chain at all, but rather a series of inconsiderable spurs and hills, interrupted at frequent intervals by broad gaps, through which the rivers, fed by the

5.—A VIEW IN THE MYSORE (DEKHAN).

drainage of the Western Ghâts, flow easily and peaceably to the sea, known, all too modestly considering its size, as the Bay of Bengal.

10. There was a time when the whole of Southern India or Dekhan was "buried under forests"; such is the description in which all ancient poets agree. It would be vastly exaggerated in the present day, for fire and the axe of the husbandman, the timber cutter, the charcoal burner, have been at work unchecked through some thirty centuries and have revelled in wanton destruction after operating the necessary clearing. The most ruthless and formidable foes of the old virgin forests are the nomadic tribes, chips of the ancient aboriginal stock, which have escaped the influences of the Aryan immigration and conquest, and lead even now, in their mountain fastnesses, the same more than half savage existence which was theirs when the first Aryan settlers descended into the valleys of the Indus. These tribes have a habit of stopping every year in their perpetual wanderings and camping just long enough to raise a crop of rice, cotton, or millet, or all three, in any spot of their native primeval forest where the proper season may find them. They go to work after a rude and reckless fashion which sets before us the most primitive form of agriculture followed by the human race at the very dawn of invention. First of all they burn down a patch of forest, regardless of the size and age of its most venerable giants, and as they do not care for the extent of the damage, and certainly do not attempt to limit the action of the fire, it usually runs wild and devours many square

miles in addition to the clearing actually wanted for cultivation. Then comes the breaking up of the soil thus summarily reclaimed, for which purpose almost any implement seems good enough. It is only a few tribes that know the use of a rough sort of antediluvian plough. Most of them content themselves with a bill-hook, a spade, or a hoe pick; nay, a common stick sometimes is sufficient to scratch the surface of the soil with—which is all that is needed; the seed is then laid in the shallow furrow, sometimes covered up and sometimes not, and the tillers sit down confidently to await results. Now a rich virgin soil, fertilized with fresh ashes, has quite enough of such treatment and a tropical rainfall to yield a return from thirty- to fifty-fold. Not infrequently several crops are raised simultaneously and on the same patch, by the simple process of throwing rice, Indian corn, millet, oil seeds, and cotton into the ground together, and gathering the crops successively as each ripens in its own season. No wonder that the nomads prefer such easy and remunerative culture to the laborious routine of regular farm work on partially exhausted soil. They do sometimes attempt to get a crop off the same clearing two or even three years in succession, but these experiments seem only to confirm them in their own easier and more attractive method.

11. It is only of late years that these lawless proceedings have encountered some resistance. It is a fact scientifically established that the wholesale destruction of forests is attended by baleful results to the country where it takes place, the worst of

which are a perceptible change of climate and decrease in the average of the rainfall. The underground moisture attracted by the roots which it feeds, being deprived of the protecting shade, dries up and evaporates; the air necessarily becomes drier, and colder or hotter, according to the latitude, from exposure to the severe northern blasts or the scorching southern sun, while, the large mass of moist emanations which a forest contributes towards the formation of clouds being cut off, the denuded district no longer supplies its own rain, but entirely depends on passing clouds and storms. These results would be particularly fatal in tropical India, living under continual dread of droughts, not to speak of the immediate pecuniary loss represented by the annual destruction of thousands of gigantic valuable timber-trees. This loss is greatly increased when we remember that many tropical trees bring a considerable income without being cut down; these are the gum-trees, with their rich yield of caoutchouc, lac, and other gums.[1] The British Government at last awoke to the absolute necessity of taking vigorous measures for the preservation of the forests still in existence and, as far as possible, the gradual restocking of those hopelessly thinned or partially destroyed. Twelve million acres of forest land are now "reserved," *i. e.*, managed as state property by

---

[1] Lac is not exactly a gum, although it looks and is counted as one. It is the resinous secretion of an insect, which forms abundant incrustations around the branches of various trees. But without the trees we should not have the gum; so it is as much an article of forest wealth as the real vegetable gums.

special state officers; in these reservations, which are carefully surveyed, nomadic cultivation and cattle-grazing are strictly forbidden, timber-cutting is limited by several regulations, and the exuberant growth of tropical creepers is ruthlessly cut down. Even the "open" forests are subjected to some control, and large patches of forest land have been turned into nurseries, to grow the finest kinds of timber-trees.

12. Fortunately such is the bountiful productiveness of the soil, and so great was the original wealth of forest vegetation, that these measures, although so belated, came in time to save, in spite of the depredations carried on through thousands of years, a mass of timber and woodland such as few spots on earth can match or even emulate. Virgin forests are plentiful even now, and cover vast mountain regions, in the Vindhya belt of highlands, and especially in the wildernesses of the Western Ghâts, of which the most conspicuous feature is the lordly teak, unanimously voted "king of forests" and "prince of timber." It is an indigenous variety of oak, which thrives best at a height of from three to four thousand feet, and grows in continuous masses, absorbing the nourishment of the soil so as not to allow any other tree or plant to come up in its domain. The only rival of the teak in size and quality of timber is the pine—or, more correctly, larch of the Western Himâlayas, admiringly named "tree of the gods," *dêva dâru* (anglicized into "deodar"). It is even more aspiring than the teak, and does not reach its full grandeur and beauty lower than six thousand

feet above the sea; but in that elevated region a trunk of from twenty to twenty-five feet in circumference is no rarity, and such is the height to which the tree shoots up, that with this thickness of trunk, it gives the impression of slimness. It was as famous in its way as the cedars of Lebanon, and ancient writers tell us that Alexander the Great used it to build his fleet. But the Himâlaya has, over the Lebanon, the advantage of being far out of the way of armies and conquests, and therefore still wears its royal forest crown unimpaired, while the Lebanon stands almost denuded, and only an occasional solitary tree tells of its former glory.

13. But, valuable and majestic as these two forest kings are, they are far eclipsed, both in beauty and dimensions, by a native tree, which may be considered the most characteristic of Indian vegetation. It belongs to the family of fig-trees, to which the soil and climate of India are so congenial that it is represented, in different parts of the continent, by no less than a hundred and five varieties. This particular variety, specially known as "*Indian* fig-tree" (*Ficus Indica*), surely may claim to be admired as the paragon not only of its own species, but of all vegetation without exception. It takes so influential and prominent a place in the life, both physical and moral, of India, and is moreover such a marvel of nature, that a description of it is not out of place even in a necessarily brief sketch, and we may as well borrow that given by Lassen in his monumental work[1]:

[1] Chr. Lassen's *Indische Alterthumskunde*, 2d ed., vol. i., pp. 301 ff.

6.—A BANYAN GROVE (SHOWING THE PARENT TRUNK) SHELTERING A SETTLEMENT OF HINDU FANATICS PRACTISING ASCETIC AUSTERITY.

"The *Ficus Indica* is probably the most astounding piece of vegetation on the face of our earth. From one single root it produces a vast green temple of many halls, with cool, shady bowers impervious to the light, and seems created expressly and exclusively for the purpose of supplying shelterless primeval humanity with ready-made dwellings. For neither is its wood of much use, nor are its fruits eatable for man, and if it inspires the Hindus and their neighbors with a profound veneration, it is owing to the surpassing marvel of its well-nigh preternatural growth, its indestructible duration and everlasting self-renewal; to which traits the mysterious gloom of its galleries and avenues adds not a little, yielding a most grateful retreat from the torrid summer heat. The trunk of the tree, at a moderate height from the ground, branches out into several stout limbs which stretch from it horizontally; from these, slender shoots—the so-called "air-roots"—grow downwards until they reach the ground, where they take root, whereupon they increase in thickness and become strong supports for the mother-limb. The central trunk repeats the branching out process at a greater height, and the second circle of limbs in its turn sends down a number of air-roots which form an outer circle of props or pillars. As the central trunk increases in height, it goes on producing tier upon tier of horizontal limbs, and these add row after row to the outer circle of pillars, not indeed with perfect regularity, but so as to form a grove of leafy halls and verdant galleries multiplying *ad infinitum*. For this evolution is carried on on a gigantic scale. The highest tier of horizontal limbs is said to grow sometimes at an elevation of two hundred feet from the ground, and the whole structure is crowned with the dome of verdure in which the central trunk finally culminates. The leaves, which grow very close together, are five inches long by three and a half broad, and their fine green color pleasantly contrasts with the small red figs, which, however, are not eaten by men."

Such is the tree, more generally known under its popular name of *banyan* than under the scientific one of *Ficus Indica*,[1] the tree which, together

---

[1] This name is supposed to come from the fact that the tree was carried westward by Hindu tradesmen called *banyans*. This accounts for its being found in places along the Persian Gulf, in parts

with the Ganges and the Himâlaya, completes the picture of India as evoked in a few apt strokes the poet's fancy (see p. 1). To the elephants that wander majestically among its shady walks, and the apes that laugh and gambol in its airy galleries, we must add the noisy parrots and other birds of no less flaming plumage, but softer voice,—and to these numerous and playful denizens the berries or small figs disdained by men yield grateful and sufficient food. It is needless to mention that these trees grow singly, not in forests—since one evidently is in itself if not a forest, at least a grove of considerable size. *How* large, indeed, can scarcely be realized without the help of a few figures. Fortunately many have been accurately measured, and several have attained historical celebrity. Thus the central trunk of one handsome banyan-tree near Madras is known to have been twenty-eight feet in diameter, and to have been surrounded by a first circle of twenty-seven secondary trunks, each about eleven feet in diameter, and from thirty to fifty feet in height, and after that by almost innumerable others, of decreasing stoutness. The largest known banyan tree had over thirteen hundred large trunks, and three thousand smaller ones. Armies of six or seven thousand men have frequently been encamped in its bowers, and it was seen afar as a solitary green hillock, until a violent hurricane half destroyed it in 1783. Besides which, being situated on an island in

---

of Arabia (Yemen), and even of Africa, although its native land is emphatically the Indian Continent, where it thrives in all provinces, except the table-land of Dekhan.

the Nerbudda, the river has from time to time carried away large slices of its domain, till it is now

7.—CLASPING ROOTS OF THE WIGHTIA (IN THE HIMÂLAYAN FORESTS).

reduced to a skeleton of its former glory. What may be its age, no one can tell. Five hundred years are historically recorded. But these trees may get to be thousands of years old for aught we can know or prove. For since each new trunk, after it has become firmly rooted and has reached a certain average of thickness, inherits the parent trunk's capacity of branching out into horizontal limbs which in their turn drop root-tendrils into the ground, and consequently absorb the nourishment of ever new soil, there is practically no reason why the multiplying process should ever stop. It is no wonder that almost every village in Hindustân has a banyan-tree which it holds as sacred as a sanctuary.

14. The companions of Alexander who enthusiastically admired the banyan-tree and gave it its name of "Indian fig-tree," leave it uncertain whether they included under that name another variety, which has obtained an even greater renown and importance from the fact that from the oldest times it has been, as it still is, the sacred tree of Indian religions. This is the *Ficus Religiosa*, very well known under its pretty native and popular names of *Ashvattha* and *Pippala*. It is frequently planted next to a banyan so as to have them mix their foliage and stems, from a superstitious notion that they are of different sex and their growing together is an emblem of marriage. The contrast between the large, massive leaves of the banyan, and the light, brilliant, continually vibrating foliage of the pippala is striking and grateful to the eye. The pippala does not reach the stupendous dimensions that the banyan does, nor are its trunks as numerous. But it has a way, wherever a seed is accidentally dropped on top of another tree—say a palm

tree—or a building, to sink several fibrous shoots through the air down into the ground, and thus in time, when these shoots have thickened and hardened into trunks, to entirely encompass tree or building, turning it into a most picturesque and at first sight puzzling object. Although the ashvattha alone is professedly held sacred, it is a crime to destroy or injure either of the two; both indifferently shelter in their verdant halls altars and images of gods, as well as the performance of sacrifices and the pious contemplations of holy hermits. Still, where neither banyan nor pippala is familiar, villagers usually pay a certain homage to the largest and oldest tree within their radius, no matter of what kind; and it is not the native trees alone which thrive and expand under that wonderful sky, but those which India shares with Europe and other moderate climes also attain dimensions unheard of elsewhere. Thus Anquetil Duperron mentions having on one of his tramps through the Dekhan enjoyed a noonday rest under an elm tree which could cover over six hundred persons with its shade, and adds:

> "One often meets in India these trees, under whose shade travellers while away the hottest time of the day. They cook there such provisions as they carry with them, and drink the water of the ponds near which these trees are planted; you see there sellers of fried rice and fruits in a small way, and crowds of men and horses from various parts of the country.

15. The same exuberance confronts us in almost any specimen of India's vegetation. Plants that grow elsewhere and in India also are sure to reach here extraordinary size and to be amazingly productive. Thus the bamboo, so plentiful in China and

8.—LIVING BRIDGE (HIMÂLAYAN FOREST.)

other countries of Eastern Asia, attains in India a height of sixty feet, and has such enormous leaves that a herd of elephants can lie concealed in a bamboo plantation. The banana, which grows wild in parts of India and thrives under the lightest cultivation all over the continent, seems to bear its luscious, nutritious fruits in even greater abundance and to be more prolific of new shoots from the same root than in other apparently as favored climes. When, at the end of the year, the long bearing stalk has been eased of its golden burden and cut down at the ground, some 180 new stalks spring up in its stead, and the yearly amount of fruit produced by a plantation of these plants is 133 times that of the same space planted in wheat.[1] Nor is the bread-fruit tree wanting in this array of tropical vegetable treasures, and as to palms, no less than forty-two varieties wave their graceful crowns over the bewitching landscapes of both Hindustân and Dekhan, and of these most are a source of wealth even more than ornament. Chief among them of course comes the cocoa-palm, which, with the manifold uses which every part of it, from fruit to root, is made to serve, supplies well-nigh all the necessaries of life to many an island where it is the natives' only resource, while in this thrice blessed land it is only one of a host. In the

[1] The banana is the same fruit as the *pisang* of the Isle of Java and the Malayan Islands. It has several local Indian names, but the scientific one, adopted in botany, is *Musa Sapientum*. It is probable that it forms a staple article of the very spare and wholly vegetable diet of Indian pilgrims and hermits, as remarked already by ancient Greek and Latin writers; whence the name: *Musa Sapientum*—"Musa of the Sages."

interior of the Isle of Ceylon is a forest of cocoa-palms numbering *eleven millions* of trees, while in Dekhan, along the western coast alone, duty was paid years ago on three millions. When to all these we add cotton, the sugar-cane, and the tea-plant, all three natives of India, besides the imported cinchona (quinine-tree) and all the native gums, spices, and varieties of grains, it really seems as though this chosen land had more than its share of the good things of creation, and it becomes more and more evident that with such a variety of resources it ought not to suffer so dreadfully even from protracted droughts, and that increase of management and improved communications are all that is wanted to put an end forever to such horrors as the famine of 1876–78.[1]

---

[1] This is how Herodotus describes the cotton plant in his chapter on India. " There are trees which grow wild there, the fruit whereof is a wool exceeding in beauty and goodness that of sheep. The natives make their clothes of this tree-wool." Of this same " tree-wool " (the exact counterpart, by the way, of the German "*Baumwolle*," cotton), they also made paper to write on, as was known to the Greeks of Alexander's time.—The sugar-cane is so much a native of India that we still call its produce by its Sanskrit name, *sharkara*, later *sakkara*, but slightly corrupted in our European languages: Latin *saccharum*, Slavic *sakhar*, German *zucker*, Italian *zucchero*, Spanish *azúcar*, French *sucre*, English *sugar*—not to mention Arabic *sukkar* and Persian *shakar*. Even the word " candy"—originally crystallized, transparent sugar, *sucre candi*—is only a corruption of the Sanskrit " *khanda*," a name designating the same article. We find no trace of a time when the art of manufacturing molasses and sugar by boiling down and clarifying the sap was unknown in India, although of course the use of the plant must have begun with chewing and sucking chunks of the cane, as is still done by the natives of the Indian Islands—and by children in the Southern American States and South

16. In so necessarily cursory a sketch of India's physical features and products, we are forced to ignore a vast number of valuable items of her vegetable wealth, and may scarcely pause to mention even such important plants as rice and indigo. The immense variety of her vegetation will be inferred from the fact that, besides the distinctly tropical and indigenous plants which have just been briefly touched upon and a great many more, there is scarcely a variety of fruit-tree, timber-tree, food plant, or ornamental plant that Europe and the temperate regions of Asia can boast, but makes its home in India and thrives there. The cause of such extraordinary exuberance is not far to seek: it lies in the great variety of climates which in India range through the entire scale from hottest tropical to moderately warm and even cold. For latitude ensures uniformity of climate only if the land be flat and otherwise uniformly conditioned. A mountainous country can enclose many climes, with their respective vegetations, within a small compass, for the average temperature is lowered regularly and perceptibly—

America.—That tea should be a native of India, not of China, will probably be a surprise to many; yet it grows wild in Assam where it sometimes reaches the size of a large tree and which is the real home of the plant, whence it was introduced into China where there is a quaint legend about it: a very studious and philosophical young prince grudged nature the hours of rest, considering them wasted, stolen from his beloved studies and meditations. One night he got into such a rage at his wretched inability to conquer the numbness which all his efforts could not prevent from sealing his eyes in sleep, that he cut off his eyelids and threw them on the earth—where they struck roots and grew into the tea-plant, that foe and antidote of the sleepy poppy.

one degree to an ascent of from 350 to 500 feet—in proportion as the elevation increases; so that a very high range is divided into many narrow belts or zones, which answer, as to climate and productions, to whole countries of entirely different latitudes. The position of the various mountain walls and ridges, by catching and directing or entirely intercepting this or that wind, and the greater or lesser vicinity of the sea, also contribute to form patches of local climate, and India, being cut up in every direction by innumerable ridges and spurs, ranging from moderate hills to the highest solid chain in the world, abounds in these, so that a complete review of her vegetation would really comprise nearly everything that grows on the face of the earth, from the distinctively tropical flora to the oak forests which clothe the first tier of the Himâlayan terraces, and the white-barked northern birch, which marks, as with a sparse, uncertain fringe, the extreme limit of mountain vegetation.

17. The same variety, and for the same reasons, marks the animal creation or fauna of the Indian Continent, both wild and domestic. Of the latter some animals appear to be indigenous, for instance the dog, which still roves wild in packs all over the Dekhan and portions of Hindustân. There are, too, some particularly fine breeds of hunting dogs, large powerful animals, which have been a boast of India from very old times, and so valuable as to have figured on lists of tribute and royal presents, almost like elephants. Herodotus tells us of a Persian satrap of Babylon under the Akhæmenian kings who

kept so many of these hounds, that "four large villages of the plain were exempt from all other charges on condition of finding them in food." It is thought that a very handsome dog, portrayed together with his groom on a terra-cotta tablet found in Babylon may be a specimen of this Indian breed. Such too, no doubt, were the dogs presented to Alexander, which were said to fight lions. Too well known to be more than mentioned is the elephant, the prince of the Indian animal world, as well as the fact that there are two varieties, one native to Africa and the other to India. But to many readers it will be an unfamiliar and amusing detail of rural economy that throughout the Himâlayan highlands the favorite beasts of burden are—sheep and cows! both, however, of a peculiar local breed fitted by nature for the work. The sheep are large and strong, and are driven, loaded with bags, to the marts on the outskirts of the ranges towards the plains, where in addition to their burden—generally borax—they bring their own wool to market, being shorn of which, they return to their mountain pastures with a load of grain or salt. The cow, on the contrary, is a small variety, the *yák*, which is also useful in a double capacity, for it is the happy owner of a particularly fine and bushy tail, which is manufactured into a rare and highly prized lace-like texture. It is a serviceable little animal, sure-footed and enduring, which safely conveys even heavy loads up the steepest paths and through the roughest gorges. It is a comfort to think that this patient servant of man at least is well cared for and does not end her life in the

37 .—TAME LEOPARDS TRAINED FOR HUNTING—READY FOR THE CHASE.

shambles, the cow being the one sacred animal of India, inviolable in life and limb, and never on any account used not only for food, but even for sacrifice. Besides, both custom and religion, in accordance with the climate and the abundance of choice and varied vegetable food, have long discouraged the practice of eating meat, and even the sacrifices ceased at an early stage of the country's history to consist of bloody offerings. For this reason, one great object of raising and keeping cattle almost vanishes out of sight in India, and domestic animals are chiefly valued for their milk, their wool, and their services.

18. Whenever we think of wild animals in connection with India, the tiger first presents himself to our mind. And well he may, for he is the most distinctively national beast, and there is no doubt whatever that Hindustân is his original home, whence he migrated into other parts of Asia, both east and west. Low hot plains, with tangled jungles to hide in, are his realm; hence it is that the royal tiger of Bengal is the handsomest, fiercest, and altogether the most representative specimen of the race. The lion was once his rival. The ancient poetry of India bears ample witness to the fact; indeed it is he, and not his more wily and bloodthirsty cousin, who is called "the king of beasts." Alexander the Great still found lions in Penjâb, where he hunted them with the hounds that were presented to him for the purpose. But the gradually changing conditions of life, the advance of civilization with the attendant destruction of the noble forests where he loved to

range, gradually made existence impossible to him, until now there are only a few lion-families left in one particular forest tract in the peninsula of Gujerât where they are strictly preserved by the Government. Not so the tiger. Nothing repressed him, and though, no doubt, the jungles of Bengal were his first and favorite haunt, he spread westward as fast as the lion retreated, for the two never have been known to dwell within hearing or meeting distance of each other. As long as he has plenty of antelopes, deer, and wild hogs to feast upon he is not a very objectionable neighbor; in fact he is, in such districts, to some extent a protector of the native agriculturist, as all those animals are exceedingly destructive to crops. When he is reduced to domestic cattle, his vicinity is of course troublesome and ruinous; but nothing can express the horror of having "a man-eater" in the district, *i. e.*, a tiger, generally an old one, which has once tasted human flesh and blood, and thenceforth, from a hideous peculiarity of his nature, will not satiate his hunger with any other prey. Tigers at all times, unlike the lion and most beasts of prey, kill more victims than they need for food, and this instinct of sheer killing seems to grow fiercer and fiercer in a man-eater. Without referring to mere sportsmen's reports, which may be suspected of romance and partiality, there are the dry statistic records with such figures as these: 108 persons killed in one place by a single tiger in three years; an average of about 80 a year destroyed by another in the course of several years; thirteen villages abandoned and 250 acres of rich paying land thrown out of cultivation from terror of a third; and a fourth, as lately as 1869, killing 127 people and stopping a public road for many weeks, until an English sportsman killed him. The aggregate of these isolated cases sums up tremendously. Thus, for the single year of 1877, we have a total of 819 persons and 16,137 head of cattle killed by tigers, and for 1882—895 persons and 16,517 cattle—which reports seem to establish an appalling average. It is some satisfaction to place to the credit side of the balance, for 1877, 1579 tigers killed by native hunters, and 1726 for 1882, which, however, cost the Government respectively £3777 and £4800 in rewards. Yet, incredible as it may appear, the loss of life from tigers and other wild beasts is as nothing compared to that caused by snakes. The serpent tribe is perhaps more numerous in India than in any other country, and the most poisonous varieties seem to have congregated there. The openness of the dwellings imperatively demanded by the climate, and the vast numbers of people sleeping in the open air, in groves, forests, gardens, etc. give them chances of which they make but too good use, swarming in the gardens and seeking shelter in the houses during the rainy season. As a consequence, death from snakebite almost equals an epidemic. In that same year of 1877, 16,777 human victims perished by this means, although £811 reward were paid for the destruction of 127,295 snakes, while in 1882, 19,519 persons were reported to have been killed by snakes as compared with 2606 by tigers, leopards, wolves, and all other wild beasts together. That year £1487 were paid in

IO. PRIMEVAL FOREST ; MONKEYS SCARED BY A LARGE SNAKE.

rewards for the destruction of 322,421 venomous reptiles.

19. The insect world is not less profusely represented than the other divisions of animated creation, and though it successfully does its best to make life disagreeable to those who have not sufficient wealth to protect themselves by costly and ingenious devices, it seems ridiculous to mention the tiny nuisance in one breath with the huge standing disaster the country possesses in its tigers and snakes. Besides, there are two insects which in almost any land would be considered a sufficient source of income, and which here step in as an incidental and secondary resource. They are the insect that produces the valuable and inimitable lac-dye, and especially the silk-worm. This latter, like the tea plant, we are apt to hold as originally the exclusive property of China, and imported thence into every country where it is raised. Yet it appears that it is as much an indigenous native of India as of China, like several other products, and, among them, that most vital one—rice. The mulberry tree, of course, is cultivated in connection with the silk industry, but by no means universally, as there are many varieties of the worm which content themselves with other plants. That which feeds on the leaves of the ashvattha (*Ficus Religiosa*) is called *dêva* (divine), on account of the sacredness of the tree, and very highly prized — nor altogether on superstitious grounds, for the thread it spins is said to be quite equal, if not superior, to that of the mulberry worm, both in glossy beauty and flexible strength; perhaps

11. LANDSCAPE AT THE FOOT OF THE VINDHYA.

this may be the effect of a gum-like substance contained in the sap of both this tree and the banyan, and which in both frequently exudes from the bark, thickens into a kind of caoutchouc, and is gathered for sale and use.

20. Even so brief and cursory a review of India's physical traits and resources would be incomplete without some mention of the mineral wealth which, for ages, has been pre-eminently associated with the name. To say "India" was to evoke visions of gold, diamonds, pearls, and all manner of precious stones. These visions, to be just, were made more than plausible by the samples which reached the west from time to time in the form of treasures of untold variety and value, either in the regular ways of trade, from the Phœnicians down, or by that shorter road of wholesale robbery which men call conquest; and indeed, but for the glamour of such visions and the covetousness they bred, India might not have seen most of the nations of Europe fight for a place on her soil, from a mere foothold to whole realms, and might have remained free from invasion and foreign rule. Yet, strangely enough, it now turns out that her chief and real mineral worth lies not so much in the gold and precious stones whose glitter fascinated the nations far and near, as in the less showy but far more permanently useful and inexhaustible minerals and ores: the coal fields which underlie most of central Dekhan; the natural petroleum wells of Penjâb, Assam, and Burma; the salt which both sea and inland salt lakes yield abundantly by evaporation, and which in

the northeast of Penjâb is quarried like any stone from a range of solid salt cliffs, unrivalled for purity and extent; the saltpetre which covers immense surfaces of the soil in the upper valleys of the Ganges; the iron which is found in almost all parts of the continent; the rich copper mines of the lower Himâlayas,—not to speak of various quarries—building stone, marble, slate, etc. As for gold, although India has always distinctly ranked as a gold-producing country, and many of her rivers have been known from oldest times to carry gold, and gold-washing has always been going on in a small way here and there and everywhere, so that the metal probably exists in many places, and very possibly in large quantities, yet the industry of gold-seeking does not appear to thrive; it is carried on in a desultory, unbusinesslike manner which yields but meagre returns. Silver is no longer found anywhere in the country, and the famed diamonds of Golconda are nothing nowadays but a legendary name, nor are other gems, with the exception, perhaps, of carnelian, onyx, agate, and lapis lazuli, found in much greater abundance; either the deposits are exhausted, or, more probably, the enormous quantities which came out of the country in the way of presents, trade, and conquest, and those which still partly fill the treasuries of native princes and temples, were due to accumulation through the many, many centuries of India's seclusion, before the land became known and open to other nations.

21. But all and more than the visionary legends of fantastic wealth coupled with the name of India gen-

erally, is realized in India's most southern and latest annexed appendage, the Isle of Ceylon. That island, about three fourths the size of Ireland, is in very truth what the adjoining continent was long erroneously thought to be: the richest mine in the world of the rarest, choicest precious stones of nearly every known kind; independently of and apart from its pearl-fisheries, which yield the most perfect pearls in existence, surpassing even those of the Persian Gulf in purity and soft radiance. Nor is the island less surpassingly endowed with regard to vegetation. The interior is one huge tropical forest, where all the palms, timber-trees, gum-trees, spice- and fruit-trees of India thrive side by side with those of Europe and other temperate zones; the cotton there grows to the size of a real tree, and justifies the apparently exaggerated accounts of the Greeks (see p.); and to all these must be added the coffee-tree which grows wild, and the wonderful bread-tree, not to speak of the vanilla vine, cinnamon, and other most valuable plants, and, of late, the successful tea plantations. In its animal creation, Ceylon is not less blest: it abounds in most kinds of handsome and useful animals, except horses, which are entirely wanting, and is renowned for its breed of elephants, the finest and cleverest, though not the largest, in India. If to all these advantages we add a soil that regularly yields three harvests a year, a glorious and most wholesome climate, not afflicted with extreme heat, notwithstanding the island's position so near the equator, but maintained on a mild and pretty uniform level by a perfect combination of sea and mountains, and, as a consequence, absence of fever and all malarial affections, we shall understand why this chosen spot, which Milton might have had in his mind's eye when he spoke of isles

> "That, like to rich and various gems, inlay
> The unadorned bosom of the deep,"

has been called the jewel casket and finishing glory of India; and we may pre-eminently apply to it the name of "Wonderland of the East," even though it assuredly beseems all this peerless portion of our habitable earth.

CHAPTER II.

THE ÂRYAS.

> "Who can see the green earth any more
> As she was by the sources of Time?
> Who imagines her fields as she lay
> In the sunshine unworn by the plough?
> Who thinks as they thought,
> The tribes who then roamed on her breast,
> Her vigorous, primitive sons?"
>
> MATTHEW ARNOLD, from *The Future.*

1. IN a work which undertakes to present, in a set of parallel pictures, the history of several nations, differing in race, culture, and religion, but covering pretty much the same span of the world's age, it is at times very difficult to keep them well apart, because the influences to which they mutually subject one another cannot be ignored, unless we are willing to content ourselves with fragmentary and fanciful sketches, leaving a good half of the characteristic traits either indistinct or unaccounted for. This difficulty increases considerably when we have to do with two nations derived from the same stock, and exhibiting such striking affinities, such undenia-

ble resemblances, as to betray their original identity at every turn and make us feel as though we can actually grasp and hold fast the time when they were as yet undivided, even though that time may lie far beyond all calculable bounds of historical research. Two such sister nations we have in the Aryan Hindus and Eranians. It is impossible to do justice to the history and culture of the one without drawing the other into the same field of vision and comparing the two,—a process which necessarily brings out their common origin, by presenting identical or similar features, obviously borrowed by neither from the other, but inherited by both from a common ancestry. It was thus that in a former volume, when treating of the Eranians, their culture and their religion, we were unavoidably led to trespass on the ground reserved for the present work.[1] We found it impossible, "in dealing with the Aryan peoples of Erân, to separate them entirely from their brethren of India, these two Asiatic branches of the Aryan tree being so closely connected in their beginnings, the sap coursing through both being so evidently the same life-blood, that a study of the one necessarily involves a parallel study of the other."[2] Thus we were actually compelled to stop for a brief glimpse at the conditions which regulated the existence of the ancestors of both in the period that has been called "Indo-Eranian," *i.e.*, the period before the future settlers of Erân and the future conquerors of India had separated, before they had

---

[1] See *Story of Media, Babylon, and Persia*, chap. ii.–v.

[2] *Ibid.*, p. 36.

severally wandered into the countries, far distant from one another and from the primeval home, of which they were to win and hold possession through well-nigh countless future ages.

2. A cursory sketch was sufficient for the comprehension of Eranian history, because the nations of this branch soon diverged very widely from the parent stock, and went their own separate and strongly individual way. Not so the peoples who descended into India and settled there. The nations of *this* branch were merely the continuation of the mother trunk. They did not break with any of their ancestral traditions, but, on the contrary, faithfully treasured them, and only in the course of time and further migrations, developed from them, not an opposition, but a progressive and consistent sequel, in the shape of a more elaborate religion and, later on, philosophical systems and speculations, based on the same principles, which, in ruder, simpler forms, had been their intellectual inheritance from the first. At the present stage of our studies, therefore, we must pause for a longer and more searching retrospect, if we mean to follow out and comprehend the long and gradual evolution of the people who, of all Orientals, are nearest akin to us in thought, in feeling, in manner, and in language. By doing so, we feel assured that we are reconstructing the past of our own race at its entrance on the career of conscious humanity, that we are learning how our own fathers, in incalculably remote ages, not only lived and labored, but thought and prayed,—nay, how they began to think and to pray.

3. A fascinating task, but not as easy as it would seem. For, if learning be a difficult achievement, far more difficult is that of *un*learning,—forgetting what we have assimilated through years of that conscious or unconscious process of absorption which not only fills but, so to speak, permeates our brains, moulds and shapes them, till our mental acquirements become part of our being, in fact the most tenacious, the most inalienable part of ourselves. Yet this is exactly what we must strive to do, if we would successfully identify ourselves with these beginnings of all the things of which we, in this our span of life, are witnessing the bloom, the fruition, the perfection, and, alas! in many cases, the decay. We must not forget for a time what forms as much a part of our intellectual consciousness, as breath or motion does of our physical existence. This mode of working backward, dropping item after item of our intellectual ballast as we go, alone enables us to divest ourselves of our obtrusive and narrow self and to put ourselves in the place of our remote progenitors, to think their eager but as yet untutored thoughts, to feel with their simple directness, their unsophisticated intenseness.

4. Behold them, then, our forefathers, the Âryas, in their early inland home—which, let it be at once understood, is neither India nor the Erân of the Zoroastrians, but some region, not as yet ascertained, though eagerly and patiently sought for,—where the ancestors of both these and many more nations have dwelt as one undivided race for many ages before that ever spying, ever prying spirit of inquiry, which

is one of the chief characteristics of our race, first stirred in their settlements. At that moment we already find a people, rude and primitive, but by no means wholly savage or barbarous, nor even what is usually understood by "a very young people." For the earliest glimpse it is permitted us to cast into their dwelling-places and mode of life shows them possessed of domestic arts and crafts which, rudimentary as they may appear to us, imply centuries of undisturbed sojourning in the land of their primary choosing, under conditions favoring the training and development of the most essential features of moral and social culture, as well as of material prosperity. A people must have passed out of the purely nomadic stage,[1] to be found established in rural homesteads; nor can it be said to be in its infancy when, after having achieved the momentous transition, it has gone beyond the solitary family life in detached dwellings—huts built on a patch of enclosed land,—and has learned to cluster these homesteads into villages and boroughs, for mutual protection and assistance,—where their daily life presents the normal and healthful combination of agricultural labor and cattle-breeding, in short the manifold occupations which, in our languages, go under the name of "farming,"—without excluding the exercise of hunting, now, however, a relaxation more than a necessity, a means of introducing wholesome variety into the monotony of the daily farm-fare, and also of repelling and destroying the ravenous night-prowlers, the wild creatures of the woods and the desert.

[1] See *Story of Chaldea*, ch. i., "The Four Stages of Culture."

Once arrived at this really advanced stage of culture, the Âryas, like all primitive races, must have advanced rapidly in the work of social organization, for we ever find intellectual improvement developing hand in hand with material prosperity. It is an attractive and instructive task to reconstruct their life from such imperfect and scattered scraps of information as we can dispose of.

5. The first feature which it pleases us to note in these early settlements of our own, still undivided, race, is the reverence for family ties and duties, firmly established and held sacred. The father acknowledges himself the protector, supporter, and nourisher of his own immediate family; brothers and sisters live on terms of mutual assistance and cheerful companionship, sharing in the manifold duties of house and farm. The degrees of relationship by marriage are determined to a nicety, and persons connected by this secondary bond are close friends and allies. Thus the family grows into the tribe; the head of the one remains the head, the king, of the other.[1] The several tribes, at first more or less closely related, live, as a rule, on terms of peaceful neighborliness and hospitality. If quarrels do occur and lead to armed strife, they mostly arise out of some dispute about flocks and herds, and, at a later time, out of the competition between kindred tribes striving for supremacy or the appropriation of more land. At the more primitive era the principal occasion of warfare was one calculated to tighten the bond of race rather than loosen

[1] See *Story of Chaldea*, ch. i., especially pp. 123–125.

it, being self-defence, the constant necessity of guarding against the raids of innumerable, lawless hordes of nomads, mostly of non-Aryan stock, who, mounted on their fleet and indefatigable steppe-ponies, kept continually hovering and circling round the pasture lands and settlements, whose prosperity excited their greed.

6. Physically, the Âryas, as we can picture them from certain indications, are of high stature, and powerful build, white-skinned, fair-haired, and probably blue-eyed. Ages of seclusion in their first home have moulded these originally local characteristics into a permanent, indelible type, which no amount of uniting with other races will ever be able wholly to obliterate. To the development of this noble *physique* their mode of life—mostly outdoor labor in moderation—and their favorable surroundings, must have contributed not a little: a temperate climate inclining to the cold, a land of alternate woods and plains, milk-food in abundance, as well as meat and wheat, pastoral and agricultural pursuits,—such conditions of existence, if continued through many centuries, undisturbed by intercourse with men of different blood and customs, must result in an exceptionally fine race. Nor are these natural advantages unassisted by art and crafts. The Âryas are prompt and skilful in wielding weapons, which, it is true, are mostly still of hewn and polished stone, shaped and sharpened at an incalculable cost of time and labor, but by no means inefficient for all their clumsiness. Besides, they have lately learned the use of metals also: gold and silver certainly, and a third metal not

fully identified yet—perhaps iron. They can fashion and handle a rude sort of plough, which, uncouth as it is, has not only survived its original inventors, but is still in use in more or less remote parts of every country of Europe, owing to the conservatism and stubbornness of the peasantry all over the world, wherever they have not been brought into direct contact and brisk intercourse with the greater or lesser centres of trade and traffic. Their garments are made of skins sewed together or of spun and woven wool. They dwell in houses provided with doors, and surrounded by yards, (or gardens), which simply means "enclosed grounds." They also have hurdles for their cattle and domestic animals—a necessary addition, for they possess very nearly every kind that we own: horses and asses, sheep and goats, pigs and geese, with the dog to guard them, the mouse to pilfer their stores, the wolf and the bear to endanger their folds; they grind their grain, they cook and bake, and have a horror of raw meat. They build boats and skiffs and navigation is known to them, though only on lakes and rivers, for they have never beheld a sea or ocean. Their minds are open to all impressions; their thoughts are busy with the phenomena of nature; but in abstract speculation they have not yet reached a very advanced stage—for they can count only up to a hundred.

7. Such we can picture to ourselves the Âryas, dwelling together as one undivided nation, speaking one language, holding one worship, one mode of life, before they yield to the impulse of migration which has seized on all peoples at certain stages of their

existence, when they—whether from want of room, or family discords, or the restlessness of awakening curiosity and unconscious sense of power, or from all these combined—begin to separate, and detachment after detachment leaves the mother trunk, never to return and never again to meet, save in ages to come, mostly as enemies, with no remotest memory of a long severed tie, of a common origin.

8. As tradition itself does not begin its doubtful records till ages after this original separation, and the dawn of history finds most of the nations which we ascribe to the Aryan stock established on the lands of which they had severally taken possession, it follows that we have just been contemplating a picture for which we have not the slightest tangible materials. No monuments, no coins, inscriptions, hieroglyphic scrawls, reach back as far as the time we have endeavored to retrace. Indeed, the first really historical monuments of any kind at our command are the inscriptions, caused to be engraved in various parts of Hindustân, on pillars and rocks, by ASHOKA, a king who reigned as late as 250 B.C. The same applies to architecture; no buildings or ruins of buildings are to be traced further back than 500 B.C. Was it then an imaginary sketch, the features of which were put together at random, supplied by fancy or any trite description of pastoral life? So far from it, we can boldly say: would that all information that comes down to us as history were as true to nature, as well authenticated, as this short sketch of an age on which not even the marvellously trained skill of modern historical investigation could fasten

by so much as a single thread. But where history throws down the web, philology takes it up and places in our hands the threads which connect us with that immeasurable past—threads which we have held and helped to spin all the days of our lives, but the magic power of which we did not suspect until the new science, Ariadnê-like, taught us where to fasten them, when we have but to follow; these threads are—our languages.

9. A hundred years ago, several eminent English scholars resided in India, as servants of the East India Company, and, unlike their coarse and ignorant predecessors, thought it their duty to become familiar both with the spoken dialects and the literary languages of the country they helped to govern. They were earnest and enthusiastic men, and the discovery of an intellectual world so new and apparently different from ours drew them irresistibly on, into deeper studies than their duties required. Warren Hastings, then the head of the executive government, representing the Company in India, cordially patronized their efforts, from political reasons as well as from a personal taste for scholarly pursuits, and not content with lending them his powerful moral countenance, gave them material assistance, and even urgently commended them to the Board of Directors at home. It was then that CHARLES WILKINS translated portions of the great national epic, the MAHÂBHÂRATA, and compiled the first Sanskrit grammar in English; that Sir WILLIAM JONES[1] translated the national code

[1] The old enemy and traducer of Anquetil Duperron.—See *Story of Media*, etc., pp. 12-15.

known as "THE LAWS OF MANU"; while COLEBROOKE wrote masterly treatises on Hindu law, philosophy, literature, and mathematics. These indefatigable learners could not but be struck with the exceeding resemblance, nay frequently the obvious identity, between a great number of Sanskrit words and the corresponding words in all or many of the living languages of Europe, as well as in the dead tongues of ancient Greece and Rome, the old Teutonic and Slavic idioms. The great future importance of this discovery at once flashed on the mental vision of these gifted and highly trained students, and comparative studies were zealously entered upon. Great and noble was the work which these men did, with results, on the whole, marvellously correct; but, as is always the case with such zealous pioneering in a new field, some of the conclusions they arrived at were necessarily immature and misleadingly positive and sweeping. Thus it was for many years universally believed that Sanskrit was the mother tongue, to which all languages could be traced. This theory was not by far as absurd as that which had been set up some time previously by certain religious zealots who, from an exaggerated regard, untutored by science, for all that is connected with the "inspired books" of our creed, went so far as to assert that Hebrew was the mother of all the languages in the world. Still it might, from its plausibility and the large percentage of truth it contained, have done much harm, by leading people to imagine that they had touched the goal, when, in reality, they were at the initial stage of knowledge;

but the question was placed on its proper ground by the somewhat later discovery of a still more ancient language, standing to Sanskrit in the relation of Latin to French, Italian, and Spanish, or Old German to English. Since then JACOB GRIMM discovered the law that rules the changes of consonants in their passage from language to language,—the law that bears his name, although it is but one among the many titles to glory of that most indefatigable, most luminous of searchers. The unity of Aryan speech is now established beyond the possibility of a doubt.

10. This common language, or—more correctly—this common ancestor of the so-called Aryan family of tongues, would prove, could it be raised from the dead, to be that of the race, whose mode of life and state of culture we just now attempted to reconstruct. Reconstruct from what? From nothing but *the words*, which are the only heirloom they have transmitted to us, their late and widely scattered successors. Only words. But as words stand for thoughts, and knowledge, and feelings, this heirloom implies all our histories, all our philosophical systems, our poetry—in fact, all that we are and will be. It is the nutshell in the fairy tale, out of which the endless web is forthcoming, unrolling fold after fold of marvellous designs and matchless variety of color.

11. If, then, in the oldest offspring of this immemorial language, we find words which we meet alike in most Aryan languages of a later growth and in our present living ones, unchanged or having undergone such slight alterations that any intelligent per-

son will immediately know them,—and if those words, all or nearly all, concern the most essential and therefore most ordinary features of social and domestic life, the simplest pursuits and relations and chief necessaries of our material existence—have we not there evidence amounting to proof, that the relations determined by those words existed, that the things called by those names were in use, the actions expressed by those verbs were habitually done, amongst and by those men, the ancestors of many of us, several, nay, many thousands of years ago? And are not the "points" thus obtained sufficient, lacking any visible or tangible materials, to arrive at something much more substantial and reliable than mere conjecture on what the life, pursuits, and ideas of those men may and must have been? Could we apply the test to the short sketch from which we started, it would bear out every single word of it,—literally "every word," for it is composed of nothing but words, which have been transmitted from the original language to all the languages of the Aryan stock, *i. e.*, later Sanskrit and the Hindu dialects, ancient Avestan and modern Persian, and the tongues of the Greek, Latin, Teutonic, Slavic, and Celtic branches.

12. Almost everybody will have noticed that words go in families. That is—several words, and sometimes a great many, are connected with or derived from one another, all expressing different forms or shadings of one common fundamental idea. On examining such words more closely, it will turn out that this common idea resides in a cer-

tain combination of sounds which will be found in all. This combination we detach from the words to which it gives their general meaning, and call it "a root." Let us take as an example the following words: "*stay*, *stand*, *stable*, *stiff*, *stile*, *stalwart*, *staff*, *stick*, *stack*, *stump*, *stem*, *stool*, *stead*, *state*, *station*, *statue*, *statute*, *stoic*," and many more, with all their numerous derivatives, like *steady*, *unsteady*, *unstable*, *standard*, *statuary*, *statutory*, etc. Different as these words are, they all ring the changes on one central idea—that of permanence, stability, remaining fixed in one place. It will readily be seen that this central idea is conveyed by the combination ST, which is as the soul of all these words. In philological parlance, ST is "the root from which they all sprang"; these and a vast number more, for ST being a Sanskrit root, it runs through all the Aryan languages, ancient and modern, and is in each unusually prolific; if counted, the words to which it serves as family bond, would go into the hundreds. Let us now take the Sanskrit root AR, of which the general and original meaning is "plough." We find it intact in Latin and Italian *arare*, in Slavic *arati*—"to plough"; in Greek *arotron*, Latin *aratrum*, Tchekh (so-called Bohemian, a Slavic language) *oradlo*—"a plough"; in English *arable*—"fit to be ploughed"; in Greek *aroura*, Latin *arvum*—"a ploughed field," whence *aroma*, originally beyond a doubt signifying the peculiar fragrance of a ploughed field, of the loose, moist, upturned earth. It has even been suggested—but the attractive suggestion has unfortunately not proved capable of sufficient scientific proof—that the name Ârya itself is connected with this root, and that the people who took it for their own originally meant to call themselves "the people who plough," in proud distinction from their sheep-raising, steppe-roaming, robber-neighbors, the Tura.[1] At the time at which we begin to know them, "Ârya" meant "noble," "exalted," "venerable"; the name had become something almost sacred, it embodied the Aryan peoples' national pride,—or a feeling deeper still, more intense, enduring, and inspiring: their pride of race, and that down to a very late period; for was not Dareios, the great Persian king, careful to preface his family genealogy in his famous inscriptions by the statement: "I am an Ârya, the son of an Ârya"?

13. Neither space nor the scope of the present work allow of our taking up the above sketch and justifying every feature of it by a thorough study of each of the words that suggest it. That would be simply embarking on a treatise of comparative philology. Still, as words have of late acquired such immense importance in the study of what may be called "prehistoric history"—an importance as great as the things found in the caves, mounds, and barrows that sheltered primitive humanity in life and death, or, in geology, the fossils and imprints which reveal the meaning of the various rocks and strata,—it will not be an unnecessary digression,

---

[1] "Ârya and Tura," in later historical times "Erân and Turân;" the same distinction ever, the same opposition, the same battle-cry. (*Erân*, *Eranian* is only a slightly altered form of *Aryan*; so is *Erin*, the national name of *Ire*land.)

if we pause awhile to trace a few of the words which are our only key, and by no means an insufficient one, to the material and intellectual life of the early Aryan world. This brief review will at the same time serve to indicate and illustrate the processes of philological research in their special bearings on historical reconstruction.

14. We have already had a hint of the great importance which attached to the cow as a factor in the life of early Aryan communities. Indeed we may safely proclaim the cow the characteristic animal of the Aryan race. We find it the companion of every Aryan people, one of the chief conditions of their existence; it stands to the Âryas in exactly the same relation that the sheep does to the Turanians. The very fact of the cow's predominance in a people's life is sufficient proof of that people's having reached the settled stage of existence—the pastoral-farming, because the cow, unlike the sheep, is unfit for a nomadic life and incapable of bearing the hardship of continual change and marching. Those who use oxen as beasts of burden and draught know very well that they have to be driven at an easy pace, by short stages, and moreover positively require one full day of rest at least in seven or eight, if they are to be kept in anything like tolerable condition. They are also very fastidious as to their food, and the least neglect in the care of them, the least pressure of overwork, cause loss of flesh and spirits, agonizingly sore hoofs, then illness and death in a very short time.

15. The Sanskrit name of the cow is GO, plural

GÂVAS, and this short radical we find running, with the modifications consequent on the character of each, through most of our languages: Old German *chuo*, modern German *kuh*, English *cow*. The Slavic branch has preserved it, like a great many others, in the form most resembling the original. Thus, Old Slavic has *govyàdo*, a herd; modern Servian *góvedar*, a cow-herd; Russian, *govyàdina*,—beef, the flesh of cows and oxen; then *gospodìn*, master; *gospòd (i)*, the Lord; *gospodàr*, the title given to South Slavic rulers; all meaning originally "master of cows," and corresponding to the Old Sanskrit *gopa*, which first means a herdsman, and later a chieftain, a king.[1] By the same evolution of compound words from a simple radical, following on the evolution of various more or less subtle shades of meaning from the plain meaning of the original radical, the Sanskrit word *gotra*, literally "the enclosure which protects a herd from thieves and keeps it from straying," gradually comes to designate a family, then a tribe, *i. e.*, the people who live behind the same walls.

16. Let us linger awhile on a few of the names expressing the closest of domestic ties, for they will give us a precious insight into the Âryas' moral life, and help us realize what we cannot sufficiently impress on our minds—that, contrary to all first (*a*

[1] The association of ideas between "a herdsman"—a leader, ruler of cattle,—and "a king," a leader, ruler of men, is obvious and close; see the Homeric poems, where the kings, especially the more wealthy and powerful, are regularly titled "shepherds," or "pastors of men."

priori) impressions and plausible prejudice born of faulty training, in adjusting our historical glasses to an unhistorical,—otherwise prehistorical, *i. e.*, unmonumental, undocumented—antiquity, the race we have to deal with was far from being a primitive—or, better, primary—block of humanity, unshaped, save to the lowest uses of material service to the one instinct of preserving life, with none as yet of the refining, ennobling stirrings of the spirit which come from experience, length of days, and leisure from bodily toil,—leisure to look and listen, to think, remember, feel. Rough-hewn they surely were, but they were the finest material ever provided for chisel to work upon, and the work *had* been going on for more years—nay, centuries, than we at first feel at all willing to concede. Whenever we address our thoughts to the human race of a few thousand years back, we pucker our lips into a superciliously condescending smile, and admire how many fine things our race could do and say when it was so very young and, naturally, ignorant. We should know better by this time ; for has not Chaldea—to take but one branch—taught us that as far as six or seven thousand years ago great civilizations had not only dawned or begun to bloom, but some had reached and even passed their maturity and were declining into that inevitable doom of decay into which others were to follow them and some, to a certainty, had preceded them. A very little calculation of probabilities will show us that mankind, at the very earliest point at which our eager grasp can secure the first slight hold of it, was *not* young, and when it had reached, say, the cave-dwelling stage, had probably existed, in the dignity of speaking, fire-using Man, more centuries than separate it from ourselves. To stand out at all where the long slim ray from the prying bull's-eye of modern research, historic or pre-historic, can, however feebly, reach it, the race—or *a* race—must have emerged out of the colorless past of tentative groping, into a stage of positive achievement of some kind—for without that, without something to hold to, our most pressing questionings must have been eluded and have been met by nought but the silence of the grave.

17. Let us then try to open the intellectual treasure-house of our earliest forebears with the golden keys they left for our use: their words. We may not yet enquire what they did with them; that they *had* them is their crowning glory and our gain, even greater than the wonders of literature in which they culminated. For, in the words of one of the greatest masters of words, their histories and their uses,[1] "our poets make poems out of words, but every word, if carefully examined, will turn out to be itself a poem, a record of a deed done or of a thought thought by those to whom we owe the whole of our intellectual inheritance. . . ." Take, for instance, the word PITAR—father, the meaning of which is threefold—"feeder," "protector," "ruler": does not the underlying connection between these at the first glance different conceptions already warrant, by the subtlety and depth of observation which they

[1] Max Müller, *Biographies of Words*, Introduction.

betray, the same writer's enthusiastic assertion[1]: "Wherever we analyze language in a scholarlike spirit . . . we shall find in it the key to some of the deepest secrets of the human mind. . . ." And does it not speak for an already highly developed moral feeling that the root PA, from which is formed *pitar*, the most generally used word for "father," does not mean "to give birth" but to protect, to support, showing how entirely the Aryan father realized and accepted the idea of duty and responsibility towards those who belonged to him by the most sacred of human ties. Each duty gives corresponding rights, just as each right imposes a duty, that the eternal fitness and balance of things may be maintained, that universal dualism, moral and physical, which is the very root and soul of the world.[2] And thus it is that it has been admitted from all time as self-evident that he who fulfils the duty of supporting and protecting a family, has the undisputed right of governing it, of imposing his will as the law of those who depend on his toil and affection for their sustenance, comfort, and safety. Hence *pati*, "master." This is, in few words, a complete definition of the word "patriarch," in which the Greeks, by a trick of language familiar to them, and, among the moderns, to the Germans, have deftly embodied the two indivisible conceptions: "father and ruler."[3]

---

[1] *Ibid.*

[2] See *Story of Assyria*, p. 106.

[3] The word "Patriarch" occurs for the first time in the Septuagint, consequently came into use at a period much later than the

This word "pitar" we can easily pursue through most Aryan languages, ancient and modern, although, as is the manner of words in their wanderings, it now takes on a letter, now drops one, now alters a vowel or even some of its consonants, until it becomes barely recognizable to the trained eye and ear of the philologist. Thus Sanskrit *pitar* (Avestan *pitar* also), can hardly fail to be at once identified in *pater* (Greek and Latin), can easily be known in *vater* and *father*, the form derived by the two northern sister languages from the old Teutonic *fadar;* the relationship is not quite as obvious in *padre* (Spanish and Italian), and especially in the French *père;* indeed, the three southern Latin sister-tongues may be said to have adopted decided corruptions of the original word; and when we come to Celtic *athir, athar* (Gælic, Welsh, Irish, Armorican), nothing short of scientific training will suffice to establish the identity.

18. The word for "mother" is even more generally in use in the various Aryan languages, and has undergone fewer alterations. The Sanskrit *mâtár*, unchanged in Avestan *mâtar*, except in accent, scarcely deviates in the Greek *mêter* and Latin *mater*, which abides in the Slavic *mater*, only slightly short-

---

golden age of Greek speech. Its immediate derivation—or rather composition—is from *patriá* or *pátra*, "a clan, a tribe," and *arkheô*, "to rule," giving the meaning, "ruler of a clan or tribe." This, however, in no wise impairs the remoter, original association of ideas between *patêr*, "father," and *patriá*, "tribe"; in fact, it still more clearly establishes the twofold—domestic and political—character of the word *patriá*, "clan,"—the family grown into the tribe, and the father of the one into the ruler of the other. Another enlargement—and the tribe has become a people, the patriarch a king.

ened by modern Russian into *matĭ*, very recognizable for once in the Celtic *mathi*, even more than in the German *mutter*, and English *mother*, from Old Teutonic *muotar;* but corrupted in the Spanish and Italian *madre*, and the French *mère*, after exactly the same fashion as the word for "father,"—evidently with conscious intention to establish a symmetry akin to alliteration—a rhyme—a trick of language by which it pleased a slightly barbaric ear and taste to couple together kindred objects or ideas. The root of this multiform word is MÂ, "to make," and also "to measure." A combination particularly suggestive, since the mother, she who "has given birth," is also she who "measures," "portions out" the provisions, the food, and the other necessaries of life to the various members of the household. From the same root we have *mâs*, the moon, the measurer of time, so that the same word means "moon" and "month," as it still does in its Slavic form, "*mêsiats*."

19. The other words expressing near relationship are no less generally preserved in the several Aryan languages. To begin with: Sanskrit *bhrátar—svásar;* Avestan, *brâtar—hvanhar;* Greek, *frater;* (only the word, at the stage of which it comes under our ken, had become diverted from its original meaning and was used in a political or social sense, to designate a member of one of the tribes or brotherhoods—*fratrías*—into which citizens were divided. For the family relationship of both brother and sister the Greeks adopted an entirely different word). Latin, *frater—soror;* Old Teutonic, *brôthar—svistar;* modern German, *bruder—schwester;* English, *brother—*

sister; Italian, *frate, fratello—suora, sorella.* (*Frate* and *suora* are used exclusively to designate religious brotherhood and sisterhood, "monk" "nun." *Frate* in this respect answers to the English *friar.*) Slavic and Russian, *brat—sestrà;* Celtic, *bráthir—suir;* French, *frère—sœur.* Take further Sanskrit, *duhitar;* Avestan, *dughdhar;* Greek, *thugatêr;* German, *tochter;* English, *daughter;* Irish, *dear;* Slavic, *dushter* (the pronunciation cannot be understood from the written word, but must be heard and imitated); Russian, *dòtcher, dotch;* Latin and her chief daughter languages, Italian, Spanish, and French, have adopted another designation, *filia—figlia—hija—fille.*

20. The secondary family ties—those by marriage—are no less nicely determined—which in itself speaks highly for an advanced state of social order,—and the words denoting them also turn up in most Aryan languages, some in many, others in but a few. One example must satisfy us: Sanskrit *dêvár,* "brother-in-law," is almost unchanged in the Russian *déver* and Lithunian *deveris,* and very recognizable in the Greek *daêr* and even the Latin *levir.*

21. We will conclude with a word embodying bereavement as universal as the family relations, and therefore reserved even more faithfully than many others through most languages of Aryan stock: *vidhavâ,* "widow"; German, *wittwe;* Russian, *vdovà;* Latin, *vidua;* Italian, *vedova,* corrupted by Spanish into *viuda* and by French into *veuve.* A word of mighty import, especially to later and modern India, as it means "husbandless," and so would, all

alone, suffice to prove that in enforcing the horrible practice of widow-burning on the ground of sacred tradition, the Brâhmans have been guilty of heinous misrepresentation; for, if the custom had, as they assert, existed from the beginning of time, there would have been no *vidhavâs*, no "husbandless women." Now they not only existed, but, as we shall see later on, are repeatedly mentioned, and once in the religious service attending the burial (or, later, the burning) of the dead, explicitly addressed, as returning from the grave or the pyre to stay among the living. All this in the book which the Brâhmans regard as the holiest in all their sacred literature. Furthermore, in their law-books, also invested with sacredness, widows are provided and legislated for at great length. So that the Brâhmans stand convicted of deliberately falsifying, at least in this one instance, their own most sacred and, as they believe and assert, *revealed* texts. And thus the English authorities, merely through ignorance of the natives' literary language and their classical literature, were placed in the atrocious necessity of tolerating this abomination or breaking that portion of their agreement with the Hindus by which they engaged not to interfere with any of their religious observances. Now that the texts themselves and their correct interpretation have been given to the world at large by the life-long labors of our great Sanskritists, the Government's hands are free to forbid and prevent, by armed force if necessary, these unnatural sacrifices. The abolition of the time-honored horrors of the widow-burning or *suttee* (more correctly written *satî*), yields us one more convincing proof of what tremendous practical issues may be waiting on the mere *study of words*, patiently, peacefully carried on by scholars in their quiet studies and libraries, so remote in space and spirit from the battle-places of the workaday world.

22. It would be easy to swell the list of such picturesque and tell-tale words. These few instances, however, must suffice—only adding the remark that the *absence* of certain words can be at times as eloquently significant by the presumptive negative evidence it supplies. We called the Âryas' primeval home an "inland home," and later stated that "they had never beheld the sea nor the ocean." This is suggested by the fact that no name for "sea" is found in their earliest known language. That name is of later growth and different in the various branches of the Aryan speech, this very difference showing most curiously how one tribe was affected by one aspect of the new element, and another by a totally different, if not opposite one. Latin and Greek call the sea "a highroad" *pontos, pontus*—from the same root as *pons, pontis*, "a bridge," and the Slavic *pont(ĭ)*, Russian *put(ĕ)*, "a road." But the Slav does not apply this name to the sea; that he calls *mórie* (Latin *mar*, Italian and Spanish *mare*, French *mer*, German *meer*, hence English *mere*, "a lake," Celtic *muir*), from a Sanskrit root meaning "destruction." A difference well accounted for, when we consider that the only seas the Slavs and Teutons were acquainted with were the Black Sea, the Baltic, and the German Ocean, all rough and

treacherous, all renowned for their fierce tempests, which must have been destructive indeed to small and imperfect craft,—while the fortunate dweller on the genial Mediterranean shores well could look at the sea, not as a barrier, but as a highroad, more useful for trade and travel than any other road.

23. Now as regards intellectual achievements and abstract speculation, we must not be too prompt to depreciate the efforts of our fathers on this ground on the plea that there is no common word for "thousand" in our languages,—or, more correctly in the parent languages of ours—Sanskrit, Greek, Latin, Old Teutonic having each fabricated a word of its own, which their respective offspring dutifully adopted with the usual tribal alterations. As to our Aryan forebears, we cannot escape the inference from this fact that they could count only up to a hundred, the numerals so far coinciding in all Aryan languages with almost comical regularity. This, however, is no proof as yet that they had no conception of thousands, or never saw things assembled in so large a number—men, cattle, etc. They may have known of thousands as so many "tens of hundreds," and counted as we ourselves still do up to a certain point: twelve hundred, eighteen hundred, and even twenty hundred, twenty-five hundred, and so on. Furthermore, the very fact of having invented a numeral system at all—and that a decimal one!—is an achievement which presupposes a longer growth and evolution both of the mind and language than all the wonders of abstract speculation which followed, and were a necessary

deduction from it, astronomical calculations included. For every one who has learned and taught knows what a weary long time the beginnings of any science or art take to master, and that, once the first principles are really and firmly grasped, the rest comes with a wonderful and ever-increasing rapidity, with a rush, as it were, partly owing to the training which the mind has undergone in the effort to step from "not thinking" to "thinking," and partly because these same "first principles" really contain the whole art or science, which is only evolved from them, as the variations from the theme, as the play from the plot, or the plant from the seed.

24. One word to conclude this, on the whole, introductory chapter. We have come to speak quite familiarly of "the Âryas' primeval home," of their separations and migrations, as though we knew all about these subjects. We are, in a sense, justified in so speaking and imagining, on the testimony afforded by the formation and evolution of languages, of which we can, to a great extent, pursue the track over and across the vast continent which, though geographically one, has been artificially divided, in conformity with political conditions and school conveniences more than with natural characteristics, into two separate parts of the world: Asia and Europe. The division is entirely arbitrary, for there is no boundary line south of the Ural chain, and that chain itself, important as it is, from its position and the treasures it holds, is anything but separating or forbidding. Of very moderate altitude, with no towering summits or deep-cut gorge-passes,

its several broad, flat-topped ridges slope down imperceptibly on the European side, and are by no means beetling or impassable on the Asiatic side either. This barrier, such as it is, stops short far north of the Caspian Sea, leaving a wide gap of flat steppeland invitingly open to roaming hordes with their cattle and luggage-wagons, with only the mild Ural River or Yaïk to keep up the geographical fiction of a boundary. Through this gap wave after wave of migration and invasion has rolled within the range of historical knowledge, to break into nations whose original kinship is demonstrated by their languages. The induction is obvious that many more such waves than we can at all be aware of must have rolled back and forward in times wholly out of the reach of our most searching methods. The diverging directions of such migrations—irregularly timed, of course—as we know of in Asia, and only a few of which can have taken the way of the Uralo-Caspian Gap: to northwest, to west, to southwest, persuasively point to a centre which, at some incalculably remote period, must have been the starting-point of these departing Aryan hives. Until within the last few years it was the almost universally accepted theory that this centre,—which the lines of march of the several nations, as well as their confronted mythical and cosmogonical traditions, pretty consistently locate somewhere in Central Asia, towards the high but fertile tableland of the Pamir region,—was also the original cradle-home of the primeval Âryas. That question, owing to new elements received into the materials and methods of prehistoric research, has been lately reopened, and treated, with varying results, by many able and erudite scholars. But, although each of them, of course, honestly and triumphantly believes that he has arrived at the only rational and conclusive solution, it is, as yet, impossible to say when and in what way the question will be finally and unanswerably settled—if ever and at all. Fortunately, it is not of the slightest practical importance for general students; in other words, for any but specialists in ethnology, craniology, etc., and least of all for the subject-matter of this volume. We do not need to pry into the darkness of an incalculable past beyond the centre of departure just mentioned, which is the first landmark of Aryan antiquity touched with a golden ray of the historical dawn. It is sufficient to know that that centre, no matter whence the primeval Âryas of all—the Proto-Âryas—may have come, has been a station on which a large portion of the race must have been sojourners for many, many centuries,—that portion of it, at all events, of which the two principal limbs, the leading sister nations of the Aryan East, Eranians and Hindus, divided almost within our ken, for reasons easy to conjecture, if not to establish with actual certainty, and some of which have been alluded to in a former volume.

CHAPTER III.

THE SOURCES OF OUR KNOWLEDGE.

1. ON the 31st of December, of the year 1600 A.D., Queen Elizabeth signed a charter incorporating into one solid body the hitherto disconnected and independent English merchants who plied the export and import trade between England and India,—or the East Indies, as the Indian Continent began to be called, to distinguish it from the islands discovered a hundred years before by Christopher Columbus and known ever since as "the West Indies," thus perpetuating that great man's geographical mistake. In virtue of this charter, 125 shareholders, with a joint stock of £70,000, entitled themselves "The Governor and Company of Merchants of London Trading to the East Indies," both charter and privileges being granted for a limited time, to be renewed on application at stated intervals. Such were the modest beginnings of that famous "East India Company," which was to offer the world the unprecedented spectacle of a private association ruling, with sovereign power and rights, a land of ten times the population of their mother country, sub-

jects in one hemisphere, kings in the other, treating with royalties on an equal footing, levying armies, waging war and making peace, signing treaties, and appointing a civil government.

2. Not that the English Company was alone or even first in the field or had things its own way in India from the beginning. On the contrary, the object of its creation was to counteract the influence of the rival company of Portuguese merchants, and to wrest from them some of those profits and advantages which they were monopolizing ever since Vasco de Gama opened the direct route to India, by doubling the Cape of Good Hope in 1498. Through the whole of the sixteenth century the Portuguese had enjoyed an undisputed supremacy in the eastern seas and on the Indian Continent, ingratiating themselves with the numerous princes, Mohammedan and native Hindu, extending their possessions by grants, by purchase, or by actual force. There is no doubt that they contemplated a gradual annexation of province after province and the eventual sovereignty of the entire country. They seemed in a fair way to achieve what they schemed, when the English Company came forward, enterprising and active, and stoutly equipped for vigorous competition, and they almost immediately began to lose ground before the new arrivals, having thoroughly alienated the people by their unscrupulous dealings, their unmitigated rapacity, and their ruthless cruelty in seeking their profits and enforcing, by fire and torture, the so-called conversion of the unfortunate population who had received them with unsuspecting and generous hospi-

tality. Step by step the Portuguese receded before the English company, one source of wealth after another was barred to them until, in 1661, they voluntarily yielded up to the English Crown the last of their important possessions, the city and district of Bombay, as part of the dowry of the Portuguese princess Catharine of Braganza when she was betrothed to Charles II. (Stuart). So ignorant were England's official statesmen at the time of the value of the gift, which they regarded as a most ungainly and unprofitable appendage, that they, in their turn, ceded it to the Company for the ridiculous consideration of an annual payment of £10 sterling!

3. Still, though so easily rid of Portuguese competition, the Company was far from running an unobstructed race for power and wealth. Their example speedily fired other nations to emulation. Within twelve years from their incorporation several East India Companies had sprung up: a Dutch, a French, and a Danish one. This last, however, as well as a German and even a Swedish one, which haltingly brought up the rear a full hundred years later, never were of sufficient account to molest the English Company or cause them any anxiety. Not so the two former. The Dutch, being confessedly the foremost maritime power all through the seventeenth century, and conducting their Indian venture not only on enterprising, but on vigorously aggressive principles, proved most formidable neighbors and rivals, the more so that they did not confine themselves to operations on the continent, but swiftly secured the partial or entire possession of the

numerous and inexhaustibly rich islands—Ceylon, Sumatra, Java, and the Moluccas—which stud the Indian Ocean, singly and in groups, forming a sort of appendage to India proper as well as a peristyle to the island world of the Pacific Ocean. It was only after a struggle, sometimes a bloody one, between the two companies, which lasted over a century, that the Dutch gradually retreated from the continent and centred all their efforts and resources on the islands which to this day obey their rule. The French Company was now the only real rival whom the English were bound to watch and fear, for its ambition was directed to precisely the same end that they pursued themselves : undivided supremacy in this, the treasure-land of the East, and as it was frequently managed by men of high ability, it seemed more than once on the point of actually compassing its object. The chief difficulty it had to contend with, and one which eventually stranded it, was the indifference of the people at home and the heartless callousness which refused it assistance of any sort at the most critical moments. It so happened that, in the middle of the eighteenth century, one of the ablest French directors, DUPLEIX, was pitted against one of England's most remarkable men, Governor—later Lord—CLIVE. The struggle between these two men, in open war and in diplomatic efforts to secure the favor of the most powerful native princes, furnishes one of the most brilliant pages of history. The signal victories gained by the Englishmen at that time, have been set down as the beginning of the modern British Empire in India, for, the French Company once beaten from the field, the competition was virtually at an end, and the French possessions do not interfere with the British rule any more than the few miles of land which the Portuguese still own on the western shore.

4. That this rule henceforth became firmly established and was more or less willingly submitted to by the people of India and such of the native princes who were still allowed, as allies or vassals of the Company, a semblance of independence and a limited range of power, England owed to the men who, at this particularly critical period, were invested with supreme authority. It was desirable that the conquest by force of arms should be followed up by a wise and mild civil administration, and it was owing to the Company's good fortune more than their wisdom that, for once, the Indian offices in their gift were filled by a set of men such as seldom are brought together to co-operate in a common field of action,—emphatically the right men in the right places. Lord Clive's successor, the illustrious and highly cultured WARREN HASTINGS, seems to have been the first English governor who took pains to understand the people he ruled. He was not an Orientalist, nor a scholar at all, either generally or specially. Had he been, he would have been far less well fitted either for his executive duties or for the part of sympathizing and impartial patronage into which he quite naturally fell towards those men, officially his subordinates, whose studies were of such material assistance to him in compassing his noble ends. As a private man, Warren Hastings

was an enlightened and refined amateur; as a statesman and the supreme ruler of a huge so-called barbarous land, whose inhabitants had, up to him, been looked on as so many million beasts of drought or burden, or—worse for them still—living treasure-casks, to be tapped, and staved in, and rifled of their contents by all and any means, he quickly gauged the importance of the unexpected help that was thus almost providentially tendered him towards his great aim: learning to *understand* the people and then govern them in accordance with modern humane standards.

5. But how do justice, wisely, comprehensively, to a people about whom one does not know the first thing? whose origin, history, worship, whose beliefs, views, modes of thought and life, are all a blank; whose manners and customs are looked down on from the foreigner's standpoint, as being all wrong, absurd, laughable, and not for one moment to be considered or respected, simply because they are unlike his own; whose laws . . . but their laws are unknown, as is their literary language—if they *have* a literature, a doubtful, or rather hitherto unmooted point. So, with the best will, nothing remains to the European governor, in his helpless ignorance, but to judge the cases that come before him, to the best of his ability, according to his own country's laws, as unknown and strange to the people as theirs are to him, or,—if thrown on his own discretion, after standards of modern Western thought and manners, which fit the Oriental's mind and life about as well as the European garb his

bodily habits and sense of beauty and fitness. Chance, which, in the vast field of Oriental discovery has, from the beginning, played so predominant a part, here again befriended the earnest searchers, by frequently putting unlooked for opportunities in their way, or placing within their reach precious finds of which they learned the value and the bearing only in using them, sometimes at first with quite a different object from that to which they were led by the threads thrust into their searching hands. Of how one may, in such studies, set out to look for one thing, and blunder on another, far richer and more valuable, we have an amusing instance on record in an experience of Sir William Jones, which opened to the amazed scholars of Europe the vast and hitherto unsuspected world of Indian fine literature.

6. It was scarcely five years since Sir William's appointment to the Supreme Court of Bengal, and four since the foundation of the Bengal Asiatic Society (1784), and in this short period the great Arabic and Persian scholar, who had brought to his comparatively late vocation—the law, the same earnestness, thoroughness, and facility that had so early lifted him to the summit in his beloved Oriental and linguistic studies, had very nearly mastered the intricate and unfamiliar Sanskrit tongue. Not that it was of much practical use in the transaction of current court business, for, as is perhaps not generally known except to special students, Sanskrit is a dead language, which stands to modern Hindustanee in the relation of Latin to Italian ; but so much was known, that the entire body of native high-standard litera-

ture, classical or special, was enshrined in that language, and Sir William, with his usual intrepidity, undertook an exhaustive study of India's national legislation, an intimate knowledge of which was indispensable to a rational and humane administration. As scholarly qualifications and competitive examinations were not dreamt of then as requirements for Indian appointments, it was necessary—if the good work now inaugurated was not to remain merely the temporary achievement of an exceptional group of men, to be obliterated by the ignorance of their successors—to place that knowledge within every functionary's reach, by transferring it into the English language. This gigantic task resulted in Jones' famous DIGEST OF HINDU LAWS,—which, however, he was not permitted to complete,—and in the translation of the INSTITUTES OF MANU, the code most widely acknowledged in India. This work, the last of a life heaped to overflowing with noble labor, but shortened by the long, never relaxing strain under a homicidal climate, was published just before his death, in 1790. It had for years been his pet project, and, the better to fit himself for it, he had devoted his few hours of comparative leisure to literary and linguistic studies in the seemingly boundless field of Sanskrit scholarship.

7. Once, when so employed, under the guidance of a competent and intelligent Brâhman master, Sir William bethought him of a passage in a well-known collection of Catholic missionaries' letters about certain "books called *Nátac*" and supposed to "contain a large portion of ancient history, without

any mixture of fable." As nothing is so hard to get in all the huge mass of Sanskrit writing as a crumb of real history, he made inquiries, having a strong inducement, as he says himself, in his desire to learn anything that might in any way be connected with the administration of justice. But he could not make much of the information that was given him, except that those books were not histories but abounded with fables, and consisted of conversations, in prose and verse, on an infinite variety of subjects, and in various dialects of India, "from which he naturally concluded that they were some sort of dialogues on moral and literary topics," until a more than usually observant and intelligent Brâhman, he goes on to relate, "removed all his doubts and gave him no less delight than surprise by telling him that the English had compositions of the same sort, which were publicly represented at Calcutta and bore the name, as he had been informed, of *plays*. . . ." Naturally, Sir William asked which was the most popular of these Nâtakas or dramas, and was answered "THE RING OF SHAKÛNTALÂ." Whereupon, he proceeds to tell,

> "I soon procured a correct copy, and, assisted by my teacher, began with translating it verbally into Latin, which bears so great a resemblance to Sanskrit that it is more convenient than any modern language for a scrupulous interlineary version. I then turned it word for word into English, and afterwards, without adding or suppressing any material sentence, disengaged it from the stiffness of a foreign idiom, and prepared the faithful translation of the Indian drama, which I now present to the public."

8. Thus, out of something very like a grammar exercise, came a revelation of beauty and high art, the unpretending form of which enhanced its effect

on the literary and scholarly world of the West. "Shakùntalâ" has been translated into nearly all European languages, sometimes in exquisite verse—but for years was known only from the great lawyer's almost interlinear prose rendering, and in this simple garb aroused unbounded enthusiasm and astonishment. Needless to say what a sudden lift was given in public opinion to the hitherto despised "natives" of a land valued merely for its wealth, by the discovery that, instead of the rude attempts at poetical expression with which the most liberal were willing to credit them, they possessed a fine literature as abundant, if not as varied, as any in the West—older, too, than any, not excepting the so-called classical ones, glittering with all the finish and the brilliancy of their country's own rainbow-hued thousand-faceted gems. For, with Shakùntalâ, the Hindu theatre was discovered, a mine as rich in legend and mythic lore as the Greek and Elizabethan dramas. With the latter, indeed, as piece after piece came to light, the Hindu drama was found to have astonishing affinities, not only in the general manner of treating the subject and working the plot, in the natural, unconstrained development of the characters and sequence of events, but down to details of form. "They are all in verse," says Sir William Jones, who, being once put on the right track, did not, we may be sure, rest content with one specimen, "where the dialogue is elevated, and in prose where it is familiar: the men of rank and learning are represented as speaking pure Sanskrit, and the women Prâkrit, which is little more than the language of the

Brâhmans melted down by a careful articulation to the softness of Italian; while the low persons of the drama speak the vulgar dialects of the several provinces which they are supposed to inhabit." Does not this description apply word for word to the Shakespearian drama? Not even prologues and epilogues are wanting—addresses to the audience by the manager, a chief actor, or an allegorical character, —with explanations of matters pertaining to the play, or the usual petitions for an indulgent hearing and kind forbearance with shortcomings, while the remarks or expressions of feeling thrown in by the secondary characters—friends, spectators, and the like—strongly remind us of the Greek chorus.[1]

---

[1] Not that any intrinsic connection between the two dramas can be supposed or admitted. Some few scholars, indeed, advance the hypothesis that the Hindu drama may have been influenced by its great Greek predecessor. They find a suggestion to that effect in the circumstance that Greek female slaves are mentioned in one play,—that the Hindu play, like the Greek tragedy, took for its heroes royal or semi-divine personages, and its subjects from the cycle of national myth and heroic romance. That the drama flourished in the Western provinces and along the Western coastland, while it had no hold at all on the Eastern portion of India, seems to them to confirm their hypothesis. But serious researches have resulted in the rejection of any direct action or intrinsic affinity. A study of the Hindu drama does not enter into the scope of this volume, except incidentally as one of the sources of our knowledge of the country and people. But it is a fascinating subject, on which full information can be obtained in the most attractive form from the following works: *The Hindu Theatre* of W. H. Wilson, with a most valuable introduction; the chapter on the same subject in Schroeder's popular but scholarly and reliable lectures, *Indiens Literatur und Cultur*; in *Études de Littérature Sanscrite* by Philibert Souppé; also *Le Théâtre Indien* (Paris, 1890), by Sylvain Lévy.

9. The Hindu drama, like the Elizabethan, bursts on us in full flush of perfection, and its beginnings, the unskilled stammerings of the voice which charms us with its plenitude of harmony, are lost to us. This is only natural, in an age and land where there was no printing-press, to create an artificial immortality and embalm for the bewilderment of future generations the still-born efforts of an infant muse: the wholesome working of that lately discovered law known as "survival of the fittest," applies to the intellectual as well as to the physical world. "Shakuntalâ" belongs to the golden age of the drama, that of a king of the name of VIKRAMÂDITYA, who reigned in the fifth century, A.D., at UJJAIN, one of the most ancient and sacred cities of India, in the present native vassal state of MÂLWÂ, and at whose court the author, KALIDÂSA, who has been surnamed "the Hindu Shakespeare," and who distinguished himself in other branches of poetry besides the drama, appears to have lived. It seems not a little wonderful that, in the remote and unknown East, a contemporary of Hengist and Horsa should indite works which could inspire such a critic as Goethe with lines like his famous epigram on Kalidâsa's favorite play:

Wouldst thou the young year's blossoms and the fruits of its decline,
And all by which the soul is charmed, enraptured, feasted, fed,—
Wouldst thou the earth and heaven itself in one sole name combine?
I name thee, O Shakùntalâ, and all at once is said.

10. Not less great than the admiration for the play as a work of art was the astonishment at the plot, when it was perceived that it is founded on one

of the most universally familiar stories of European folk-lore: that of the lover who, stricken by a wicked spell, forgets his love—whether sweetheart or bride—and recovers his memory of her only on seeing the golden ring he gave her, and which is brought back to him under a variety of romantic circumstances—sometimes by the maiden's or wife's own contrivance, as when she arrives to find him on the point of wedding another and manages to have the ring dropped into the goblet of wine presented him at the feast—sometimes by sheer accident. The latter is the solution adopted by Kalidâsa, and—doubly wonderful—the accident is the same which makes the subject of one of the best known and most popular stories bequeathed us by Greek antiquity. The ring is discovered in the stomach of an exceptionally fine fish caught in a stream into which Shakùntalâ had accidentally dropped it, and the fisherman, accused of stealing it, is brought into the presence of the king for judgment; the ring is produced, and, the moment it catches the monarch's eye, he awakes as from a trance and asks for his wife. Now, who does not remember the same ring-and-fish incident as told by Herodotus in his story of Polykrates, the too fortunate tyrant of Samos, who casts into the sea his most costly and highly prized ring, to propitiate the Deity by a voluntary sacrifice, and sees it reappear the same night at his table, cut out of the body of a huge fish presented to him by the fisherman as too fine for any but the royal board? There is no love in the case, and the Greek uses the incident to point a moral of his own, but the incident itself is there, in both, identical.

11. Another play by the same poet, VÎKRAMA AND URVASÎ, or THE HERO AND THE NYMPH, develops a mythical incident made as familiar to us by a popular story from a similar source. A celestial nymph loves and marries an earthly king, warning him, however, that she can abide with him only so long as he will be careful she shall not behold him disrobed. For many years they enjoy unalloyed happiness, when her former companions, the nymphs and sprites, who had sorely missed her, resolved to bring her back by stratagem and contrived, by sending an opportune flash of lightning in the night, that the condition of her existence on earth should be violated. In that flash she saw her lord divested of his robes,—and, with a wail, forthwith vanished. King Vîkrama mourned for her and sought her all over the world, until, after long, sorrowful wanderings, he found her and they were miraculously reunited. Even this brief epitome will at once have suggested to the lover of storydom the adventures of EROS AND PSYCHE as told by that bright story-teller, the precursor of Boccaccio and Chaucer, Greek APULEIUS, in spite of a few circumstances being altered or even inverted. In the Greek legend it is the lover who is divine and the woman is a mortal, forbidden from beholding his face or form not only disrobed, but in any way whatever. And he is not shown to her by any external agency, but she deliberately seeks him with a lighted lamp at the dead of night. Yet the external agency is supplied by the promptings of her sisters, who wish, out of envy or affection, to get her back, and urge her to the disobedience which is her undoing.

As natural, it is she who wanders and seeks for the lost one, to whom she is reunited in the end. And this story too, like that of Shakùntalâ, can be matched by one of a vastly different age and clime, the northern mediæval legend of LOHENGRIN, THE KNIGHT OF THE SWAN. He too is a more than human being and the maiden he weds is warned that she must ask him no questions as to his past—nor so much as to inquire who he is—for though he must satisfy her, that moment he leaves her. Like Psyche, she listens to evil promptings, breaks the command, and pays the penalty. In all these stories, vastly differing in details, substance and spirit are the same.

12. That such resemblances could not come under the head of casual coincidence was clear to the most superficial of the "general reader" class, and a momentary curiosity was pretty universally aroused as to what might be their cause and meaning. But the scholarly world—philologists, Orientalists, mythologists—was far more deeply stirred. This was confirmation of much knowledge that had been coming in thick and fast for some years,—ever since the English residents in India had begun to study Sanskrit, and made and promptly published the startling discovery of that ancient tongue's close kinship with all the languages, old and modern, of Europe. Confirmation, too, that completed observations already made in the parallel field of mythology, and embodied by Sir William Jones in a celebrated paper on the affinity—if not identity—of the divinities of the Brahmanic religion with the gods and goddesses of the classic world; an identity which

often extended to minute details, as in the case of KÂMA, the child-god of Love, bearer of a bow and arrows of flowers, whose very name, meaning DESIRE, seems merely translated into the Greek EROS, and the Latin CUPID. Owing to the same few scholars' indefatigable zeal, which was soon to arouse in Europe the emulation of such men as FRIEDRICH WILHELM VON SCHLEGEL and WILHELM VON HUMBOLDT, the field was widening almost hourly, and the great Hindu epics, the RÂMÂYANA and the MAHÂBHÂRATA, were becoming known,—in fragments at first, as the students went on on the simple plan of translating the selections given them to read by their native teachers, mostly Pundits of renown. But these fragments were like those scattered erratic granite blocks which show what the primeval mountains of the earth were made of. And it was evident that these epics were treasuries of national heroic legends, myths, and stories which all went to prove the same thing, besides being an absolutely inexhaustible mine of information not only on the customs and manners, but also, and even more, on the spiritual life of the Hindu people—the ways of their thinking in religion, philosophy, and ethics.

13. Poetry in India, like the country itself and everything in it—its scenery, its vegetation, all its nature—is on an enlarged scale with regard not only to copiousness of fancy and exuberance of imagery and diction, but to the actual size of its productions, the bulk of words. The dramas, long indeed, do not so far exceed the proportions familiar to our

training. But what shall we say of the two epics, especially the Mahâbhârata (more than twice the length of the Râmâyana), with its 110,000 *shlokas* or couplets of two lines, each more than double the length of an ordinary English blank verse line! Only to compute such a mass of words is a problem in arithmetic, and the result must be appalling to a student of even more than average working powers. But then these two gigantic repositories really constitute between them a national encyclopedia, not only of heroic and mythic legends and poetical creations, but in at least equal measure of the nation's philosophy, its religion, its political and social theories, and many more grave and profound matters which, in other countries, endowed with a clearer perception of proportions and the fitness of things, are not admitted into the scheme of what should be merely works of art, for purposes of entertainment of an elevating and ennobling nature. Of these Hindu poems, overflowing with wealth of every kind, but nondescript of form and absolutely promiscuous of contents, we can say that they take us through portals of tropical flowers and labyrinthine groves of ambrosial foliage and enticing dalliance, into a sterner world on a higher plane, where the pleasure-seeking mood changes to contemplative and vague questioning, while further still loom the shades of the ascetic anchorite's forest home, and beckon the snow-bound peaks of disembodied thought, in whose rarefied atmosphere nothing can breathe save God-centred meditation and absolute renunciation.

14. The way is long, and our knowledge of each stage indicated in the ITIHÂSAS (legendary and semi-historical, heroic poems) is supplemented by a mass of literature, the profoundest and abstrusest the world has known, and which to classify alone is a serious work both of memory and discernment, so that mere catalogues of manuscripts—their titles and a brief indication of their subject-matter—are among the most valuable contributions to Orientalist libraries. What we would call the scientific department is very respectably represented by a number of works on arithmetic, mathematics, astronomy, and grammar, this latter having been carried by the Hindu scholars to a perfection of subtility and precision never equalled by those of any other nation, ancient or modern. Then come jurisprudence and social science, expounded in elaborate works which have for their text books, 1st, the DHARMA-SÛTRAS and the DHARMA-SHÂSTRAS, a number of codes of various antiquity and authority, the best known of which is the MÂNAVA DHARMA-SHÂSTRA, or "Institute of Manu" (already mentioned), and, 2d, the GRIHYA-SÛTRAS, collections of practical rules for the conduct of life, domestic and religious. These manuals, which are meant for the use of only the priestly class, the Brâhmans, are far older than the SHÂSTRAS, to which they have in a measure served as foundation. Then there are the six systems of philosophy and metaphysics, which cover pretty well the ground explored and battled over by most schools of the West, from antiquity down to our own day: deism, pantheism, idealism, materialism, skep-

ticism, and even cynicism. Lastly, the PURÂNAS, literally "Old Stories," or, rather, "Tales of Eld," which might be, in a general way, likened to the Itihâsas, with this very distinctive difference, that —while these and the smaller and sometimes quite short epic poems called KÂVYAS give us the exploits and adventures of human and semi-divine but still mortal heroes,—the Purânas treat only of gods and their doings, of the creation and other kindred subjects, sacred if not wholly religious. In fact, their cycle is methodically classed under the following five heads: 1st, the creation of the world, or Cosmogony; 2d, its successive dissolutions and renovations; 3d, the genealogy, *i. e.*, the origin and parentage of the gods and patriarchs, or Theogony; 4th, the reigns of the great patriarchs and ages of the world; 5th, the history of the ancient, heaven-born dynasties of kings. The bulk total of these collected works, which contain almost the whole distinctively theological literature of the later development of the Brahmanic religion, or HINDUISM, is enormous. There are eighteen so-called "great Purânas," making together 400,000 *shlokas*, the longest heading the list with 81,000, and the shortest closing it with 10,000. Of these, some are already translated into various European languages, wholly or in portions; and the contents of all are well known, and, on the whole, thoroughly studied. They vary in importance and popularity, but greatly surpass in both the sixteen so-called "lesser" or "secondary" Purânas, the best known part of which is their titles, as they are not common, and lacking in interest or attractiveness, some even being written in prose.

15. Needless to enumerate the minor classes of works which make up the balance of Sanskrit literature: lyrical and other poems, stories in prose and verse—those of real interest to us being the so-called "beast-stories," the source and models of all the fable-literature of the Aryan world,—works on medicine, various crafts, fine arts, etc. They are generally of very late and many of actually modern date, except the beast-stories which, if comparatively late in form, are, as to contents, as old as the race itself, for most of the animal types and a great many of their adventures belong undoubtedly to its primeval treasury, which accounts for their universal adoption by all its branches. It is the vast and massive classes of literature, briefly outlined in the preceding paragraphs, from which we derive our most important and comprehensive knowledge of India; but they, too, are for the most part comparatively late productions, embodying stages of culture of very different periods, times ranging through more than twenty centuries, and some quite modern. Now twenty centuries do not take us back to a very remote antiquity—at least it does not seem such to our minds, trained by the last half-century of historical research to grapple with very different chronological problems, our horizon having been widened and moved further and further back until our mental vision now easily reaches the end of a vista of *seventy* centuries.

16. The first explorers of India's past already

felt the incompleteness of their efforts in that direction. They entered on their studies with appetites whetted by the few significant disclosures vouchsafed them by chance, and with a keen relish for further revelations along the same line, which was to take them to the glorious goal already dimly visible in the far distance: the primeval unity of all the so-called Aryan nations, in speech, in thought, in worship. They were the more prepared for arduous labor that they could not, as they very well knew, look for assistance to the faithful auxiliaries of the archæologist in other Oriental fields: the pickaxe and the shovel. The field of Indian research, up to a very late period, is absolutely bare of monuments —including under that name everything tangible, from a temple ruin to a rock inscription and to a fragment of statuary or pottery. All the monuments the Sanskritist can turn to are books, or more correctly manuscripts, and of these the mass kept daily increasing till it threatened to become unmanageable. Yet, even while almost buried under the abundance of valuable material, they felt that their progress was slow, heavy, unsatisfactory. Still, if the polar beacon-light, on which they kept their gaze unswervingly fixed, did not come nearer, and at times almost seemed to recede, it never disappeared, never went out. Soon they began to see the way that led to it straight, at first vaguely, then more and more clearly, at the same time that they felt an invisible barrier, not of their making, rise up between them and their soul's desire. This barrier was a purely moral one—a silent opposition on the part of the

English students' native teachers, Brâhmans all of them, of high social standing and great learning according to the nation's standard. Up to a certain point their English pupils found in them willing and sympathetic guides and helpers. But just as sure as they came to a passage that seemed to open a gate into the very fields where they longed to explore, their eager questioning was met with feigned ignorance, assumed indifference, or evasive rejoinders, generally of the purport that these were things that could not interest foreigners or repay their trouble, seeing they had no importance save for natives.

17. So much the Englishmen quickly made out: that all the subjects which they soon learned were to be kept closed from them, either by passive resistance or devices to divert their attention, were the very ones it most imported to them to find out about, invariably bearing on matters of ancient religion or law. They also discovered that these subjects and all the literature treating of them were considered sacred and, as such, to be jealously guarded from the sacrilegious prying of unholy strangers; furthermore, that, the Brâhmans as a class being specially entrusted with the guardianship of all things sacred and national, they did not wish their pupils, who were also their masters, to learn too much about matters the knowledge of which might enable them to strengthen their own power at the expense of the Brâhmans' own, and to unravel, on occasion, the plotting and scheming of the latter, as well as expose the fallacy of many of their claims and assertions. THE VEDA was the name of the forbidden knowledge—

literally, for the word *means* "knowledge." It was applied, as the English students found out, sometimes to the sacred books of the ancient religion of India, and sometimes to the body of literature that had gathered around them in the course of time. Those books, four in number, were said by the Brâhmans to be a direct verbal revelation from the Most High, and were soon understood by the scholars to be the fountain-head of India's religion and law both. All their efforts were henceforth bent in this direction, but they could accomplish very little, even when they contrived to get hold of portions of the precious texts, as they met another and not less disheartening obstacle in the fact that the language proved to be an older form of Sanskrit, which it was as impossible for them to master unassisted as it would be for us to understand without previous study the Anglo-Saxon writings of Bede or Alfred the Great.

18. The second generation of Sanskrit workers fared better, because the more enlightened Brâhman Pundits began to drop some of their reserve and forget their apprehensions before their English pupils' earnestness and singlemindedness. It is not improbable that their patriotic feelings, too, may have been flattered, and their hopes aroused of better government at the hands of men who were striving so hard for knowledge of the people they were called on to rule. How, for instance, could such a man as Henry Thomas COLEBROOKE fail to command their respect and sympathy, when they saw him, a youth of scarcely twenty, resist the

temptations which beset him in the midst of the wealthy, pleasure-loving, and dissipated English official society, and take refuge in his midnight studies unaffected by the allurements of the gambling-table?[1] Be it as it may, when Colebrooke, fifteen years after his arrival in India, after completing the compilation and translation of the *Digest of Hindu Law* begun by Sir William Jones, came out in the same year (1797) with a study of his own—*Essays on the Religious Ceremonies of the Hindus*,—the work "showed very clearly that he had found excellent instructors, and had been initiated in the most sacred literature of the Brâhmans," even had he not explicitly testified in his writings that Brâhmans had proved by no means averse to instruct strangers, and that they did not even conceal from him the most sacred texts of the Veda.[2]

19. Sir William Jones, in founding the Bengal Asiatic Society, became the initiator of systematic and consecutive research in the newly opened quarry. His friend and fellow-laborer, Charles Wilkins, lived to be greeted in his native land, at the close of an unusually long and well-filled life, with the title of "Father of Sanskrit Studies." And well earned was the recognition, since he often had sacrificed the tastes which drew him to purely scholarly pursuits in his chosen field, in order to devote himself to the drudgery without which the establishment of the Society must have remained barren of practical

[1] Colebrooke's Letters.

[2] Max Müller, *Chips from a German Workshop*, vol. iv., p. 371 (New York edition, Scribner, Armstrong, & Co., 1876).

results. It was he who organized the first Sanskrit printing office, with absolutely raw material in the shape of native printers and other workmen, who had to be, each individually, shown the very a-b-c of their craft. And not only that, but the type had to be designed and cast, so that Wilkins, in his own single person, was by turns, or all at one time, draughtsman, founder, compositor, type-setter, printer, and proof-reader. Yet these two men, great as were their merits, are regarded now, in the light of a century of marvellously successful work, rather as the precursors and prophets of a science of which Colebrooke is acknowledged the true messiah. For, if his predecessors opened, so to speak, the garden of Sanskrit *belles-lettres*, he it was who began that determined digging down amidst the roots and through the subsoil and stratified layers of words and facts which at length brought down the searchers to the very hard pan of positive knowledge. Religion, law, social institutions (especially that of caste), native sects, grammar, astronomy, arithmetic, and sciences generally, as known to the Hindus—in each of these provinces he showed the way and started the work mapped out for those who were to succeed him by some standard pieces of research, which, for skill and depth of treatment, have never been outdone, even if many of the positions he took up on the high-water line of the knowledge of his time, were naturally swamped by the advancing tide of science.

20. No province of Oriental research is as rich as the Sanskrit field, both in materials and in illustrious workers. Their name is legion; the mass of their

scholarly achievements, as piled on shelf upon shelf, in rows of more or less ponderous volumes, or scattered in loose essays and studies through numberless special periodicals in every European language, is such as to appal not only those that aspire to follow in their footsteps as original searchers, but even, if not still more, those who elect the more modest portion of popularizing their works, *i. e.*, of making the world at large interested in and familiar with their aims, their methods, and the results attained so far, and who, in order to do this successfully and reliably, must master the greater portion of what has been done, keeping well up to date, as this is work that never pauses, and each day may bring forth a discovery or a point of view more important than the last. To give the names of even the most illustrious of this admirable host were a hopeless attempt, besides that mere names are always unprofitable. Many will turn up of themselves in the following pages, in connection with their work, and the bibliographical list appended to this volume, as to the preceding ones, will, it is hoped, in a great measure, supply the want of information on this subject.

CHAPTER IV.

THE VEDAS.

1. WITH the vague and sweeping approximativeness with which we are wont to lump our knowledge or imaginings of all such things as are removed very far away from us in space or time, or both, we rather incline to think of "India" as one country, one nation. How ludicrously wide of the mark such a fancy is, has already been shown, and will appear repeatedly as we advance. Yet it is in so far excusable, that to the European mind, India is identified with one race—the Aryan; that her history is to us that of this race's vicissitudes on the Himâlayan continent, on which it has been supreme so long, materially and spiritually; that the history of Indian thought and speech is pre-eminently that of the Aryan mind,—until even now, when races have become so inextricably mixed that there are no longer any Aryan peoples, but only Aryan languages and, perhaps, traits of intellect and character, we turn to India as one of the fountain-heads of Aryan life.

2. Not *the* fountain-head. For we know beyond

the need of demonstration that Âryas descended into India after long periods both of stationary life and migrations, in the course of which they traversed the immensities of Central Asia; we further know almost to a certainty that these Âryas were a dissevered branch from a far greater and more numerous nation, to which we have given the name of INDO-ERANIANS, and which everything—especially the evidence of language and religion—shows to have lived undivided down to a comparatively late period, while and after other swarms had flown, in other directions, away from that primeval Aryan mother-hive, which, like all beginnings, must remain forever wrapped in mystery, though we can partly surmise what its language must have been like—the root of our flexional culture-tongues, and its myths,—the primary conceptions of nature in the working of her divinized forces.[1] We also have good reason to suspect that diversity of feeling in religious matters, deepening in time to a schism, may not have been foreign to the separation.[2]

3. When Zarathushtra embodied this revulsion of feeling, which had attuned his people's minds to loftier teachings, in his great religious reform, and gave forth that profession of faith which once forever stamped them with the stern earnestness, the somewhat sadly serious spirituality which was to distinguish them from all ancient nations,[3]—the separation

---

[1] See *Story of Media, Babylon, and Persia*, pp. 37 *ff*.

[2] *Ib.*, pp. 98–100.

[3] *Ib.*, pp. 102–104.

 12.—A LANDSCAPE IN LAHORE (PENJÂB).

must have been an accomplished fact, perhaps for some time already. It is then that we can imagine the first Aryan detachment—soon to be followed at intervals by others—emerging, still awe-struck and bewildered, with a sense upon them as of a wonderful escape, from the sinuous and beetling mountain passes through which they had followed at a venture the bounding, tumbling Indus where, with a sharp southward bend, the river for which a continent is named, digs and breaks its rocky bed out of gloom and wildness, into a region of sunlight and peaceful plains.

4. It was the PENJÂB. A land of many rivers and broad valleys, of mountains grading down into hills, wooded, forest-clad, of moderate clime and ever-bearing soil. It had everything to invite settlers—and to keep them a long, long time, even to isolation. For a glance at the map will show that this garden in the shape of a corner or triangle, while fenced from the outer world on two sides by a well-nigh impassable barrier, is on the third side separated from its own continent by a wide belt of desert; and its wonderful system of rivers is entirely its own; their course,—with the exception of the giant, Indus,—begins and ends within its limits. Five bountiful streams descend from various points of extreme Western Himâlaya, their courses converging, uniting by twos, now here, now there, until their waters blend into one short but wide, deep, and rapid river which has always borne the collective name PANTCHANÂDA, "The Five Rivers"—a name which was transferred, unaltered, to the land itself, and of

which "Penjâb" is the Persian form.[1] The Indus, the while, has been gathering volume and swiftness all by itself, without any contributions from affluents, of which it receives only a few inconsiderable ones in the upper portion of its course before it emerges into the open land. It advances, solitary, majestic, to where the Pantchanâda brings it the united tribute of "The Five," and then rolls down towards the sea, such a mighty, often storm-tossed, mass of waters, that the early poets habitually described it by that very name,—*Samudra*—which they used for the accumulation of atmospheric moisture in the shape of rain-clouds—the celestial ocean—and which was given later to the sea itself when the Âryas from the Penjâb, probably by navigation down the Indus, reached at last the Indian Ocean.

5. There is a name under which the land we know as Penjâb was even more widely designated both in the early or Vedic, and the later, so-called

[1] The five rivers can show up between them about five times as many names, which, to a beginner, is confusing. Their modern names are different from those of the Epic Brahmanic period, while the very oldest have been discovered in the Vedic literature of a remoter era still. Then the Greeks, who knew this portion of India tolerably well, had their own names for them, with a slight assonance to the native ones. The list begins with the westernmost, modern JHELUM, the Epic and Vedic VITASTÂ, of which the Greeks made HYDASPES; next comes Vedic ASIKNÎ, Greek AKESINOS, now TCHENÂB; these two unite and for a considerable distance flow on in one stream of double volume and rapid current, as indicated by the picturesque Vedic name MARUDVRIDHÂ, "The Wind-Swelled"; its later Sanskrit name, TCHANDRABHÂGÂ, hellenized into SANDROPHAGUS, it still retains. There is a pretty story of this river having set a term to Macedonian Alexander's Indian campaign; its Greek

Classic periods: it is SAPTA-SINDHAVAH,—"the Seven Rivers." This is the Hapta-Hendu of the Eranians,—the land mentioned in the famous geographical chapter of the Avesta among the earliest creations of Ahura-Mazda, and in the rock-inscription on the tomb of Dareios I. in the list of the Persian Empire's tributary provinces. It is, indeed, a far more correctly descriptive name, as it takes due count of the Indus,—the SINDH of Indian antiquity[1]—and includes a seventh river, of high and even sacred legendary fame, the SARASVATÎ, which may be described as the eastern boundary of this first Aryan dominion in India, since it skirts the edge of the Indian desert already mentioned. That river has, in the course of ages, undergone some rather peculiar changes. It springs from the western slopes of the slight watershed which divides the river-system of the Penjâb and the Indian Ocean from

---

name meaning "Devourer of Alexander," the conqueror is said to have accepted it as an evil omen and decided on returning. The modern RÂVÎ or IRÔTI is easily recognized in the Epic IRAVÂTÎ, but not in the Vedic PARUSHNÎ or the Greek HYDRAOTES, while both SHUTUDRÎ and the later SHATADRÛ are little altered in the Greek ZADADRES, and leave a slightly reminiscent sound in the modern SUTLEDJ; just as in the name of the VIYAS or BIAS there is a faint echo of the Vedic VIPASÂ, transparently hellenized into HYPASÌS, HYPANÌS, or, closer still, VIPASÌS. Of the five, the Sutledj is by far the most considerable, in length and volume, and the most frequently mentioned—almost as the Indus' twin sister river; "Indus and Sutledj" go together just as "Ganges and Djumna," the two leaders of the other twin system, that of the Gulf of Bengal.

[1] "Sindh" means "River." This is another instance of a country's principal stream being styled by the inhabitants "The River" *par excellence.*

that of Eastern Hindustân and the Gulf of Bengal, and used to accomplish its travels in the customary manner, and end them in the Indus, as indicated on the map by the punctured line which designates its original course. But the Sarasvatî does not seem to have had the vigor of its sister-rivers. Perhaps from scantness of water at the start, or from the spongy nature of the soil which, being dry and sandy, absorbed too much of its volume—be it as it may, its waters gave out, and at some time it stopped midway and got lost in the sands of the desert. This must have happened already at a very early period, for quite ancient manuscripts mentioned the place as a landmark, observing that such or such a locality is distant so or so many days' march from where the Sarasvatî disappears into the ground. What is left of it is now known, in its upper course, as the SARSUTÎ, and, lower down, it changes its name to GHARGHAR. At the present time it has no importance save that which it derives from old poetic and legendary associations and from having been one of the original "Seven Rivers" that graced and nourished the first Aryan settlements in the land—"the Seven Sisters," or "the Seven Mothers," as the ancient bards often gratefully and prettily addressed them in their songs.

6. A people's life and pursuits were mapped out for it in such a country: agriculture and cattle-breeding—the cornfield and the pasture, the barn and the dairy, together with the few simple auxiliary crafts which make primitive farming self-sufficing—pottery, carpentering, hide-tanning, spinning, and

 13.—SOURCES OF THE GANGES.

14.—THE GANGES AT GANGATRÎ.

weaving,—these were the departments which claimed nearly the whole attention of the Aryan settlers, the joint and divided labor of their men and women. It would have been strange if the many wide and deep rivers had not encouraged boat-building, even ship-building and navigation; so that, while the general formation of the land, divided by intersecting mountain spurs into countless valleys, favored the establishment of separate and independent tribes, the many easy ways of communication fostered neighborly intercourse, and laid the beginnings of commerce. These almost ideal conditions for a nation's development, moreover, though full of the promise of great prosperity, did not in the least dispose it to indolence or effeminacy. For, generous as was the soil, it repaid labor, but would not, like many tropical zones and isles, support the human race in idleness; balmy as was the climate part of the year, it was not enervating, and winter, snow-clad, was a yearly visitant. Then there were wild animals, especially wolves and bears, to be kept at bay. Last but not least, ample scope was afforded these first Âryas of India for the development of manly and even warlike qualities by their position in a land which they had occupied and held in defiance of a brave and numerous native population who kept up armed resistance probably for centuries, and receded or submitted only step by step. Not for several hundred years did this conquering colonization, pushing slowly eastward, cross the watershed and enter the valley of the Ganges.

7. The natives, whom the Âryas for a long time

gathered under the general Old-Aryan designation of DASYU,[1] belonged to a black, or at least a very dark race, and everything about them, from their color and flat noses, to their barbarous customs, such as eating raw or barely cooked meat, and their Shamanistic goblin-worship,[2] was intensely repulsive to the handsome, gentler mannered and, to a certain degree, religiously refined and lofty-minded Âryas, who strenuously kept away from them and were especially intent on avoiding the moral contamination of association with them precisely in matters of religion and of worship. There is every reason to believe that this spirit of fastidious exclusiveness was the occasion of their collecting and ordering into one body the hymns and sacred songs embodying the religion they brought with them, and which probably had not yet at that early period assumed the finished poetic form under which it has at last descended to us. This work was accomplished by a number of specially gifted men, poets and priests both, the RISHIS of India's oldest and sacred literature, at more or less long intervals and at different periods, ranging over certainly the whole of five hundred years, probably much more. The result is the collection known as the RIG-VEDA,—"the Veda of praise or of hymns,"—or, to give the full title: the RIG-VEDA-SAMHITÂ.

---

[1] Meaning simply "peoples," "tribes"; a meaning which the word, under the Eranian form DÂHYU, retains all through the Avesta and the Akhæmenian inscriptions, while in India it soon underwent peculiar changes, as will be seen.

[2] See *Story of Chaldea*, p. 180, and the chapter "Turanian Chaldea" generally.

8. The word *samhitâ* means "collection." It is here used to denote the collection of original MANTRAS (hymns, sacred texts),[1] 1028 in number, which compose the Rig-Veda, free of all additions in the way of explanations, commentaries, and the like. This is, without the shadow of a doubt, *the oldest book of the Aryan family of nations*,—in contents if not in actual tangible shape, for writing did not come into use for centuries after even the latest of the Rig-hymns had finally assumed the poetical garb in which they have come down to us, and which cannot have been later than 1000 B.C., while it was probably much earlier. And when close study of the hymns has given us the training necessary to discern, from intrinsic evidence of language and matter, the oldest portions even of this stupendous collection,—most probably about 1500 B.C. and rather earlier than later,—we are forced to the admission (for which, however, we are not unprepared, having already had glimpses, beyond the Indo-Eranian period, of a primeval or Proto-Aryan era)[2] that many, both of the words and the conceptions that confront us there, already mark a secondary stage of development and are the result of historical growth.

9. The earliest religious life of the Penjâb Ârya and its outer forms, as they can still faintly be traced here and there through the later complications of

---

[1] An old Indo-Eranian word, familiar to us under the Eranian form *Manthra* from the Avesta. (See *Story of Media*, etc., pp. 30, 49, 86.)

[2] See *Story of Media*, etc., p. 37.

the Rig-Veda, are beautifully simple—almost entirely family worship. The head of the household is also its spiritual representative and leader; he lights the flame of the daily sacrifice, which he feeds with the simple offering of melted butter and cakes, singing the appropriate hymns. But this latter feature already contained the germ of a much more artificial state of things. What *were* appropriate hymns? The selection implies a form, a ritual. The 1028 songs are divided into ten separate books or collections *(mandalas)* some of them subdivided into smaller groups, the authorship (more probably compilation) of each being ascribed to some particularly renowned saintly poet-priest—Rishi—of olden times. The historical authenticity of these names is of course more than doubtful, as they became, in the course of time, encrusted with such a growth of myth and legend as to leave almost no loophole for anything like sober, reasonable conjecture. On the whole, it may be assumed, with no small degree of probability, that behind these names would be found not only individuals, but also whole families in successive generations, in which both priesthood and poetic gifts were hereditary. It is these families who will have made the selections and gradually established the more and more systematized forms of worship which, by the time the Aryan conquest and colonization had, in their steady eastward progress, reached the valleys of the Upper Gangâ and Yamunâ, had expanded into the most elaborate and intricate ritual and sacrificial ceremonial the world has ever known, in the hands of an exclusive and privileged priesthood, who, under their final name of BRÂHMANS, had in the interval grown into that all-powerful caste, which, for nearly thirty centuries, has held India prostrate—the most perfect theocracy of any land or age, possibly rivalled only by the Egyptian.

10. Where there is a liturgy, there needs must be prayer-books. Such was the origin and such the use of two other *samhitâs* or collections included among the sacred books under the titles of YAJUR-VEDA and SÂMA-VEDA. Both consist of hymns and fragments of hymns (*mantras*, "texts") taken out of the Rig, and arranged in a certain order so as to accompany each action and incident of any given religious service, and especially sacrifices—these latter in particular having become so numerous and varied as to require the ministrations of a great many priests,—on solemn occasions as many as seventeen,—of unequal rank and having entirely different, very strictly prescribed and limited duties. Some are to mutter their *mantras*, some to recite them rapidly and moderately loud, others to intone, and others again to sing them. The *mantras* of the Sâman, which can be traced to the Rig with a very few exceptions—78 out of 1549—are all to be chanted. Those of the Yajur mostly come from the same source, but are interspersed with passages in prose, containing explanations and directions for the guidance of the priests who make use of this liturgical manual.[1] They are grouped in two uneven halves

[1] These explanatory interpolations are thought to be the oldest existing specimens of Aryan or Indo-European prose-writing.

or parts—the "Black Yaju" (TAITTIRÎYA SAMHITÂ) and the "White Yaju" (VÂJASANEYÂ SAMHITÂ)—an arrangement insufficiently accounted for by a very grotesque legend.

11. For a long time these three *Samhitâs*—the Rig, the Yaju, and the Sâman—the bulk of them in reality reducible to only one, the Rig,[1]—formed the entire body of sacred lore, under the collective title of TRAIVIDYA, *i. e.*, "the threefold Veda," or "the threefold knowledge." It was only at a considerably later period, for which no precise date can be suggested, that a fourth one was incorporated in the sacred canon—the ATHARVA-VEDA. It may therefore, in one way, be called a comparatively modern addition. Yet in another it may probably lay claim, at least in part, to a higher antiquity than even the Rig-hymns. Nothing could well be imagined more different in contents and more opposite in spirit than these two *samhitâs*. That of the Atharvan contains a comparatively small number of *mantras* from the Rig, and those only from the portions unanimously recognized as the latest, while the bulk of the collection along with some original hymns of the same kind and, in many cases, of great poetic beauty, consists chiefly of incantations, spells, exorcisms. We have here, as though in opposition to the bright, cheerful pantheon of beneficent deities, so trustingly and gratefully addressed by the Rishis of the Rig, a weird, repulsive world of darkly scowling demons, inspiring abject fear, such as never

[1] The Yajur-Veda contains some original matter, which has been found to be not later than the Rig.

sprang from Aryan fancy. We find ourselves in the midst of a goblin-worship, the exact counterpart of that with which we became familiar in Turanian Chaldea.[1] Every evil thing in nature, from a drought to a fever or bad qualities of the human heart, is personified and made the object of terror-stricken propitiation, or of attempts at circumvention through witchcraft, or the instrument of harm to others through the same compelling force. Here as there, worship takes the form of conjuring, not prayer; its ministers are sorcerers, not priests. The conclusion almost forces itself on us, that this collection represents the religion of the native races, who, through a compromise dictated by policy after a long period of struggle, ending in submission, obtained for it partial recognition from the conquering and every way superior race. It is easy to see how the latter, while condescending to incorporate the long abhorred ritual into their own canonical books, probably at first in some subordinate capacity, would, so to speak, sanctify or purify it, by supplementing it with some new hymns of their own, addressed to the same deities as those of the Rig and breathing the same spirit.[2] If, as is more than probable, this is the history of the fourth Veda, the manner of its creation justifies the seemingly paradoxical assertion that it is

[1] See *Story of Chaldea*, chapter iii., "Turanian Chaldea," especially pp. 153-170.

[2] We have seen something of the kind in the fusion of the old Shamanism of Turanian Chaldea with the nobler religion of the Semitic priestly rulers, actuated most probably by a similar policy of conciliation.—See *Story of Chaldea*, pp. 174-179, and especially pp. 235-237.

at once the most modern of the four, and, in portions, more ancient than even the oldest parts of the Rig-Veda. As a *samhitâ*, it is a manifestly late production, since it bears evidence of having been in use in the valleys of the Gangâ and the Yamunâ; but the portions which embody an originally non-Aryan religion are evidently anterior to Aryan occupation.

12. It would be a mistake to suppose that the *mantras* of the Yajur and the Sâman are reproduced from the Rig-Veda with absolutely literal accuracy. Indeed this is far from being the case, and although there never is any difficulty in identifying the texts, a careful collation of them shows many, at times quite considerable, discrepancies. This fact is very easily accounted for. The oldest known manuscripts of the Rig-Veda do not date back much earlier than 1500 A.D. Yet, two thousand years before that, about 600 B.C., the study of it, exclusively pursued in several theological schools, by the simple but arduous process of memorizing, was so accurate and minute that, with a view to establish the text and prevent interpolations, every verse, word, and syllable had been counted. From treatises written at that period we learn that the number of the words is 153,826, that of the syllables 432,000, while that of the verses is differently computed and varies from 10,402 to 10,622. Now it is quite possible, as every-one may find out by trying on a passage of either prose or verse, to alter a quotation, without materially injuring the sense, by changing some of the words and substituting others of the same length, so that the ear will detect no difference. Indeed this

often happens when quotations are made from memory. How easily would such corruptions occur where there was no written standard of the canonical text to check and correct them! The wonder—a great, standing wonder—is that the text was preserved so unimpaired, on the whole and in detail. But where deviations did occur, of course each particular school would not admit them, but stood by its own text as being the only pure one, and thus it came to pass that we have several versions of the Rig-Veda slightly differing in details. Furthermore, when the Rig *mantras* were arranged in liturgical order as prayer-books or sacrificial manuals for the priests, the compilers might slightly adapt them to this or that action of the ritual, and all these causes more than account for the divergences in the *samhitâs* of the Yajur-Veda and the Sâma-Veda.

13. To be studied with such exceeding care, to have its every syllable numbered and treasured as so many crumbs of gold, a book must needs be, not only sacred, but old. The fear of losing some of the spiritual wealth is closely followed by that of losing the full appreciation of it—of ceasing to understand it. Then begins the period of commentaries. Everything has to be explained. The language has become antiquated. The poetic metres—very rich and varied in the Rig-Veda—are out of use, and must be studied laboriously as we study those of our dead languages. Allusions to once familiar things are no longer understood. Myths are lost track of; their true meaning is forgot. Names that once were household words and told their own tale, have become

empty sounds. In short, times have changed and the thread is broken. On the other hand, these new times must be anchored on to the old. All these new things—new notions, new customs, new laws, new rites, new social conditions—must be accounted for, justified, consecrated by the old, now almost unintelligible, for these are the sole, universally acknowledged, holy fountain-head of the entire national life—social and spiritual. It will be easily seen what a feat of intellectual gymnastics such a task must have been, nor will it be wondered at that there was enough of it to keep several generations of priestly specialists occupied. The beginning was made with the prose passages intermixed with the *mantras* of the Yajur-Veda, and which converted that compilation into a manual for uses that had not been contemplated by the old Rishis, but had gradually grown out of sundry slender roots which twined their nearly invisible threads below the bare surface of the ancient simple worship.

14. Such was the origin and purport of the numerous theological works which, under the name of BRÂHMANAS (composed by Brâhmans and for the use of Brâhmans), formed the staple literature of the Aryan Hindus through several centuries, belonging as distinctively to the second stage of their establishment in the northern half of the Himâlayan continent, that gravitating around the Upper Gangâ and Yamunâ, as the early portions of the Rig-Veda belonged to the first stage, with the Sindh for the main artery of their material life. In this way the Brâhmanas mark the transition from Vedic culture

to the later Brahmanic social order and modes of thought—indeed help to bring on that transition, some evidently belonging to the beginning, others to the end of that intercalary period.

15. As was but natural, this work gave rise to numerous theological schools, each of which jealously guarded and handed down its own version of this or that Brâhmana, just as was the case with the Vedas themselves. This of course materially increases the difficulties that beset our students, especially when one remembers that each of the four Vedas had several Brâhmanas attached to it. Many are lost, or not yet found, but it is doubtful whether they would add much valuable knowledge to that imparted by those which are open to our inspection, the survivors naturally being the most important and popular works. Perhaps the most interesting portion of each Bráhmana is the appendix with which each is supplied, under the title of ÂRANYAKA —"belonging to the forest"—for the use of such Brâhmans as had retired from the world into forest hermitages, to spend there a few quiet years, or the latter end of their lives. Four Âranyakas are known to us.

16. As already remarked elsewhere, all religions that have sacred books, and, in consequence, an immutable canon of law and belief, claim for them a superhuman origin.[1] They are to be accepted, obeyed, believed in, as being supernaturally dictated or revealed to their human authors by the Deity. The body of Scriptures which the Hindus gather under

[1] See *Story of Media*, etc., pp. 17-19.

this head is unusually large, as it comprises not only the *mantras* of the Vedas but the whole of the Brâhmanas, including the philosophical UPANISHADS. They call it SHRUTI, "what was heard," in opposition to SMRITI or "what was remembered,"—only remembered, and therefore liable to error, to be respected as invested with a sort of secondary sacredness, but not necessarily and implicitly believed, as a matter of salvation. All the law books, including the great code of Manu, are *Smriti*, so are the Itihâsas (see p. 94), the Purânas (95), and another important class, of which anon. It would seem to the unbiassed mind as though the Rig-Veda alone, being the corner-stone and fountain-head of India's entire spiritual life, would be entitled to be enshrined in it as *Shruti*—revealed, repeated from "what was heard" by the Rishis who were the chosen vessels and instruments of the divine message to men. This would be logical, but would not have suited the Brâhmans at all. This most ambitious and crafty of all priesthoods made such exorbitant, nay monstrous demands on the credulity, docility, and liberality of the people over which they claimed—though they may never have quite established—absolute power, both spiritual and temporal, that not even such a contemplative, indolent, physically enervated race as the once vigorous Âryas were changed into by a long sojourn amid the relaxing, debilitating influences of semi-tropical Eastern Hindustân, would have submitted to them tamely and unresistingly, had they not become imbued with the conviction that they were obeying the will of Heaven. Now all these things that the Brâhmans claimed for themselves were not in the Rig-Veda,—to begin with the claim to revelation itself, which the old poets did *not* put forth for their hymns, of which, indeed, they emphatically speak as their own creation, boasting that they made this or that new song, "as the carpenter fashions a wagon." It had all to be spun out of embryonic hints contained in scattered texts, meanings made out, twisted, and made to fit where needed. The text was nothing, the interpretation was everything. This was supplied by the Brâhmanas, and so it came to pass that a huge body of literature—larger than we even yet can realize, since many Brâhmanas have been lost or not yet found—by a host of authors, of a score of different theological schools, and ranging over between five and eight hundred years, was enveloped in one shroud of mystery and sacredness and labelled SHRUTI, "Revealed." Of course such a high-handed proceeding could not but give rise to contradictions and glaring inconsistencies. Thus, the Brâhmanas are continually referred to by the names of their authors or at least schools, and spoken of as "old" or "new," which is downright heresy, as *Shruti* can, properly speaking, be neither old nor new, having pre-existed, unaltered, through all eternity. But theological casuistry will thread its way out of worse difficulties.

17. *Smriti*,—which might be comprehensively paraphrased by "venerable tradition"—embraces a vast range of subjects and of time, as we have seen. But there is one set of literary productions of this

extensive class which specially belongs to the Vedas, and supplements the Brâhmanas and Upanishads. They are manuals on certain principal subject-matters connected with and partly contained in them and which go to the making of the perfect Vedic lore required of every Brâhman. These subject-matters are six in number, and, by their nature, show the kind and minuteness of the study to which the Veda—especially the Rig-Veda of course—has been subjected from very early times. They come under the following heads:

1. Phonetics (pronunciation and accentuation),—SIKSHÂ.
2. Metre—CHHANDAS.
3. Grammar—VYÂKARANA.
4. Explanation of words (etymology, homonyms, and the like)—NIRUKTA.
5. Astronomy—JYOTISHA.
6. Ceremonial—KALPA.

An exhaustive knowledge of these six things is considered so essential to a full understanding of the Veda and the proper idea of the infinitely complicated forms of worship evolved out of the Rig, that they are said to belong to it organically as members to a body, and are very realistically called VEDÂNGAS, "limbs of the Veda," as necessary to its articulate perfection.

18. It follows from this that, in speaking of "the six Vedângas" we do not mean six distinct books or treatises, as is sometimes superficially concluded, but six subject-matters which are contained in the Veda as part of its substance and which are to be abstracted

thereout and developed for purposes of study. We continually apply a similar process to Homer, or to Shakespeare. We might just as well speak of Homeric accentuation, Homeric metre, Homeric grammar, Homeric mythology, Homeric astronomy, Homeric worship, and say that these six subjects or studies are "the pillars of Homeric scholarship." It further follows that, if there were six Vedângas, the numbers of works or manuals treating of them could multiply indefinitely—which is just what did happen. One feature, however, was common to all these works; as they were only meant to specialize and epitomize knowledge which for the most part was already scattered, in a loose and desultory form, through the Brâhmanas, they were compiled in short paragraphs or aphorisms compact and concise—a sort of telegraphic memorandum style,—in which brevity often degenerates into obscurity and at times into an almost unintelligible jargon, that provides enough hard nuts to crack for a few more generations of special students. These collections are called SÛTRAS, literally "strung together," or rather "sewn together," from the root *sîv* or *syû*, "to sew." [1]

19. The Hindu scholars must have found this epitomic hand-book style particularly convenient and helpful to the memory, for they applied it to many other than specially Vedic subjects: law, philosophy, medicine, crafts. These subjects belonging to the "remembered" or "traditional" half of classi-

[1] Sometimes the Sûtras are comprised under the term "Vedânga."

cal literature, *Smriti*, the Sûtras that treat of them are designated as SMÂRTA-SÛTRAS, to distinguish them from those that treat of matters connected with "revelation," or "what was heard,"[1] *Shruti*, and which go by the general name of SHRAUTA-SÛTRAS. Of these, as of Brâhmanas, there are several sets annexed to each Veda, and they embrace a large variety of subjects, minute subdivisions of the general matter classed under the headings of the Vedângas, till we actually find a set of Sûtras on the art of adapting the words of the sacred hymns to music. It may be confidently asserted that India is the only country in the world where grammar, prosody, versification, are a portion of the nation's *sacred* literature, and indeed partly of its revealed scriptures, since the bulk of the material worked over by the Sûtra-compilers in their peculiar style, is really found in the Brâhmanas and, in one case, in the Veda itself—meaning the prose portions of the Yajur-Veda. However incongruous and almost grotesque this may appear at the first glance, if unexplained, it becomes quite logically intelligible when the connection is made plain and pursued from the start.

20. The sacredness attaching to these branches of

---

[1] It is quite natural that revelation should be conceived of as coming through the sense of hearing in an age so much anterior to writing, and even later, when, preferably and *on principle*, the entire sacred literature was committed by students to memory, being received orally from the teacher's lips. Yet, curiously enough, parts of *Shruti* are usually spoken of as *seen*. Thus a certain Rishi is said to have *seen* certain hymns of the Rig-Veda which have come down under his name.

study, usually considered as emphatically a part of the layman's education, accounts for the extraordinary pains and care early bestowed on them, and which culminated in the most elaborate, profound, subtle, and finished investigations of language ever achieved by any people. It will be noticed that such questions make up four out of the six Vedângas: Phonetics, Metre (or versification and prosody), Etymology (comprising homonyms and synonyms), and Grammar proper. In the intricate system of sacrificial rites, based on forms pure and simple, into which the once beautiful Vedic worship quickly and surely degenerated, one misplaced accent, one mis-pronounced word, one falsely given quantity, was supposed not only to destroy the beneficial virtue of a sacrifice, but actually to turn it against the sacrificer. Yet how easy to commit such a slip when using only half intelligible words and forms in a language which, from being at all times a more or less artificial, literary idiom, was fast coming to be a dead one! What wonder then if nice points of grammar and prosody became of vital importance, and exercised for centuries the choicest faculties, the unremitting efforts of the national intellect; if each theological school fiercely vindicated and clung to its own version of a passage—nay, its own pronunciation, its own accentuation of this or that word, producing a long and varied series of scientifically elaborated treatises (Sûtras), the larger number of which, judging from quotations in those that were preserved, have evidently been lost, only the best having survived the natural selection of unwritten literature, the productions of which must stand or fall exclusively on their own merits.

21. We have now arrived at the end of a survey, not incomplete, if necessarily brief, of what can, in the stricter sense, be called Vedic Literature. In a wider sense, all the literature of India may, theoretically, be said to come under that head, since the Veda—the Rig-Veda in the last instance—pervades and dominates her spiritual life, even as her own Himâlaya sways and regulates the conditions of her material existence. But the special and distinctive Vedic literature is that which follows directly from the Veda and revolves around it, treating only of such matters as it either contains or suggests. It naturally falls into three very obvious main divisions: 1, the Mantra period—the period of collecting the songs with no special object beyond that of preserving them; 2, the Brâhmana period—the period of commentary and a certain amount of exegesis, with the patent object of establishing the supremacy of the Brâhman caste; 3, the Sûtra period—the period of concise special treatises for practical use at school and sacrifice. Chronologically, these periods do not strictly succeed one another, any more than the so-called culture ages—of stone, of brass, of iron—but overlap both ways over and over. Thus, if the second period corresponds to a well-defined stage of the Âryas' conquest of India—that of their advance eastward and their establishment in the valleys of the Gangâ and Yamunâ—the third may be said to straggle down actually into modern times, since the monumental commentary on the Rig-Veda,

the Brâhmans' standard authority, was written by SÂYANA as late as the fourteenth century of our era.[1]

---

[1] PÂNINI'S no less monumental grammar, though a much earlier work (4th cent. B.C.), and by its subject belonging to the Vedângas, can hardly be classed under strictly Vedic literature, for the language which he found and dissected with an acumen and thoroughness unrivalled even by Greek grammarians, is not that of the Veda at all, and Vedic forms of speech are studied by him as curious philological relics.

CHAPTER V.

THE RIG-VEDA: THE OLDER GODS.

1. WHEN we prepare to investigate one of the world's great religions, and before we enter on an analytical study of details, we naturally incline, in our desire to feel firm ground under our feet, to ask the preliminary question: What is its character? in what category should it be classed? to what division of the spiritual world does it belong? Polytheism? Pantheism? Animism? or what other? When it is the Rig-Veda into which we are about to plunge, we doubly feel the need of some such guiding thread, some anchor to rest upon, for its 1028 hymns, bristling with names and allusions, produce, on a first perusal, a labyrinthine, chaotic, wholly bewildering impression. But alas, a direct, plain answer to such a question is seldom, if ever, possible, and, in the case of the Rig-Veda, perhaps a little less so than in that of any other analogous spiritual document. The growth of a long series of centuries, elaborated in many million busy, subtle brains, containing a great race's spiritual food for as many centuries to come and materials for endless transformations, could not

possibly be so simple and transparent a thing as to admit of a sweeping definition in one word. The study of the Zend-Avesta showed us how many varied elements, and how intricately stratified, go to the making of a great national religion. The same unconscious work of time and influences confronts us in the Veda, but by so much more many-sided and complicated by how much the contemplative, introspective character which the Âryas developed in India is more involved and self-absorbed than that of their sternly simple, active, and hardy Eranian brethren.

2. Let us, however, attempt to answer the question with which we began the present chapter, just to see how far and deep it will carry us. Even a cursory first study of our text will establish the following points: A great many gods are named and invoked in the Rig-Veda; consequently, the religion it embodies is decidedly POLYTHEISTIC; the spirits of deceased ancestors come in for a large share of honor and worship, so that ANIMISM may be said to be a conspicuous feature of it; an early tendency to view the deity as pervading the universe, both as a whole and in its minutest parts, animate or inanimate—a view exhaustively expressed in such words as these: "He whose loins the seas are" is also "contained in this drop of water"—early reveals a strong attraction towards PANTHEISM; while many are the passages which explicitly inform us that the various gods are only different names of "that which is One"—more than hinting at a dim, underlying MONOTHEISM. There is no doubt that the purer and

more abstract conceptions could be traced to the later of the many centuries which it took to evolve the Rig-Veda in its final form, if we but had a sure key to its chronology; as it is, we have only, as in the Avesta, the internal evidence that goes so far in the hands of trained criticism, to support and guide our impressions, our conjectures. But one thing appears sure: Vedic religion at no time, until opened to alien and grosser influences, was idolatrous. In this respect the Âryas of India were in no wise behind their brethren of Erân: nature was their temple; they did not invite the deity to dwell in houses of men's building, and if, in their poetical effusions, they described their Devas in human form and with fanciful symbolical attributions, thereby unavoidably falling into anthropomorphism, they do not seem to have transferred it into reproductions more materially tangible than the spoken word—into the *eidolon* (portraiture,—of limner's, sculptor's, or potter's hand) —which becomes the *idol.*

3. And if the Rig-Veda may be shown to contain the germs of most of the religions and even philosophical systems which subsequently covered the spiritual soil of India with crops of such bewildering luxuriancy, the main character of this book of books, in nearly half its *mantras*,—answering, no doubt, to the earlier and main period of their composition and collection,—is simple and easy to define; at this earliest and unalloyed stage, the religion which we see faithfully mirrored in them is NATURALISM, pure and simple, *i. e.*, the worship of the Powers of Nature as Beings, generally beneficent, with only a very

few absolutely Evil Ones, such as Darkness and Drought; these latter, however, are not worshipped, nor even propitiated, but unconditionally abhorred by men, fought and conquered by the Powers of Good. In this unalloyed naturalism, we can watch the birth of myths and catch it, so to speak, in the act, by the simple proceeding of translating the names of each divine or semi-divine being as it confronts us in an invocation or in a bit of story (for long and especially connected and consistent stories are the works of a later, elaborating, and compiling age). We then perceive, to our astonishment, that they are not names at all, but either matter-of-fact common nouns, direct designations of the natural object under consideration, or else a verbal noun expressing some characteristic action of that object—as "the Pounders," "the Howlers," names of the Storm-Winds—or an adjective, a more or less ornate epithet, describing one or other of its characteristic properties or aspects. So that, by merely dismissing the capital initials, we reduce an incipient story—a primary myth containing all the live germs of future poetic and legendary development—into a fanciful, poetical description of a natural phenomenon—like the various stages of the sun's progress, the incidents of a thunderstorm, the dramatic episodes of a drought. Special illustrations of these positions are scarcely needed here, since all the following pages will, in a measure, consist of such illustrations. But, before we investigate the Vedic natural pantheon, it may not be amiss to repeat the definition of the word MYTH given in another volume,[1] because it should be borne in mind through all the study on which we are entering, and will be found to cover each single case subjected to it. This it is: "*A myth means simply a phenomenon of nature presented not as the result of a law, but as the act of divine or at least superhuman persons, good or evil powers.* Reading and practice will show that there are many kinds of myths, but there is none which, if properly taken to pieces, thoroughly traced and cornered, will not be covered by this definition." The beauty of the Vedic myths is that they need no cornering, no taking to pieces, mostly being themselves embryonic, and resolving themselves, at a touch, back into the natural elements out of which they directly emanated, without as yet materializing into any such flesh-and-blood reality as, say, the biography of a Greek god.

4. We shall never know exactly what the inheritance was which the Âryas of the Sapta-Sindhavah received from the time—the so-called Indo-Eranian period—before the separation of the two sister races, the original material out of which grew the Rig-Veda. But there are some large primary conceptions in it which clearly confront us in the Zend-Avesta also, and which we are therefore justified in ascribing to the original, primeval Âryas, the ancestors of both. We may be tolerably well assured that so much of these primary conceptions as we can trace in the Rig-Veda unalloyed with elements betokening local Indian conditions and influences, represents the

[1] See *Story of Chaldea*, p. 294, and Ch. VII. (on Myths) generally, which should be carefully re-read.

earlier stage of the religion which was to become so complicated and manifold. It is not impossible to disentangle these simpler outlines from an intricate aftergrowth, and we are not surprised to find them representing the purest naturalism, with just so much moral consciousness and religious feeling as cannot be absent from the spiritual life of a highly gifted race.[1]

5. The poets, the thinkers, and contemplatives of all nations have been attracted to what lay beyond the experience and testimony of their material senses, and have conceived the universe as divided into several "worlds," visible and invisible. Obviously the oldest of such speculations, the starting-point for all subsequent ones, is the conception of "the two worlds"—Heaven and Earth. Many names are given to each in the Rig-Veda, but in their special connection as a divine couple, who between them and by their union have given life to all creatures and are ever supplying them with the means of preserving that life, they are addressed, jointly and inseparably, as DYÂUS AND PRITHIVÎ. The latter name is singularly direct and unimaginative; it means simply "the Broad," and if it offers any interest, it is from the suggestion of antiquity it contains, since that is scarcely the epithet which would be chosen, out of many, as specially distinctive, in a land of towering peaks and steep-sided ridges, and therefore it does not seem too unlikely

[1] The chapter on "Aryan Myths" (Ch. III.) in the *Story of Media, Babylon, and Persia* should by rights be re-perused here, and would undoubtedly prove of great assistance.

that the name, as the conception, may have been familiar prior to the Aryan descent into the Penjâb, carrying the mind back to the period (Indo-Eranian?) of dwelling on flat, boundless plains and steppes.

6. Of far more positive interest and wide-reaching significance is the name of the other divine consort, Heaven—Dyâus. The word means "the Sky." But this meaning has back of it another, the true original meaning, which shows the word to be only a descriptive designation. It comes from the root DIV, "to shine, to be brilliant"—and how could a tropical or semi-tropical sky strike the poetic and artistic eye more characteristically than as "the Shining," "the Brilliant"? Say "the Shining One"—and the thing is done; the magic wand has touched the inanimate object, and it has become a *being*, a *person*, a *power*—in classical language, a god. And what a god! The original universal god of almost all Aryan peoples and such as, in later times, adopted the Aryan speech and, with it, the Aryan traditions and turn of mind. For Vedic Dyâus—and still more in the immemorial association of ideas and words, DYÂUSHPITAR, "Heaven, the Father," is no other than Greek ZEUS, ZEUS-PATER, Latin DIES-PITER, JUPITER, then DEUS, "*a* god," and Christian DEUS, God, and lastly our modern DIO, DIOS, DIEU, with all the kindred derivatives from the original Sanskrit—and probably Aryan—root: "divus," "divine," and others. The name of Dyâus is, more frequently than that of any other deity, coupled with the epithet ASURA, and that alone vouches for the immeas-

urable antiquity of this, probably the most primeval of Aryan cults, since the word Asura, which was originally a designation common to all beneficent Beings, shifted its meaning to the exact opposite, and came to signify evil Beings,—demons or fiends, whose opposition and frequently open warfare against the Powers of light and all good is a standing feature of later Hindu mythology. When the transformation took place is not, of course, to be determined; but it may be proved to have done so within the span of time covered by the Rig-Veda, for the word occurs in the great collection in both senses,—the favorable one in such passages as are otherwise shown to belong to the earlier portion. As Asura begins to mean an Evil Power, another word has to be found to designate the Good Powers generally, and that word is DEVA, coined out of the same root which gave the name of the oldest Aryan god. So the Âryas of India first spoke of their "Bright Ones" in a general way, then the notion and word both hardened and crystallized into the special meaning which we attach to the word "gods." The Eranian sister race, in the meantime, retained Asura (Eranian "Ahura") in its original meaning, which Zarathushtra and his followers intensified and sanctified by making it an integral part of the name of the Most Holy himself, the supreme and only Lord, Ahura-Mazda, while the word "deva," doubtless to show their abhorrence of their former brethren's polytheistic tendencies, was degraded into the designation of the fiends—the "Daêvas" of the Avesta, the "Divs" of later Persian spirit lore—the servants of the Evil One, Angra-Mainyush. The coincidences and divergences are too pointed and systematic to be casual, and give almost decisive weight to the hypothesis that religious antagonism was not foreign to the—probably late—separation of the Indo-Eranian family, which seems to have remained united longest of all the branches of the original Aryan stock.

7. Every natural object fills more than one part or function in the economy of the universe, has more than one quality or aspect wherewith to strike an observer—a variety easily expressed in speech by a number of adjectives and verbs or verbal nouns. If that observer be poetically inclined and therefore subject to moods, he will scarcely be disposed coolly to enumerate all these qualities and actions, producing a sort of dry descriptive litany; he will be more specially struck, according to the mood of a given moment, by this or that particular aspect of the object of his contemplation; he will let his fancy dwell on that aspect, suffer himself to be entirely possessed by it, and develop it in his song to the exclusion of all others, until the reflection in his poet's soul is rendered tangible in form to his fellow-men, and becomes, although unsubstantial, a perfect, indelible creation. And what is this creation, seen first by the poet in his mind's eye, then by his cunning word made visible to the world? heard first by him in his mind's ear, then poured by his cunning metre into music for all? this creation first *revealed* to him in that semi-trance of the soul, when the poet is lifted into a world which is not that of every day and where voices speak to

him and visions come to him he knows not how? Is it a song? a picture? it is all that and more: it is a god. What he has seen and heard, and rendered, is so complete, so real that he is the first to forget that what he started from was really only one of many aspects or qualities belonging to an already familiar deity (divinized natural object, or power), and lo! the magic wand of language wielded by fancy has done its work, *as the epithet or noun becomes a name, the quality or action it expresses becomes a person, and where there was one god, there now are two*, henceforth imagined and worshipped distinctly and separately, in total forgetfulness of their original identity. And what was a poetical description of certain attributions, certain effects, becomes the god's personal history, the story of his adventures.

8. This is the way that gods—and myths—are born. And nowhere can the process be caught in the act, so to speak, as in the Rig-Veda, where poetical creation often hovers so closely over the boundary line between reality and myth as to make it doubtful to which it finally belongs. And no apter illustration of the process can we have than in the person of the other Sky-god, VÁRUNA, who, from a simple attribution, rose to be perhaps the sublimest figure of the Vedic pantheon. All ancient peoples used to say that "the heavens cover or encompass the earth and all it contains," sometimes adding "like a tent" or "like a roof"—and meant it literally, not metaphorically, for to their unscientific minds, which knew nothing of optical delusions, but accepted unquestioningly the impres-

sions conveyed to them by their senses, the blue vault *was* a blue vault, solid and immutable—nay the very type of solidity and immutability, a veritable *firm*ament—a designation, by the by, which shows how words will survive exploded notions (like the *rising* and *setting* of the sun) and sometimes perpetuate in the popular mind the errors which gave them birth. Now Sanskrit has a root VRI "to cover," —a prolific one, which can be traced in many words of kindred meanings,—and one of its most direct formations is this very name of Váruna. It is as though we called the sky "the coverer, the enfolder," and indeed there would be nothing amiss with any one of our modern poets referring to "the all-covering, enfolding heavens." Only, we would admire the line as a beautiful, picturesque bit of imagery, but it would not crystallize in our minds into a person and a name (even setting apart the impossibility of such a thing on religious grounds); *that* is a faculty specially belonging to those remote ages of the world's youth, which have on that account been nicknamed "the *mythopœic*," *i. e.*, "myth-making," ages —a faculty which could grow only out of an exuberant fancy, revelling in the novelty of things, unrestrained by knowledge, and therefore ready of belief. It must be well understood, however, that things went thus *at the very beginning* (whenever the beginning was), but that habit and routine soon asserted their deadening influence, and that what had been play of poetical fancy, then effusion of faith, settled into conventional form of speech, into stereotype phrase. It is, unfortunately, at this stage, further stiffened by set forms of worship, that the unconscious creations of the myth-makers generally reach us, even in the earliest monuments in our possession, and we cannot, therefore, be sufficiently grateful for such stray glimpses into the earliest workings of the myth-making brain as the Rig-Veda—and that alone—still occasionally affords.

9. But—to return to Váruna. Scattered through the Rig-Veda are several hymns indited specially in his honor, sometimes alone, oftener in connection with some other god. In Book VII., attributed to the legendary Rishi Vasishtha, and at all events preserved and used as a sacred heirloom by the priestly family of that name, these hymns are most numerous. They abound with short descriptive invocations and passages which, if pieced together, would give a very lifelike presentation of the god with all his direct and personal physical attributions and, what is still more interesting, his connection with sundry natural phenomena that cannot possibly be dissociated from the sky in its several aspects. The fundamental idea expressed by Váruna's name (as explained above) is distinctly traceable in many of these passages, but in none so much as in the following three, which may be said to contain a paraphrase or amplification of the name of the "all-enfolder": he is said to "cover the worlds as with a robe, with all the creatures thereof and their dwellings" (VIII., 41), to "enfold the heavens," and to "measure out the earth and mark her uttermost bounds" (the horizon, where sky and earth seem to touch). The same idea--the keynote to the god's special identity—will

be clearly seen to lurk in this bit of grand poetic imagery: "He has encompassed the nights around; he has, by his wisdom, established the dawns; he visibly encompasses all things" (VIII., 41). What particularly strikes in this last passage is the moral quality of wisdom which is added to the god's physical attributions. This is the beginning of the process of spiritualization which all nature-gods undergo at some stage of their career: from being "the Sky" he becomes the "god *of* the Sky," and as such presides over all the numerous phenomena of which the sky is the seeming scene; the alternations of light and darkness come under his rule, as well as the heavenly bodies themselves, and as nothing is more obviously and strikingly obedient to a law, so regular in a certain immutable round as these very phenomena, Váruna rose to be the supreme embodiment and guardian, then the maker of that law and, by an easy and natural transition, of *all* law and order, moral and cosmic both—"King of gods and men" in mythic phrase. "King" is the title more especially consecrated to him, though he is also frequently given that of Asura. As always happens in such cases, the god's physical and spiritual nature blend, and merge into each other, and separate again, until it is very difficult at times to decide when certain descriptive phrases apply to him as the material sky itself, or as a power outside of it and governing it. The hymns consecrated to him contain some very grand poetry and, at all events, it is quite transparent and easy to comprehend after what has just been said. Sun and moon are said to be his eyes, but his relation to the former is expressed in especially varied and fanciful imagery. Sometimes the sun is Váruna's golden steed, sometimes the golden-winged bird, his messenger, that dives into a sea of light; then again it is a golden swing hung up on high; on one occasion, in a riddle-style very familiar to the Rishis, Váruna is said to hold up the mighty tree by its top in the groundless space, with its roots up,—the tree-top being again the sun and the roots its beams.

10. Besides "the two worlds" (*rodasî*, Heaven and Earth), which are the first divine couple of all mythologies, there is a third which, from peculiar local conditions, early assumed a still greater importance in the eyes of the Âryas of India and almost monopolized their passionate interest. This is the world "which lies between the two others" —*antariksha*, the Atmosphere or Air-region,—where the winds do battle, where the clouds gather and disperse, where the waters collect until they form a giant reservoir, a mid-air or celestial sea,[1] which then is poured down on the earth to feed and refresh her. From its seeming position, this fateful region might well be made a dependence of the sky and given into King Váruna's keeping. This is why he is said to have hollowed out paths for the rivers which flow by his command; and, on earth, the Seven Rivers are once called "his sisters"; while in another very remarkable passage he is likened unto a sea, into which all the rivers flow yet never fill it—

[1] Compare the Vouru-Kasha of the Avesta, *Story of Media*, etc., p. 64.

a striking image for the cloudy, rain-laden sky. Of course he is also the giver of rain which, as so frequently throughout the Rig-Veda, is called "the milk of the kine," *i. e.*, the rain-clouds, which hold the waters as the cow the milk in her udder.

11. A few coherent passages culled from various hymns to Váruna will now prove intelligible, and merge the fragmentary features of this sublimest of Vedic deities into a more complete and harmonious figure. One Rishi sings:

"Sing a hymn, pleasing to Váruna the King—to him who spread out the earth as a butcher lays out a steer's hide in the sun.—He sent cool breezes through the woods, put mettle in the steed [the sun], milk in the kine [clouds], wisdom in the heart, fire in the waters [lightning in the clouds], placed the sun in the heavens, the Soma on the mountains.[1]—He upset the cloud-barrel and let its waters flow on Heaven, Air, and Earth, wetting the ground and the crops.—He wets both Earth and Heaven, and soon as he wishes for those kine's milk, the mountains are wrapt in thunder-clouds and the strongest walkers are tired. . . ." (V., 85.)

"Váruna laid out the sun's path, and sent the waters coursing to the sea [celestial or atmospheric—*samudra*]; for the days he appointed their wide tracks and guides them as a racer does his mares.—His breath is the wind that rushes through the air. . . (VII., 87.) He leads forth the great, the holy sun-steed, that brings a thousand gifts.—When I gaze upon his face, I seem to see him as a blazing fire, as the King causes me to behold the splendor of light and darkness in the heavens. . . . (VII., 88.) The stars up there, that are seen at night, where do they hide in the day? But Váruna's ordinances are immutable and the moon goes shining brightly through the night. . . . (I., 24.) He who knows the path of the birds as they fly through the ample space,

[1] Soma is the plant from which the sacrificial beverage is prepared, of which much more later on—the Haoma of the Eranians. See *Story of Media*, etc., p. 65.

and on the sea the ships, . . . he who knows the track of the wind, . . . he is seated in his mansion protecting the law, Váruna, Almighty King, and looks down attentively from there on all that is hidden, on all that has been and is still to be done. Arrayed in golden mail, he wraps himself in splendor as in a garment[1] and around him sit his spies [the stars at night, the sunbeams by day]."—(I., 25.)

12. The "law" of which Váruna is keeper, the "immutable ordinances" which he has established and jealously maintains, are THE RITA—originally the COSMIC ORDER, which regulates the motions of the sun and moon and stars, the alternations of day and night, of the seasons, the gathering of the waters in clouds and their downpour in rain; in short, the order that evolves harmony out of chaos, and the visible scene of whose working is the sky. That this order is the result of a higher Law is clear—a law which the gods themselves (the Sun, the Moon, the Winds, etc.) can never transgress; and that it is a beneficent law, is no less evident. Therefore Rita is holy, is true, it is "the right path"—the Right itself, the Absolute Good, which is at once transferred from the tangible and visible into the invisible and abstract world—from the physical into the spiritual. There is a moral Rita as there is a material one, or rather the same Rita rules both worlds. What Law is in the physical, that Truth, Right, is in the spiritual order, and both are Rita. Therefore the god who is the ordainer and keeper of the physical law is also the guardian

---

[1] Compare the attributions of Ahura-Mazda in the Avesta. See *Story of Media*, etc., p. 61.

and avenger of the moral law, the punisher of sin. The Ârya loved light—the light of day and of the sun—with a passionate adoration and transports of gratitude, equalled only by his loathing and fear of darkness, with its dangers and snares, in any form; and lying and wrong-doing,—in a word, sin—was to him moral night, with all its horrors. Now Váruna was the dispenser of both light and darkness; when displeased with mortal man, he turned his face from him, and it was night. The accepted poetical expression of this fact was, "Váruna binds the sinner with his fetters." For man felt as helpless in the dark as though bound and given over without defence to the dangers he could not see. Disease was another of Váruna's fetters, and lastly—death. To Váruna, therefore, man when oppressed with the consciousness of wrong-doing, of sin, cries out for pardon and mercy. And there are in the Rig-Veda a few penitential hymns which, for beauty and depth of feeling, rival the best of the kind in any literature. Vasishtha's (in Book VII.) are the most impressive.

13. The poet thinks back with rapture of a time when he was high in Váruna's favor; he describes a glorious vision he once had, when it was given him to behold the god face to face; he was taken on board Váruna's own ship, and together they glided over the celestial waters, with gently rocking motion; and there in that ship, on that day of blessedness, the god gave him the wondrous power of song, to be his Rishi so long as days and dawns follow one another. But there has been a change: in some

way, unknown to himself, Vasishtha has angered his divine friend, who has heaped woes on him, and sent sickness to chastise him, and from the depth of his misery he sends forth his moan:

> "What has become of our friendship, when we used to commune so harmlessly together? when I was allowed access to thy house of the thousand gates?—If thy friend, O Váruna, who was dear to thee, if thy companion has offended thee, do not, O holy one, punish us according to our guilt, but be thou the poet's shelter." (VII., 88.)
>
> "I speak unto myself: when shall I be once more united with Váruna? Will he again accept my offering without displeasure? When shall I, consoled at heart, behold him reconciled?—I ask, wishing to know my sin; I go to ask the wise. They all tell me the same in sooth: 'King Váruna it is who is wroth with thee.'—What, O Váruna, was that worst of misdeeds for which thou smitest thy worshipper and friend? . . . Absolve us from the sins of our fathers, and forgive those which we committed ourselves. Release Vasishtha like a calf from the rope.—It was not our own will—it was seduction, an intoxicating drink, passion, dice, thoughtlessness. The stronger perverts the weaker; even sleep brings on unrighteousness." (VII., 86.)
>
> "Let me not yet, O Váruna, enter into the house of clay. Have mercy, almighty, have mercy!—If I go along, trembling like a cloud driven by the wind, have mercy, almighty, have mercy.—Through want of strength, thou pure one, have I gone astray: have mercy, almighty, have mercy!—Thirst came upon the worshipper, though he stood in the midst of the waters: have mercy, almighty, have mercy!—Whenever we, being but men, O Váruna, commit an offence before the heavenly host, whenever we break thy law through thoughtlessness, have mercy, almighty, have mercy!" (VII., 89.)

These hymns of Vasishtha's form a cycle, a whole more complete and personal than is usual in the Rig-Veda, yet will bear supplementing with a few more short passages of particular significance, from other, scattered hymns, like the following:

"However we may transgress thy law, day by day, after the manner of men, O Váruna, do not deliver us unto death, nor to the blow of the furious, nor to the wrath of the spiteful. My songs flee to thee . . . as birds to their nest . . . as kine to the pastures . . . (I., 25.) Take from me my own misdeeds, nor let me pay, O King, for others' guilt. . . . (II. 28.) That I may live, take from me the upper rope, loose the middle, and remove the lowest.[1] (I., 25.)

14. A peculiarity of the worship of Váruna in the Rig-Veda is that he is invoked, more often than alone, jointly with his brother, MITRA ("the Friend"), who represents sometimes the sun itself, and sometimes Light generally, or again the Power who rules the sun and brings him forth to shine on the world at the proper time. In this mild, wholly beneficent deity we recognize the Mithra of the Eranians, with whom the Avesta makes us so intimately acquainted—only he has paled somewhat and become more impersonal, although he has retained all the qualities which distinguished him before the separation of the two races, especially that of the all-seeing and truth-loving god.[2] But somehow he has lost his individuality (only one single hymn—III., 59—is addressed to him personally and separately), and has almost merged it with that of Váruna, all of whose attributions, functions, and honors he shares. The sun is said to be "the eye of Mitra and Váruna," as well as Váruna's alone, and Light is the chariot on which both gods, inseparably, ride through space on their appointed path,

---

[1] We must imagine a man bound to a post—round the shoulders, the middle of the body, and the ankles.

[2] See *Story of Media*, etc., pp. 67–72.

and of which it is once said that it is golden at break of day, while its poles take the color of a gray metal at the setting of the sun. They are joint keepers of the Rita, avengers, but also forgivers, of sin—in short, there is not a thing said of Váruna that is not repeated of both, not a thing asked of Váruna that is not requested of both, only perhaps not quite so emphatically, with not quite the same wealth of striking imagery. Then it is Mitra's own particular business to wake men and call them to the duties of a new day. Hence in time he somehow comes to be associated with the phenomena of light, and Váruna to be considered as more especially the nocturnal sky, although originally there is no such distinction, and he is proved by a hundred passages to have been the lord of both day and night. But it took root, and the commentators already assert it positively. This was the beginning of a curious transformation which made of the Váruna of the later, Brahmanic, pantheon a being entirely different from the sublime Sky-god of the Rishis, although the change can be traced, step by step, back to the Vedic presentation. Thus, in the later mythology, Váruna is merely—a Water-god: stripped of all his celestial attributions, nothing is remembered but his association with the waters—the atmospheric sea and rain-rivers,—and this watery realm is transferred to the surface of the earth. Then again, of his moral nature only the sterner, the forbidding, side is retained; he is the punisher only, and the persistent use of the conventional expressions: "fetters," "ropes," "nooses," suggests a certain cruelty and malignancy utterly foreign to the majestic and just, but also merciful, King of Heaven, who is expressly said to "take pity even on the sinner."[1]

15. Váruna and Mitra are both ÂDITYAS. That means Sons of ADITI. Aditi, in consequence, is habitually entitled "Mother of the Gods," and is, undoubtedly, herself a divine person, or, as we would say, a goddess. But the goddess of what? Or what does she represent in the order of natural objects or phenomena in which all mythical conceptions have at *some* time, originally, had their roots? To decide this question is the more difficult that *aditi* originally is merely an adjective, and used as such quite as frequently as in the other way, so that the interpreter is frequently confronted by a doubt as to the proper manner of rendering the word in a

[1] Although not a sign of anything ignoble can be discovered about the Váruna of the early Rishis, it must be admitted that in their efforts to render the various aspects of the multiform Sky-god, they did not always keep clear of the quaintness, amounting to grotesqueness, which is such a disturbing feature of classical Indian poetry, such a blemish of Indian art. It is fortunate that the men of the early Vedic ages did not yet attempt to render word-pictures in plastic form, for when Váruna is said, on one occasion, to be "four-faced," in right transparent reference to the four cardinal points——an Indian chisel would not have failed to represent a human figure with four faces, if not four heads on one neck. And from the hosts of nightmare monstrosities which people the later temples, it is easy to imagine what Indian art would have produced in the way of sculptural illustration to such passages—rare it is true—as that where Váruna is described as having three shining tongues in his mouth,—sun, moon, and lightning—(Atharva-Veda), or as "pushing onward with his tongue," or lastly as "climbing up the heavens and dispersing the foes' evil spells *with his flaming foot*" (the sun again! Rig-Veda, VIII., 41).

given passage. On the other hand, as is usually the case with such ambiguous expressions, the literal meaning of the common adjective gives us a very helpful clue towards the solution of the problem presented by the name. "Aditi" means "not bound, not limited," but it is difficult to determine by *what* the being thus described is "not bound." Sometimes it manifestly refers to unboundedness in space, so in this verse, partly quoted already, of a hymn to Mitra-Váruna:

> "Mitra and Váruna, you mount your chariot, which is golden when the dawn bursts forth, and has iron [1] poles at the setting of the sun; from thence you see what is boundless [*aditi*, space], and what is limited [*diti*,[2] the earth], what is yonder and what is here."

At other times the boundlessness of time—eternity or immortality—is suggested by the context, and the bonds, freedom from which is expressed, are those of death. This is clearly indicated by the following beautiful passage, supposed to be spoken by a living man musing on his own coming death.

> "Who will give me back to the great Aditi, that I may see again father and mother? Agni [fire], the first of immortal gods, . . . he will give me back to the great Aditi, that I may see again father and mother." (I., 24.)

---

[1] *Ayas* is translated "iron" for convenience, but, though it is the name of a metal and philologically answers the *eisen*, "iron" of our modern language, it has been impossible as yet to ascertain what was "the third metal" mentioned in the Rig-Veda, there being no doubt about gold or silver.

[2] The particle *a* is negative, which means that, being prefixed to a word, it annuls the meaning conveyed by that word. So *diti* means "bound, limited"; therefore *aditi* means "*not* bound, *not* limited."

This alludes to the custom of cremation and its accepted religious meaning. Fire, while consuming the body, conveys the spirit to the boundless—and bondless—world, where it is reunited to those who went before. In another, and very quaint passage, a horse about to be sacrificed is to become *aditi* (adjective)—a phrase which becomes intelligible when we know that animals offered in sacrifice were supposed, literally, to go to the gods, there to lead forever a sort of beatified existence.

16. It will be noticed that Aditi (as a person or divine being), whether representing boundlessness in space or in time, or generally freedom from bonds of any kind, always seems to mean not only that, but something more, tending always higher and deeper into pure abstraction, until in the following passage, it is broadened into the most abstruse metaphysical symbolism:

> "Aditi is the sky. Aditi is the intermediate region [*antariksha*—the atmosphere]; Aditi is father and mother and son; Aditi is all the gods and the five tribes; Aditi is whatever has been born; Aditi is whatever shall be born." (I., 89.)

This remarkable effort at an exhaustive definition describes not only boundless space, eternity, and immortality, but universal, all-embracing, all-producing nature itself, or—to grasp the last and highest metaphysical abstraction—Infinity, THE INFINITE. Such is the final meaning, which has been abstracted and condensed from the name and conception of Aditi, by the most philosophical students, out of all the passages directly referring to or bearing on this creation of the contemplative Indian mind. Of all who have treated this ofttimes puzzling subject, no one has used more beautiful language or more convincing argument than Professor Max Müller. "Aditi," he says, "is now and then invoked in the Veda as the Beyond—as what is beyond the earth, and the sky, and the sun, and the dawn." This gives the gist of the question, which then is developed in one of the master's most exquisite and brilliant pages:

"Aditi is in reality the earliest name invented to express the Infinite, not the Infinite as the result of a long process of abstract reasoning, but the visible Infinite, visible by the naked eye, the endless expanse beyond the earth, beyond the clouds, beyond the sky. . . The idea of the Infinite was revealed, was most powerfully impressed on the awakening mind by the East. It is impossible to enter fully into all the thoughts and feelings that passed through the minds of the early poets when they found names for that far, far East from whence even the early dawn, the sun, the day, their own life seemed to spring. . . . Aditi is a name for that distant East; but Aditi is more than the dawn. Aditi is beyond the dawn, and in one place the dawn is called 'the face of Aditi.' That silent aspect awakened in the human mind, the conception of the Infinite, the Immortal, the Divine. . . . Aditi is not a prominent deity in the Veda, nevertheless hers is a familiar name, that lives on in that of the Âdityas—the sons of Aditi. . . ."

17. Varuna and Mitra then are Âdityas. We know now what is the far from literal meaning of such terms as "Sons of Aditi": Sons of Eternity,—Sons of Immortality,—Sons of boundless Time and Space,—there is nothing but what is metaphorical, appropriate, and poetically beautiful in all these names for the deified impersonations of Sky and Light. They are shared by several more divine beings, who seem but paling reflections of their great brothers. Of

these only one, ARYAMAN, is frequently addressed with words of praise and homage, though never alone, but jointly with Mitra and Váruna. A fourth, BHAGA, quite impersonal and only occasionally mentioned along with the others, is of great interest to us because of his name, which, in a very slightly modified form, BOGH, has been adopted by the entire Slavic branch of the Indo-European family of nations as that of God—the one God of Christian monotheism. The Âdityas are said to be seven ; yet only two more are named occasionally in the hymns ; the seventh remains in a shadow of uncertainty, while now and then an eighth is spoken of ; once or twice the Fire-god would seem to be that eighth.[1] But all this is very vague and misty. One thing, however, is evident from the hymns to all the Âdityas, which are quite numerous : they all share,—and so does Aditi herself—in the special attributions so characteristic of Mitra and Váruna ; they are all keepers of the Rita and its innumerable ordinances, they all are guardians of purity and truth ; avengers—and also forgivers—of sins, healers and givers of health, and the prayer "to be held or made guiltless before the face of Aditi and the Âdityas" is a familiar and oft-repeated one.

---

[1] Just as Âtar is once mentioned in the Avesta as an eighth Amesha-Spenta, though otherwise the "Bountiful Immortals" are always seven in number. That there is some affinity between the original conceptions—Amesha-Spentas and Âdityas—has always been suspected, and the names do not militate against it, seeing that Âditya, in the sense of "Son of Immortality" would not match badly with Amesha, "Immortal." See *Story of Media*, etc., pp. 41 and 78.

18. This is a prayer often—and naturally—addressed to AGNI—Fire—the purifier and men's most intimate friend and protector, towards whom they turn with the same "respectful tenderness and affectionate familiarity" which we found so striking a feature of the Eranians' worship of the same deity under his Eranian name of Âtar.[1]

"O Agni [the Vedic Rishi invokes], accept this log which I offer to thee, blaze up brightly and send up thy sacred smoke; touch the topmost heavens with thy mane and mix with the beams of the sun. Thou Lord of wealth, drive away from us the enemies, give us rain from heaven, and food inexhaustible, and drink a thousand-fold. Thou youngest of the gods, their messenger, thou goest, O sage, wisely between the race of gods and that of men, meaning well by both." (II., 6.)

Among the hundreds of hymns to Agni treasured up in the Rig-Veda, few indeed could be found that did not contain *some* allusion—description, simile, epithet—to the absolutely literal and material nature of the original fire-worship in Aryan India. Dr. Muir has collected a vast number of such characteristic expressions, sometimes consisting of one or two words, sometimes of a whole descriptive sentence which, if strung, or rather grouped, together, would compose the most complete, the most vivid and picturesque portrayal of the dread, yet familiar element in its various aspects of regulated beneficial activity, of resistless power or devastating fury. "Fed by wood, with blazing, tawny mane, he sends up his smoke like a pillar to the sky, or like a wavering banner. Though headless and footless, he rushes

[1] See *Story of Media*, etc., p. 79 *f.*

through the woods like a bull lording it over a herd of cows, roaring like a lion or like mighty waters. He envelops the woods, consumes and blackens them with his tongue; with his burning iron grinders, his sharp, all-devouring jaws, he shears the hairs of the earth, like a barber shaving a beard. When he has yoked his wind-driven coursers to his car, the beautiful, fleet, ruddy steeds that can assume all shapes, he bellows like a bull and invades the forests; the birds are terrified at the noise when his grass-devouring sparks fly round, and his wheels mark his path with blackness. He is a destroyer of darkness and sees through the gloom of the night. The world which had been swallowed up and wrapped in darkness, and the heavens, are manifested at his appearance, and the gods, the sky, the earth, the waters, the plants, rejoice in his friendship."[1]

19. To the beings and things that rejoice in Agni's friendship, should be added first and foremost—men. Familiar and even bold as the Aryan Hindu generally was in his intercourse with his Devas, whom he readily addressed as "friends," Agni alone of immortals appears to him so close and dear as to be entitled "brother": "Father Heaven, guileless mother Earth, brother Agni, be gracious to us!"[2]

---

[1] J. Muir, *Original Sanskrit Texts*, vol. v., pp. 211–213. The sentences, sometimes single epithets or brief similes, which are here grouped into a consecutive description, are scattered through the entire collection of hymns, and picked out of a far larger number gathered by Dr. Muir.

[2] "*Dyaush pitah, Prithivî mâtar adhrug, Agne bhrâtar* . . ."

implores one poet. For, "friendly to mankind, he despises no man; kindly disposed to the people, he lives in the midst of every family" (X., 91, 2); he is a father, mother, brother, kinsman, and friend, and one of his habitual and preferred surnames is "AGNI VAISHVÂNARA," *i. e.*, "Agni that belongs to all men." And indeed, what other deity actually dwells with man—"the immortal among the mortals"—as his guest and constant companion, his assistant in humble household tasks, his light-giver and home-maker? No wonder he is called the special protector of householders, nay the householder *par excellence*, making the hearth sacred and all the acts of which it is the centre and agent. Yet, dear as Agni is held in his capacity of domestic friend, he is still more revered when, as mentioned in the hymn quoted above (p. 156), he goes back and forth as "the messenger between the two worlds," or "the two races" (of gods and men), the mediator through whom alone constant intercourse between the two is kept up. But it is not the Agni of the hearth—the Domestic Fire—who fulfils this high mission; it is the Sacrificial Fire, whose holy flames are not desecrated by any mean office, but are enkindled at every prayer time—dawn of day, noon, and sunset are the three regular prayer times, the AGNIHOTRAS—to receive and consume the offerings of the worshippers, principally melted butter, milk curds, and cakes. Melted butter especially was poured abundantly on the flames, as it produces a brilliant and vigorous blaze, hence such epithets bestowed on Agni as "butter-haired," "butter-backed," "butter-formed," and "gleaming with butter." As no sacred function—from great, solemn religious ceremonies like the coronation of kings or other public special occasions to the humblest householder's family prayers—could be performed without one or more sacrifices, it was but natural that Agni should have been said to know all about sacrifices and ritual, indeed to have instituted sacrifice, first among the gods, then among men, have been entreated to conduct the sacrifice in flawless order and make it acceptable to the gods, and that among the many honorary titles bestowed on him, should have been that of "divine HOTAR" or priest:

> "Agni rectifies all these mistakes which we ignorant men commit against your prescriptions, O ye most wise gods. Those matters relating to sacrifice which we mortals of feeble intellects, with our imperfect comprehension, do not understand, may Agni, the venerated priest [*hotar*] who knows all these points, adjust, and worship the gods at the proper seasons." (X., 2, 4-5.)

20. The kindling of the fire on the altar was itself the most sacred of all religious ceremonies and a complicated one, requiring time and exertion. For the fire originally was not lit from another flame or blown into life from embers, but produced anew by friction out of two peculiarly shaped pieces of wood. This proceeding was given a mysterious—or rather mystical—significance and called "the Birth of Agni." The parents of the ever newly born god (therefore "the eternally young, or "the youngest" —YAVISHTHA) were the "two sticks," or pieces of wood,"—the ARANÎ—out of which friction called

forth the spark. The simple apparatus might be called a fire-drill or fire-churn, since the action consisted in rapidly twirling the upper piece (generally made of Ashvattha-wood, *Ficus Religiosa*,—hence its sacredness, see p. 29) in the lower hollowed piece, of some softer wood. The incongruity between the sacredness ascribed to the action, the mysteriousness of the result, and the almost ludicrously commonplace tool, appears to have struck those earnest worshippers, in whom faith by no means excluded thought, somewhat as a puzzle, which, however, their sense of reverence prevented them from carrying to the extent of scoffing or scepticism. Innumerable are the passages which most simply and realistically describe the familiar process, then express an almost childlike wonder that a god should have such homely, feeble beginnings. "This process of generation has begun; let us rub out Agni as heretofore. This god is deposited in the two pieces of wood. . . . He is produced of them like a new-born infant." In one place wonder is expressed that a living being should spring out of dry wood; in another, that, born of a mother that cannot suckle him, he should grow so rapidly and at once begin his work as messenger. "This I declare, O Heaven and Earth," one poet exclaims, horrified, "the son, no sooner born, devours his parents. But," he hastens to add, "I, a mortal, cannot judge a god; Agni is wise and knows."

21. So far, nothing can be plainer than the material nature of the god. There is even very little anthropomorphism about it. It is the pure, undisguised element of Fire. Nor is any abstraction

attempted when Agni is entreated to disperse the fiends (of darkness) with his club, or is said to look on the world with a thousand eyes. All this clearly lies within his attributions as light-giver and dispenser of heat on earth. But it is not on earth alone that light and heat abide; not to earth alone is their action limited. A people less thoughtful and observant than the ancient Âryas could not fail to associate the phenomena of lightning with those of fire, or, when contemplating the sun—SÛRYA—in his exuberant glory of light and heat, to come to the conclusion that their own fire—whether mildly illuming the household hearth, blazing, butter-fed, on the altar, or devouring forests and hostile forts—was but his earthly substitute, or rather that the two were *one*, of one substance, variously manifested. And indeed, this is the view most explicitly expressed in this one brief line: "Agni is Sûrya in the morning, Sûrya is Agni at night." It is an accepted and oft-repeated saying that Agni has more than one abode, sometimes two, and then again—more truly—three: on earth, as fire; in the heavens, as the sun; in the atmosphere, as lightning. From this to identifying all three together is but one step, and it is frequently taken. The humble birth—from "two dry sticks"—which suited the god in his earthly manifestation, no longer accounted for his existence in those exalted spheres; "Son of the Waters"—ÂPAM-NAPÂT[1]—is

[1] The name is certainly older than the Aryan colonization of India; it must be Indo-Eranian at least, if not older still, since we find it in the Avesta as one of the habitual surnames of Âtar. See *Story of Media*, etc., pp. 37, 45, 80.

the mystic but appropriate name of Agni, the Lightning, who, after lying long hidden in the celestial cloud-ocean *(Samudra)*, flashes forth from it, in very truth " water-born." It is only an obscurer form of the same myth when Agni is alluded to as "the son of seven mothers," or, " of many mothers," or of "the Mothers" generally, because then the clouds, under the name of ÂPAS, "the waters," are taken individually, separately, from the mass of suspended waters, which is imagined as the celestial sea, the *Samudra*.

22. Like the Eranians, the Âryas of India held that Fire dwelt not only in water, but in plants. Both positions seem, at first sight, untenable. Yet we saw how easily the first of them is justified by fact, and a moment's thought shows that the second is but the sequel of it. For, placing ourselves for a moment on their standpoint, fire could not be brought out of plants (wood comes of trees and trees are plants) if it were not in them. Fire—heat—hidden in the plant, is what moves the sap, quickens the growth ; it is the latent principle of the plant's life. But how did it get into them ? Very simply : it descended straight from heaven, *with the waters* which are its native element, in the showers which, with thunder and lightning, pour down on the thirsty earth. In the rain Fire descends, not upon, but *into* the ground, and thence rises into the plants as sap and life ; do we not say " vital *spark* " ? There is no lack of passages in the Rig-Veda which more or less transparently describe this very process. For instance : " His road is the flood that pours through

the arid space; he reaches earth with the clear waters; he devours what is old (wood), and penetrates into new plants." (I., 95, 10.) And again: "When he is brought down from the highest Father [Dyâus, Heaven], he climbs into the sapful plants . . . to be born again, ever most young."

23. This is undoubtedly one of the ways in which Agni was supposed to have descended to the earth. But this manifestation is accomplished in a very roundabout way and continually repeated. The question remained, in what more direct manner he came among men for the first time in his more familiar and visible form—for Agni's original home is *not* sought on earth. It is said: "Agni was born first in heaven; his second birth is with us; the third in the clouds, imperishable. . . ." (X., 45, 1.) The Âryas, no doubt, had several myths embodying their beliefs or traditions—speculations or reminiscences —on this fascinating question, which has not only not lost any of its interest in the course of the ages, but rather gained more, in the first place because we are better able to measure and appraise all that fire has done for our race, in the second because we have hardly arrived nearer to a reliable or at least plausible solution, and we are so made that curiosity never relents until satisfied. But the Rig-Veda is not a book of mythology. Myths are not told by the old Rishis, but only alluded to as things well known to their audience,—just as a modern preacher might refer to Jonah's adventure with the whale or the Hebrew boys' fortitude before the fiery ordeal, without every time narrating at length the familiar

Bible stories. From such brief snatches and allusions we gather that Agni was brought from afar by some superhuman agency; and he has always to be *found*, fetched out of hiding, so strongly had the notion of the latent presence of fire in water and plants taken hold of men's fancy. The finder who is most frequently named is MÂTARISHVAN, a being whose nature is not explained, and who is said to have brought Agni "from heaven," "from the gods, very far away," and to have given him, "as a gift," to the BHRIGUS, an equally mysterious race, nearly connected with humanity, however, as they, in their turn, after again concealing him in the wood, brought him forth and gave him to men—or to MANU, apparently the first man, whose name stands for the entire race; which can only mean that the illustrious priestly race of the Bhrigus claimed that their ancestors taught men to "bring forth," *i. e.*, kindle fire by friction. As Mâtarishvan is certainly the lightning ("Agni is manifested to him the very moment he is born in the highest heaven"), this very coherent if incomplete story is not at all spoiled by the fact that Agni is himself repeatedly called by that name. It is more confusing to find that, once in a while, he is spoken of as being found without Mâtarishvan's assistance. For instance: "The wise Bhrigus followed him, the hidden one, as one hastens after cattle that has strayed; they found him in the waters and placed him in the homes of men." But then philology by a careful comparative study of the name and the large family of its kindred or derived words in the Aryan languages, both ancient and of later formation, has proved that the mythical Bhrigus had something to do with such things as "flame" and "blaze," if not with the lightning itself. The affinity strikes us still more clearly when we are told that "ATHARVAN drew Agni forth, by friction, out of the blue lotus-blossom" (a not unusual poetical name for the vault of heaven), since the name at once suggests a fire-priest, being identical with that of the Eranian priests of Âtar,[1] besides being, probably, one of the oldest names for Lightning itself, not to mention the Sanskrit words *atharê*, "flame," and *atharyu*, "blazing," a by-word of Agni.[2] As there was a class of priests called Atharvans,—those specially appointed to the care of the different fires at great sacrifices,—this is another instance of the connection claimed by classes or families of men with semi-mythical progenitors. The ANGIRAS, another highly reverenced family of hereditary priests and Rishis, are also mentioned in the Rig-Veda as having first kindled Agni. And "Angiras," in the singular, as the name of an individual, is now that of the human but half-mythical ancestor of the priestly race, and now unmistakably a name of Agni himself. The confusion produced by so many names is not as great as might appear at first sight, because one soon detects an underlying general idea, which is neither more nor less than the kinship between Agni and his mortal worshippers, indeed points to a belief in the celestial and fiery origin of the human race.

---

[1] See *Story of Media*, etc., pp. 150–152. This is also the only trace in the Rig-Veda of the older Eranian name of Fire.

[2] See *ib.*, p. 42.

24. Truly, the association of ideas is very obvious. Of the heavenly birth and descent of Fire (which name, it must not be forgot, covers the conception and manifestations of Heat generally) no doubt was entertained, whether in its patent—obvious—form, as sunlight and lightning, or in its latent—hidden—form, as the elementary principle concealed in the waters and the plants, and ever ready to escape therefrom. Now the warmth of the living body is a still clearer indication of the divine presence, and Agni may be said to have descended into men in the same way that he has descended into plants—not to mention another possibility: that of his passing into the human frame in the guise of the vegetable food it consumes, and then from generation to generation, as the "vital spark," which, being perpetuated by heredity, is not destroyed even by death. In this sense also the god is "immortal among mortals." Well may he be called, "he of many births." Numerous are the passages in which "community of race" —kindred—is claimed with gods for men, explicitly, though in a general way: thus the verse "We have in common with you, O gods, the quality of brothers in the mother's bosom" is fully explained by this other: "Heaven (Dyâus) is my father, who bore me; my mother is this wide earth (Prithivî)." The oldest Rishis are styled "heaven-born," and one poet invokes them all by name (Angiras and Manu in the number), as "knowing his race" and the fact that "it reaches up to the gods, its stock is among them." And if these claims and assertions seem too vague to be directly referred to Agni, no doubt is possible before the positive statement that he "gave birth to

men" and "found a way for his descendants" and the direction to men "to invoke him as the first father."[1] Marvellous to watch is this dim perception of the unity of nature, the kinship of man with the entire universe (or at least our own solar system), so lately established by modern science, struggling into expression at that early age, with nothing but poetic intuition to guide.

25. We have now learned to know Agni: 1st, in heaven as the Sun; 2d, in the atmosphere, as Lightning; 3d, on earth, as the Domestic, and 4th, as the Sacrificial, Fire. We have still to be introduced to the god in his fifth aspect, in which he plays an exceedingly important part in the Hindu Ârya's life: as consumer of corpses and guide of departed souls to the abodes of "the Fathers." For, unlike the Eranians, the Hindu did not hold that the impure contact of death could pollute the holy element, but on the contrary ascribed to the latter the power of purifying and sanctifying all things its flames consume or only touch.[2] Yet the "funereal Agni" was

---

[1] This theme, of man's celestial and fiery origin, is treated with great erudition and convincing mastery by Abel Bergaigne, in his colossal work *La Religion Védique* (vol. i., pp. 31 *ff.* chapter entitled *Origine Céleste de la Race Humaine*).

[2] What would the Eranians have said to the modern Brahmanic custom of floating corpses down the Ganges, to be carried out to the ocean by the sacred river's sanctifying waters! This dreadful custom is especially in force at Benares, the great city near the junction of the Ganges and Djumnâ, the holiest spot of all Brahmanic India. There the dying are actually carried to the river and plunged into it to breathe their last in the sacred waters, not only singly, but at certain times in crowds. Of course all these practices were abominations to the Parsis. See *Story of Media*, etc., pp. 124 *ff.*

kept separate from all other forms of fire, and was not allowed either on the sacrificial altar or on the hearth.

26. There is an entire book of the Rig-Veda—the ninth—which, contrary to all the others, is devoted to the praises of only one deity—SOMA. Like Agni, with whom he is most intimately associated, Soma has many forms, and more than one dwelling-place; like Agni, the place of his birth is not on earth; like Agni, the form under which he first presents himself is an unmistakably material one: Agni is the fire and Soma is a plant. Only, whereas Agni, under this his earthly form, was put to many and widely differing uses, the Soma plant had but one: an intoxicating beverage was prepared from it, which was offered at sacrifices, being partaken of by the worshippers and poured into the flame on the altar. And like the Fire-worship, the Soma-cult takes us back to the so-called Indo-Eranian period, the time before the separation of the two great sister-races, for we have seen the Soma, under the name of HAOMA, play exactly the same part in the worship and sacrifices of the Eranian followers of the Avesta. Indeed we probably have here one of the very few relics of an even earlier time—that of the undivided Âryan, or as it is sometimes called, "the Proto-Aryan period."[1] For, as we noticed in its place, the Avesta bears evident traces of the use of the Haoma at the sacrifices being a concession made by Zarathushtra

[1] Such is the opinion of most students of both sacred books, convincingly expressed in two special studies by that eminent and deep-seeing scholar, Windischmann.

15.—DYING HINDU BROUGHT TO THE GANGES TO BREATHE HIS LAST IN THE WATERS OF THE SACRED RIVER.—(MODERN CUSTOM.)

to old-established custom, not without subjecting it to a reforming and purifying process.[1]

27. In India, as in Erân, the Soma is mountain-born.[2] It is said that King Váruna, who placed the Sun in heaven and Fire in the waters, placed the Soma on the mountain. Like Fire, it is brought to men by superhuman agency: "The one," says a hymn already quoted, "was brought from heaven by Mâtarishvan, the other by the falcon from the mountain." The Soma used in India certainly grew on mountains, probably in the Himâlayan highlands of Kashmir. It is certain that Aryan tribes dwelt in this land of tall summits and deep valleys in very early times—probably earlier than that when the Rig-hymns were ordered and collected, or the already complicated official ritual which they mostly embody was rigidly instituted. From numerous indications scattered through the hymns, it appears probable that this was the earliest seat of the Soma worship known to the Aryan Hindus, whence it may have spread geographically with the race itself, and that, as the plant did not grow in the lower and hotter regions, the aridity of some parts disagreeing with it as much as the steam-laden sultriness of others, they continued to get "from the mountains" the immense quantities needed for the consumption of the gradually widening and increasing

[1] See *Story of Media*, etc., pp. 118–121.

[2] It should not be forgotten, however, that it can hardly be the identical plant. Scholars are pretty well agreed that the Aryan sacrificial liquor, though retaining the same name, may—or indeed must—have been prepared from different plants in the different lands where Âryas settled.

Aryan settlements. A regular trade was carried on with the Soma plant, and the traders belonged to mountain tribes who were not Aryan, and, therefore, irreverently handled their sacred ware like any other merchandise, bargaining and haggling over it. This is evidently the reason why Soma-traders were considered a contemptible class; so much so that, when customs hardened into laws, they were included in the list—comprising criminals of all sorts, breakers of caste and other social laws, followers of low professions, as usurers, actors, etc.—of those who are forbidden to pollute sacrifices by their presence. To an Aryan Hindu, the man who owned the Soma and did not press it was a hopeless reprobate. In fact he divided mankind into "pressers" and "not pressers," the latter word being synonymous with "enemy" and "godless barbarians." They were probably itinerant traders, and the bargain was concluded according to a strictly prescribed ceremonial, the details of which seem singularly absurd and grotesque, until one learns that they had a symbolical meaning. The price (probably for a given quantity, though that is not mentioned) is a cow—light-colored, or, more precisely, reddish-brown, with light-brown eyes, in allusion to the ruddy or "golden" color of the plant—which must not be tied, nor pulled by the ear—*i. e.*, not handled roughly.

28. The Soma used in India is thought to be the *Asclepia acida* or *Sarcostemma viminale*, a plant of the family of milk-weeds. It is described as having hanging boughs, bare of leaves along the stalks, of light, ruddy color ("golden"), with knotty joints,

containing, in a fibrous, cane-like outer rind, an abundance of milky, acid, and slightly astringent sap or juice. It is this juice which, duly pressed out,

16.—THE SOMA PLANT.

mixed with other ingredients, and fermented, yields the intoxicating sacrificial beverage. The process—the most sacred and mystic act of the Vedic and

Brahmanic liturgy—is alluded to in the Rig-Veda innumerable times, but in such fanciful and often enigmatical ways that we might be puzzled to reconstruct it, had we not in some of the Brâmanas most precise directions, amounting to a thorough and detailed description of the operation. Though pages might easily be written on the subject, the following brief description after Windischmann must suffice, as it is both graphic and comprehensive:

". . . The plant, plucked up by the roots, collected by moonlight on the mountains, is carried on a car drawn by two goats to the place of sacrifice, where a spot covered with grass and twigs is prepared,[1] crushed between stones by the priests[2]; and is then thrown, stalks as well as juice, sprinkled with water, into a sieve of loose woollen weave, whence, after the whole had been further pressed by the hand, the juice trickles into a vessel or kettle which is placed beneath.[3] The fluid is then mixed with sweet milk and sour milk, or curds, with wheaten and other flour, and brought into a state of fermentation; it is then offered thrice a day and partaken of by the Brâhmans. . . . It was unquestionably the greatest and holiest offering of the ancient Indian worship. . . . The gods drink the offered beverage; they long for it; they are nourished by it and thrown into a joyous intoxication. . . . The beverage is divine, it purifies, it is a water of life, gives health and immortality, prepares the way to heaven, destroys enemies," etc.

---

[1] The *vedi*, made of the famous *kusha* grass, and called "the seat of the gods," for whom it was prepared, and who were supposed invisibly to occupy it, when they came to receive the sacrifice offered them, on being formally invited thereto. It was therefore meet that the Soma should be laid on this consecrated spot before the ceremony of pressing began.

[2] A mortar is also mentioned in the Rig-Veda, but rarely. As a mortar was used in the preparation of the Eranian Haoma (*Story of Media*, etc., pp. 118–121), this was very probably the older custom, a relic of the forgotten Indo-Eranian period.

[3] These vessels were, very appropriately, made of the sacred ashvattha-wood (*Ficus religiosa*).

The fieriness of the drink, its exhilarating and inspiriting properties are especially expatiated upon. The chosen few who partook of it—few, for besides the officiating priests, only those were allowed a taste who could show that they had provisions enough stored up to last them three years—give most vivid expression to the state of exaltation, of intensified vitality, which raises them above the level of humanity. Some such effusions are neither more nor less than bragging; for instance (X., 119):

> 1. I think to myself: I must get a cow; I must get a horse: have I been drinking Soma?—2. The beverages carry me along like impetuous winds: have I, etc.—3. They carry me along as fleet horses a chariot: have I, etc.—4. The hymn has come to me as a cow to her beloved calf: have I, etc.—5. I turn my song over in my heart as a carpenter fashions a chariot: have I, etc. . . .—7. The five tribes seem to me as nothing: have I, etc.—8. One half of me is greater than both worlds: have I, etc.—9. My greatness reaches beyond the heavens and this great earth: have I, etc.—10. Shall I carry this earth hither or thither? Have I, etc.—11. Shall I shatter this earth here or there? Have I, etc.—12. One half of me is in the heavens and I have stretched the other down deep: have I, etc.—I am most great; I reach up to the clouds: have I, etc.[1]

The effects of the exhilarating beverage are not always described in such exaggerated strains. The following passages, culled here and there, although

---

[1] Until very lately this hymn was supposed to be spoken by the battle-god Indra after quaffing the sacrificial liquor. A. Bergaigne shows that it comes much more appropriately from an exhilarated mortal.

"We have drunk the Soma," exclaims another; "we have become immortal, we have entered into light, we have known the gods. What can an enemy now do to us, or what can the malice of any mortal effect?"

enthusiastic, depict no abnormal condition of body or mind, but may be produced by the moderate and wholesome use of a rich stimulant:

"He, the wise, has entered into me, who are simple."—"Make me burn as with fire, O Soma, . . . prolong our life as the sun renews the days each morning. . . . Our intelligence is excited by thee . . . thou hast descended into all our limbs. . . . Disease has fled, powerless . . . the powerful Soma has descended into us and our days are lengthened."

29. Through all this runs a consciousness of the presence of something divine in the liquor which can produce such wonderful effects in those who partake of it. And indeed, this liquor is only the earthly form of the celestial Soma, or, more correctly, it is a symbol of the celestial Soma, the god Soma. When the sacrificer, after pouring a small quantity of the sacred beverage into the flame on the altar, describes how the gods—especially the battle-god INDRA—quaff Soma by the pailful, by the barrel, and only then feel strengthened for their daily strife against the powers of evil, he certainly does not mean it literally. There *is*, however, a divine liquor which gives the gods (the Powers of Nature) strength and immortality, without which they would lose their might, their eternal youth, their life even, without which the world—*our* world at least—would become barren and dead, and uninhabitable; and that heavenly liquor, the veritable AMRITA or drink of immortality, is—the rain, the dews, perhaps it were more correct to say, the moisture which is diffused through nature, exhilarating, vivifying, calling forth and fostering life in all its forms. Of the gathering and flowing

of this fountain of life—the *amrita*, the celestial Soma—the sacrificial process is an apt illustration: the skin on which the pressing stones are disposed is the cloud, and the stones themselves are the thunderbolts; the sieve is the sky, the liquor that falls through it in more or less abundant drops is the rain, and the large vessel or kettle into which they fall is the *Samudra*—the celestial sea that holds all the atmospheric waters. The likeness—the symbol—is never lost sight of. Nothing can be clearer than this invocation: "Drink exhilaration from the heavenly Soma, O Indra, drink it from the Soma which men press on earth." This identification of Soma with the waters and with plants accentuates very strongly his affinity with Agni which we noticed from the start and—to make a long line of proof and argument as brief as our limited space commands—we may at once arrive at the conclusion that Soma, in this phase of the myth, is a form of Agni, in a word, is *liquid fire*.[1] It is no wonder, therefore, that the two should be so constantly associated together and even invoked jointly in numbers of hymns specially addressed to them.

30. But even the celestial Soma, the drink that invigorates the gods and gives them eternal youth and immortality,—in short, the *amrita*—cannot rationally

---

[1] We saw that the fiery or vital principle is conveyed into the heart of plants, and into the human frame, by water. For exhaustive studies on this, as it may be called, most sacred mystery of the Aryan faith, see A. Kuhn, *The Descent of Fire and the Celestial Beverage;* A. Bergaigne, the chapters on Agni and Soma in *La Religion Védique;* and Hillebrandt, *Vedische Mythologie*, vol. i.

have been *the god* Soma. Water, moisture, could not possibly, at any time, be thought of as *a person.* This water, this moisture, must be produced, or at least held in keeping,—then given out, distributed, by a being, a Power that *could* be imagined as a person, and when we find that power, we have the god. The parallelism between Soma and Agni which we traced throughout this study points to the *a priori* conclusion that, Agni being the Sun, Soma must be the Moon, and the fact instantly occurs to us that in the mythology of the post-vedic, so-called "epic" or "classical," period, down to our own day, Soma has always been and is the moon. Very peculiar and consistently developed are the later Brahmanical theories about the moon as expounded in the Purânas, but always hinging on this one fundamental fact, that the moon is the reservoir of *amrita*, the drink of the gods, and both in these and the poetical works it has a number of epithets alluding to this. During the light part of the month (while the moon is visible), the gods drink from it—and it swells the more as they drink—the sweet *amrita* which makes them immortal. During the dark half of the month (while the moon is invisible), the PITRIS—the spirits of the dead—drink from it, when it gradually decreases. Its beams are woven of cool watery atoms which penetrate into the plants, refresh and vivify them. Another has it the other way; the gods approach the moon at its full, and the dead on the night it is new. The same in the Upanishads, which are earlier than the Purânas. "The Moon is King Soma, the food of the gods." The same, more frequently, more insistently, in the Shatapatha-Brâhmana, the most important of all. "This King Soma, the food of the gods, is the Moon. . . . When it decreases, then they feed on it." ". . . The Seasons are King Soma's royal brothers, just as a man has brothers." Whose brothers can the seasons be but the moon-god's?

31. And so it turns out that moon-worship occupies a prominent place in the Aryan religion, and that the ninth book of the collection is exclusively devoted to this worship, the ritual of which is specially contained in the Sama-Veda. This book, and for that matter, the numerous Soma-hymns scattered in the other books of the Rig, teem with allusions too transparent and direct to need explanation, provided the lunar nature of the deity they celebrate is thoroughly comprehended, whereas they would be hard to make even tolerable sense of, even allowing most amply for archaïc mannerisms of thought and imagery, under the supposition that the god Soma is *only* the sacrificial beverage of Aryan worship or the celestial beverage of the gods—the vivifying moisture diffused through the universe. Some of the similes are very graceful and pretty. Soma is a well of sweetness in the midst of the sky; a golden drop hung up in the heavens; a bowl of ambrosia (*amrita*), nay, an ocean (*samudra*) of the drink of gods. Soma is a wise god, for does he not know the times and the seasons, bring round the months, and fix the days and hours for the rites, and the prayers, and the sacrifices which are the gods' due? Soma also is a warrior god, vigorous and well armed,

equipped for battle against the demons and monsters who people the "dark forest"—night, and whom he dispels, and also for the defence of the precious spring of life which he has in his keeping, and which evil beings, hostile to the Devas—the Asuras—are ever on the watch to steal. To whom but the moon could lines like the following apply: "Soma stands above all the worlds, similar to the divine Sûrya," or, "he has clothed himself in the radiance of the Sun, and, full of wisdom, surveys the races?" Lastly there is a myth in which Soma is married to Suryâ, the Sun-maiden, and the very hymn (X., 85) which tells this myth with unusual length of detail and circumstance, begins with this passage, the most explicit and decisive of all, which indeed sums up in few words the results to which we have laboriously worked our way:

> "Through the Law [Rita] the earth stands firm, the heavens and the Sun, through the Law the Âdityas stand, and Soma stands in the sky. . . . Soma is placed in the midst of these stars.
>
> "When they crush the plant, he who drinks regards it as Soma. *Of him whom the priests regard as Soma, no one drinks.*
>
> "Protected by those who shelter thee and preserved by thy guardians, thou, Soma, hearest the sound of the crushing-stones; *but no earthly being tastes thee.*
>
> "When the gods drink thee, O god, thou increasest again. . . ."

It is impossible more fully to realize the symbolism of the Soma sacrifice. Yet there is no lack of passages which as plainly express the conception that the god descends personally into the plant, giving up his own body and limbs to be broken for the good of men and gods, and that a mysterious communion is established between the god and his worshipper, who has tasted the sacred drink, that this drink is part of the divine substance. This thread of mysticism runs through the whole Rig-Veda: We have tasted Soma,—the god has descended into us,—we have become like unto the gods—immortal life is ours.

32. The following beautiful prayer, a poetical gem of purest water, may be considered as the crowning expression of the Aryan Soma-worship in its noblest, most spiritual form (IX., 113).

> "Where there is eternal light, in the world where the sun is placed, in that immortal, imperishable world place me, O Soma!
>
> "Where the son of Vivasvat reigns as King, where the secret place of heaven is, where these mighty waters are, there make me immortal!
>
> "Where life is free, in the third heaven of heavens, where the worlds are radiant, there make me immortal!
>
> "Where wishes and desires are, where the bowl of the bright Soma is, where there is food and rejoicing, there make me immortal!
>
> "Where there is happiness and delight, where joy and pleasure reside, where the desires of our desire are attained, there make me immortal!"[1]

There is not one line here, not one image that offers the least difficulty to interpretation if the identity of Soma and the Moon be accepted as the basis thereof—as there is not one that does not present almost insuperable difficulty on any other supposition. The "bowl of the bright Soma," the "radiant worlds" (the stars), the world of "eternal light," of "the mighty waters"—how beautiful and how self-evident, when we know that the moon is the abode

[1] Translated by Max Müller.

of the dead who partake of its "honeyed sweetness," even as the gods and, like the gods, quaff length of days in the draught. There is, however, one line in this passage which introduces us to two new mythical persons: Vivasvat and his son.

33. This son is YAMA, whom we have already learned to know in the Avesta as YIMA, SON OF VIVANHVANT,[1] but in how altered a garb! The Rig-Veda knows very little about Vivasvat except his name and that he is Yama's father; yet that he had been a god and had the power of one is proved by such prayers as the following, addressed to him: "May the shaft of Vivasvat, the poisoned arrow, not strike us before we are old!" "May Vivasvat grant us immortality. Let death go its way and immortality come. May he protect our people to their old age." But this is only a faint trace, an obliterated memory of the position he must have occupied in a remote Indo-Eranian past, for in the Avesta, consistently with the anti-polytheistic tendency of the creed, Vivanhvant is a mere mortal man, a saintly priest, the first who offered a Haoma sacrifice, while his son Yima is also a mortal, the first king, the ruler of a golden age.[2] But if the father has lost ground in India, the son, Yama, fills one of the most prominent and picturesque positions in the Vedic pantheon, as the king of the dead, the mild ruler of an Elysium-like abode where the shades of

---

[1] See *Story of Media*, etc., pp. 89-94.

[2] The name, which means "the Luminous," has been taken to indicate a sun-god, and the conclusion is borne out by the entire Brâhmana-literature. See on this question, however, ch. vii.

the PITRIS (the departed fathers of the living, answering the Avestan Fravashis),[1] lead a happy, dreamy existence.

34. The bare facts are these: Yama was the first to die and we all follow him to the world which he was the first to enter, and where, therefore, he assumed the part of host, receiving those that joined him as they came, and naturally becoming their king and ruler. He has messengers who roam the world spying out those who are to die, and whom they drive or escort to his realm. These messengers, generally two in number, most frequently take the shape of dogs of weird and fantastic appearance, and are probably meant to personify the morning and evening twilight—a most apt poetical image, since it can certainly be said that each morning and evening brings some recruits from the living world to that of the dead. It is remarkable that the most explicit and pithy text is contained in the Atharva-Veda:

> "Him who first of mortals died, who first went to that world, the gatherer of men—King Yama, son of Vivasvat, honor ye with an oblation."

"Death is Yama's wise messenger." A wonderful thought, wonderfully expressed, which we also find in the Atharva-Veda. Birds of evil omen also, are mentioned in the Rig as Yama's messengers, and one poet prays that the thing which such a bird announces with its cry may not come to pass. The dogs are called SÂRAMÊYA or children of SARAMÂ,

---

[1] *Story of Media*, etc., pp. 83-84, 154.

and described as spotted, broad-snouted, four-eyed, and Yama is entreated to bid them protect the guests they bring him on the road.[1]

35. The world over which Yama rules is not repulsive, dark, or in any way dread-inspiring, being situated, as we have seen, in the highest heaven, in the sphere of the sun, in the midst of radiant worlds, and no idea of judgment or punishment attaches to it. In the Rig-Veda Yama is the king of the dead, not as yet their judge and chastiser. That came later, and in the Brahmanical literature of the classical period Yama appears stripped of all gracious features and tricked out in all the cheap horrors of the vulgar devil. How different from the mild, benignant deity, to whose gentle rule the earlier Aryan Hindus lovingly, trustfully committed their departed dear ones![2]

36. The question naturally arises: what natural phenomenon originally was disguised under the myth of Yama Vaivasvata? The answer as naturally suggests itself: the setting sun, for that is one of the scenes in the grand drama of nature which always most forcibly suggested the belief and hope in a future life.[3] And in the poetical language of early myth-makers, bristling with bold metaphor, the setting sun can very well be said to be the child of the morning sun (Vivasvat). But then it is by

---

[1] See *Story of Media*, etc., pp. 93, 94 (*Sagdîd* ceremony), and p. 165 (the dogs guarding the Chinvat Bridge).

[2] See, for details and texts, ch. ix., *Early Culture*, in connection with the Vedic funeral rites.

[3] See *Story of Chaldea*, pp. 337–339.

no means sure, as will be seen,[1] that Vivasvat was always the sun, and quite recently a school of interpreters has arisen who would identify Yama, like Soma, with the Moon.[2] It cannot be denied that the arguments they bring in favor of this solution carry great weight. They point out, among other things, that the "seat of Yama" is avowedly in the "third heaven," in "its most secret (*i. e.*, remotest) place," and that the *setting* sun cannot be said to occupy that position; that the moon easily could appear to the unscientific eye of the early myth-makers as a smaller, *younger* sun—the child of the sun, who dies (disappears) after running his course; that the two, with the inconsistency so characteristic of myths, which delight in presenting the same divine beings under different aspects, to place them in different mutual relations, might just as easily have appealed to the imagination as twins —as in point of fact they *have* been considered by most ancient peoples, and that the very name "Yama" is a word signifying "twin." Yama is often spoken of as having been the first man, the progenitor of the human race. But that honor belongs to another son of Vivasvat—*Manu* (*i. e.*, Man), and was mistakenly transferred to Yama, on the strength of an imperfect argument, namely, that he who was the first to die must have been the first man who lived. But Yama is nowhere styled "the first

---

[1] In ch. vii.

[2] A. Hillebrandt argues the point at great length, and decides it in this sense, in the first volume of his *Vedic Mythology*, already mentioned.

of men," only "the first of *mortals*." Now the word "mortal" (*martya*) is very frequently used to denote "man"; but two other words—*manushya* and *jana* occur quite as frequently[1]; yet neither is used when Yama is spoken of. The persistency with which he is called the first of *martyas*, "mortals," is scarcely accidental. Not man alone is mortal in the conception of ancient myth-making peoples: the gods themselves would die did they not continually renew their life and vigor by draughts of the divine Soma, the water of youth and immortality; the sun dies when it sets, or faints at the numbing touch of winter; the moon dies when, after waning away before our eyes, it disappears. True, after death comes resurrection; but that does not belong here. We must be content with establishing the fact that Yama is invariably styled the "first of *mortals* who died," not "the first of mortal *men*."

37. Another Vedic deity who can be traced with certainty to a pre-Eranian (or Proto-Aryan) past is VÂYU or VÂTA, the Wind. Not the violent storm-wind, but the wholesome, cooling breeze, that clears the atmosphere, purifies the air, brings health and life to men and animals prostrated by heat. Vâyu holds a modest place in the Rig-Veda. Few hymns are addressed to him alone, but he is frequently joined with other gods, and always men-

[1] It is impossible not to admire the ingenious and pithy names by which those who spoke the ancient Sanskrit tongue designated the human race: *martya*, "the mortal"; *manushya*, "the thinking" (the root *man* being the same as that of *mens*, *mind*); *jana*, "the begotten," "the born" (same root as in *gens*, *genus*, *gen*erate, etc.).

tioned with respect and gratitude. He is a "Son of Heaven" (Dyâus), and not only is he invited to partake of the Soma libations, but when he comes with other gods, the first drink is his by right.[1] The following short hymn (X., 168) shows the high esteem in which this unobtrusive deity was held and how sensitively alive the fancy of those ancient poets was to the picturesque and the mysterious—also how a thing may strike in the same way spirits separated by ages and continents.

"I celebrate Vâta's great chariot: it comes rending the air, with noise of thunder. It touches the sky as it goes and makes it ruddy, whirling up the dust on the earth.—The flying gusts rush after it,—as maidens to a festival . . . .—As he flies along on airy paths, Vâta never rests on any day . . . . For what place was he born? and from whence came he,—the vital breath of gods, the world's great offspring? The god, where'er he will, moves at his pleasure; his rushing sound we hear,—his form was never seen.[2] . . ."

38. With this god we close the cycle of Vedic gods—Dyâus, Váruna, Mitra, Agni, Soma, Yama, Vâyu—whom we can trace with absolute certainty to an Indo-Eranian past and identify with corresponding divine beings in the Avesta. Further researches no

---

[1] There is, in one of the Brâhmanas, a story invented to account for this privilege. It tells how several gods once ran a race for the first drink of Soma, and Vâyu (naturally!) won. This is the way in which the Brâhmanas dispose of all obscure or puzzling points—by stories made up to explain them. The result is generally obscurity doubly intensified, confusion inextricable, often sickening absurdities, and *some*times—gems of philosophy and poetry.

[2] "The wind bloweth where it listeth, and thou hearest the sound thereof, but canst not tell whence it cometh and whither it goeth."—St. John, iii., 8.

doubt will bring to light more affinities, more likenesses,—as indeed not a few have already been hinted at. But suggestions, conjectures, can find no place in works the object of which is to place before the larger public—the uninitiated laymen of science—the results actually achieved, the conquests that may be considered final. The divine personages into whose exalted circle we shall now step are of Indian growth, bear the unmistakable impress of the land and conditions of life which the migrating Âryas found on the hither side of the Himâlaya and the Indus.

APPENDIX TO CHAPTER V.

THE CHURNING OF THE AMRITA.

THE accompanying illustration represents one of the most famous legends told in the Mahâbhârata and some of the Purânas, and is a good specimen of the literalness with which Indian art sets to work to reproduce the details of a mythical story, just as the legend itself is a fair sample of what the learned Brahmanic poetry of the classic or epic ages made of the simple and transparent myths of Vedic times. We have just admired and fully explained the myth of the *amrita*, the food of the gods, of which the sacred Soma-drink is the earthly imitation. The Brâhman poets amplified it into a story, given with varying details in different versions, but of which the main features are the following:

The devas were at war with the asuras (the evil demons), who repeatedly conquered them, so that they lost heart, and were fain to ask the assistance of Vishnu, the god to whom later theology ascribed the mission of general adviser to the gods and preserver to them and the created worlds. Vishnu promised them that their strength should be restored if they would do as he would direct. First they must collect specimens of all the plants and herbs that grow in the world and cast them into the Sea of Milk, then they must churn that sea, and they would thus obtain the Amrita, the drink of strength and immortality. But as the labor would be very great, he advised them to suspend hostilities with the Asuras and invite them to join in the work: "I will take care," he said, "your foes shall share your toil but not partake in its reward." The Asuras readily took the bait and worked with all their might. When the herbs were thrown in, the mountain Mandara was taken for a churning stick *(pramantha)*, and the King of Serpents, VÂSUKI—others say SHESH or SHESHNA—allowed himself to be used as the rope to twirl the stick. So all pulled with a will, the devas on one side, the Asuras on the other, while Vishnu himself, taking the form of a tortoise, took the mountain on his back to steady it. Great was the tumult that ensued. The milky waves rose and tossed and foamed, as though lashed by a mighty storm. Then all sorts of rare, wonderful, and useful things and beings began to emerge from the heaving bosom of that mysterious deep. First rose from them the sacred Cow, then in succes-

17.—THE CHURNING OF THE AMRITA.
(VISHNU'S THIRD AVATÂR OR INCARNATION—THE "KURMA" OR TORTOISE AVATÂR).

sion the divine many-headed horse, the elephant, a troop of Apsaras (water-maidens); the goddess of beauty appeared, seated on a lotus blossom ; deadly poison also was churned out of the waters; Vâsuki claimed that as his perquisite, to be given to his serpents. According to some versions the four Vedas also came out of that memorable churning. But on our picture they seem to be represented as one of the divine beings who do the churning—as a person with four heads and four arms, with a book in one hand. Last of all came forth the physician of the gods, radiant, triumphant, bearing aloft the cup with the precious beverage. Both devas and asuras made a rush for it and there ensued a raging battle. But the devas had managed to secure the first draught, and being fully invigorated by it, had no difficulty in beating off their late allies and hurling them into the dark abysses.

CHAPTER VI.

THE RIG-VEDA: THE STORM-MYTH—THE SUN-AND-DAWN MYTH.

1. WE already know that the main, most vital fact of India's physical life, that on which it hinges for good or for evil, is the timely arrival and beneficent violence of the southwestern monsoon, or, as the unscientific would say, the spring thunderstorms. This is what may be poetically termed the great atmospheric drama, with its incidents of war and conquest, its armies and its heroes. Here the imagination of the old Âryas of the Seven Rivers, with their characteristic naturalistic tendencies, revelled unstinted. Here, in the Middle-Region—*antáriksha*—was Cloudland, which men watched day by day as the familiar but never palling scenes were enacted over and over again,—where INDRA—the Thunderer—was king, and the MARUTS—the Storm-winds—were his friends and helpers; where the clouds were sometimes actors and sometimes scenery, where the precious Cows were fought for, for whose milk the long-suffering earth hungers and thirsts.

2. And here we are brought to the root of that

strange and apparently ineradicable superstition of Aryan India—the sacredness of the Cow. It has been suggested as one of the reasons, that the cow is the distinctive animal of Aryan life. For, absolutely unfitted by nature for the hardships of a nomadic existence, or for the torrid heat of the open steppe, it needs the protection of forest glades, the coolness of streams, the rest and sweetness of meadows exactly suiting the farming stage of culture which immediately follows on the nomadic and precedes or co-exists with the city-building stage,[1] since its wants and the care it demands are such as can be supplied only under favorable and settled conditions of life, even though still very primitive. And in that stage —the first in which the Aryan race appears to the historical vision—we can scarcely realize what a wonderful, god-given, all-sufficient treasure this gentle, homely, patient companion must have seemed to a people broken up into families or small clans, wholly dependent each on its own dairy and patch of tillage. The sweetest, most wholesome of foods flowed from her udder, easily transformed into the butter which, melted and clarified, fed the sacred flame on the home-altar, while her mate, the fiery bullock, supplied meat for the burnt-offering, or, tamed and trained, became the obedient laboring steer. There were no bounds to the gratitude and reverence, the loving care they paid this living embodiment of a kindly providence, until they came to consider the cow as something holy and half divine. It became

[1] See *Story of Chaldea*, ch. i., "The Four Stages of Culture," especially pp. 123-125.

to them the sacred animal, the object of almost worship, which it remains to this day among their descendants in India.

3. To this sacredness, founded on such homely, positive grounds, a more imaginative reverence was added by the active poetical fancy which filled the world with the mythical creations that were to beggar the invention of all coming ages. The real, live, earthly cow had her glorified double in the heavens, or, rather, the Middle-Region, *antáriksha;* there roam the herds of dark, light, or dappled cloud-kine, whose udder pours down their pure sweet milk, the rain, in life-giving showers, for men and animals, and plants. And, as though to show how intimate the connection between the two, they both—the cloud and the cow—have the same name—GO,—and that again is a root expressive of motion, walking. The clouds moving across the sky may first have suggested a likeness to kine moving across the pasture; with a little observation the comparison completed itself. The heavenly pastures and the heavenly herds, and, consequently, the gods as heavenly herdsmen, just as the heavenly ocean with the cloud-ships, are standing mythical images, on which the poetry of all times has rung endless changes. In fact, the most cursory perusal of the Rig-Veda places the Middle-Region before us as a sort of mirror-world, showing an exact reflection, only magnified and glorified, of this lower world, with all its doings, relations, and conditions. This applies to all the incidents of what may be called the atmospheric drama, a perfect counterpart of the wars or

perhaps rather the tribal raids of earth, and which, like the latter, takes the homely form of a conflict for the possession of cattle, or of women and maidens, these being the two staple articles of intertribal booty, the standing objects of mutual covetousness and clan feuds.

"The phenomena of thunder and lightning," remarks Mr. Muir in his study on Indra, "almost inevitably suggest the idea of a conflict between opposing forces; even we ourselves, in our more prosaic age, often speak of the war or strife of the elements. The other appearances of the sky, too, would afford abundant materials for poetical imagery. The worshipper would at one time transform the fantastic shapes of the clouds into the chariots and horses of his god, and at another time would seem to perceive in their piled-up masses the cities and castles which he was advancing to overthrow." [1]

Or mountains.[2] There is nothing a solid dark bank of clouds, with its broken outlines against the horizon, more resembles, and many a mariner longingly looking out for land has been deceived by this mirage of the sea. These castles, these mountains with their deep, dark caves, are the fastnesses wherein wicked robbers hide the stolen cows or

[1] Muir's *Original Sanskrit Texts*, vol. v., p. 98.

[2] *Párvata* (from a root meaning "to swell") means both "cloud" and "mountain"; so "*pur*" means "fortress" and "cloud." Vedic Sanskrit has many more such homonyms, which, while strongly impressing us with the nearness to nature of the old poets and their fine sense of the picturesque resemblances between earth-land and cloud-land, have for us moderns the disadvantage that they actually blur the line between the two, and frequently render it almost impossible to make out whether a given incident—such as storming of fortresses, hurling enemies down mountains and the like—is to be taken in a mythical or historical sense. They seem to us to have lived in both worlds and scarcely themselves to have known one from the other.

maidens, over whom the dragon cloud-fiend, AHI, the Serpent, who loves to lie on the top of mountains, and the shaggy monster, VRITRA, the Enfolder, keep watch, until the Thunderer's lightning spear pierces and tears them to pieces, while the castle walls or mountain sides burst open under the resonant blows of his fiery mace, and the captives come forth. "For" (if we may be permitted to quote from a former volume of our own) "there are clouds and clouds, and not all by any means bode or bring rain. If some generously pour down the precious, pure liquid which is life and drink to the parched, pining earth, others keep it back, wickedly hide it, swell and spread with the treasure they cover and enclose, and will not give it up until pierced and torn asunder by the lightning spear of the angry thunder-god."[1] And those whose ill-fortune it has been to live through a genuine drought in a semi-tropical clime, will heartily endorse the remark that nothing can be more disheartening, when every breathing and growing thing, nay, the inanimate soil itself, with its gray, dusty, rifted surface, is panting and gaping for rain to bring moisture and coolness, than to see the clouds collecting and floating across the sky day after day without discharging their contents.[2]

---

[1] See *Story of Media, Babylon, and Persia*, pp. 44-47.

[2] See Muir, vol. v., p. 98. The author's personal experience includes several "dry spells" in Central Italy, and a real, unmitigated two years' drought in Texas—the most terrible in fifty-nine years. Aggravating as the relentless blue sky was on the former occasions, it was nothing to the exasperation of gazing daily on a cloudy, sometimes an overcast, sky, knowing that not a drop would fall from it. The feeling was distinctly one of animosity against some invisible, but sentient and malicious power.

And now that we clearly understand what may be called the plot of the drama—very simple and in substance always the same—we may introduce the actors and let the various scenes unfold themselves, keeping, as we did in the preceding chapter, to the only really forcible and impressive method: that of letting the ancient poets speak, *i. e.*, quoting as much as possible from the Rig-Veda itself.

4. It is generally understood that Vedic worship knew of no temples or images of its gods, and this must of course apply to Indra, the king of the Middle-Region—him who may well be termed the champion-god of Aryan India.[1] Yet one is almost tempted to doubt the fact in his case and that of his faithful comrades and escort the Maruts—the Storm-Winds[2]—who ride forth to battle with him, an eager, rushing troop—so realistic and complete are the descriptions of their personal appearance, strength, and warlike equipment, down to the smallest details. Indra is shown us borne on a shining chariot, a golden whip in his hand, the thunderbolt in his arm, helmeted with gold, and not only are his long, strong arms spoken of, and the beauty of his nose and ruddy cheeks, but we are told how his

---

[1] This name has been the theme of much and vigorous philological discussion. The most convincing explanation, because the simplest and most pertinent, is that which connects it with the root IND—"sap, drop,"—a root which we find again in Sindhu-Indus ("river") It is very plain that "India" is the land of Indra and the Indus.

[2] Literally "the Smashers," "Grinders," as this is one of the meanings contained in that extremely serviceable and prolific root MAR.—See Max Müller's *Science of Language*, Second Series, pp. 332 *ff.* (New York Edition, Scribner, 1875).

golden beard is violently agitated by the swift motion, as he guides his mettlesome steeds and hurls his bolts around. Again the Maruts. Not much is left to the imagination when they are presented to us as driving chariots borne along with the fury of boisterous winds by their swift tawny horses or dappled deer, and described as follows:

"Spears rest upon your shoulders; ye have anklets on your feet, golden ornaments on your breasts, ornaments on your ears, fiery lightnings in your hands, and golden helmets on your heads."

Together with Indra they are bidden by Agni, the priest-messenger, to the sacrificer's banquet; together they quaff huge quantities of the invigorating soma, and together rush to do battle against Vritra, whom they helped Indra to overcome, to pierce through and through, to cut to pieces, till his remains strew the mountain side, and the waters which he imprisoned leap merrily forth, and roll and tumble and pour down on both worlds. Brush and color could hardly give a more vivid picture—and for that picture Indian warrior kings and their gorgeously arrayed body-guards have surely sat. It is anthropomorphism running riot. The question is not: how did the hero of the Middle-Region become the war-god of men, the champion and protector of his Aryan and native worshippers? but: how could he have helped becoming both?

5. Anthropomorphism, however, seldoms keeps long within such sober bounds—certainly not in India. In its tendency to bring the superhuman within the mind's ken, by clothing it in human,

familiar garb, it but too easily slips into exaggeration, and, in exalting the object of worship, is apt to represent greatness by material size. Scarcely any of the Indra hymns, which are more numerous than those to any other deity, are free from this taint of fancy, or rather weakness of expression, to which, however, together with some images of the most grotesque grossness, we owe some of great poetical beauty. Let us pick out a few at random, as they occur scattered through the hymns.

6. Nothing is more frequently impressed on the worshipper than Indra's physical immensity and strength. He is "so superior to men, heaven and earth do not suffice for his girdle," and "when he grasps the two boundless worlds, they are but a handful to him." "He contains all that exists as the tire of a wheel contains the spokes"; indeed, "as the axle passes both wheels, so his greatness surpasses both worlds"; but, "not a hundred heavens and a hundred earths, with a thousand suns—no, not all created worlds could contain *him*." But it is Indra's soma-drinking capacities which inspire the poets with the most extravagant absurdities; he is said to drink it in pailfuls—tubfuls—thirty lakes at a sitting; he is invited to drink freely, like a thirsty stag, or a bull roaming in a waterless waste. The acme is reached when he is credited with two bellies, which are compared to two lakes, and which he is requested to fill—which he does with a will, if we are to believe the translator who reads a certain verse as saying that Indra cannot wait for the soma to be drawn for him, but gulps down cask, fau-

cet, and all[1]; it is doubtless after an exploit of the kind that he is admiringly described as staggering about at the sacrificial feast, tottering like a boat on the waters—"soma in his belly, great might in his body, wisdom in his head, and lightning in his hand." It is in this "exhilarated" condition that the hero-god performs his most notable deeds and most brilliantly earns his highest title, that of VRITRA-HÂN—"Slayer of Vritra," the cloud-demon of Drought. The same idea re-appears in a spiritualized form in the hymns in which Soma the god is invoked jointly with Indra and both are besought for help against fiends or earthly foes, when they impartially share the credit and praise. In one place Soma is called "the soul of Indra."

7. As the god of war on earth between men and men, Indra is not merely the Âryas' champion and helper in single battles, he is the leader of the Aryan eastward movement generally; it is he who guides them from the Indus to the Yamunâ, and makes their path one of conquest: "Look forward for us, O Indra, as a leader, and guide us onward towards greater riches. Take us safely across, lead us wisely and in safety." Nothing could mean more clearly: pushing eastward, crossing rivers, dislodging *dasyus*.

8. It must be admitted that the goods which the Ârya pleads for to Indra are always of the most material kind. When it is not rain or the dispersion of darkness, it is cows, horses, many sons healthy and strong, gold and riches of every kind, victory in war, and "the riches of the enemies." He is essentially

---

[1] Mr. E. D. Perry of Columbia College.

the creation of a rushing, active, coveting time—a "storm and stress" period,—and his personality has none of the spiritual charm which radiates from such contemplative conceptions as Vâruna or Aditi, or the philosophical play of fancy which makes the elusive forms of Agni and Soma so truly divine. Still, there is something very touching and tender in the confiding familiarity with which he is addressed in some few passages, as in the following:

"Come, O Indra, brother. . . . Here thy friends have lived from oldest time; look now on thy later friends, and the youngest. . . . For thou wast our fathers' friend of old and willingly didst grant them their wishes. . . . We call on thee, who dost not make thy ear deaf to our voice, but hearest us from afar. . . . For thou, O gracious one, hast always been both father and mother to us . . . the most fatherly of fathers.

"The old songs hasten to thee ever anew . . . like harnessed steeds, like kine that lick their young calves, like wives that fondle and cling to the stateliest of husbands. . . . O stay, go not from us, thou mighty one, when I offer thee the well-pressed soma. I take hold of thy robe, as a son of his father's robe, with my song. . . ."

9. If we believe his worshippers, Indra certainly is not insensible to so much love and trust. The hymns abound in lists of the things he does for them and gives them: he threshes their foes as corn-sheaves on the threshing-floor; he comes to his friends with both hands full of riches, and benefits shoot from him as boughs from a tree—and he is asked to shower down wealth on his worshippers as the hook shakes the ripe fruit from the tree. . . . He is the helper of the poor—the deliverer and the comforter—a wall of defence—his friendship is indestructible—it is no idle phrase when one poet exclaims: "We are thine and thou art ours! . . ."

"The days dawn prosperously for him who says: Come, let us press the soma for Indra! . . . That king's power is never shaken in whose house Indra drinks strong soma mixed with milk; he flourishes in peace, conquers in war, and dwells securely at home, enjoying high renown." It is but just to say that Indra is very exclusive in his friendships, and "will have nothing to do with the wretch who does not press the soma"—*i. e.*, with such native peoples as have not become converted to the Aryan faith.

10. That one whose favors were so very substantial, and who was so lavish of them, should be the object of selfish and envious solicitations, is but natural. Many are the passages in which Indra is warned against rival petitioners, with a naïve directness which is highly amusing, for instance:

"I will harness the bays to Indra's chariot and draw him down by a new song. Do not let other hymn-singers—and there are many—turn thee from thy way."—(II., 18, 3.)

"Speed thee hither, Indra, with thy mettlesome bays; let no one snare thee, like a bird in a net, but drive straight on, as through a flat country."—(III., 45, 1.)

No less amusing are the remonstrances, nay, downright upbraidings, with which one or other worshipper does not fear to assail his favorite god if he thinks himself slighted or inadequately remembered:

"Gracious are thy hands, O Indra, and beneficent when they bestow gifts on the singer. Where tarriest thou? Why hastest thou not to the drinking-bout? Or art thou disinclined to give?"—(IV., 29, 9.)

"Why do men call thee generons, thou wealthy one? A giver thou art, so I hear: then give to me. Let my hymn be blest with treasure, O mighty one. . . ."—(X., 42, 3.)

Most characteristic of all in the way of chiding is the following, though there is no lack of separate passages where the god is called "stingy," and "tardy," and "grudging":

"Had I, O Indra, so much wealth as thou possessest, I should freely give to my worshipper, thou source of wealth; I should not leave him in poverty.—I would lavish riches on him day by day, wherever he might be; for nothing is more valuable to us than thou art—not kindred, not even a father."—(VII., 42, 18–19.)

Or this:

"Were all the riches mine, O Indra, which thou ownest, my poet should be wealthy.—I would help him, bless him with gifts, O Lord of Might, were I the Lord of Kine. . . . For no god nor mortal can hinder thy liberality, O Indra, when it is thy will to give."—(VIII., 14, 1, 2, 4.)

11. When scholars tell us that Indra is a creation of a later and different epoch from that of the old sky-gods Dyâus and Váruna, a growth, moreover, of India's own soil—(it were perhaps more correct to say Penjâb's)—they by no means rest their assertion on mere circumstantial evidence. There is, in the Rig-Veda itself, ample evidence of the impetuous Storm- and War-god having supplanted the two great Asuras, and that by no means peaceably, without strife and bitterness dividing the followers of the new worship and the old—until the latter were carried away by the tide of the times and public feeling. If the interpretation of scattered single lines or expressions might still leave room for doubt, the following entire hymn (IV., 42) does not. Nothing could be more explicit. It is in the dramatic form of a dialogue: each god

speaks for himself, and the poet decides between their rival claims.

"(*Váruna speaks*): I am the King: mine is the lordship. All the gods are subject to me, the universal life-giver, and follow Váruna's ordinances; I rule in men's highest sanctuary.—I am King Váruna; my own are these primeval heavenly powers. . . . —I, O Indra, am Váruna, and mine are the two wide, deep, blessed worlds. A wise maker, I created all the beings; Heaven and Earth are by me preserved.—I made the flowing waters to swell; I established in their sacred seat the heavens; I, the holy Âditya, spread out the tripartite (or threefold) universe." (Heaven, Earth, and Atmosphere.)

"(*Indra speaks*): I am invoked by the steed-possessing men, when pressed hard in battle; I am the mighty one who stirs up the fight and whirls up the dust, in my overwhelming strength. All that have I done, nor can the might of all the gods restrain me, the Unconquered; when I am exhilarated by libations and prayers, then quake both boundless worlds."

"(*The priest speaks*): That thou didst all these things, all beings know; and now thou hast proclaimed it to Váruna, O Ruler! Thee, Indra, men praise as the slayer of Vritra; it was thou who didst let loose the imprisoned waters."

12. There is another hymn—a much later one, as shown by the far abstruser tone and more elaborate diction (X., 124)—which tells (or commemorates) the same story. There the poet summons Agni out of the darkness to conduct the sacrifice. The divine *hotar* then announces that he is loth to forsake an old friend and go among strangers, but that he "has long observed the guest of the other party," has travelled through many places, and he concludes:

"I now say farewell to the Father, the Asura; I go from him to whom no sacrifices are offered to him to whom men sacrifice.—In choosing Indra, I give up the Father, though I have lived with him many years in friendship. Agni, Váruna, and Soma must give way; the power goes to another, I see it come."

13. Indra clearly was the god for a struggling, conquering, unscrupulously pushing people, rather than the great Âditya—majestic, serene, and just. In what way the supremacy was, so to speak, officially transferred to him, there is nothing to inform us. There is quite a number of passages, even of whole hymns, full of allusions to Indra's birth, childhood, early exploits, and the like. But the wording is so obscure, most of the things alluded to are so utterly unknown to us, that nothing coherent or satisfactory can be made out of all these texts. Heaven and earth are said to quake with fear before his anger at his birth. His mother (who is she?) seems to die almost as soon as he is born; then he is said to have taken his father by the foot and hurled him down. There are also hints of conspiracy to kill him in his sleep or on his wanderings, and he himself is made to say: "Pressed hard by hunger, I cooked dogs' entrails; I found no god who would take pity on me; I saw my wife deeply bowed with grief; then the eagle brought me sweet Soma."[1] It would be vain to try to piece a consistent story out of these shreds: for there are plenty of other lines, even in the same hymn, which point to different versions of the same events. All that we can gather from the above quotations, and other passages, is the plain allusion (in mythical language) to the antagonism and persecution of which he is the object, on the part of the other gods, *i. e.*, the followers of the older gods.

14. Neither do we know when or how the feud

[1] See for more on this subject, ch. vii.

between "the gods" was laid. But certain it is that harmony was restored at some time, for we meet with numerous hymns addressed to Indra and Váruna jointly; they peacefully share at last the government of the world, each in his own line. This is expressly intimated in a text: "The one [Indra] loves to slay foes, the other [Váruna] always maintains his ordinances." Indra is also frequently addressed jointly with several of the greater gods—with Agni, Soma, Vâyu, and others. Vâyu and Agni, indeed, became in the course of time most closely associated with him—till, at the later period of Brahmanic theology, the three—Rain, Fire, and Wind—formed a sort of mystic trinity or triad.

15. The personality of Indra, though sufficiently transparent, still has enough of complexity in its duality (Storm-god and War-god) to suggest evolution from simpler material, from a more directly naturalistic conception. We shall hardly go wrong if we seek the latter in PARJANYA, the Storm-god pure and simple, originally neither more nor less than the rain-cloud or the thunder-cloud itself, for *parjanya* is frequently used in the Rig-Veda as a common noun for *cloud*.[1] Of several texts, one is absolutely decisive: "Even during the day the Maruts shed darkness by the water-bringing *parjanya*." Now nothing but a cloud can shed dark-

[1] The word is said to come from the same root as *párvata—cloud* and *mountain*. This god has a special interest for us moderns, because he remained the highest god of a large branch of the Aryan race—the Slavo-Lithuanian, who still worshipped him for many centuries after Christ, under the scarcely altered name of PERKUNAS = PERKONS = PERÙN.

ness during the day. Agni is asked to "send the rain-bringing *parjanya* hither"; then the plural is used: "the *parjanyá* [clouds] bring joy to the earth." But these are isolated survivals. The Rain-and-Storm god (for India knows little of our quiet rains) is almost always separated from the cloud, which is sometimes his chariot, sometimes the barrel or skin filled with the water which he pours down on the worlds; then he is the "Son of Heaven," who "speaks a gleam-accompanied, resounding word which brings refreshment."

16. Parjanya has one peculiar feature: he pours the seed on the earth; it enters the plants and there becomes the germ. His name is hardly ever mentioned without some allusion being made to this important duty of his, and he is in consequence directly invoked as the special guardian of plants: "Parjanya, who brings us food through the plants." Does not this forcibly remind us of that curious Old-Eranian belief that the seeds of all plants were carried down to earth by the rain?[1]

17. From all this it will be seen that Parjanya very possibly goes back to the oldest Aryan period, and might fairly claim a place, in Aryan India, among the "Older gods," the subject-matter of our preceding chapter. But, with every presumption in favor of the suggestion, which great scholars endorse,[2] the link is broken, direct proof is wanting, no

---

[1] See *Story of Media*, etc., p. 65.

[2] See especially the two exhaustive papers by Geo. Bühler, in the *Transactions of the London Philological Society*, 1859, pp. 154 *ff.* (English), and in Benfey's *Orient and Occident*, vol. i., pp. 214 *ff.*

corresponding name being found in Indo-Eranian antiquity. One thing is sure: that Indra and Parjanya are distinct mythical persons, not convertible quantities. We have a text which says expressly: "Great Indra, who is like to Parjanya in power." It is extremely probable that at one time they were, so to speak, parallel gods, *i. e.*, that two different Aryan tribes worshipped the Storm-and-Rain god under these two different names, with some differences also in their functions; that Indra happened to be the god of the more pushing, warlike tribes, and thus early developed into the champion of Aryan conquest, and by his growing popularity quickly eclipsed his former brother.

18. Among the five or six hymns to Parjanya, there is one—V., 83—which is one of the very few Vedic pieces of complete and faultless poetical beauty, without anticlimaxes or any of the puerilities or vulgarities which so often leave us disappointed with otherwise fine effusions:

"1. Sing unto the strong with these songs, laud Parjanya, with praise worship him. Loud bellows the Bull; he lays down the seed and fruit in the herbs.—2. He cleaves the trees asunder, he slays the Rakshasas; all living creatures fear the wearer of the mighty bolt. Even the sinless trembles before him, the giver of rain, for Parjanya, thundering, slays the evil-doers.—3. As a driver who urges his horses with his whip, he makes the rainy messengers appear. From far arises the roar of the lion when Parjanya makes the cloud full of rain.—4. The winds rage, the lightnings shoot through the air, the herbs sprout forth from the ground, the

---

(German). One of the greatest contemporary Vedic scholars, Ludwig, on the other hand, specially identifies Parjanya with the spring monsoon. If so, he might very well be of Indian growth, yet older than Indra.

heavens overflow, refreshment is borne to all creatures when Parjanya blesses the earth with rain.—5. Thou, Parjanya, shield us well, by whose doing the earth is shaken, by whose doing the hoofed herd is supported, by whose doing herbs of all kinds sprout forth. —6. . . . . Oh come to us with the thunder-cloud, pouring down the waters, Asura, our father.—7. Roar, thunder, give fruit, fly roundus with thy chariot that is filled with water. Pull strongly the downward-bent, well-fastened water-skin; may the heights and the valleys be made even.—8. Lift up the great barrel, pour down; loosened may the streams rush forward. Drench heaven and earth, give good drink to the kine. . . .—10. Well hast thou poured down the rain, now cease; thou makest that we can pass over the dry plains; thou hast made the herbs to sprout that we may eat, and hast received praise from the creatures."

19. The Rig-Veda was not generally known, even in name, sixty years ago, except among English and a few German scholars,—certainly not in Russia. Yet we find in the works of the great Russian poet Pushkin a short poem, which might be a free paraphrase on this hymn to Parjanya. We must be permitted to translate it for our readers, as it suggests interesting comparisons, and may serve as an additional warning not to be too prompt to suspect connections or imitation wherever there is similarity of thought or imagery. Besides, the poem is both short and beautiful.

THE CLOUD.

Thou latest straggler of a storm that's fled!
  Alone thou floatest o'er the joyous blue,
And castest, on thy envious course and sad,
  O'er day reviving an ungenial hue.

It was but now thy shade the sky o'erspread.
  And from thy gloom the threatening lightning broke,

And from thy womb the mystic thunder spoke,
And with thy rain the thirsting earth was fed.

Enough then! hie thee from the peaceful scene!
Refreshed is earth, and long dispersed the storm;
The zephyr courts the trees and sweeps thy form
Far from the azure of the sky serene.

20. But little need be added specially about Indra's companions in battle, the warlike Maruts—the Storm-Winds. They are the sons of PRISHNÎ, the Cloud-cow,[1] and of RUDRA, rather a subordinate deity in the Veda, though undoubtedly very old, but who, in later Brahmanism and especially Hinduism, rose to the highest rank. He is thought by the latest scholars to be a personification of the stormy sky, as opposed to the serene sky—Váruna. Ludwig suggests that the oldest conception of Dyâus—the Sky in its entirety, in all its manifestations—split itself into those of Váruna and Rudra, the latter representing the elementary, the former the spiritual and moral side of the original conception[2]—of course a later evolution, yet older than Indra. Rudra undoubtedly is a wielder of the thunderbolt: it is his deadly arrow, with which he is entreated not to strike the worshipper, or his children, or his cattle, but, if need be, to draw his mighty bow against "somebody else." "The Terrible" *(rudra)* is his name, and terrible he is; and the

[1] Prishnî, "speckled," from the root PRISH, which, however, also means "sprinkle" (the connection between the two is obvious)—a play on homonyms or *pun* quite in the taste of all ancient mythical poetry, and a liberal source of stories, riddles, and puzzles.

[2] *The Rigveda*, vol. iii., p. 320.

flattering things which are said of and to him, about his beauty, his splendor, his healing powers, must be taken as the deprecatory utterances of fear. The best that is expected of him is to spare. It will be seen how widely this deity differs from Indra.

21. The Maruts themselves are frequently called Rudras. They appear always in troops; sometimes they are twenty-seven, sometimes sixty-six; then there are said to be thousands of them—ways of saying "a great many." They are all alike; no distinctions are made between them, either of age or appearance; they always act in a body and are "of one mind." Sometimes they drive along "with golden mantles waving, sometimes "cloaked in rain," and once they are shown "clothed in the woolly cloud" as they "split open the rock with might." Their chariots, drawn by self-yoked dappled mares or spotted deer, fleet as birds, now are "laden with lightning," now with buckets and barrels of water which they pour down as they go, singing loudly. Their very sweat is rain, and pleasant to the ear is the crack of their whips (the whistle and whizz of the wind that ushers in a storm). They are boisterous and noisy. The hymns are simply inexhaustible on this theme, and rise on some occasions to naturalistic poetry of great beauty. No enemy is there to face them, not in heaven nor on earth; they make the mountains to tremble, they rend and shake the trees like wild elephants; the earth totters and quakes before them with fear "as an aged king." Of course they are entreated for all the usual good things of which Indra is commonly the dispenser,

and they are not spared rebuke any more than Indra when they do not respond promptly enough to their votaries' instances:

> "Were ye but mortals, O sons of Prishnî, and your worshipper were an immortal—ye should not be neglected as the insect (?) in the grass, nor should ye go the road to Yama [die]; nor be perpetually subjected to distress and danger."

22. Great and constant as is the friendship between Indra and the Maruts, there are some few traces in the hymns of a dispute between them, with mutual reproaches and self-assertion. Now a dispute between gods always means one between their votaries, and verses like the following may point to some ancient schism between priests of the Maruts and priests of Indra, each party probably contending for their favorites' respective claims to superior prowess and power. In the principal of the passages in question, Indra rebukes the Maruts for having left him to fight the serpent Ahi single-handed, immediately adding that he is strong and powerful enough to overcome his enemies by his own might alone. They reply:

> "Thou hast indeed done great things, O mighty one, with us for thy helpers, through our equal valor. But we Maruts, O strong Indra, can perform many great deeds by our power when we so desire."
>
> *Indra retorts:* "By my own inborn might, O Maruts, I slew Vritra. Through my own wrath I grew so strong. It was I who, wielding the lightning, opened the way for the shining waters to run down for men."
>
> *The Maruts:* "In truth, O hero, there is nought thou canst not conquer. Thou hast no equal among the gods. . . ."

Indra: "Mine then must be the supreme power. What I have begun, I carry out wisely; for, O Maruts, I am known as the Strong One. . . ." (I., 165.)

In conclusion, Indra expresses himself as pleased with their praise and homage, and the old friendship is renewed—on the distinct understanding that Indra is the greater. And so he has the best of it here, as he had in his dispute with Váruna.

23. We have now pretty thoroughly studied those gloomy scenes of what we called the Atmospheric Drama which are known in mythological language as the STORM-MYTH. But there is another drama, enacted not in the Middle-Region, but on a higher plane—in the highest heaven itself; nor are the chief actors beings of war and violence, but the most beauteous and gentle of Powers—the light-and-life-giving Sun, and the loveliest of heaven's daughters, the Dawn. Wherefore the scenes in which they take part have received the collective name of SUN-AND-DAWN MYTH. Their parts—as those of genuine protagonists or "first subjects" should—embrace both love and war: love towards each other (for in some way Sun and Dawn must always be closely connected), and war with the beings of opposite nature to theirs: Darkness in all its forms, and consequently some of the foes of Indra and the Maruts—obscuring clouds and blinding mists.

24. The Sun-and-Dawn drama presents more variety of incident than the Storm drama, for the reason that these two mythical persons offer richer poetical material to a lively imagination which, according to the moment's mood or fancy, can

place them in different relations to each other and to the other and lesser powers which complete the cast. Thus, if the Dawn is the born enemy of Darkness, which to dispel and rout is her only business, she is also the twin sister of Night, as they are manifestly both daughters of Dyâus, the Sky, and both work in harmony in their alternate times, keeping the eternal ordinances of Rita and the Âdityas (see pp. 146, 155). Then again she has another sister, even more brilliant, but also older, sadder than herself—the evening Gloaming, doomed to be devoured by the demon Darkness, the shaggy Beast, which the bright young sister vanquished in the morning. Or yet—Dawn and Gloaming are one: the maiden, dazzling in her beauty, arrayed in saffron and rosy robes, drives her golden chariot through the portals of the East, closely followed by her lover the young Sun, whose advances she receives, coy, but not unwilling, until her delicate, ethereal being shrinks from his more and more fiery touch and she flees to the ends of the heavens, vanishes, and is lost to her gay lover; he, meantime, not being free to tarry (for the path laid out by Rita must be run), pursues his way, meets foes—the cloud-demons of many shapes, the crawling mist-serpents, whom he transfixes and dispels with his golden spear—meets other loves too, especially the dangerously fascinating Apsáras, the water-maidens that sail the sky on light shifting cloudlets—until, weary, shorn of his power, yet glorious still, he sinks low and lower, sometimes serenely victorious, sometimes still fighting his darkling, crowding foes, whom he disperses by a last mighty effort, like a dying hero; and here at last he, the old Sun, beholds again his love of the morning—no longer the radiant, hopeful Dawn, but the subdued, the saddened Gloaming. For one brief while the lovers are united at their career's end; for one brief moment the joy of their meeting irradiates the West, then, in each other's embrace, they sink to their rest—to their doom, and Darkness, their arch-foe, engulphs them. To-morrow's young rising Sun is their child—if the popular fancy cares to look for a sequel to the day's drama, which is not usual in early Indian poetry. It prefers the fiction of the old Sun being somehow rejuvenated, cured, liberated, and reappearing youthful and vigorous in the morning.

25. It is very evident that these are only one or two of a great many possible poetical interpretations of the same natural phenomena, and that each such interpretation must shape itself into an image, an incident, a story. What endless material for love stories, love tragedies! Each such utterance, separately, is only a more or less apt and beautiful poetical figure, simile, metaphor. But if collected and fitted and pieced into a system, then consistently carried through, some very queer and even distressing features will appear—distressing, *i.e.*, so long as we have not the key to mythical language and take its sayings as we would so many bald statements on human affairs. So, while the Sun is the eternal foe of Darkness, still, as he is seen to emerge out of darkness, he may, in a sense, be said to be the "Child of Darkness," and it follows that he of necessity must kill

his father, just as Agni must needs devour his parents as soon as born (see p. 160). Again, it is no faulty poetical figure to call the Sun the child, or the brother, of the Dawn—and then it may very well happen that he loves, or weds, his mother or his sister, or kills her! Bad enough to place gods in such awkward positions; at least the devout votary has the resource, like Agni's worshipper, to abstain from judging the acts of great deities (see p. 160). But bring down all this to earth—as all nature-myth has invariably been brought down, to become Heroic Epos—and see in what a fine tangle the later poets will find themselves, what horrible deeds they will calmly relate of their most cherished ancient heroes and founders of royal houses, without the least consciousness or recollection of the original real meaning of what they tell! Fortunately there is little system or consistency in the Rig-Veda—at least, so far as combining and connecting the different myths with which it teems. So we can take each one on its own merits, untroubled by moral qualms or logical misgivings.

SÛRYA—THE SUN.

26. To begin with plain fact, SÛRYA is the Sanskrit common noun designating the Sun; the root contained in it gives it the meaning of "brilliant, shining." And Sûrya is, in the Rig-Veda, the material, visible luminary, "created" by the gods (or even some particular god), and obedient to their bidding. But Sûrya is not only the sun, he is also the Sun-god, powerful, independent, subject only to

the ordinances of the great Âdityas, themselves governed by Rita, the supreme Cosmic and Moral Law. This distinction—surely unconscious, and which we find in the presentment of all the Nature-gods—between their physical and moral essence, accounts for the difference in the tone of the several hymns, and even different parts of the same hymns, addressed to this deity. These invocations are mostly fine poetry, and the figures used explain themselves.

27. One quality has been universally ascribed to the divinized Sun in every age, by every ancient race: that of being "all-seeing." The association of this quality with the giver of light and the disperser of darkness is too natural to suggest mutual borrowing, and we need not wonder if we find a striking resemblance between the Old Chaldean and the Old Aryan hymns to the Sun, not only in this particular, but in several other poetical conceptions.[1] Sûrya, a Son of the Sky (Dyâus), we have already learned to know as the Eye of Mitra and Váruna.[2] Now, in Oriental phraseology, the Eyes of the King are his spies, so it is but natural that he should observe all the deeds of men, and report them to the great Âdityas, the guardians and avengers of Law and Right. That the expression was really understood in this manner is proved by the frequent prayer to Sûrya to "report men sinless before the Âdityas,"—which looks singularly like a request, in child-slang, "not to tell on them," and so not bring them into

---

[1] See *Story of Chaldea*, pp. 171, 172.

[2] Once Sûrya is called the Eye of Agni also (I., 115).

disgrace and punishment. Thus one of the Vasishthas sings:

"If thou, O Sûrya, at thy rising wilt report us truly sinless to Váruna and Mitra, we will sing to please the gods. . . . Sûrya is rising, O Váruna-Mitra, to pace both worlds, looking down on men, protector of all that travel or stay, beholding right and wrong among men. He unharnesses his seven HARITS[1] . . . and hastens dutifully to your throne, ye twain, surveying all beings, as a shepherd his flock. . . . Sûrya emerges from the sea of light, he whose path the Âdityas laid out. . . ." (VII., 60.)

". . . He unweaves [ravels up] the black mantle, his rays cast off the darkness, rolling it up as a hide and dropping it into the waters.

"Not hanging on to anything, not made fast, how comes it that he falls not from such height? By whose guidance does he travel? Who has seen it?" (IV., 13.)

Even more rapturous is the following greeting:

"The gods' bright face has now arisen, the Eye of Mitra, Váruna, and Agni; Sûrya fills heaven, earth, and atmosphere, the breath of life of all that stands and moves. . . . The beautiful golden Harits, the bright ones, hailed by songs of joy, they mount to the highest heaven, and in one day their course encircles heaven and earth. . . . And when he unharnesses the mares, the veil of darkness spreads over all things." (I., 115.)

We have learned to know the Sun as a horse, and as a bird. These images both remain standing symbols of the god, and there even are two hymns (I., 163 and X., 177), rather obscurely and mystically worded, celebrating him as "the Bird adorned by

---

[1] Sûrya's seven steeds or mares—as also the Dawn's—are generally called HARITS ("brilliant, ruddy"); they are of course his rays, as the first verse of I., 50, expressly shows (see farther on). It should be noted, however, that the steeds of other gods—Indra's and Agni's, for instance—are also sometimes called so.

the Asura" (Váruna), and as "the Horse who neighed as soon as he was born, emerging out of the waters [or mist]," the Steed with the "falcon's wings and the gazelle's feet." So the Dawn is said to bring "the Eye of the gods" to "lead forth the white and lovely horse." There are few entire hymns addressed to Sûrya, but of these the following (I., 50), has become famous for its rich imagery and its unusually finished literary form:

"1. The god who knows all beings rises aloft, drawn by his rays, that he, Sûrya, may behold all things.[1]—2. Straightway, like thieves, the stars with their brightness slink away before the all-seeing god.—3. His rays are visible to all mankind, blazing like flames.—4. All-conspicuous on thy rapid course thou createst light, illumining the whole firmament.—5. Thou risest for the race of gods and for that of men, that all may behold thy light.—6. With that same glance wherewith Váruna, the illuminator, surveys the busy race of men,—7. Thou, O Sûrya, searchest the sky and the wide space, making the days, spying out all creatures.—8. Seven mares bear thee on, O far-seeing Sûrya, in thy chariot, god of the flaming locks.—9. Sûrya has harnessed the seven Harits, daughters of the car, self-yoked.—10. Gazing out of the darkness up at the highest light, we have reached Sûrya, a god among the gods."

INDRA AND SÛRYA.

Sûrya's relations to Indra are rather peculiar. The grim warrior god appears to treat him sometimes in a friendly and sometimes in a hostile way. True, there are many passages—in hymns to Indra, be it noted—which would place the sun-god in his direct dependence, by actually saying that he was *created*

[1] This is the rendering of the French scholar A. Bergaigne; others translate, "that all may behold Sûrya." Either meaning would be appropriate and satisfactory.

by Indra; but this must be taken only as a piece of exaggeration from excessive zeal on the part of the worshipper to ingratiate himself with the deity he is invoking—a trick of Vedic priestly poetry which has long been noticed as one of its most peculiar and characteristic features. When, however, Indra is said to have prepared the way for Sûrya, or "caused him to shine," it is no more than good myth-rhetoric. For we can well imagine—from personal observation—the sun-god so overwhelmed in battle with Ahi, Vritra, and other cloud-demons as to be unable to extricate himself and overcome his foes without the help of the Thunderer's weighty arm; in plain prose—a thunderstorm clears the sky and allows the sun to shine. It is, in substance, the same myth as that contained in a passage which tells how "the gods lifted Sûrya out of the sea [*samudra*] wherein he lay hidden" (X., 72). Not less transparent is the request to Indra that he should "hide the sun," here likened to a wheel, and direct his bolts against SHUSHNA, the Demon of Drought. But this short verse also very clearly shows how Sûrya, on certain occasions, could be regarded by Indra, on behalf of men and nature generally, as an enemy and a nuisance, to be suppressed, at least temporarily, at all cost. For when battle is to be waged in earnest against the wickedest of all fiends, the blazing disc, or wheel, of the sun is hardly a desirable auxiliary. So that we do not wonder at the climax when Indra is praised for having, with the help of Soma, broken a wheel from Sûrya's chariot and sent it spinning downhill, thereby laming "the great wizard."

INDRA AND USHAS.

27. On the same principle we can understand how the Dawn herself—USHAS, the beautiful, the auspicious[1]—could be treated by Indra at times with the utmost severity; in seasons of drought, is not the herald of another cloudless day, the bringer of the blazing sun, a wicked sorceress, a foe to gods and men, to be dealt with as such by the Thunderer when, soma-drunk, he strives with his friends the Maruts to storm the brazen stables of the sky, and bring out the blessed milch-kine which are therein imprisoned? Indra's treatment of the hostile Dawn is as summary as his treatment of Sûrya, though at other times he is as ready to help her, and "lay out a path" for her, and "cause her to shine" or "light her up." It is the same myth; and fortunately we have it in a far clearer and completer form. Smashing the obnoxious one's car seems to be the one method which occurs to the great foe-smiter, who is more earnest than inventive.

> "This heroic task also, this manly deed, O Indra, thou didst perform, that thou didst smite the woman who planned mischief, the Daughter of the Sky [Dyâus]; this Ushas, who was exalting herself, thou didst strike her down. Ushas fell in terror from her shattered car when the mighty one had felled it to the ground. There it lay, broken utterly, while she herself fled far away." (IV., 30.)

This feat of Indra's is recounted in a hymn which rehearses a list of his finest exploits. It is evidently looked on as one of his highest claims to glory and

---

[1] Ushas—from a root meaning "to burn," "to glow."

gratitude, for it is repeatedly alluded to in different books. In one passage, the fair Ushas is represented as having taken the lesson to heart and flying of her own accord, leaving her chariot standing, from fear of Indra's bolt, while in another the latter is said to have smitten certain enemies as he had broken Ushas' car.

USHAS, THE DAWN.

28. What strikes us most in all this is the exulting and insulting tone in which the poets celebrate the defeat of the goddess who is, except on this one occasion, their greatest favourite, their heart's desire, —one might almost say their pet. Some twenty hymns are addressed wholly to her, and she has a place in numerous others; and everywhere the poets' fancy exhausts itself in brilliant and dainty imagery, in a variety of loving and admiring epithets. Again and again she is likened to a beautiful woman or maiden, who reveals herself in all her loveliness; and it must be confessed that these descriptions, as a rule, recall Oriental harem life (or the *Zenana* of Indian princes), too realistically to be relished by the general reader in their original crudity. So that such passages, scattered through most of the Rig books, may best be summed up in the very comprehensive lines of Mr. J. Muir.[1]

"Like a beautiful young woman dressed by her mother, a richly decked dancing girl, a gaily attired wife appearing before her husband, or a female rising resplendent out of the bath,—smiling and

---

[1] *Sanskrit Texts*, vol. v., p. 194.

confiding in the irresistible power of her attractions, she unveils her bosom to the gaze of the beholder."

A few characteristic verses culled from various hymns will be more interesting and instructive than descriptions detached from the texts:

"The shining Ushas has been perceived; she has opened the doors [of the sky]; setting in motion all living things, she has revealed to us treasures—[the golden treasures of light that were hidden by darkness]—Ushas has awakened all creatures (I., 113, 4).—. . . She hastens on, arousing footed creatures, and makes the birds fly aloft (I., 48, 5).—The birds fly up from their nests and men seeking food leave their homes (I., 124, 12).—[Arousing] the prostrate sleeper to move, [impelling] one to enjoyment, another to the pursuit of wealth, [enabling] those who see but a little way to see far; . . . [arousing] one to wield the royal power, another to follow after fame, another to the pursuit of wealth, another to perform services, Ushas awakes all creatures to go their different paths in life (I., 113, 5, 6).—Inasmuch as thou hast made Agni to be kindled—[for morning worship]—. . . and hast awakened the men who are to sacrifice, thou hast done good service to the gods (I., 113, 9).—She has yoked [her horses] from the remote rising place of Sûrya; . . . Everything that moves bows down before her glance; the active goddess creates light; by her appearance the magnificent Daughter of the Sky drives away our haters. Ushas has repelled our enemies. . . . In thee when thou dawnest is the life and breath of all creatures. . . ." (I., 48, 7–10.)

The dispeller of enemies—not only of the powers of darkness, but also of thieves and other malefactors who are sheltered by darkness, of bad dreams, phantoms, spells, and all the evil brood of darkness—is quite naturally likened to a warrior brandishing weapons. But rarely. The poets dwell almost entirely on the lovely and even the pathetic aspects of their favorite. And indeed there is no lack of pathos and sadness in the conception of a beauteous and gracious being who, herself immortal and ever youthful, though old as Time, serenely and inevitably, in obedience to the highest Law, (she is "the preserver of Rita," "born in Rita,") both prolongs and shortens life, each new day being both her gift to men and the tribute she levies on their sum of days. The pathos is deepened if the bringer of food and joy, the dispenser of life and death, is herself a mortal, a creature of a day—nay, of an hour,—one of many as brilliant and as ephemeral as herself, as she needs must be if each day is thought as having a dawn to itself. In the hymns to Ushas we find her addressed and referred to almost in one breath both as the one ever-returning or born again, and as the fleeting unit of an endless series:

" . . . As thou wast invoked by the poets of old, . . . reward our praise also, O Ushas, with gifts and with brilliant light! (I., 48, 14).

"Maintaining the ordinances of the gods, but wasting away the lives of men, Ushas has shone forth, the last of the numerous Dawns that are past, and the first of those that are coming (I., 124, 2).

"Shine on us with thy best rays, O divine Ushas; give us a long life! (VII., 77, 5).

"Ushas has dawned before; let her now dawn again. . . . (I., 48, 3).

"Born again and again, though ancient, shining with an ever uniform hue, she wastes away the life of mortals as a clever gambler the stakes—(I., 92, 10).

"Ushas follows the track of the Dawns that are past and is the first of the unnumbered Dawns that are to come.— . . . How great is the interval that lies between the Dawns that have arisen and those which are yet to arise? Ushas yearns longingly after the former Dawns and gladly goes on shining with the others [that are to come]. Those mortals are gone who saw the earliest Ushas dawn ; we shall gaze upon her now ; and the men are coming who are to behold her on future morns.— . . . Perpetually in former days did the divine Ushas dawn ; and now to-day the radiant goddess beams upon this world : undecaying, immortal. . . . " (I., 113, 8–13.)

The hymn from which the last extract is taken (I., 113) is the longest and most sustainedly beautiful of those addressed to the " desire of all men," —that which closes with the magnificent *finale*, the grandest lyrical effusion in the whole Rig-Veda :

" Rise ! Our life, our breath has come back ! The darkness is gone, the light approaches ! Ushas has opened a path for Sûrya to travel ; we have reached the point where our days are lengthened. The priest, the poet, celebrating the brightening Ushas, arises with the web of his hymn ; shine, therefore, magnificent Ushas, on him who praises thee. . . . Mother of the gods ! manifestation of Aditi ![1] banner of the sacrifice, mighty Ushas, shine forth ! Arise ! lend a gracious ear to our prayer, giver of all boons !" (I., 113, 16–20.)

We seem to see the uplifted hands, the worshipping upturned eyes, amid the glories of the awakening Eden-like nature—and we long for a burst of Wagner's song and harmony. It seems as though nothing short of Brynhild's waking invocation, " Hail, O Sun," could worthily render the grandeur, simplicity and whole-hearted adoration in this archaïc ode.[2]

[1] See p. 154.

[2] Nor is the association far-fetched. For Brynhild and Sigfrid are originally the Sun-and-Dawn lovers of Teutonic mythology, as is now fully understood by the veriest dabbler in music and folk-lore.

THE TWO SISTERS.

29. There are some verses in this same hymn which very beautifully and completely describe the Dawn's relations to her sister, who of course is no other than Night.

> "The ruddy Bright-one with her bright Calf [the Sun][1] has arrived; to her the Dark-one has relinquished her abodes; kindred to one another, immortal, alternating Night and Morning go on changing color.—The same is the never-ending path of the two sisters, which they travel by the gods' command. They strive not, they rest not, the majestic Night and Dawn, of one mind, though unlike."—(I., 113, 2–3.)

Once or twice the Bright-one is said to be born of the Dark-one (the Dawn to be daughter of Night), but in the great majority of texts they are sisters—the two beauteous Daughters of the Sky, equally beneficent, equally welcome, and equally—but alternately —bringing refreshment and vigor to all that lives; "alike to-day, alike to-morrow, fulfilling the fixed ordinance of Váruna," never transgressing it, never omitting to be at the proper time at the appointed place. Evidently Night is not here conceived as the wicked foe of men, the devouring Beast, the river or sea of darkness, but as the kind friend, the bringer of rest and coolness, the gentle fosterer and restorer. Both sisters are great weavers. They are perpetually weaving mantles and veils—golden, shining, or black, each after her manner; and one undoes the weaving of the other. Ushas shows herself beaming at the borders of the sky, having thrown off the dark

[1] This peculiar surname will be explained farther on.

covering, as she drives on her beautiful chariot drawn by the self-yoked ruddy steeds (I., 113, 14); Sûrya rolls it up like a hide (VII., 63, 1,) unweaves, ravels it up, and hides it away (IV., 13, 4). Yet even this work the sisters perform amicably: "Jointly they weave the out-spread curtain" (II., 4, 6). So close indeed is their relationship, though each goes when the other comes—Ushas "chases far away her sister"—and so harmoniously do they work together, that the poet at last wonderingly asks: "Which of them is the older and which the younger? Who knows, O ye sages? They carry (between them) all that exists, revolving as on one wheel" (I., 185, 1).

30. Ushas' relations to the Sun are as natural, but more varied. She "shines with the light of her lover," Sûrya, who "follows her as a lover follows a maiden." But she flies before him and he never can join her; it were disastrous for her if he did, for the delicate Dawn never could stand the full blaze of her lover's splendor; indeed one poet urges her—not very politely—to hasten and make no delay, that Sûrya may not scorch her like a thief or an enemy (V., 79, 9). But sometimes she is Sûrya's wife—though he is her brother too, both being children of Dyâus—and sometimes his mother. As such she appears in that peculiar passage where she arrives with her "bright Calf." For there Ushas, the fair, the resplendent, appears in the form of——a Cow!

31. Vedic heavenly zoölogy is a curious thing; and confusing, unless one has the patience to study out its main features and underlying principle, after which it becomes, on the whole, tolerably intelligi-

ble. The phenomena are many; the animals are few; so they have to do duty for different things. They are, if we may so word it, *homonyms* in their way. Thus the Horse, the well-attested emblem of the Sun, once in a while stands for the Sky—as when the Pitris are said to have adorned the black horse with pearls (the moonless starry sky). Serpents are not always drought-clouds; there are the serpents of darkness. Nor are cows always rain-clouds; there are also the ruddy, bright cows—the Kine of Light, and the black cows—the Kine of Darkness. Looked at in one way, Night is the dark stable in which the bright cows are shut up; Ushas opens the stable and they bound forth joyously and "scatter around her like a herd." These are of course the rays of the dawn which shoot forth in all directions—and lo! Ushas appears in the *rôle* of shepherdess. Vedic imagery could not stop there. From a "leader of cows," she became "the mother of cows," and consequently a cow herself; a lovely bright one of course; hence her child, the Sun—as calf! But even so her bond with her sister Night is not severed, and both are invoked together as "the two cows which give milk of different colors from similar udders." This fully explains the otherwise obscure passage where Indra is said to have put dark milk in the black cows and light milk in the ruddy ones.

32. We must not forget one last attribute of Ushas, not the least of her charms in the eyes of her by no means disinterested votaries—her great wealth. It is not only that, at her coming, she reveals the treasures of golden light,—the herds of

ruddy cows,—which had been hidden by her sister Night. She is the dispenser, in an indirect way, of far more substantial treasures. By going from house to house, arousing all sleepers, whether poor or rich, to their day's work, she fosters honest endeavor and helps it to its earnings.[1] But even this is too slow and commonplace a way to wealth to content those priests who are forever crying out to the gods, in the name of the worshippers, for riches on a large scale—herds of cattle, horses, booty from enemies, wives (really female slaves), and sons, strong, stalwart, and numerous,—and, in their own, for "great gifts" and "liberality," *i.e.*, the highest possible pay for their priestly services from kings and wealthy patrons generally. These great boons, these windfalls, the gods reserve for the pious sacrificer and "soma-presser," the zealous performer of appointed rites and singer of hymns. But, to be efficacious, the singing, the rites, the sacrifice, must take place at the appointed times, of which the most sacred and important is the hour of sunrise. Ushas, therefore, who "causes Agni to be kindled" on the morning altar, who gives the signal for the "joyful voices" to be raised, and "brings the gods to the sacrifice" jointly with their messenger Agni, puts men in the way of obtaining all they so much covet, and thus becomes a dispenser of wealth. Not improperly, therefore, is she addressed in such strains as this,

---

[1] *Morgenstund' hat gold im Mund* ("Early morn has its mouth full of gold"), the homely old German saw instructs us, while "Early to rise," and "The early bird," are the despair of every nursery.

which may stand here for numberless similar passages:

"Dawn on us with prosperity, O Ushas, Daughter of the Sky, with great glory, O luminous and bountiful goddess, with riches! —Bringing horses and cattle, all-bestowing, they [the Dawns] have often come to shine. Send riches then to me also, O Ushas, incline the Kings to dispense gifts. . . . Those princes, O Ushas, who at thy approach incline their thoughts to liberality, Kanva, the chief of his race,[1] here celebrates.—(I., 48, 1-4.)

"May the soma-presser obtain such Dawns as rise upon the liberal mortal (Dawns), rich in kine, in sons all stalwart, and in horses. . . ."—(I., 113, 18.)

Always the same thing: the bargain between the worshipper and the deity he invokes. To the "liberal mortal," who grudges neither soma, nor fire, nor cakes and hymns, nor fees to the priests, a liberal return is due from the gods. It is to be noticed that, however varied the Vedic Âryas' mythical (*i. e.*, poetical) vocabulary may be, their begging is remarkably monotonous. They ask precisely the same things of every deity—quantities of them—and in almost precisely the same words.

THE ASHVINS.

33. Numerous are the Children of the Sky. We will close the brilliant galaxy with the renowned couple of twins, the ASHVINS, or Horsemen, the brothers of the Sun and the Dawn. They are almost as great favorites as the latter. Many hymns are addressed to them, and they are incidentally men-

[1] This hymn is one of a collection attributed to the priestly family of the Kanvas.

tioned or invoked in a great many more. No other deities, scarcely Indra himself, have become the heroes of such a number of what we may call "story-myths." Indeed, so many and different things are told, asked, and expected of them, that when the Rig-Veda had lost its living actuality, and commentators went to work on it, they were fairly puzzled to determine their original nature, *i. e.*, the natural powers or phenomena which they represent. For they are not only horsemen (or more probably "descendants of the horse," since they themselves never ride, but drive their own chariots like the other gods)—they are also the physicians of gods and men, workers of miracles, rescuers from storms, best men at weddings, protectors of love and conjugal life. This is certainly confusing; and no less so are the answers given by different commentators to the query: "Who—or rather what—are the Ashvins?" Yet some indications we owe them which helped our scholars in their researches; but a careful and minute study of the Rig texts has, as usual, proved the surest guide, and the question may now be considered as settled.

34. The Ashvins' connection with the Horse *(ashva)* gives assurance of their heavenly luminous nature, and this is confirmed by the many epithets conferred on them. Like their sister Ushas, they are beautiful, gracious, bright, swift, immortal, young, though ancient. This latter feature alone would point to a regularly recurring phenomenon of the morning. Then, they are the earliest risers and arrive the first at the morning sacrifice, *ahead* of the

Dawn, who is said to come immediately *after* them; the worshipper, to greet them with his song has to get up *before* the dawn; and they are asked to come to the house on their chariot "to which the twilight is yoked," for the sacrifice held "at the first lighting up of the dawn." Indeed they come earlier still; their chariot appears "at the end of the night," and they are invoked also "in the last watch of night," as well as "at break of day"—two moments, to be sure, which come very close together; with the difference, however, that at the former it is still dark and at the latter it is not quite light. They are "dispellers of darkness" and "killers of Rakshasas" like all luminous beings; they "open the doors of the fast-closed stable rich in cows" (the Dawns, or the rays of the Dawn). These things are explicitly said and repeated in numbers of texts,[1] and leave no doubt as to the original place of the Ashvins in the order of natural phenomena: they represent the twilight hour which precedes the dawn, luminous, but not yet brilliant—a delicate touch quaintly expressed by giving them a team of gray asses—animals that are not quite horses and subdued in color. Not always though. Nothing is immutable in the Rig-Veda. So the chariot of the Ashvins is quite as often drawn by horses. One poet is struck by some fancy, some nice characteristic detail, and gives it. Another takes it up, or sets it aside, at his pleasure—or, for that matter, he does so himself. It is all a question of moods, not deliberate invention.

[1] See for a large and convincing collection of them in Myriantheus' valuable monograph *Die Açvins*.

35. The most decisive witness in favor of this identification of the Ashvins with the morning twilight, we find in this thoroughly Vedic riddle: "When the dark cow [Night] sits among the ruddy cows [the rays of the Dawn], I invoke you, Ashvins, Sons of the Sky," *i. e.*, "when night has not quite gone and morning is just coming." Possibly it was this text which clinched the question for Yâska, one of the great native commentators, who in his *catalogue raisonné* of Vedic deities (the *Nirukta*), after mentioning the opinions of other students, gives as his own that

> "Their time is after the (latter) half of the night when the (space's) becoming light is resisted (by darkness); for the middlemost Ashvin, (the one between darkness and light) shares in darkness, whilst (the other) who is of a solar nature—*âditya*—shares in light."[1]

This also explains why there should be *two* Ashvins, twins. For twilight, the well-named, is of a complicated and essentially dual nature: beginning in darkness, ending in light. Hence, too, there is a difference between the brothers. Yâska, in the passage partly quoted above, says that "one [of course the elder] pervades everything with moisture, the other with light." Again, one is a hero and conqueror (he who stands the brunt of the first fight with darkness), and the other is the wealthy, fortunate Son of the Sky (whose time is when the fight is won, of which good news he is the bearer,

[1] Translation of Professor Goldstücker. The words in parentheses are put in by the translator to relieve the, to us, obscure conciseness of the Sanskrit original.

while the treasures of returning light begin to be revealed). Still the two moments are so close together that the twins are regarded as inseparable, and compared to all sorts of things which go in pairs—the two eyes, the two ears, the two breasts, a bird and his mate, two wheels, etc., etc. In the course of time, a certain spirit of symmetry asserts itself, and the ritual decrees that the Ashvins shall be invoked twice, morning and evening, making them to personate both the twilight before sunrise and that after sunset—though in express contradiction to the following text (V., 77, 2): "Invoke the Ashvins in the morning; the evening is not the time for gods—it is displeasing to them" (naturally, since the gods are *devas*, "bright"). It will be seen how easily this could lead to identify the Twins, one with the morning twilight, the other with the evening twilight,—and even with Day and Night,—which has been done repeatedly, contrary to the very essence of the myth, which makes them *inseparable*, not *alternate*. Ritualism at last prevails entirely, and we find—still in the Rig-Veda—a third invocation of the Ashvins at noon, evidently in accord with the three daily offerings. This is the beginning of confusion, and affords us at the same time a glimpse of the stratification of periods in the Rig-Veda—like that in the Avesta—resulting in the obliteration, or at least blurring, of the original conceptions.

36. Once we have succeeded in determining the elementary nature of the joy-bringing Twins, we also have the key to their various acts and deeds, which

are always gracious and beneficent, wherein they differ widely from most other gods. They are invariably mild, helpful, merciful. They are the great Physicians, who heal the sick, make the lame to walk, the blind to see. But their patients are always the same: the Old Sun, who reaches the goal of his long day's journey weary and sick unto death —when the foe he has fought and vanquished, grim Darkness, at last overcomes and blinds him—and who is made young again and vigorous, and seeing, by the returning light which the Ashvins—the morning twilight—conquer and bring; or else it is the Old Dawn—the evening gloaming—who runs the same dangers, undergoes the same infirmities and decay, and is led forth, rejuvenated and radiant, by her ever youthful brothers. They are best men at weddings, protectors of love and marriage, because they bring the Dawn-bride before the face of her Sun-lover, or reunite the separated lovers. On one occasion, indeed, Ushas is said to have mounted on the Ashvins' car—(was it not on the memorable occasion when her own was shattered by the ungallant Indra?)—and to have chosen them for her husbands.—They are rescuers from stormy waters, because night is a dark and stormy waste of waters, full of dangers and monsters, into which the worn-out Sun fatally sinks, and in which he might perish, did not the ever helpful heralds of Light take him into their swiftly flying ship and carry him safely across to the other—the bright—shore, from which he rises aloft, in fully restored vigor and splendor.—And will not those who do all these kindly offices, who work these miracles for gods, do the same for suppliant men? We know that every myth ends by coming down to earth and being humanized. It will strike every one how many and varied stories could and must have been spun out of this peculiarly attractive and prolific myth of the Ashvins.

37. We cannot close the gallery of the Vedic Beings of Light without devoting a few lines to one who, though holding a rather modest rank, shares in their honors, and is always affectionately and reverently remembered. We mean PÛSHAN, pre-eminently a friend of men, and whose career is one of almost homely usefulness. The great French Vedic scholar, A. Bergaigne, sums it up in one brief page, so lucid and comprehensive, that we cannot do better than reproduce it:

> "Pûshan is, first of all, a pastoral and agricultural deity. He is requested to direct the furrow; his hand is armed with the ox-goad; he is principally the guardian of cattle, who prevents them from straying, and finds them again when they get lost. He is, therefore, prayed to follow the cows, to look after them, to keep them from harm, to bring them home safe and sound. His care extends to all sorts of property, which he guards or finds again when lost. He is also the finder of hidden treasure,—cows first on the list, always. Lastly, Pûshan guides men, not only in their search for lost or hidden things, but on all their ways generally. In a word, he is the god of wayfarers as well as of husbandmen and herdsmen. He is called 'Lord of the Path,' he is prayed to 'lay out the roads,' to remove from them foes and hindrances, to guide his worshippers by the safest roads, as 'knowing all the abodes.' . . . ."

A very human field of action—almost a picture of rural life. But all the foregoing pages have been written to little purpose, if it does not strike the reader at once that it is a reflection of the usual heavenly pastoral,—itself, of course, originally copied from the earthly model. We are, by this time, sufficiently familiar with the aërial pastures and roads, along which the heavenly cattle—whether Cloud-Kine or Kine of Light—roam and stray, get stolen or lost, and are found again. So do we know who they are that guard, and follow, and find them, and bring them back. But not these alone are heaven's "hidden treasure." Agni lies hidden and is found, and so is Soma, whom Pûshan is expressly said to have brought back "like a strayed ox"; and immediately: "Pûshan, abounding in rays, found the king, who lay hidden, and who now shines forth on the sacrificial grass." This at once establishes Pûshan's claim to a place in the highest heavens, at the very source of light itself. It is there that he is the lover of his sister Sûryâ, the Sun-maiden, and sails his golden ships across the aërial ocean.

So much for this gentle deity's naturalistic aspects. His loftier symbolical character will become apparent in connection with a different—and later developed—order of ideas.[1]

[1] See A. Bergaigne, *La Religion Védique*, vol. ii., pp. 420–430.

CHAPTER VII.

THE RIG-VEDA: LESSER AND LATER GODS.—STORY MYTHS.

1. CLASSIFICATION, on the whole, is unsatisfactory. The worst of it is, the things classified won't dovetail nicely, but are sure to overlap both ways or to fall short. Yet, when one has on hand an overwhelming mass of material, and is, moreover, limited to a scant selection from it, one would flounder helplessly without the assistance of such a guide, even though it be lame and to some extent misleading. This is a disadvantage under which all great subjects labor. And of all great subjects there is none both vaster and more complex than the Rig-Veda; none that grows and expands more bewilderingly under handling; none that more elusively resists classification and—to use a very modern yet already somewhat trite expression—popularization. For popularization means: presenting the results of the work of specialists in an untechnical form, intelligible and attractive to the large mass of average, general readers. And how are "results" to be presented where so very few have been finally established? in a branch of learn-

ing which is in the very fervor of research, discovery, comparing theories, correcting errors or hasty conclusions,—so that it is a current saying among brethren of the craft that no book on Ancient India can reach its last chapter without the first ones being rewritten.[1] Method, therefore, is, after all, the best safeguard, and careful sorting and sifting—classifying in short; under reservation and with frequent qualifying of one's own definitions.

2. To begin with the title of this chapter. It should be well understood that the adjectives "lesser and later" are not meant to apply to one and the same deities, or at least not always. The more a divine person goes into abstraction, and the farther it becomes removed from the natural phenomenon which it originally represented, or the more it accentuates certain details of that phenomenon, the later, as a rule, we can place it. Thus the high moral conception of the Sky-god Váruna cannot but have been evolved out of that of the primeval Dyâus, the material visible sky. Again, when we meet three goddesses (very subordinate and rarely mentioned in the hymns), representing the three phases of the moon—the growing, the full, and the waning,—we may be very sure that the worship of the moon itself preceded them. Though of course it is never possible even to suggest a particular time for such

[1] The truth of this saying the author can vouch for from experience. Such scholars as may glance at the present volume and be inclined to fault-finding, will therefore please consider that, with the best-meant efforts to "keep up to date," a book, to *be* a book, must be printed *some* time, and by that fact, in the present case, of necessity fall behind.

evolution where there is absolutely no chronology—or at least the nearest approach we can make to one is to conclude, from internal evidence alone, that such or such parts of the Rig-Veda, such or such hymns, deities, conceptions, are "very early," "early," "later," "very late," within the period—unknown to us with any precision, but certainly embracing several, probably many, centuries—covered by the collection. Superlatives, like "earliest and latest," are out of the question where the limit escapes us at either end.

3. As to the designation, "lesser gods," it requires to be qualified even more. In the first place, by what standards do we know the lesser from the greater? We have only one, a very simple one: the place each occupies in the Rig-Veda—the number of hymns addressed to each, the frequency with which a given deity is mentioned in hymns addressed to others. It seems a crude standard; yet on the whole it is not deceptive. Judged by it, Indra, Agni, Soma, at once stand out as the three kings of the Vedic Pantheon—and so they are. It would seem as though the tone of the hymns—the degree of fervor in the invocations and praise, the qualities and power ascribed to the different deities, should go for something in deciding such a question; but they hardly do, on account of the way the old Rishis have, as already noticed, of exalting the god they address, for the moment, above all the others, and ascribing to all in turn the same greater cosmical functions, such as spreading out the heavens, supporting the universe, keeping apart heaven, earth, etc., even to creating

other gods, or, at all events, being first among them. The other standard, therefore, is the safest. But it stands only for the time, whatever that was, when the selection of the hymns was made, and—to borrow a word from other theologies—the canon of the Rig-Veda was established. That time was preceded by a past which we have no means of fathoming, and followed by a future as vast, in which the religion of the Rig-Veda was to pass through all the evolutions of Brahmanism and Hinduism. Some of the persons and myths of the Vedic Pantheon, therefore, are very old, while some again are just beginning to assert themselves. To the former class, probably, belong among others Parjanya and Rudra. If so, the greatness of Rudra, as we saw, is in abeyance in the Rig-Veda, but it was to rise again and reach a higher climax than ever, when he became the dread Shiva—the Destroyer—of the great Brahmanic Triad.

4. Of the second class the most notable is VISHNU, a solar deity and form of Agni, who holds a very modest place in the Rig-Veda, where he appears as a friend and comrade of Indra, stands by his side at the killing of Vritra, and helps him to "open the stable and let out the cows." One peculiar trait is attached to him, and mentioned whenever he is addressed or spoken of: he is the god of the three strides. Purely naturalistic interpreters think of the expression as referring to the strides of the Sun-god to the three stations of his course, at morning, noon, and evening. But closer study shows that there is a far deeper significance behind the seemingly simple myth—the three strides of Vishnu cover or pervade, earth,

heaven, and the highest world of all, invisible to mortals, as clearly intimated by the verse: "We can from the earth know two of thy spaces; thou alone, O Vishnu, knowest thine own highest abode" (VII., 99, 1). However that may be, nothing in the Rig-Veda presages the coming greatness of the god, the future second person—the Preserver—of the Brahmanic Triad, the rival of Shiva in the devotion of millions of worshippers, till all Brahmanic India became divided into two immense and fanatical sects, the Shivites and the Vishnuites. It appears, however, that the earliest beginnings of these sects may be faintly traced as far back as the Rig-Veda, from a passage in one of the so-called historical hymns which relate the early struggles and wars of the Penjâb Âryas.[1]

5. The god—SAVITAR—to whom is addressed the GÂYATRÎ, the most holy text in the whole Rig-Veda, to this day the daily prayer of millions of human beings—cannot properly be classed among the "lesser gods"; but that he belongs among the later ones is shown by the complexity and by certain abstruse aspects of his being. That he is first and foremost a solar deity goes without saying. But a very puzzling fact about him is that he is sometimes identified with the sun—Sûrya,—and sometimes expressly distinguished from him—or it. Savitar is, as Muir says, "pre-eminently the golden deity"—golden-eyed, golden-armed, golden-handed, driving a golden car along ancient, dustless paths, beautifully laid out through space. There are

[1] See ch. viii., p. 303.

passages in which the two names—Savitar or Sûrya—are used convertibly and indiscriminately; for instance: "God Savitar raised his banner high, providing light for all the world; Sûrya has filled earth and heaven and the vast 'middle region' (*antariksha*, the atmosphere) with beams." They are unmistakably separated when Sûrya is called Savitar's beautiful bird (IV., 14, 2); or Savitar is said to be "invested with the rays of Sûrya," or to "bring Sûrya." Sûrya of course, in such cases, is to be taken as a common noun, standing for the material sun, and Savitar assumes towards it the relation of a higher being directing its movements, disposing of and distributing its light.

6. Another peculiarity of Savitar is that he represents not only the bright sun of the golden day, but also the invisible sun of night, *i.e.*, the sun in the mysterious, invisible land between West and East. He is associated as much with light as with darkness—the friendly darkness that brings repose and sleep to all that breathes. There are indeed hints of the kind in the descriptions of Sûrya, whose mares, "the Harits, draw without end now the bright light and now the dark" (I., 115, 5), and who seems to have a night-horse, which reverses the course of his chariot[1]; but they are few and vague; while the semi-diurnal, semi-nocturnal nature of Savitar is one of that deity's essential characteristics. Those outstretched hands of his, which shower light upon the worlds, also "firmly guide the starry host"; after

[1] See the chapter on ETASHA (the horse in question) in A. Bergaigne's *La Rélígion Védique*, vol. ii., pp. 330–333.

arousing all creatures in the morning—"those with two feet and with four"—they bring them to rest in the evening. In all the hymns addressed to this god, which are held in a peculiarly noble and lofty strain, this great and beneficent function of his is gratefully mentioned.

"He who hastens hither through the dark aërial space, who lays to rest whatever mortal is, or immortal, God Savitar on his golden chariot comes towards us, surveying all creatures." (I., 35, 2.)

". . . Where is Sûrya now? Who knows it? Over which heaven do his rays extend?" (I., 35, 7.)

"With golden hands comes hastening Savitar the god, pursuing busily his work 'twixt heaven and earth; he drives away oppression, leads Sûrya forth, through the dark realm of air he hastens up to heaven." (I., 35, 9.)

Here we see that, when Savitar comes in the evening, the sun becomes invisible and shines on some other world; when he comes in the morning, he brings back the sun. The difference between the two deities is made very plain, and we can best sum it up by saying that though, in translating, "Sûrya" can always be rendered by "the Sun," "Savitar" cannot.

The "Evening Hymn" to Savitar (II., 38) is one of the finest in the collection.

". . . . 2.—The god his mighty hands, his arms outstretches in heaven above, and all things here obey him; to his commands the waters are attentive, and even the rushing wind subsides before him. 3.—Driving his steeds, now he removes the harness and bids the wanderer rest him from his journey; he checks the serpent-smiter's[1] eager onset; at Savitar's command the kindly night comes. 4.—The weaver rolls her growing web together, and in the midst the workman leaves

[1] A bird of prey.

his labors ; the god arises and divides the time, [night from day],—God Savitar appears, the never-resting. 5.—In every place where mortals have their dwelling, the house-fire far and wide sheds forth its radiance, the mother gives her son the fairest portion, because the god has given him desire to eat. 6.—Now he returns who had gone forth for profit ; for home the longing wanderer's heart is yearning, and each, his task half finished, homeward journeys : this is the heavenly Inciter's ordinance. . . . 8.—The restless darting fish, at fall of evening, seeks where he may his refuge in the waters ; his nest the egg-born seeks, their stall the cattle; each in its place, the god divides the creatures."[1]

7. So far the hymn might be addressed to the visible sun, "to him who clothes himself in all colors" when he climbs up the heights of heaven, and "wraps himself in a brown-red mantle" as he descends from them ; but Savitar is decidedly the *invisible* nocturnal sun, when the poet expressly says: "Thou dost journey through the night from West to East." Yet all this transparent naturalism by no means exhausts the complex and somewhat mystical personality of this god. He has also a lofty moral side ; for

---

[1] From the German translation in Kaegi and Geldner's *Siebenzig Lieder des Rig-Veda*, English version of R. Arrowsmith in the English edition of Kaegi's *Rig-Veda*.—Many readers will probably be struck by the great similarity, not only in the spirit, but even in the separate images, of this hymn, and the lovely Greek poem beginning "*Hespere, panta fereis,*" which has been so beautifully paraphrased by Byron in a famous stanza of *Don Juan* (Canto III., cvii.) :

> O Hesperus ! thou bringest all good things—
> Home to the weary, to the hungry cheer,
> To the young bird the parents' brooding wings,
> The welcome stall to the o'erlabor'd steer ;
> Whate'er of peace about our hearthstone clings,
> Whate'er our household gods protect of dear,
> Are gather'd round us by thy look of rest ;
> Thou bring'st the child, too, to the mother's breast.

while Sûrya is only asked to "declare men sinless" before the Âdityas, Savitar is implored by the repentant sinner in strains exactly similar to those addressed to the great Âditya, Váruna himself.

"Whatever offence we may have committed against the race of gods, through feebleness of understanding, or through violence after the manner of men—against gods and also against men,—in spite of all, O Savitar, take from us the sin." (IV., 54, 3.)

Considered all in all, and taking into account also the etymology of the name, *i. e.*, the meaning of the root from which it is derived and which is constantly alluded to in the characteristic epithets—Inciter, Enlivener, and the like—bestowed on the god, Savitar appears to represent pre-eminently the life-giving, generative force of nature, chiefly, but not exclusively, as manifested in the action of the sun. These qualities would easily be transferred to the spiritual world, when Savitar would naturally become the Enlightener, the quickener of the spirit, who, as he wakes all creatures to life and work, also wakes up the intellect, the moral faculties of men. This view also fully justifies such lofty epithets as "Lord of Creatures [*prajâpati*], having [and perhaps giving] all forms" (*vishvarûpa*), which it would be difficult to fit to a mere solar deity.[1] As the worship of Fire in all its visible and invisible forms and abodes is really at the bottom of the Vedic religion, and the Sun itself is at times regarded only as one of its forms, Savitar could scarcely fail to be more or less identified with him, either as Sun or as Lightning. Many

[1] Even Savitar's golden chariot is said to be *vishvarûpa*, omniform.

passages point to this abstruser mystical doctrine, as well as the name of Apâm Napât (Child of the Waters)—Agni's own surname—which is given him more than once. His connection with Soma and the Soma sacrifice is also beyond doubt, and he is said to have given immortality to the gods. The heavenly Soma being no other than the *amrita* or drink of immortality, this well accords with the nature of a vivifier and creator.

8. There is a remarkable verse (III., 55, 19) which gives us the following startling combination:

> "TVASHTAR SAVITAR, the god of many forms [*vishvarûpa*], has produced and nourished all creatures, and all these beings are his own. . . . He created both the world-cups, [heaven and earth]; all they are both filled with is his own."

In this passage (and in one other where they appear joined together in the same way), one of these names would seem to be an epithet of the other, or else they are identical, *i. e.*, two names of one and the same person. Yet Tvashtar in all other cases stands out alone as an independent, though not very clearly characterized, deity. He has been called somewhat sweepingly "the artificer of the gods," and that certainly covers one side of his nature to which his name alludes, as it is said to be derived, with a slight alteration, from a root meaning "to make, to construct." He is seldom mentioned in the hymns without some such epithet as "skilful-handed," "most cunning workman," and the like. For it was Tvashtar who forged Indra's thunderbolt, the golden, with a thousand points and a hundred edges, and who sharpened the axe of another god, BRAHMANASPATI, the "Lord of Prayer"; it is he, "the omniform," who gives their shapes to all living things, even to the unborn young of men and animals; he also knows the art of making the best cups from which the gods drink the Soma; especially, he fashioned one wonderful sacrificial cup which was his pride of workmanship and with which he had a peculiar experience.

9. There were three brothers, the RIBHUS—some say pupils of Tvashtar—who rivalled him in skill. They had fashioned Indra's chariot and horses, and the Ashvins' three-wheeled chariot; they had rejuvenated the wonderful cow which produces all things at will; nay, they made "the two Old Ones," their "two parents," young again. But they were not gods; only pious men and sacrificers. Once Agni, the messenger of the gods, came to them and gave them this message: "Ye are to make four cups out of the one; this is why I come hither. If ye perform this, ye will receive equal honors with the gods." They did perform the astounding feat, whereupon they boldly drove to heaven in their chariot, to "gracious Savitar's abode," where they received from him the gift of immortality, and consequently the right to partake of the heavenly Soma and to be invited to men's Soma-sacrifices. But Tvashtar was incensed at the liberty taken with his greatest work and chose to consider it a sacrilege; he even proposed to the gods to "kill these men" (of course before they had yet tasted the *amrita*), and was so mortified when his malice was baffled, that he slunk

away and hid himself among "the gods' wives" (I., 110 and 161).

10. "Of what was made that one cup out of which you cunningly fashioned four?" This direct question is asked by one of the Rig poets (IV., 35, 4). It has been, and still is, asked by our scholars. But answered—that is another matter. The difficulty is in this case particularly great, because the personality of Tvashtar is almost too much blurred for recognition. He is evidently a very ancient god, fallen from his high estate, with a cycle of myths hopelessly incomplete and mutilated, and partly deformed by later rehandling. Still it is said that "out of the clash of opinions springeth light"; and after careful comparison of a score of interpretations, differing in some points, agreeing in others, the following may be ventured upon as coming probably near to the mark, because offering a comparatively unstrained construction of the remarkable myth of Tvashtar and the Ribhus, and fitting tolerably well the various passages which touch on it.

11. TVASHTAR-SAVITAR-VISHVARÛPA—"the Omniform[1] Maker and Vivifier"—was originally one divine person. Then—and this is a common and universal process of mythological multiplication—the single but threefold designation split itself into three separate ones. Men invoked now Tvashtar, now Savitar, till their original oneness was wellnigh obliterated; even Vishvarûpa—"omniform" or "multiform"—though an epithet not unfrequently

[1] "Omniform" not only in the sense of assuming all forms, but of *giving* them, being, in Muir's words, the arch-type of all forms.

bestowed on various deities, such as Agni, Soma, Indra, took an individuality of its own and became a son of Tvashtar who tends his cattle, and is one of Indra's most hated enemies. This is how things stand in the Rig-Veda, where only two passages, by giving the complete combination of three names, revive an all but obliterated memory.[1] It is probable that Tvashtar-Savitar was a Sky-god, whereupon Savitar retained all the gracious, vivifying qualities of a heavenly power specially connected with the beneficent Sun, while Tvashtar became his counterpart and represented the stern, baleful, and threatening aspects of the heavens, standing to Savitar much as Rudra to Váruna (see p. 209).[2] Under this explanation it appears quite natural that Tvashtar should be the special—and morose, grudging—keeper of the heavenly Soma. The sacrificial cup which he makes for the gods is, therefore, most probably—the Moon, "the bright bowl of Soma" (see p. 180). The Ribhus are the genii of the Seasons. It is very possible that originally there was also only one Ribhu—the Year, who then easily split himself into three brothers—the three seasons; for the Vedic Âryas divided the year into only three seasons—the rainy, the hot, and the fall. The Ribhus' great feat consisted in dividing the one Soma

[1] Hillebrandt (*Vedische Mythologie*, i., p. 514) remarks of Tvashtar: "All that is said of him warrants the supposition that we have before us the ruins of a large cycle of myths, which, having been originated outside of the Rig-Veda tribes, did not greatly arouse their interest."

[2] May not, at some untraceable time, the three names together have been joint descriptive predicates of the primeval Sky-god, Dyâus?

bowl into four—the phases of the moon: the growing, the full, the waning, and the dark.[1] The finishing touch to this myth is the twelve days' rest which they took "in the house of Savitar." These are the twelve intercalary days added by the early Indian astronomers to the 354 days of the lunar year, at the time of the winter solstice,[2] a period of rest during which the sun and the seasons themselves seem to stand still, awaiting the beginning of the new year, when they commence their work, "producing vegetation on the mountains and waters in the valleys." The other magic feats of the Ribhus are as easily explained. It is the seasons that fashion Indra's chariot and horses, for the great thunderstorms come only at certain times of the year; they restore the youth of their old parents, Heaven and Earth; likewise that of the ever-productive cow—the Earth. As to Vishvarûpa, a monster with three heads, which are all struck off by Indra, he clearly represents the "omniform" clouds, which may well be the offspring of the Sky regarded as a malignant being, an evil magician.

12. But it is not only in the person of his son that Tvashtar experiences Indra's hostility. He is himself the object of it, chiefly as the grudging keeper of

---

[1] This is the explanation of Hillebrandt; only he makes out Tvashtar to be the moon itself. Ludwig, on the other hand, agrees with him about the Ribhus being the seasons, but he sees in Tvashtar the sun, and the cup to him is the year, which the Ribhus divide into the four seasons. It will be seen that neither of these theories "fits" so well as a whole and in details as that given in the text.

[2] The solar year of 365 days was introduced much later, probably in connection with the worship of Vishnu.

the heavenly Soma, in the use of which Indra, as we know, brooks no stinting. From the confused and fragmentary accounts of the god's childhood and early exploits, we see that he possessed himself of the coveted beverage by violence, and then proceeded to vent his ire and try his newborn strength upon the keeper of it, whom he overpowered and hurled down, seizing him by one foot. (See p. 204.)

For Tvashtar is Indra's father. Two texts establish the fact beyond a doubt:

> " *Tvashtar* fashioned for him the thunderbolt to be wielded in battle." (I., 61, 6.)
>
> " The thunderbolt which *his father* fashioned for him some time ago just suits his arm." (II., 17, 6.)

Indra, scarce born, drinks the Soma *in the highest heaven* (III., 32, 10). The mother who bore him poured it out for him *in the house of his great father* (III., 48, 2). Scarcely has the babe tasted the stimulating beverage, when his strength grows on him:

> "Vigorous, victorious, of might transcendant, he shaped his body to his will; just born, *he overcame Tvashtar*, stole the Soma, and drank it in the vats." (III., 48, 4.)

" Who made thy mother a widow?" asks the poet (IV., 18, 12). Evidently Indra himself, by slaying his father.—" Who wanted to kill thee while resting or travelling?" Probably Tvashtar, in anger at being robbed of the Soma.—" What god came to thy assistance when thou didst seize thy father by the foot and hurl him down?"

Here we have the whole myth, complete and clear;

only, after the manner of the Rig-Veda, we do not get it in a connected form, but must fish it out in bits from texts out of the different books. There is nothing there that does not fit in beautifully with the identification of Tvashtar as a Sky-god of sombre and malevolent aspect, supplanted in the devotion of the Indian Âryas by the more popular—and more immediately useful—Warrior-god. Many more short texts could be picked out which would confirm this remarkable myth, but could not make it more complete. And what more natural than that the Lightning—for the god who wields the thunderbolt is nothing else in reality—should be the son of the frowning, angry sky?

13. But we have not done with Tvashtar yet. He figures in another story-myth, as remarkable as that of the cup, and one that has given as much food to disputed interpretations, both among native commentators and modern European scholars. It is the myth of the birth of the Ashvins. The story is told completely, though, as usual, not without obscurity, in the following too famous passage (X., 17, 1–2):

> "Tvashtar makes a wedding for his daughter and all the world comes to it. The mother of Yama, the wedded wife of the great Vivasvat, disappeared.—They [the gods] hid the immortal one from mortals and having created another just like her, they gave her to Vivasvat. Then SARANYÛ bore the two Ashvins and, having done so, she deserted the two twins." [1]

[1] "Or the two pairs of twins." This would include Yama's twin-sister YAMÎ, though she is not named in the text. She does, however, appear once in the Rig, in a most peculiar dialogue with Yama. But this piece is of very uncertain date, and bears the imprint of quite late Brahmanism. So that Yamî may very well have been a subsequent addition, for symmetry's sake, and also because the name of Yama generally means "a twin."

We already know that Yama was a son of Vivasvat. We now find that the Ashvins were Vivasvat's sons also, and grandsons of Tvashtar, and learn that their mother was that ungracious god's daughter. So far we know *who* Saranyû was. But *what* she was is the question that has been so differently answered by the various schools of learned mythologists. "The Dawn," say those who are inclined to see the Sun and Dawn in most heavenly couples. "The Stormcloud," reply those who think that the atmospheric drama absorbed the attention of the Penjâb Âryas almost to the exclusion of other natural phenomena.[1] Neither of these interpretations is exempt from a certain lameness. For the Dawn can hardly be the mother of the early twilight which *precedes* her, even allowing for Vedic inconsistencies, though there is nothing amiss with the myth which makes her the Ashvins' sister or even their bride, who on one occasion is said to have mounted their chariot. Again, the Stormcloud seems to have even less to do with a phenomenon of light: the two belong to different worlds—the Atmosphere and the Sky. But Saranyû's name is too suggestive: it means "the fleet," "the running," and nothing occurred to the first investigators that it would fit, except the Dawn or the Stormcloud. A younger scholar proposes a far more plausible solution:

"When we are told," he says, "that the Ashvins arrive at the end or in the last watch of night and gradually spread over the whole

[1] As leaders of the first-named school we may consider Professors Max Müller and Angelo de Gubernatis, while in the van of the latter stands the no less eminent Adalbert Kuhn.

horizon, dispersing or destroying the darkness and bringing daylight to all creatures, we surely cannot take either the Dawn or the Storm-cloud for their mother, but must, in the order of nature, look for some other phenomenon which precedes the dawn and even the twilight represented by the Ashvins, and that can be no other than—Night. The adjective *saranyû* should therefore be completed by the noun *naktê*, and then interpreted as 'the fleet night' (in coming and in vanishing)."[1]

14. That the Night should be the daughter of the Sky in its unamiable aspect (Tvashtar) and the mother of the Twilight Twins, is satisfactory; that she should first be the mother of Yama,—if Yama be, as Hillebrandt so ably contends, the Moon,—is highly so. As to her husband, "the great Vivasvat," he is often, and in post-vedic times always, identified with the Sun; not always or necessarily, however, in the Rig-Veda. For "Vivasvat," like most proper names, is originally an adjective, signifying "bright, luminous." Now there are other bright and luminous things besides the sun; what they are, the context in each separate instance must help us to find out. And the context of many passages in the hymns show beyond a doubt that Vivasvat can also represent the bright, luminous *Sky*. Here are some:

"Mâtarishvan, the messenger [of the gods] brought Agni from afar, from *vivasvat* [the Sky]." (VI., 8, 4.)

"With your chariot, fleeter than thought, which the Ribhus fashioned, come O Ashvins,—the chariot at the harnessing of which

---

[1] Dr. L. Myriantheus, *Die Açvins oder Arischen Dioskuren* (1876), p. 57. He points in confirmation to the Homeric expression "the fleet night," and to the fact that Leda, the mother of the Greek Dioskouroi (the "Sons of Zeus"—the exact equivalent of the Âryan *nâpatâ-diva*, the "Sons of the Sky"), has long ago been identified with Night.

the Daughter of the Sky [the Dawn] is born, also Day and Night, both splendid, from [or out of] Vivasvat [the bright, luminous sky]." (X., 39, 12.)[1]

And especially:

"After staying overnight with Vivasvat, O Ashvins, come hither to drink Soma, drawn by our songs." (X., 46, 13.)

Vivasvat being their father, it is not strange that they should stay with him; in other words, the twilight may be imagined as waiting overnight in the sky before appearing.[2]

To sum up: Saranyû, the fleet Night, is the daughter of Tvashtar, the stern and frowning Sky, who gives her to wife to Vivasvat, the luminous Sky; she becomes the mother of Yama, the Moon; then the gods conceal her, the immortal, from mortals: the Night vanishes; but, in doing so, she gives birth to the Twilight Twins, the Ashvins, whom she perforce must leave as well as her first-born. The myth is simple and transparent enough; only the second or substituted wife remains unaccounted for. But the commentators tell us that she gave birth to MANU, the mythical sage and sacrificer, the progenitor of the human race, thus formulating the ancient

[1] This alludes to the later and already corrupt belief in the Ashvins coming both in the morning and at night.

[2] See Myriantheus, *Die Açvins*, pp. 4–13. We may as well mention here the curious custom of giving to sacrificers, by courtesy, the name of *vivasvat*. By the act of sacrificing, the worshipper enters into communion with the gods, becomes, for the time being, one of them. Thus in Egypt, every man received after death, by courtesy, the title of "Osiris," because it was hoped he had attained blessedness in the bosom of the god.

belief in the heavenly origin of mankind.[1] Who she was, *i. e.*, what she was meant to represent, has never been found out. The myth itself, however, in the attempt at explanation, was handled and rehandled, added to and ornamented, until it became almost hopelessly obscure, and it was necessary to return to the original Rig texts, and them only, in order to restore it to its meaning in the order of natural phenomena.

15. There is another mysterious being, another mother of twins, whose name, SARAMÂ, shows her to be somewhat akin in nature to Saranyû—also a "fleet one," a "runner." With her offspring, the twin SÂRAMÊYAS dogs, the messengers of Yama, we are already acquainted (see p. 182).[2] She herself appears to have been Indra's special messenger, employed by him on diplomatic and scouting errands. We have an unusually detailed and complete narrative of one such expedition in the Rig-Veda. The Panis—the avaricious traders and robbers—had stolen the milk kine on which the race of men chiefly depends for nourishment. Indra prepared to go to their rescue in company with Brihaspati—the Lord of Prayer—and the nine ANGIRAS, the heavenly singers and sacrificers. But he first sent

---

[1] Manu is often used simply in the sense of "man." The etymological meaning is "the thinker." The other habitual designation of our race is "mortal," as opposed to the "immortals"—gods. Man, therefore, was to the old Âryas "he who thinks" and "he who dies"—surely a definition as profound as comprehensive.

[2] Probably on account of her connection with these dogs, Saramâ was subsequently made out to be herself a dog. There is, however, no allusion to this in the Rig-Veda.

Saramâ to reconnoitre. She went "on the right path" and found the strong stable, a cave in the rock, through a cleft of which she heard the cows' lowing. She went on until she came across the Pani-robbers, between whom and herself there ensued the following dialogue, one of the most remarkable pieces in the Rig-Veda (X., 108). The Panis begin:

The Panis: "With what intention did Saramâ reach this place? for the way is far and leads tortuously away. What is thy wish with us? Didst travel safely? [or "how was the night?"] How didst thou cross the waters of the Rasâ?"[1]

Saramâ: "I came sent as the messenger of Indra, desiring, O Panis, your great treasures. This preserved me from the fear of crossing, and thus I crossed the waters of the Rasâ."

The Panis: "Who is he? what looks he like, this Indra, whose herald you have hastened from afar? Let him come here, we will make friends with him, then he may be the herdsman of our cows."

Saramâ: "Ye cannot injure him, but he can injure, whose herald I have hastened from afar. Deep rivers cannot overwhelm him; you, Panis, soon shall be cut down by Indra."

The Panis: "Those cows, O Saramâ, which thou cam'st to seek, are flying round the ends of the sky. O darling, who would give up to thee without a fight? for, in truth, our weapons too are sharp."

Saramâ: "Not hurtful are your words, O Panis, and though your wretched bodies were arrow-proof, though the way to you be hard to go, little will Brihaspati care."

The Panis: "That store, O Saramâ, is fast within the rock—'t is full with horses, cows, and treasures; Panis watch it who are good watchers; thou art come in vain. . . ."

Saramâ: "The Rishis will come here, fired with Soma, Ayâsia, and the Angiras, the Nine. They will divide this stable of cows. Then the Panis will spit out this speech [wish it unspoken]."

The Panis: "Of a surety, Saramâ, thou art come hither driven

---

[1] The Rasâ—a mythical river, deep and dangerous: the waters of Darkness or of Death.

by the violence of the gods: let us make thee our sister; go not away again. We will give thee part of the cows, O darling."

Saramâ: "I know nothing of brotherhood or sisterhood; Indra knows it and the awful Angiras. They seemed to me anxious for their cows when I came; therefore get away from here, O Panis, get far away."

Saramâ's scouting having proved more successful than her diplomatical effort, she returned to those who sent her, to act as guide. Swift and sure of foot, she walked before them, taking them along the broad and ancient heavenly path which leads to the one goal. As they approached the rock, which she was first to reach, the loud singing of the Angiras mingled with the lowing of the cows in the cave. Indra and Brihaspati now came up; the rock opened with a great crash under the blows of Indra's mace, and Brihaspati led forth the cows, driving them along as the wind drives the storm-cloud. The Panis were dismayed; VALA, the cave-demon, mourned for his beautiful cows as the tree mourns for its foliage when it is stripped bare by frost.[1]

16. This beautifully and dramatically developed story-myth speaks for itself, and it is only the identification of Saramâ, which gives rise to the usual difference of opinions. She, too, has been said to be the Dawn, and the Stormcloud; but she is so specially characterized as the precursor of a violent thunder-storm that, if a naturalistic interpretation

---

[1] The narrative is given in words taken from the Rig-Veda. Only the passages are so short and scattered, it would be cumbersome to give chapter and verse for them all. This particular myth, with the active part Brihaspati plays in it, was a great favorite, for it is alluded to innumerable times, though Saramâ is mentioned only in half a dozen texts.

be adopted,—no doubt the original one,—one is more tempted to concur in that which makes her out to be the wind which precedes a heavy rain. It is only the wind that can be called the scout of the heavens; only the wind that may be said to try to bring away "the cows" from the solid black mountain banked up against the horizon, and to be unable to accomplish it until the storm-god and his troop follow the "broad trail" opened for them and break open the rock. This explanation is greatly confirmed by the fact that Saramâ's canine offspring, the Sârameya dogs, undoubtedly are the evening twilight twins (probably in symmetrical opposition to the morning twilight twins, the Ashvins), who have inherited their mother's scouting and cattle-driving qualities,—only the cattle they are after are men (see p. 182),—and most certainly represent the twilight *together* with and inseparably from the breeze which, in Southern climes, invariably rises immediately after sunset.[1] That, like the Ashvins, these twins may, in the course of time, have been separated into morning and evening, is more than likely; indeed one Brâhmana, in one of those rare passages of profound poetical beauty ("rare" in every sense of the word), which reward the patient searcher, calls Day and Night, "the outstretched arms of Death."

17. So much for this most lucid nature-myth. But nature-myths have a way of becoming transformed

[1] The name *Sârameya* has been philologically identified beyond a doubt with that of the Hellenic god *Hermes*, the messenger of the gods, the sweet whistler and musician, *the stealer of cows and guide of the dead*—and Hermes is certainly the wind.

in the course of time; and if they do not actually descend to earth and become the stories of old-time heroes and sages, they can undergo changes to suit the developing spirit of the race and age without being taken from their celestial habitat. This appears to have been the case with the myth of Saramâ, even before it assumed its fixed and finished form in the canon of the hymns.[1] For in this form latest research finds good reason to see a combination of nature-myth and spiritual, or rather ritualistic, elements, introduced by those all-pervading priestly influences which were soon to culminate in the tyranny of Brahmanism. In this transformed myth Saramâ represents no longer a power of nature, but that of the human Prayer, more correctly the sacred word—the *mantra*; for, as early as the Vedic times, prayer was no longer the spontaneous outpouring of the heart, as it must have been at least sometimes and with some of the first composers of the hymns, the ancient Rishis, but a strictly regulated reciting of texts considered as sacred and powerful in themselves, with a sort of talismanic power, and credited with compelling force over the elements, *i. e.*, the gods. It will be seen that Saramâ, as a personification of this Prayer, can well be imagined as "going on the right path" ("the path of *rita*," represented on earth by the sacrificial rite), "finding the cows," frightening the robbers, then guiding the god to the strong stable and standing by while he breaks it open. This secondary interpretation will be very convincing if we consider

[1] See Bergaigne, *La Religion Védique*, vol. ii., pp. 311–321.

who Indra's attendants are on this occasion: not the Maruts, but the Angiras—a troop of priestly demigods, supposed to be divinized ancient sacrificers, in reality themselves personifications of the sacred hymns which they go on everlastingly singing on their aërial way. Now the heavenly form of the sacred song is the voice of the thunder. When the loud singing of the Angiras mingles with the lowing of the captive cows, of course we know we have to imagine the long swelling and rolling thunder of a southern storm, answered by muffled mutterings from the distant mountains, while the "loud crash" with which the cave-stable is burst open is the short rattling clap of the bolt that strikes. For all heavenly music is produced either by the thunder or the wind or the rain. And thunder is the Sacred Word, the Sacred Hymn *par excellence*, the prototype of all speech, the language known to gods, but not understood of men.[1]

18. Then—Indra's companion. It is not Vishnu, or Soma, or even Agni in his direct natural form; it is BRIHASPATI or BRAHMANASPATI—Fire in his most august, sacrificial, and sacerdotal form, the "Lord of Prayer," the leader of hymns, the institutor of worship and rites; in a word, the divine *hotar* and *purohita*, the priest of god and men, having himself the name of "Angiras"—the leader of the Nine, and the divine personification of both the holiness and the power of the *brahma*—Prayer, as represented by the sacred songs—*sâman*, or sacred texts—*mantra*.[2]

---

[1] See farther, pp. 269–270.

[2] *Brahma*, from a root meaning "to penetrate, to pervade; it is also contained in the name Brihaspati.

When therefore he is called *pathikrit*—"path-preparer"[1]—we are not puzzled as to what path is meant: it is the same that "the old Rishis have prepared," that on which Saramâ led the gods, the broad and ancient heavenly path which leads to the one goal—the path of Sacrifice. In the hymns addressed to this priestly deity, he is credited with all the deeds and works elsewhere ascribed to Indra and all the other great nature-gods, whose supremacy thus seems to be centred in him or rather transferred to him, and numberless short interpolated passages bring him into older hymns where he is manifestly out of place. Indeed we have in him the connecting link between pure Vedism and rising Brahmanism. For not only are the Brâhmans the men who wield the power of the *brahma*, but the line of abstract speculation, initiated by this creation—and reflection—of the priestly class (soon to be a caste), gradually supersedes the old joyous, vigorous nature-worship, and culminates in the evolution of the *brahma* (neuter noun) into an all-pervading but latent spiritual essence and presence, and its final manifestation in the person of the supreme god and creator BRAHMÂ (masculine), the head of the great Brahmanic Triad.

19. It has been remarked that "all the gods whose names are compounded with *pati* ["lord of—"] must be reckoned among the more recent. They

---

[1] The exact equivalent of the Latin highest priestly title, *pontifex*—literally "bridge-maker." *Pons, pontis* originally meant not a bridge, but a path: a bridge is a path across a river. The Teutonic and Slavic languages have retained the old meaning.

were the products of reflection."[1] It should never be forgotten, at the same time, that such secondary mythical persons (abstractions) must of necessity have developed out of primary ones (nature-gods), and the Rig-Veda shows us exactly how it was done. "Brahmanaspati" is repeatedly used in the hymns as an adjective, an epithet of Agni. It does not follow from this that, after the epithet is detached from the name it qualifies and has become a separate person, that person should be considered as always identical with the bearer of that name, for with an individuality it also assumes individual life, and begins its own course of evolution; but the original connection between the two will always be apparent, as that of Brihaspati with sacrificial fire. Thus again Savitar, Soma, Indra, each in turn receive the epithet of PRAJÂPATI—"lord of descendants," or, as the word is more commonly translated, "lord of creatures." In the late stage of Vedic theology, the dawning era of abstractions, we always have Prajâpati mentioned, and occasionally invoked as a separate deity. It is only in post-vedic Brahmanism, however, that he attains the supreme honor of being identified with Brahmâ himself. Another connecting link; another product of the period of transition. Such also is VISHVAKARMAN —"the fabricator of the universe," originally a title given to Indra, Sûrya, and other great gods, then an independent deity, tending, in true Vedic fashion, to absorb the functions, qualities, and

---

[1] Roth, "Brahmâ and the Brâhmans," *Journal of the German Oriental Society*, vol. i., pp. 66 *ff*.

honors of all other gods. Two hymns are consecrated to him (X., 81 and 82), where he is described as

"the one god who has on every side eyes, on every side a face, arms, feet; who, when producing heaven and earth, shapes them with his arms and wings. . . . Who is our father, our creator, maker,—who every place doth know and every creature,—by whom alone to gods their names were given,—to whom all other creatures go, to ask him."

Among these gods of the second formation we may also class HIRANYAGARBHA,—"the Golden Embryo," or "the Golden Child," evidently originally a name of the Sun,—who goes the same way of abstraction which leads these gods to the supreme rank. A most beautiful hymn (X., 121) is addressed to him, but it properly belongs, as well as the greater portion of those to Vishvakarman, among those that illustrate the beginnings of speculative philosophy in the Rig-Veda.[1]

20. These gods of what we call the secondary or speculative formation, whose connection with the primary nature-gods is clearly discernible, should be carefully distinguished from deities of a third class still—the purely allegorical—*i. e.*, mere personifications of abstractions and qualities that never had any existence in physical nature, such as Faith (SHRADDHÂ), Liberality (DAKSHINÂ, in the sense of largess to the priests) Wrath (MANYUS, the righteous wrath which animates those who fight demons and earthly foes). This, as we have seen, is the favorite myth-form of the moralizing Eranians,[2] and

---

[1] See farther on, chapter xi.

[2] See *Story of Media*, etc., pp. 72 *ff*.

does not at all come natural to the Âryas of India in the earlier time of their cheerful nature-worship. It is therefore but scantily represented in the Rig-Veda, but blossoms forth abundantly in the late portions of the Atharva-Veda, where Time, Desire, the Breath of Life, etc., are addressed as divine persons, with all the pompousness of the earlier hymns to Indra, Agni, Soma, and the others. In the Brâhmanas this element predominates more and more.

21. It may have been noticed that the feminine element is almost absent from our sketch of the Vedic Pantheon. So it is from the Rig-Veda itself. There is really only one "great goddess," with an individuality, a story, and functions proper to her and to no other divine being, and that is Ushas, the Dawn. Saramâ is not a goddess; still less Saranyû "The wives of the gods"—the *Dêvapatnîs*—are spoken of vaguely, collectively, but they are easily transformed into "wives of the demons—*Dâsapatnîs*,"—for they are in reality neither more nor less than "the waters" or "cows," which are eternally fought for, captured, and rescued. And when these "wives" so far emerge out of their misty unreality as to be coupled with one or other particular god, they assume their husbands' names with a feminine ending: VARUNÂNÎ, INDRÂNÎ, AGNÂYÎ, ASHVINÎ. They are only pale, unsubstantial reflections.

22. Neither can the Waters and Rivers properly be called goddesses, though they are treated with extreme reverence, and frequently invoked as the holiest and purest of created things. When "the Waters"—ÂPAS—are spoken of in a general way,

the heavenly waters are meant, as a rule—the Mothers of Agni, and one of the abodes of Soma; hence their mysterious and exceeding holiness, which is naturally transferred to the terrestrial waters, if only because the latter play an important part in sacrifice as one of the ingredients of the Soma-beverage. Yet, although the Waters' mystical purifying powers are certainly alluded to in such texts as ". . . these divine ones carry away defilement; I come up out of them pure and cleansed," there is no doubt that their physical qualities were fully realized and appreciated: their cleanness, their wholesomeness, their bountifulness as the fosterers of vegetation and of cattle, and as wealth-givers. They are then thought of chiefly in their form of rivers, and are compared, often very poetically, to various things loved of the people: now to stately milch-cows, now to fleet and graceful mares; they are playful sisters, they are kindly mothers. There is a famous "River-hymn"—*Nadîstuti* (X., 75)—celebrating by name the rivers of early Aryan India, a treasure of prehistorical geography. For there we find all the rivers of the Sapta-Sindhavah (see pp. 107, 108, note), besides several which it has been impossible so far to identify with certainty. They may possibly belong to a more eastern and less familiar region than the old Riverland, a region only just entered by the Âryas in their slow onward march—mainly in search of new pastures and more room to spread in.[1] For this is the only hymn in the whole

[1] "We have come to a pastureless land . . ." (the sandy tract west of the Djumna) ". . . The earth, though wide, is too close for us: show us the way in battle, O Brihaspati! . . ."

collection in which unmistakable mention is made of the Gangâ and Yamunâ (Ganges and Djumna), showing it to be one of the very latest. But they are merely named, as two among many; while fully half of the verses are devoted to the glorification of the Sindhu (Indus) who

"flashing, sparkling, gleaming, in her majesty, the unconquerable, the most abundant of streams, beautiful as a handsome, spotted mare, rolls her waters over the levels."

Evidently the centre of gravity of Aryan spiritual life had not yet been displaced.

23. Among the rivers there is one which, from the extreme reverence cherished for it, and the manifold aspects it assumes, comes nearest to the rank of a real goddess, a divine Person, receiving oblations and invited to partake of Soma. It is the SARASVATÎ. We have seen (p. 109) that, in the late Vedic period and the whole of post-vedic classical antiquity, the name and the great sacredness attaching thereto, belong to a rather insignificant river, which at the present time loses itself in the sands of a tract of desert, and which even in its early and palmier days could never have possessed much importance, unless it were, as at one time, the farthest eastern boundary of the Aryan domain beyond which Agni "Vaishvanara" ("who burns for all men") had not been carried—*i.e.*, the sacrificial flame, personifying Aryan conquest and Aryan propaganda. Nor is it possible that *this* Sarasvatî should ever have been described in such superlative terms of admiration as the following: (VII., 95, 1–2):

"With great noise of waters, bringing nourishment, Sarasvatî breaks forth; she is to us a firm bulwark, a fortress of brass. Like to a warrior in the chariot race, she speeds along, the *sindhu* [river], leaving all other waters far behind.

"Sarasvatî comes down the purest of streams, from the mountains to the *samudra*;[1] bringing wealth and prosperity to the wide world, she flows with milk and honey for those that dwell by her banks."

In early Vedic times, (and the book in which this passage occurs is a late one) there was only one river that justified such a description—the Indus. Indeed this passage has led to the positive identification of the Sarasvatî *as* the Indus. This undoubtedly was the original name of the great river of the West, till it came to be familiarly spoken of simply as *Sindhu*, "*the* River." After the Âryas had advanced a considerable distance eastward, crossing river after river, they reached one which arrested their progress for a time. Settlements arose along its course, and it inherited the name that for some reason was dear and sacred to the Âryas. For what reason? From ancient memories and association. For "SARASVATÎ" is the exact Sanskrit equivalent of the Old-Eranian "HARAQAITI," the Avestan name of the great river (modern HELMEND) of Eastern Erân—Afghanistân and Kabul—where some of the separating Indo-Eranian tribes certainly sojourned before they summoned courage to face the stony wall of the Suleïman range and thread its wild, narrow passes. Was it not natural

[1] *Samudra*—"gathering of waters"; in the Rig-Veda *not* the sea or ocean, but the broad expanse formed by the reunion with the Indus of the "five rivers," whose waters are brought to it by the Pantchanâda (see p. 107).

that they should have thus perpetuated the memory of what had long been home? This beautiful and natural solution is suggested by the results of latest researches,[1] and confirmed from a most unexpected quarter by a curt mention in the Atharva-Veda (VI., 100,) of *three Sarasvatîs*—a mention which, being long unexplained, has been another of the puzzles which confront scholars at every step. Probably no explanation was needed at the time, of things which had not passed out of remembrance.

24. Sarasvatî in post-vedic times is chiefly praised and invoked as the goddess of eloquence, though she never lost her identity as river-goddess. We ourselves speak of "a rich, a free, an easy flow of words," of "fluency of speech," of a "torrent of eloquence," —so the poetical imagery which underlies this transformation will not appear far-fetched or strained. In the Rig-Veda we do not yet find her thus specialized, but she is associated with sacrifice and the hymns in a way to leave little doubt that, in the later portions of it, she already represented the eloquence of sacred poetry, possibly even the different sacred metres which were extolled and deified to such an extraordinary extent in the Brâhmanas.

25. The same may be said in a still greater measure of another goddess, VÂCH,[2]—personified Speech, —who in the Rig-Veda already (in the latest book of course, the tenth) is invested with much of the

---

[1] See chiefly Hillebrandt *Vedische Mythologie*, vol. i., pp. 99-100. It will be noticed that the Helmend ends, not in a sea, but *in a large lake*, to which the name of *samudra* would apply perfectly.

[2] *Ch* pronounced as in *church*.

usual pomp of Brahmanic metaphysics, as a "most adorable," "widely pervading," wealth-bringing deity of "many abodes," but not to extravagance; the personification—or rather allegory—does not pass the bounds of fine, even noble poetry, and is moreover distinctly traceable to the natural phenomenon from which it is evolved. For sublimity, few conceptions can equal this of our race's earliest poets—a conception which lingers still in the mythical poetry of later nations in other lands. Primeval speech is the voice of the gods, speaking in thunder and storm; it is *Vâch*,—the Sacred Word, majestic and compelling, beneficent and wise—in its heavenly abode. But it is not for men. To them Vâch descends in the form of Speech, and lo!

"1 . . . men with their earliest utterances, gave names to things, and all which they had lovingly treasured within them, the most excellent and spotless, was disclosed. 2. Wherever the wise have uttered speech [*vâch*] with discrimination, sifting it as meal with a sieve, there friend knows friend and auspicious fortune waits on their words. 3. Through sacrifice they followed the track of Vâch, and found her entered into the Rishis. Taking her, they divided her into many portions, and now the seven Rishis sing her praise. 4. One man, seeing, sees not Vâch; another, hearing, hears her not; to another she willingly discloses herself, as a well-attired and loving wife displays her person to her husband. 5. One man is said to be secure in her favor—and he is not to be overwhelmed in poetical contests; another lives in unprofitable brooding: he has only heard Vâch, and she is to him without fruit or flower. 6. He who forsakes a well-meaning friend, he has no portion in Vâch, and what he hears he hears in vain: unknown to him is the path of virtne. 7. And even those who enjoy her with equally understanding eye and ear, are unequal in the moving of the spirit: some are lakes which reach up to shoulder and to mouth, and some are shallow waters good to bathe in. 8. When competing priests practice devotion in sayings born of the spirit's might, one lags far behind in wisdom, while others prove themselves true priests. 9. One sits and produces songs like blossoms; another sings them in loud strains; one discourses sapiently of the essence of things; another measures out the sacrifice according to the rite. 10. And friends are proud of their friend, when he comes among them as leader of the poets. He corrects their errors, helps them to prosperity, and stands up, ready for the poetical contest." (X., 71).

The beauty, dignity, and ennobling uses of speech could scarcely be appraised with finer feeling or apter touches; or the difference between him who seeing, sees not, and hearing, hears not, and him to whom the gift is given; between the spirit deep as the lake and the mind shallow as the bathing pool; between him who blossoms into song, and him who unprofitably cudgels his brains and for whom the goddess has neither fruit nor flower. Only, we must beware of putting more modern a sense into passages of this kind than they will bear. We must remember that the poetry we have to do with here, though god-given, is not the free, unfettered gift that it is to us: the goddess must be sought *through sacrifice*, which means that she comes loaded with all the shackles of rite, ceremonial, sacred metres, etc. The poetical contests are for the composition of hymns, the errors which the victorious priest corrects are errors in sacrificial *technique*, the prosperity to which he helps is that obtained, nay compelled, from the gods by correctly regulated prayer (*brahma*). Still, the poet who "fashioned" this hymn, builded better than he knew, and, if freed from extraneous, priestly matter, it remains an exquisite thing for all time.

Not so another hymn (X., 125) consecrated to Vâch, where the goddess is the Brahmanic abstraction and nothing more, or that most characteristic passage where she undergoes the inevitable transformation into a cow. The poet is discontented. Maybe he is *purohita* to a prince who is not over lavish with sacrifices—which are expensive—and fees and gifts have been coming in scantily. He puts his plaint in the mouth of the goddess Vâch, whom he presents as saying:

"I, Vâch, the skilled in speech, who assist all pious practices,—I, the divine cow who has come from the gods,—I am neglected by evil-minded man."

26. We will conclude our selection with a short poem (it can hardly be called a hymn) in praise of Aranyânî, the goddess of forest solitude (*Waldeinsamkeit*), or rather—the personified Forest. Not that she is of much importance as a divine being; indeed she appears to have been invented for the occasion by some poet-hermit whose soul was attuned to her mysterious charm. But it is a pretty thing; and besides, it shows that forest life, which was to become so distinctive a feature of later Brahmanism, is—like almost everything that ever held a place in the spiritual life of Aryan India,—to be traced to the fountain-head of it, the Rig-Veda. We must imagine the thousand strange sounds and delusions which seem to encompass the solitary listener of an evening in the darkening forest:

"1. Aranyânî, Aranyânî! thou seemest to have lost thyself there; why dost thou not ask the way to the village? Does terror not seize thee?—2. When the owl's shrill call is answered by the parrot, which hops about as though to cymbals' rhythm, then does Aranyânî rejoice. —3. Here, there is a sound as of browsing cows; there, houses appear to be seen; then there is a creaking at eventide, as though Aranyânî were unloading carts.—4. Here one man calls to his cow—there another fells a tree; then one dwelling in the forest at night fancies that some one has screamed.—5. Aranyânî is not herself murderous, if no one else assails (a tiger, etc.); and after eating of sweet fruit, a man rests there at his pleasure.—6. I sing the praise of Aranyânî, the mother of wild beasts, the spicy, the fragrant, who yields abundance of food, though she has no hinds to till her."

CHAPTER VIII.

THE RIG-VEDA: EARLY HISTORY.

1. EVERYBODY knows what is meant by CASTE in India. Everybody has a more or less clear perception of the hold this baleful system has established on about one sixth of the human race, and of its well-nigh ineradicable evil effects,—of the insuperable barrier it opposes to the best-meant efforts of the country's European rulers. We are not here concerned with the modern development of the system—the endless divisions and subdivisions resulting from intermarriages, originally forbidden,—which make official life in India so bewildering a task. But we must dwell awhile on the original division of the social body into four distinct, well-defined classes: (1) the Priests—BRÂHMANS; (2) the Warriors—KSHATRIYA or RÂJANYA; (3) the Working class—VAISHYA (farmers, craftsmen, and traders);—and (4) the Menial class—SHÛDRA; in other words: those who pray; those who fight; those who produce and barter; and those who serve.

2. This is the division into which, more or less distinctly, every nation naturally splits itself at the

very start of its organized existence. The peculiarity which characterizes it in India from very early times is that nowhere else were the distinctions so harshly set, the separating lines drawn so deep and straight; nowhere else were men so sternly doomed to live and die within the pale of the social status into which they were born, with nothing left to individual choice, no narrowest door ajar through which to pass into another—wherein, in fact, lies the very essence of caste as distinguished from mere class barriers, which may be high and forbidding, but not utterly impassable. Lastly, nowhere else did the priesthood claim such absolute pre-eminence, demand such unconditional submissiveness, such almost servile self-abasement from all other members of the community—to this extent that for a Brâhman to marry a maiden of the warrior caste was a condescension or derogation, although to that caste belonged the kings and princes, the rulers of the land. What other priesthood ever had the hardihood to proclaim in so many words that "there are two classes of gods: the gods in heaven, and the Brâhmans on earth"? Let us see how the great Brahmanic code—the Laws of Manu—defines the duties and mutual relations of the four castes (I., 88–91):

"To Brâhmans he [Brahmâ] assigned teaching and studying the Veda, sacrificing for their own benefit and for others, giving and accepting of alms.

"The Kshatriya he commanded to protect the people, to bestow gifts, to offer sacrifices, to study the Veda, and to abstain from attaching himself to sensual pleasures.

"The Vaishya to tend cattle, to bestow gifts, to offer sacrifices, to study the Veda, to trade, to lend money, and to cultivate land.

"One occupation only the Lord prescribed to the Shûdra: to serve meekly the other three castes."

The position claimed for the Brâhmans in this first, general definition, is comparatively modest, certainly not unreasonably arrogant; but we turn a few pages and the lawgiver goes into details and makes his meaning clearer.

"A Brâhman," we read, "coming into existence, is born as the highest on earth, the lord of all created beings, for the protection of the treasury of the law.

"Whatever exists in the world is the property of the Brâhman; on account of the excellence of his origin, the Brâhman is, indeed, entitled to it all.

"The Brâhman eats but his own food, wears but his own apparel, bestows but his own in alms; other mortals subsist through the benevolence of the Brâhman. . . ."

". . . Know that a Brâhman of ten years and a Kshatriya of a hundred years stand to each other in the relation of father and son; but between those two the Brâhman is the father. . . ."

". . . A Brâhman, be he ignorant or learned, is a great divinity. . . ."

". . . Though Brâhmans employ themselves in all sorts of mean occupations, they must be honored in every way; for each of them is a very great deity. . . ."

The whole duty of kings is pithily summed up under these three heads: "Not to turn back in battle; to protect the people; to honor Brâhmans." "To *worship* Brâhmans" is the expression repeatedly used; "to enrich them" is a point emphatically inculcated, and the king is solemnly warned not to provoke them to anger under any circumstances, "for they, when angered, could instantly destroy him, together with his army and vehicles." Many are

18.—THE SIXTH AVATÂR (OR VISHNU INCARNATE AS PARASHU-RÂMA, THE EXTERMINATOR OF THE KSHATRIYAS).[1]

[1] The cow is Vasishtha's sacred and miraculous cow, the emblem of Brahmanic prayer and sacrifice.

the worldly privileges and exemptions which they demand and enjoy. Still, it is very certain that the material power was in the hands of the warrior caste and that the Brâhmans did not get quite as much in practice as they claimed in theory, and were perfectly aware that conciliation was, after all, their wisest policy. Indeed, after some of the most outrageous bragging and bullying, the priestly lawgiver suddenly descends to reasonable ground and lays down the following shrewd axiom, which, in all times and countries, has been the basis of the mutual understanding between Church and State:

"Kshatriyas prosper not without Brâhmans; Brâhmans prosper not without Kshatriyas. Brâhmans and Kshatriyas, being closely united, prosper in this world and the next.[1]

3. It will have been noticed that only the three first castes are enjoined to study the Veda. No mention of this duty is made among those of the fourth, the servile, caste. But this is not all. The Shûdras were not only not expected, they were for-

---

[1] Post-vedic Brahmanism, however, retains a vivid memory of a bitter struggle for supremacy between the Brâhman caste and that of the Kshatriyas. It is given in the form of a story both in the Mahâbhârata and the Purânas: The Kshatriyas had become so arrogant and oppressive that the interference of Vishnu himself was needed to repress them. The god took human form and was born in the family of the Bhrigu, a priestly race of divine descent, as PARASHU-RÂMA ("Râma with the axe") who became the exterminator of the warrior caste. "Thrice seven times did he clear the earth of the Kshatriya race and filled five lakes with their blood"—after which *he gave the earth to the Brâhmans!*

bidden, to share in the sacred inheritance of those whom to serve was their only mission. Their presence at a sacrifice would have polluted it; the sacred *mantras* were not to be sung or recited within hearing of a Shûdra, and had a Brâhman instructed one of the servile caste in the knowledge of the Veda, he would have been guilty of a wellnigh inexpiable offence. When a boy of one of the three higher castes attained a certain age, considered as "years of discretion,"[1] he was "initiated," *i. e.*, admitted under solemn ceremonies into the religious community, after which he was placed under a *guru* or spiritual guide, invariably a Brâhman, for instruction in the Veda. This initiation was regarded as the youth's second birth, his birth into the spiritual life, wherefore the three higher castes took pride in the appellation of "twice-born" (*dvi-ja*). From this distinction the Shûdras, of course, were excluded. This is declared most explicitly in Manu's Code:

> "The Brâhman, the Kshatriya, and the Vaishya castes are the twice-born ones, but the fourth, the Shûdra, has no second birth. There is no fifth caste."

4. This brief survey of the original caste system has led us away from what is, properly speaking, our allotted subject, for we have strayed into post-vedic times. But the digression was necessary in order, precisely, to conclude it with the statement that castes, as a firmly established institution, were not

[1] Any time between the eighth and sixteenth year for a Brâhman, between the eleventh and twenty-second for a Kshatriya, and between the twelfth and the twenty-fourth for a Vaishya.

as yet a feature of the Vedic period. Had they been, the fact must have transpired, even if indirectly, in the Rig-Veda, which faithfully reflects the state of society prevailing at the time that the collection was forming; and this is not the case, except in one solitary and noteworthy instance: the ninetieth hymn of the tenth book (X., 90), known as the "Purusha-hymn," PURUSHA-SÛKTA. The hymn, as a whole, is exceedingly obscure and of entirely mystical import. It describes the act of creation in the guise of a huge sacrifice performed by the gods, in which the central figure and victim is a primeval giant, a being named Purusha (one of the names for man), probably because mankind is represented as being produced by this being or, more correctly, out of various portions of his body. This is the only passage of the hymn with which we are here concerned. Purusha, it is said, "is this whole universe, whatever has been and whatever shall be." Probably in a latent state, since the gods proceed to evolve out of him worlds and animals and men:

> "When the gods divided Purusha, into how many parts did they cut him up? What was his mouth? What his arms? What his thighs and feet?
>
> "The Brâhman was his mouth; the Râjanya was made his arms; the Vaishya he was his thighs; the Shûdra sprang from his feet."

Now the tenth book, as a whole, is of later date than the rest. It was made a sort of receptacle for odd hymns and such as, important in themselves, did not fit well into the scheme of the others, or were attributed to odd authors, while each book (except the tenth and the first) usually bears the name of one priestly poet or family of poets. Intrinsic differences in language, spirit, range of thought, etc., bear witness to the fact. The Purusha-Sûkta especially comes under this head; and, by bringing the caste system as far back as the late Vedic period, shows how easy must have been the transition from that to the so-called Brahmanic or classical period, there never really having been a violent break between the two. The Brahmanic writings all endorse the Purusha myth, with the only difference that Brahmâ, the Creator and highest deity of the post-vedic creed, is substituted for the older name, and the mystic sacrifice is not mentioned. This is why the Brâhmans always boast of "the excellence of their origin," their interpretation of the legend being this: that those who came from the Deity's mouth, as the noblest organ, are born to teach and to command; they embody his Mind, his Word; those that came from his arms are born for action and defence; those that come from his thighs have the mission of carrying and supporting the nobler parts of the social body; while humble service is clearly the lot of those lowly ones who proceed from the divine feet.[1]

5. Although the castes and their names occur but once in the course of the entire Rig-Veda, there is another distinction which recurs throughout the col-

[1] Ludwig suggests that there is a hint at caste—or at least the incipient conception of caste—in the hymn to Ushas (Rig-Veda 1136), where it is said that the goddess "arousing one to wield the royal power, another to follow after fame, another to the pursuit of wealth, another to perform services, awakes all creatures to go their different paths in life." (See p. 222.)

lection, no matter to whom the different books are ascribed, and which divides the peoples who dwelt in the Penjâb, and, later on, those who occupied the more easterly portion of Hindustân, into two main categories opposed to each other, each comprising numerous subdivisions, *i. e.*, nations or tribes, many of whose names have been preserved by contempo-

19.—BRÂHMANS OF BENGAL (= ÂRYAS).

rary bards: this division is that into ÂRYAS and DASYUS. Who the former are we know well, and a natural association leads us to the conclusion that the latter are no other than the native—or non-Aryan—peoples whom the Aryan immigrants found in the land, and whom, after a long period of struggle, they reduced into more or less reluctant submission. There is no doubt but that we have here the first beginnings of caste, for this sweeping division is singularly like the modern one into "twice-born" and Shûdra. Besides, the name for caste is even now *varna*, which means "color," and we shall presently see that the difference of color between the white conquerors and the dark-skinned natives is continually alluded to by the Vedic poets. Then, too, the word Dasyu, with the changes of meaning

20.—LOW-CASTE BENGALESE (= DASYUS).

it has undergone, tells an eloquent tale. It is an old Aryan word, and the Persians continued to use it in its original harmless sense of peoples, nations. In Dareios' historical rock inscriptions we find it so used, also in opposition to Âryas, to designate the populations of the provinces. In India it took a hostile shading—that of "enemies," whence it easily passed into the cloudland of Vedic mythology, with the meaning of "fiends," "evil demons,"—the powers of darkness and drought—the "foes" whom Indra eternally combats and conquers with the help of the Maruts, the Angiras, and other beings of light. Logical and natural as the transition is, it adds very greatly to the difficulties of Vedic interpretation, because, when Indra or Agni are besought to drive away and annihilate the Dasyus, or are said to have destroyed the fastnesses of the Dasyus, it is frequently all but impossible to decide *which* "enemies" are meant—the earthly or the mythical ones.[1] The last change which the word underwent is very significant: it ended by meaning simply "slave, servant," (slightly altered into *dâsa*), thus telling of conquest completed, and closely answering the more modern Shûdra. We may, then, set down as correct the equation: Ârya — Dasyu = "twice-born"—Shûdra. And if any more proof be wanted of the fact that the servile class was made such by conquest, we have it in a passage of Manu's Code, which forbids the twice-born to associate with a Shûdra "*even though he were a king*." What can a Shûdra king be but a native sovereign?

6. It were impossible to exaggerate the loathing and contempt with which the Âryas regarded those whom they were robbing of land and liberty. These feelings primarily aroused by that most ineradicable and unreasoning of human instincts, race antagonism, find vent in numberless passages of great value,

[1] How easy and natural the step from "foe" to "fiend" we see from the very word "fiend," which originally meant both. The "arch-fiend" is the "arch-enemy" of mankind,—*Erz-feind* the Germans call him even yet.

because they enable us to piece together a tolerably correct picture of what those aborigines must have been, and in what manner they chiefly contrasted with their conquerors. The difference in color and cast of features is the first to strike us, and in that, as already hinted, we trace the beginnings of caste distinction. "Destroying the Dasyus, Indra protected the Aryan color," gratefully proclaims one poet. "Indra," says another, "protected in battle the Aryan worshipper, he subdued the lawless for Manu, he conquered *the black skin.*" "He [Indra] beat the Dasyus as is his wont . . . he conquered the land with his fair [or white] friends. . . ." Other names given by their Aryan conquerors are "goat-nosed" and "noseless" (*anaso*, evidently an exaggeration of "flat-nosed"), while the Aryan gods are praised for their beautiful noses. The Dasyus are accused of having no sacred fires, of worshipping mad gods, of eating raw meat, and, lastly, it would appear that they were held to be dangerous sorcerers: "Thou [Indra] hast made the Dâsa's magic powerless against the Rishi." Needless to add that difference of language completed the barrier which the victors later strove to render impassable.

7. Although the opposition of Ârya to Dasyu or Dâsa, of "twice-born" to Shûdra, is a perfectly established and intelligible fact, it were a mistake to see in "Dasyu" or "Shûdra" the names of a particular nation: they applied to all that were not Aryan, somewhat after the manner that, in classic antiquity, all went by the name of "Barbarians" who were not Greeks or Romans. It is suspected

that "Dasyu," in a slightly different form, *may* have been originally the name of a people whom the Indo-Eranian Âryas encountered and fought in their wanderings before they entered the Penjâb.[1] If so, the name early became a common one for "enemies," then "subjects," and its origin was thoroughly forgotten by both Eranians and Âryas of India. In point of fact, the fair-complexioned worshippers of Agni, Indra, and Soma found *two* widely different races in possession. These were undoubtedly broken up into numerous tribes, with different names and under different kings,—as, for that matter, were the Âryas themselves. The Rig-Veda teems with names which at first produce a bewildering impression of chaotic confusion; but we shall see that the patient labors of a band of ingenious and untiring searchers have already succeeded in bringing some kind of order into this confusion, and evolving out of it something that may be called a twilight of history. This groping in a particularly obscure past, unguided by even the scantiest monumental evidence, is materially aided by an observant study of the mixed

[1] Nor were these "enemies" always and necessarily of non-Aryan stock. The *Dahae* (possibly the original "dasyus") seem to have been "a tribe nearly akin to the Eranians," located "in the Kirghiz-Turkman Steppe, which extends from the Caspian Sea beyond the Yaxartes (now Syr-Daryà)." See Ed. Meyer, *Geschichte des Alterthums*, vol. i., § 425, p. 525, and Hillebrandt, *Vedische Mythologie*, vol. i., pp. 94–116. In this most important chapter it is also suggested to identify the wealthy robber tribe of the *Panis* with the *Parnians*, whom the Greek biographer Strabo describes as nomads—a sort of Eranian Bedouins—having their abodes along the Oxus (modern Amu-Daryá), and that of the *Pârâvatas* or "Mountaineers," a people whom the Vedic Âryas fought, with the *Parouêtai*, dwelling in the mountains, also of "foreign" Aryan stock. (*Ibid.*, pp. 97, 98.)

population of India in our own times. "India," writes Mr. Hunter, he who, of living men, has the most thorough and comprehensive knowledge of the immense empire, "forms a great museum of races, in which we can study man from his lowest to his highest stages of culture.

"A museum of races" indeed; and no one could say so with better authority than the writer of the above lines, since he compiled and published a dictionary of the non-Aryan languages of India, which comprises *139* languages and dialects! Of these but very few, of course, can lay any claim to literary worth; yet the names of several, such as Tamil, Telugu, Kanarese, are familiar to philologists, and hold their well-defined place in the lists of important human speeches. They form two groups, representing two distinct and widely different types or families of languages, answering to the two main stocks or races to which respectively belong the various non-Aryan peoples—the Dasyus of Vedic antiquity, the Shûdrà of classical Brahmanism, the "low-castes" of modern Hinduism.

8. These main stocks are the KOLARIANS and the DRAVIDIANS. Both came into the land at a prehistoric period far anterior to the Aryan invasion, from two opposite sides: the Kolarians from the east, or northeast, the Dravidians from the northwest—possibly through the very passes which later admitted the Aryan tide. If, as is probable, they found an older aboriginal population, no traces whatever are left of that—unless some of the numerous sepulchral mounds be theirs, and of the rude monuments made of unhewn stone and of upright slabs,

forming the combinations known in Western Europe by the Celtic names of "dolmens" and "menhirs," and circles and avenues, like those of Stonehenge in England, and Karnak in Brittany. Even these crudest forms of monumental art cover presumably several centuries, for, although they betray no attempt at either writing or decoration, they represent two stages of culture, since in some only flint implements and the roughest of pottery are found, while others contain iron weapons, gold and copper ornaments. It is thought that the Kolarians came first, and after spreading over the regions now known as Assam and Bengal, encountered the Dravidian current, which was pushing on from the other end, somewhere in the Vindhya highlands, about the centre of the land, where they converged,—or rather collided, and crossed each other, the weaker Kolarians being broken up by the shock, and dispersing among the valleys and forests of this most intricate, though but moderately high mountain-ridge, while the more hardy, more vigorous Dravidians swept on and through the ridge, and flooded the South.[1]

---

[1] Mr. J. F. Hewitt, whose novel and extremely valuable papers on the "Early History of Northern India" (*Journ. of the Roy. Asiat. Society*, 1888 and 1889) are freely used throughout this chapter, makes the following very explicit statement: "Wherever the three races have formed part of the now amalgamated population, the Kolarian tribes were the earliest settlers, as we always find them driven into the worst lands in districts where they live together with the other races. That they came from the East is shown by the following facts: First, they themselves always say that they did so; secondly, the most powerful and purest Kolarian tribes are found in the East; thirdly, their languages are allied to those used on the Brahmaputra and the Irâwaddy by the Kambojans and the Assamese."

21.—PRIMITIVE STONE MONUMENTS IN NORTHERN INDIA.

9. The descendants of the two non-Aryan races are, even at the present day, easily distinguished by their different customs, traits of character, and religions. The Kolarians are by far the gentler. As their chief representative tribe may be considered the SANTALS, who were a million strong in 1872 and who have their home among the hills abutting on the Ganges in Lower Bengal. They are among the more advanced of the pure-blooded non-Aryan tribes and have not adopted anything whatever from their conquerors' civilization. They have no castes or kings, but live in free village communities. Their religion amounts to little more than spirit and demon worship: besides the spirits of the forefathers—which the Kolarians, like the Dravidians, the Aryans, and all known races, worshipped originally from fear of their ghosts—there are those that dwell in each mountain, forest, river, well; there is the race-god, the clan-god, and the god or spirit of each family. These tutelary spirits are supposed to dwell in large, ancient trees. This is why—for the modern Hindus have incorporated into their Brahmanic creed this native superstition along with many less harmless ones—there is in or just outside almost every village some gigantic tree which is at once temple, shrine, and meeting-place, often, too, the only hostelry for pedestrians to rest in; the vast circle of shade which such a tree casts around thus becomes the centre of village life; it even does duty as a mart or fair ground, where peddlers and itinerant venders of cakes, fruit, etc., dispose their booths and stands, jugglers, and snake-charmers exhibit their

tricks. Sacrifices are offered to the resident spirits—of cakes, honey, milk, if the people are Hindus, of small animals and fowls if they belong to other races,—and the branches flutter gaily with the ornaments and ex-votos hung upon them. If such a tree, as is

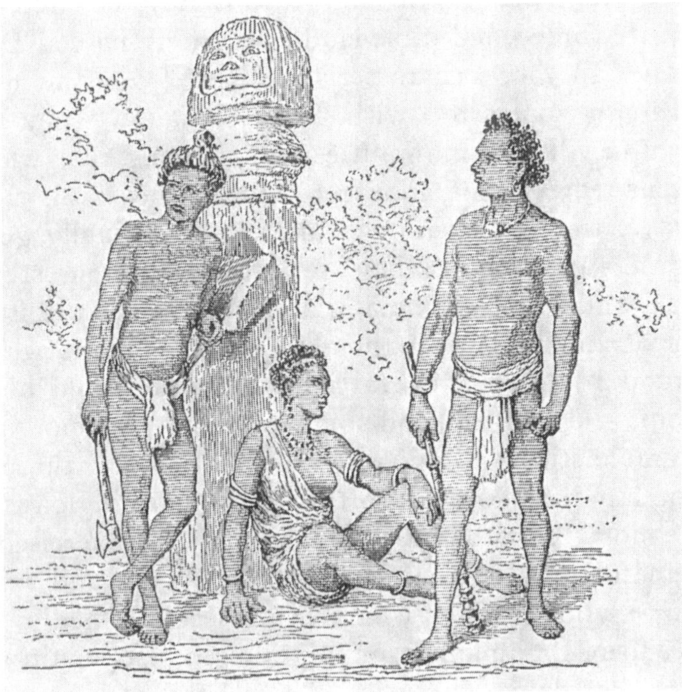

22.—SANTAL TYPES.

often the case, happens to be a banyan, with its mysterious, self-planted avenues, and its tiers of leafy galleries, it becomes a suburb in itself, and the effect, to a foreigner's eyes, is indescribably picturesque and original. These solitary, sacred trees appear to be a survival of the very ancient practice observed by the Kolarians when they first began to clear the forests which barred their way—that of leaving a portion of it untouched and sacred to the forest spirits.[1]

10. Of the Dravidian race, tribes are scattered through the central Vindhya region, while its bulk has, from pre-Aryan times to this day, covered the entire three-sided table-land sweepingly named Dekhan. In moral characteristics they, from the first, strongly contrasted with the Kolarians. They too live in village communities, but under a rule which leans more to the monarchic type, and, in all their ways, they show more public spirit. Equally good traders and farmers, they are patient, laborious, steadfast, and loyal—the material out of which the English trained some of those Sepoy Regiments which stood by Clive and Hastings through untold hardships and dangers, and some of which—far more admirable still—did not waver in their loyalty through the late rebellion. Unfortunately, their religion is of a most barbarous character, and has exercised a baneful influence on that of the Aryan and semi-Aryan population, which professes the medley of Vedism, Brahmanism, and native gross superstitions, now known as Hinduism. They share the Kolarians' belief in spirits and goblins, and their priests are conjurers versed in all the practices and tricks of

---

[1] That the Kolarians were the first to clear the forests and till the land, Mr. Hewitt is very positive ; he even thinks that, although they learned the use of iron very early, and cut the trees with iron weapons, the great number of stone axes or *celts* found in various localities makes it probable that they did some clearing work with stone implements before they found out the use of iron.

Shamanism. But this is a subordinate part of their religion. The most essential feature of it is the worship of the Earth, in the form of both god and goddess, as the giver and maintainer of life, and the adoration of the Snake as the Earth-god's special emblem. The Snake-god or King of Snakes is the wise and gigantic serpent *Shesh*—a name which casts a singularly vivid side-light on one of the many puzzles with which the Rig-Veda still teems. In several of those passages in which the priestly poets exhaust their ingenuity inventing abusive epithets for their Dasyu foes, they call them, with scathing contempt, *Shishna-devas*, literally: "whose God is Shishna or Shesh." The inference suggests itself almost irresistibly, and, moreover, leads us to suspect that many a passage wherein serpents and dragon-monsters are mentioned, may have a more direct and realistic meaning than was hitherto supposed. Thus, with regard to the ever-recurring battle between Indra and Ahi, "the Serpent," invariably ending with the Aryan champion-god's victory, we cannot help asking ourselves: have we really *always* to do with a nature-myth? is that battle *only* an incident of the atmospheric drama, and is the Serpent always and inevitably a Cloud-Serpent? By the light of later ethnological studies, another and even simpler interpretation lies temptingly near: may not the serpent sometimes personate the Serpent-god of the Snake-worshippers—the *Shishna-devas*—and the battle between the Aryan champion-god and the Dasyu sacred emblem thus resolve itself into a poetical version of the long race-strife? It is certain, at all events, that, in the enthusiasm and novelty of recent discovery, mythical interpretation has been greatly overdone, and, just as the word "Dasyu," which was at first declared to designate only the demons (of darkness, drought, or winter) whom the bright *devas* fought, is proved to apply quite as often to earthly, human foes; so the cloud-serpent of the uncompromising myth-theory may very well turn out to be, quite frequently, an allegorical presentation of the object of those foes' superstitious adoration. We are often brought down to earth from Cloudland with as unceremonious a shock.

11. Be that as it may, it is certain that snake-worship, utterly un-Aryan as it is, made a profound impression on the white invaders, so much so that, in the course of time, an Aryan snake-god—ARIÂKA—was invented; an impression plainly discernible, too, in the prominent place given to the NÂGAS (snakes and, snake-people, half-human, half serpentine in form and possessed of supernatural wisdom) in the later classical poetry. They play an important part, too, in modern Hinduism, which has instituted a yearly festival in honor, not of mythical serpents, but of the real, live snakes, which do not appear to strike this apathetic people with a loathing and terror at all proportionate to the havoc they play with human life (see p. 40). This festival, which comes round towards the end of July, is of a decidedly propitiatory character. Pilgrims flock to the Nâga-shrines which abound in certain districts; the cities teem with snake-charmers, whose weird charges eagerly crawl around the pans with milk

295 23.—FESTIVAL OF SERPENTS.

placed at intervals on the ground in all the principal thoroughfares, before the admiring eyes of a devout and festive throng.[1]

12. Repulsive and uncanny as this, to us unnatural, worship appears, it is, on the whole, harmless, and we might dismiss it with a shrug. Not so the crowning feature of the Dravidian religion—human sacrifices, which have been in constant and universal use among all the tribes of this ancient race until put a stop to by the English quite lately—in the case of the KANDHS and GÔNDHS, two representative and advanced Dravidian tribes, not till 1835. Human victims—either bought or kidnapped—were offered to the Earth-god regularly twice a year, at seed-time and harvest-time, and on special occasions, when some public need or calamity appeared to call for conciliation or atonement. Nothing can be more averse to the Aryan spirit than such sacrifices, at least at the stage of moral development at which we become acquainted with the race; yet such is the influence of long contact and habit, that we find even this horrible practice adopted by modern Hinduism in one of its two principal sects (Shivaism). The pure Brahmanism of the post-vedic and classical periods was not guilty of any such compromise, and such was the horror with which these aborigines in-

[1] It is worthy of notice: 1st, that temples dedicated to serpents are not found in the North of India; 2d, that the priests of such temples are never Brâhmans, but belong to the lower castes. Indeed, the old Aryan spirit is so much alive still in the noble castes, that they hold the serpent to be of evil omen and a Brâhman, if he happens to see one in the morning, will give up for that day whatever work or errand he may have on hand.

spired the Aryan Hindus, that their always exuberant fancy transformed them into a race of cannibal giants,

24.—GÔNDH TYPES.

fiends, and wizards, possessed of supernatural powers and every evil art that magic can lend, even to that of flying through space and assuming any form at will—thus transferring to them the attributes of the old Vedic cloud-demons whose place they took in the classical mythology of the race. These RAKSHASAS, whose horrible aspect and murderous wickedness make them the counterpart—or possibly the prototype—of our nurseries' Ogre, are described as taking especial delight in defiling sacrifices, disturbing the devotions of pious forest hermits, or leading them into unseemly temptations, carrying off pure and holy maidens, and opposing, by force or wile, the advance of the fire-worshipping, Soma-pressing "friends of the Devas." The Râmâyana is full of their evil prowesses; indeed the Rakshasas clearly stand out as the main obstacle encountered by Râma in his campaign against Ceylon, which embodies in heroic and epic guise the Aryan invasion of the South,[1] although it was in reality neither so rapid, nor quite so successful as the national poem would lead us to think. It was not so much an invasion as an advance, and we can easily imagine that it must have been an achievement of no small difficulty for a body of men necessarily very inferior in numbers, in the face of a compact population, brave, stubborn, and strongly organized. Such the Dravidians are now, when they number over twenty-eight millions south of the Vindhya, and there is not the slightest reason to doubt that such, in the main, they were at the early time of their long patriotic struggle.

---

[1] See Frontispiece—the Rakshasa king of Lanka, RÂVANA, with ten heads and ten pair of arms, each wielding a different weapon, defending his island at the head of his hosts of black giants.

13. We are often told to look on the non-Aryan peoples of modern India if we would picture to ourselves those whom the Aryan immigrants had to deal with from the moment they set foot in the land of the Seven Rivers. "Many of the aboriginal tribes," writes Mr. Hunter, "remain in the same early stage of human progress as that ascribed to them by the Vedic poets more than 3000 years ago." The instances of which he proceeds to give a list show conclusively that, in this wonderful country, the human race presents as great a variety as the animal and vegetable worlds, and covers the entire range of possible development, from pole to pole, of highest culture and spirituality, reached ages ago by some of its denizens, down to the lowest depths in which degraded humanity *can* drag itself and be human still. We seem to listen to the grotesque fancies of a dream—wild even for a dream—when we are told of people who live, or at least huddle together for shelter, in kennel-huts, six feet by eight, wear no clothing but bunches of leaves fastened to a string of beads that encircles the waist, and use flint weapons, not having even words for any metals in their language, thus affording us a startling glimpse of the Stone Age, a survival not even of the highest type of that age's civilization. Yet such a tribe, under the graphic name of "Leaf-wearers," actually exists, in the hilly districts of Orissa, not very far from Calcutta; it was ten thousand strong in 1872, and though a considerable portion were persuaded by the English authorities to adopt some kind of clothing and given the neces-

sary cotton material, it is reported that many have since returned to their foliage costume. Not much higher rank certain broken tribes who live in the mountains south of Madras, with no fixed dwellings of any sort, wandering about in the wildest recesses, only resting or seeking temporary shelter under little improvised leaf-sheds—existing on jungle products, mice, and other such small animals as they can catch,—and worshipping wicked demons, so that the question which naturally occurred to them when

24.—ANCIENT TYPE OF DWELLINGS DISCOVERED IN THE HIMÂLAYAS, AMONG NON-ARYAN TRIBES.

missionaries told them of a great and all-powerful God was: "And what if that Mighty One should eat us?" Some hill-tribes of Assam are described as "fierce, black, undersized, and ill-fed." Until very lately they lived on their more peaceable and industrious neighbors of the plains—in what manner can be gathered from the names of two such clans, which, translated, mean respectively, "The Eaters of a Thousand Hearths" and "The Thieves who Lurk in the Cotton-field."

14. Doubtless, such were some—many, of the aborigines, or Dasyus, whom the Aryan immigrants found in possession, and whom they drove before them or reduced to subjection, certainly with no gentle hand. But it were a great and fatal mistake —fatal to sound historical criticism—were we to imagine that the entire population of the land stood on this lowest level of barbarism. It is to be feared that this error was, at one time, only too generally entertained; but it could proceed only from a super-

25.—ANCIENT TYPE OF DWELLINGS DISCOVERED IN THE HIMÂLAYAS, AMONG NON-ARYAN TRIBES.

ficial study of the Rig-Veda, or from insufficient means of research on a field so very lately opened; or—and it is probable that this was a frequent and fruitful source of error—from too blind a confidence in certain theories which, indeed, had an ample foundation of truth, so that the fault lay not so much in them as in the exaggerated enthusiasm which accepted them too unconditionally, to the exclusion of other elements. Comparative Mythology is a new science even now. Its first discoveries, some forty years ago, coupled with those of its twin-science, Comparative Philology, were so startling that they dazzled its votaries. The Sun-and-Dawn Myth and the Storm Myth, ubiquitously identical, were a revelation, the "*Open Sesame*" to a long list of puzzles, in which problems of race, language, religion, poetry, had been heretofore tangled into a very jungle of mostly unanswerable questions, which, however, pleasantly untwined at the touch of the new talisman—the key, as was believed, to every lock. A band of brilliant scholars took hold of the Rig-Veda and subjected it, hymn after hymn, verse by verse, to the mythological system of interpretation which it had first suggested and splendidly justified, and under their deft, ingenious fingers there grew a world of gods and demons, a world that was not of earth and in which humanity had no part, save in the persons of priests and worshippers. By a sleight-of-hand, of which the trick became very easy to catch, *every* king or hero became an impersonation of the Sun or the Thunderer, *every* maiden was the Dawn, *every* enemy a fiend of Darkness or Drought, and in this manner all the proper names, with which the Rig-Veda bristles, were accounted for *mythically*, without leaving a loophole for History to put in a timid claim. A closer, more dispassionate study, conducted by a later, more cool-headed generation of scholars—cool, because not elated with the fever of the discoverer, the pioneer—revealed that many of the hymns were invaluable historical documents, commemorating real events, and perpetuating the names of the leading actors therein. And it becomes patent that probably a majority of the common names, which were sweepingly set down as names of fiends and other supernatural agents, really are those of tribes, peoples, and men, while many an alleged atmospheric battle turns out to have been an honest, sturdy hand-to-hand conflict between *bona-fide* human, mortal champions.

15. It is a thousand pities that the Rig-Veda does not contain history in the direct narrative or epic form, but only in that indirect and fragmentary form which is known as "internal evidence." The reason is that the book represents, not a simple and primitive stage of culture, as has been, somewhat rashly, taken for granted for a number of years, but, on the contrary, an advanced and complex one, which had developed some essential social institutions, such as royalty, aristocracy, and priesthood, in clean-cut, strongly set frames, on the background of an already long and eventful national past. The consequence is that the hymns which we may designate as in a specially direct sense "historical" ones, are full of allusions to occurrences which every one is supposed to know about, of names familiar to all. And where the occurrences and the names do belong exclusively to the world of Myth, that also was too well and too generally understood to require explanation. Thus it comes to pass that the kernel of historical fact for which we seek is, to us late-comers, unaided as we are by any thinnest thread of memory or tradition, imbedded in an almost impenetrable thickness of hardest outer shells and prickliest burrs. Yet

enough very essential facts have already been elicited by close and minute study, to form an interesting and on the whole not unreliable general presentation of the Aryan advance from their first quarters in the Penjâb eastward to that vast region watered by the historical Ganges and Djumna, which became the centre and headquarters of the race when the Vedic era had glided by and merged into the Brahmanic period.

16. Scant as we think the material which the Rig-Veda supplies for a reconstruction of an age too remote to be called epic, let alone historical, the results obtained are yet important enough to justify an epitome of them even in a popular work so necessarily limited in scope and space as the present. A few broad strokes of the brush will sketch an outline which will keep filling itself in with every added detail or scrap of internal evidence, from the moment the point of view and the perspective are properly established—and it is these which will have to be shifted considerably from the originally accepted, long maintained lines, producing, on the whole, an entirely different picture, and one which, while it opens out a vista into a remoter past than was heretofore credited to our knowledge of India, presents some (if we may so express it) startlingly modern features; only another way of reasserting what has been found out by philosophizing students of our race so many ages ago as to have become a truism, namely that "history repeats itself," and that "there is nothing new under the sun."

17. Thirty-five years ago no one would have

thought of connecting India (pre-Aryan India), with archaïc Babylonia, and if a solitary fact pointing that way was once in a while picked out by an exceptionally inquisitive and observant mind, it was suffered to remain unexplained, as a sort of natural curiosity, for the inferences it suggested were too startling to be more than hinted at. Eminently such a mind was the late François Lenormant, and he laid great stress on the use of the word *manâ* as early as the Rig-Veda, to denote a definite quantity of gold[1]—a word which can be traced to ancient Chaldea, or Semitic Babylonia, with the same meaning, and which afterwards passed into the Greek monetary system (*mnâ*, still later latinized into *mina*). Well, this little fact simply points to a well established commercial intercourse between Dravidian India (for the Kolarians never came as far west as the land by the Indian Ocean) and Babylonia or Chaldea. And now, years after, chance brings two more discoveries, individually as trifling; yet, linked together, the three form a chain of evidence as complete as it is strong. In the ruins of Mugheir, ancient Ur of the Chaldees, built by Ur-Êâ (or Ur-Bagash) the first king of united Babylonia, who ruled not less than 3000 years B.C., was found a piece of Indian teak.[2] This evidence is exceptionally conclusive because, as it happens, this particular tree is to be located with more than ordinary accuracy: it grows in Southern India (Dekhan) where it advances

[1] Rig-Veda viii., 67 (or 78), 2: "Oh bring us jewels, cattle, horses, *and a manâ of gold*."

[2] Sayce, *Hibbert Lectures for 1887*, pp, 18, 136, 137.

close to the Malabar coast, and nowhere else; there is none north of the Vindhya. Then again, the precious vocabularies and lists of all kinds of things and names which those precise old Babylonians were so fond of making out and which have given us so many startling surprises, come to the fore with a bit of very choice information, namely that the old Babylonian name for muslin was *sindhu, i. e.* that the stuff was simply called by the name of the country which exported it.

18. This is very strong corroborative evidence of several important facts, viz. that the Aryan settlers of Northern India had already begun, at an amazingly early period, to excel in the manufacture of the delicate tissue which has ever been and is to this day —doubtless in incomparably greater perfection—one of their industrial glories, a fact which implies cultivation of the cotton plant or tree, probably in Vedic times already[1];—that their Dravidian contemporaries were enterprising traders; that the relations between the two races were by no means of an exclusively hostile and warlike nature. For, if the name *sindhu* proves the stuff to have been an Aryan product, it was certainly not Aryan export trade which

---

[1] It is well known that our name for the fine and dainty fabric called "muslin" (*mousseline*) is derived from that of the city on the Tigris, Mosul, which, throughout the Middle Ages and to the present day, has been famous for its fabrication. How long before—who can tell? An imaginative and inquisitive mind might wonder whether, if all the links could be recovered and joined together, this particular industry might not be traceable to those almost prehistoric commercial relations between Dravidian India and Chaldean Babylonia. Did the latter learn the art from India and import the cotton from there—and did the Assyrians carry it north along with other arts? A stupendous issue to hang on so frail a thing!

supplied the foreign markets with it, for there was no such trade, the Âryas of Penjâb not being acquainted with the sea, or the construction of sea-going ships. It is clear that the weaving of fine stuffs must have been an Aryan home-industry; that Dravidian traders—probably itinerant merchants or peddlers—collected the surplus left over from home consumption, certainly in the way of barter, the goods then finding their way to some commercial centre on the western coast, where the large vessels lay which carried on the regular export and import trade. All this internal evidence is still further strengthened by another item of information which, though coming from a very different quarter, dovetails into it exactly. Professor Max Müller has long ago shown that the names of certain rare articles which King Solomon's trading ships brought him, were not originally Hebrew.[1] These articles are sandal-wood (indigenous on the Malabar coast and nowhere else), ivory, apes and peacocks, and their native names, which could easily be traced through the Hebrew corruptions, have all along been set down as Sanskrit, being common words of that language. But now, quite lately, an eminent Dravidian scholar and specialist brings proof that they are really Dravidian words, introduced into Sanskrit.[2] This is a dazzling ray of light, and proof so conclusive, when added to an already strong and compact case, that further corroborative evidence would be welcome, but scarcely necessary.[3]

---

[1] *Science of Language*, First Series, pp. 203, 204 (1862).

[2] Dr. Caldwell, Introduction to his *Comparative Grammar of the Dravidian Languages*.

[3] Compare the sculptures on Shalmaneser's Black Obelisk, *Story of Assyria*, pp. 185–195.

19. The late Greek historian Arrian mentions a maritime city, PATÂLA, as the only place of note in the delta of the Indus. This city, very probably the port from which the muslin went forth, and which is identified with modern Hyderabad, is renowned in legend and epos as the capital of a king of the Snake race—*i. e.*, a Dravidian king—who ruled a large part of the surrounding country. This native dynasty is closely connected with the mythical traditions of the two races, through its founder, King VASUKI—a name which at once recalls the great Serpent Vâsuki, who played so important, if passive, a part on a memorable mythic occasion (see p. 187). The connection between the Dravidians of Northern and Western India and the first Babylonian Empire,—the Babylonia of the Shumiro-Accads, before the advent of the Semites[1]—becomes less surprising when we realize that there was between them something more than chance relations, that they were in fact of the same race or stock—that which is broadly designated as Turanian. Philology points that way, for the Dravidian languages are agglutinative; craniology will not disprove the affinity, for a glance at the Gôndh types on illustration No. 23, and the turbaned head of Tell-Loh (Accadian Sirgulla) will show the likeness in features and shape.[2] But even more convincing is the common sacred symbol—the Serpent, the emblem of the worship of Earth, with its mystery, its wealth and its forces. The Accadian supreme god Êa was worshipped at his holiest shrine at

---

[1] See *Story of Chaldea*, ch. iii., "Turanian Chaldea," and ch. iv.

[2] *Ibid.*, p. 214.

Eridhu under the form of a Serpent, and as Eridhu was the centre from which the first Chaldean civiliza-

26.—HEAD OF ANCIENT CHALDEAN. FROM TELL-LOH (SIRGULLA.) SARZEC COLLECTION. (ABOUT 4000 B.C.)

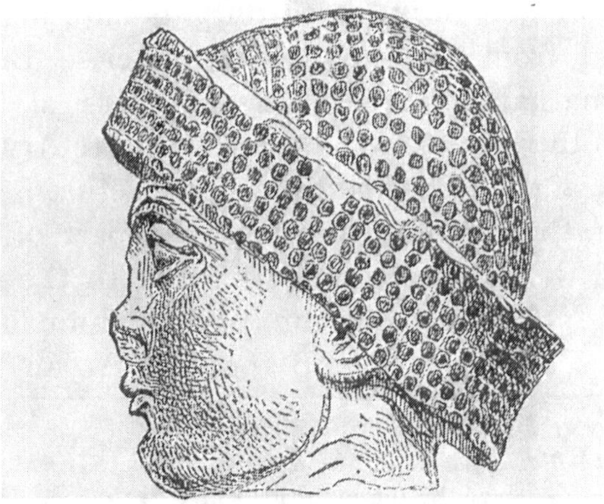

27.—SAME, PROFILE VIEW.

tion started and spread, so the serpent-symbol was accepted as that of the race and its religion.[1] The

[1] See *Story of Chaldea*, pp. 215, 246, 287.

Turanian Proto-Medes also, before they were conquered by the Aryan followers of Zarathushtra,[1] worshipped the snake-symbol of Earth, which afterwards was identified by the Eranian Mazdayasnians with Angramainyush, the Evil One, the Spirit of Lie and Death. This Proto-Median Serpent, like his Dravidian brother, had the honor of being admitted into the Aryan Mythic Epos. The snake-king (originally snake-god) AJI-DAHAK ("the Biting Serpent") figures in the mythical legends embodied in the Eranian SHAH-NAMEH ("Book of Kings") as the wicked Turanian king AFRASIAB, whose shoulders were kissed by the Evil One, when there sprouted from them two living snakes, who had to be fed daily on human brains—a pretty close equivalent of the Dravidian human sacrifices,—until the invincible Eranian hero, as in duty bound, delivered the world from the threefold monster.[2] But the most remarkable bequest left to classical Aryan India by the intimacy between her pre-Aryan inhabitants and their Chaldean race-brethren, is the legend of the Deluge, in which the part of Hâsisadra and the Biblical Noah is given to the Aryan sage and progenitor of the present human race, MANU. The story has no roots in Aryan myth,

---

[1] See *Story of Media*, etc., pp. 144, 267, 268.

[2] The *Shah-Nameh* is the Eranian national epic. It was written, in the eleventh century, by the poet FIRDÂUSI, at the suggestion of his patron, the great Sultan Mahmud of Gazna. It purports to be the history of Persia from the earliest times down to that monarch's reign, but is really, at least the first half of it, a complete collection of the hero-myths of the Eranian race, embodying the glorious memories of the life-long struggle between Erân and Turân.

in which it stands alone, unconnected with any of its legends, being evidently torn out of its own native cycle of the Izdubar poems. It would form too long a digression in the middle of a chapter; we will therefore do it justice best by reserving a separate appendix for it.[1]

20. There is one fundamental axiom which should be firmly kept in sight from the outset, as, by so doing, much confusion and wrong theorizing will be avoided. It is *that a people who speaks a certain language does not necessarily belong to the race which originated that language.* This proposition, when applied to individuals, will appear self-evident. But in dealing with whole communities, national or tribal, especially in more or less remote antiquity, it has for a time been strangely overlooked. There prevailed a general tendency to forget that a community, as well as an individual, may acquire a foreign language from a variety of reasons. It may do so from choice (retaining its own the while), for friendly purposes of trade and political intercourse; or from necessity, if not compulsion, on being reduced to subjection by an alien conquering race. Conciliation follows on conquest; intermarriage completes the work of amalgamation; mixed races are the result; the language at first imposed as a stamp of bondage remains as a pledge of amity; frequently, if the invading race is intellectually the higher, to the exclusion of the original, native tongue. But a language does not mean merely a bundle of words and names; it means a subtle, all-pervading influence,

---

[1] See pp. 335 *ff*.

and the race that adopts, no matter from what motives, another race's language, ends by absorbing also what that language carries with and in itself: the spirit, the soul which that race breathed into it, as embodied in its religion, forms of worship, social institutions, popular poetry, and ethics. These things, when once they have gained a hold, spread and propagate by all manner of channels, and thus it may come to pass that a people will speak a language, follow a religion, practise forms of life, originally not their own. It is therefore utterly unscientific to say, for instance, "such and such a people speaks an Aryan language; consequently it is of Aryan stock"; for ethnology, with its attendant sciences, physiology and craniology, may positively demonstrate that it is no such thing; at all events our decision must wait on their verdict. Without being scientific, the Âryas of India knew this well: it is expressly inculcated in their standard code, the Laws of Manu, that "all those tribes in this world" which do not belong to the three twice-born castes are Dasyus, *whether they speak the language of the Mlekkhas* (Barbarians) *or that of the Âryas* (X., 45). The only warranted conclusion in such a case would be that the said people had at some time been subjected to a powerful, transforming Aryan influence; as to the people of Aryan race who were the bearers of that influence, they may, or may not, have passed away from the land or region to which they left the most enduring part of themselves—their spirit.

21. This hypothetical case represents a reality which confronts us all through history, in all times

and parts of the world. But it is comparatively rare for a morally victorious race to vanish from a land, whose population its influence affected so deeply and so lastingly, without leaving any traces of its physical presence. At this late age of the world, when intercourse and amalgamation have shaken most of the barriers between race and race, and pulled down so many, mixed races are the rule, the mixture running through innumerable grades and shadings; and, in proportion as one or another stock predominates in a given fraction of humanity, the spiritual characteristics belonging to it assert themselves. This is precisely what we see in modern India. The whole of the huge continent is permeated with Aryan influences. To the Aryan race it owes its name, its culture in the main, its distinctive national language and literature. Yet what lack of uniformity! Side by side with the Sanskrit dialects are spoken about 150 non-Aryan languages and dialects; the variety in physical types and features is as great, ranging from the noble Aryan to the low Negroïd; the official national religion, Brahmanism, encloses in its fold several powerful sects which are manifestly growths of widely different spiritual soils; and no wonder, when, of the 200,000,000 which make the Indian Empire (not including the Feudatory Provinces), the census of 1872 showed only 16,000-000 of Brâhmans and Râjputs (corresponding to the Kshatriyas, originally called Râjanyas),—"the comparatively pure offspring of the Aryan or Sanskrit-speaking Race"[1]; while 11,000,000 represented

[1] W. W. Hunter, *The Indian Empire*, etc.

"the great Mixed Population, known as the Hindus, which has grown out of the Aryan and non-Aryan elements, chiefly from the latter"; the rest being the recognized non-Aryan tribes or Aborigines.

22. It will be a surprise to many that the Aryan population of the Indian continent should be so out of all proportion small when compared to the descendants and representatives of those races which the Aryan immigrants found in possession. The same difference must have existed on a still greater scale in those earliest times—and would alone suffice to stamp as irrational the theory of Aryan supremacy having been established by sheer conquest and force. Of course there was fighting, and raiding, and driving of native tribes into mountain fastnesses, while others were reduced to a state of bondage. But this would account for only a very small portion of the Âryas' success; for the laws of overwhelming numerical odds can be defied only within certain limits, even by the bravest. But it has ever been one of our race's chief and truest claims to glory, that it has asserted, extended, and maintained its superiority far more by moral means than by physical force. Three agencies were, beyond doubt, mainly active and successful in propagating Aryan intellectual influence and, as a consequence, Aryan material rule: commercial intercourse, foreign diplomacy helped by an innate spirit of adventure, and missionary work. Intermarriages, of course, did the rest.

23. It has always been a characteristic custom among Aryan nations for their warriors to work off their exuberant energies by going forth in search of

adventures abroad, frequently in the form of robbing raids or piratical expeditions, but quite as often by taking military service with neighboring, or even remoter, states or sovereigns, singly or in bands. Opportunities of the kind must have been plentiful with the Aryan youth of the Seven Rivers, surrounded as they were with numerous tribes, with whom war must have been a habitual occupation. This naturally paved the way for political alliances, and there were those at home who were not slow to decide that such was the surest, and in the end quickest way to extend and establish Aryan influence. These were the spiritual leaders of the people, the priestly class which was in time to develop and crystallize into the Brâhman caste. In the Rig-Veda we find these most influential persons belonging to the families of hereditary poets and bards—Rishis—whose names are handed down as the composers of the sacred hymns. Seven of the books in the collection are attributed each to one of these Rishis, who are shown by many allusions and direct assertions in the text to have been attached to the royal families of different tribes, where they occupied the position not only of *purohitas* or family priests and national bards, but evidently also that of royal advisers and ministers —a custom which meets us as a fully developed and sacred institution all through the later Brahmanic period. But it turns out, on closer inspection, that these royal houses and the tribes they rule, are by no means always Aryan, and it is startling, at first, with our still lingering prejudices, to find an Aryan priest glorying in the position of bard and *purohita* to a

Dasyu—*i. e.* native—king and people. Yet we have to get familiar with the fact, which opens out a whole vista of missionary work, conversions, priestly ambition—and sound national policy.

24. Every one who has lived in India knows—and the English learned it to their cost at the time of the great mutiny—what almost unlimited influence the wandering home-missionaries have over the population. When such a *guru* (spiritual instructor) makes his rounds, the people of the villages which he honors with a visit pour out to meet him and carry him to their homes under demonstrations of respect almost amounting to worship. Within historical, even modern times, such men have been known to rise to the highest positions at the courts of native potentates, as prime ministers or as unofficial, but all the more powerful, private advisers of the master. Such must have been the Aryan missionaries of the Vedic times, who carried the worship of Agni and Soma into the lands of the Serpent together with Aryan speech and customs. The process of conversion must have been a simple matter enough. A ceremony of initiation, significantly named "a second birth,"—a simple confession of faith—and the impure brood of the Serpent was transformed into the "twice-born" child of the bright Devas and admitted into the Aryan spiritual community, the Aryan political confederacy. Now there is in the Rig-Veda a short verse which, under the name of GÂYATRÎ, is to this day considered the most sacred of all texts, endowed with miraculous powers, and has, through over a score and a half of centuries, been repeated

28.—RECEPTION OF A GURU OR SPIRITUAL INSTRUCTOR.

thrice a day at least, with fervent faith, by numberless millions of human beings. It reads as follows in the translation:

> "Of Savitar, the heavenly, that longed for glory may we win, and may himself inspire our prayers."—(III., 62, 10.)

This text at first sight appears so insignificant as to make the exceeding holiness attached to it something of a puzzle. Our perplexity however vanishes if we assume it to have been the confession of faith demanded of converts—as this would fully account for its sacredness, which endures unimpaired to this day. We can have no proof that this *mantra* was used for this particular purpose, but there is nothing to make it improbable. Its briefness and simplicity make it appropriate; it is comprehensive too, as the sky-and-sun-worship, a form and development of fire-worship, might well be taken as the symbol of the bright Aryan nature-religion in opposition to the mystic and gloomy earth-worship represented by its weird emblem, the Serpent. This supposition is still further and very greatly favored by the circumstance that the Gâyatrî is found in the collection attributed to the Rishi Vishvâmitra. And here we come on the thin end of a wedge which, being inserted at this early time, sprung a cleft which runs through the entire epic and religious life of India: the schism between the two Brahmanic schools which have their names from the two—probably real—Vedic Rishis VASISHTHA and VISHVÂMITRA.

25. To keep strictly within the information supplied by the Rig-Veda itself—Vasishtha was the

bard of the TRITSU, the leading and purest Aryan tribe, and Vishvâmitra was the bard of the BHÂRATAS, their great enemies and one of the most powerful native tribes. He at one time had been with the Tritsu, and for whatever cause he left them—not improbably personal revenge—he played a conspicuous part in the confederacy which attempted to check the Aryan advance and increasing power. There is a hymn (53), in Book III., that of the Vishvâmitra family, which evidently alludes to this very thing. In the first part of the hymn it is said that when Vishvâmitra conducted King Sudâs' sacrifices, Indra was gracious to him for the Rishi's sake, and a great blessing is pronounced on the king, and his war-steed and the expedition on which he starts. Then, quite suddenly, Vishvâmitra is made to declare, in his own person, that his prayers protect the tribes of the Bhâratas, and the hymn ends with four verses of imprecations against enemies who are not named, but whom tradition so positively identified with Vasishtha and his family, that the priests of this house in later times never uttered these four verses, and tried not to hear them when spoken by other Brâhmans. It is most probable that the Vishvâmitras resented some distinction conferred upon the Vasishthas, possibly their appointment as *purohitas* to the Tritsu royal family, and went over to their most powerful enemies, the Purus and Bhâratas. The Tritsu and their allies were victorious in the ensuing struggle, known as "the War of the Ten Kings," and both the bards have left descriptions of it and of the final battle on the banks of the Purushnî, in some spirited hymns, the most undoubtedly historical of the collection. At a later period the followers of Vasishtha and his descendants represent the narrowly orthodox Brahmanic school, with its petty punctiliousness in the matter of forms, rites, observances, its intolerance of everything un-Aryan, its rigid separatism. This school it was which stood guard through all these ages, and up to our day, the champion—and possibly originally the institutor, of Caste; who advanced and upheld all the exaggerated claims of the Brâhman priesthood, to divinity, to the rule of the world, and ownership of all it holds, to supernatural compelling powers over nature and the gods themselves through sacrifice and ascetic practices, and the like. The followers of Vishvâmitra and his descendants, on the other hand, represented the school of liberalism and progress, of conciliation and amalgamation; it was probably through their efforts chiefly that Aryan speech and worship and, as a consequence, Aryan supremacy, spread among the native princes and their tribes. But it must also have been owing to this their policy of conciliation that many of the beliefs and practices of the once loathed aborigines gradually crept into Aryan worship, and gained a footing there, paving the way for the mixed forms of Hinduism in the future. Their orthodox antagonists blamed and despised them for this laxity, wherein they saw a danger which they strove to avert by redoubled zeal in keeping high and strong the bulwark of Caste; and while they could not deny the holiness and authority of one who ranks with their own Rishi in the Rig-Veda itself, they found a vent for their hatred and spite in the assertion that Vishvâmitra was not originally a Brâhman but a Kshatriya, and had obtained the highest rank only by superhuman feats of asceticism which *compelled* the gods to grant him the consecration he desired. The feud between the two bards and their respective descendants is a favorite theme in later Brahmanic literature, where it is invested, both in poetical and theological writings, with the usual exuberance of fancy and extravagance of detail and incident. We find nothing of the kind in the Rig-Veda, where the beginning of the difference is not narrated at all, and only shows from the context of the so-called historical hymns. Very significant, in the light of these, is the line in which Vishvâmitra praises his adopted tribe, the Bhâratas, calling them "far-sighted people,"—probably in opposition to his former patrons, the orthodox and narrow-minded Tritsu. All this shows us the institution of the castes in a novel and most natural, convincing light: as a reaction, on the part of the strictly orthodox worshippers of Agni and Soma, against the alarmingly broad and levelling tendencies of the missionary work done by some enthusiastic preachers who combined religious zeal with far-seeing diplomacy. High Church against Low Church. The native converts, received at first on equal terms, began at a later period—probably that of the early Brâhmanas—to be admitted only on condition that they should occupy a subordinate position—whence the Shûdra caste. It will be noticed, however, that both systems—the orthodox and the

21

liberal, help to carry out what Mr. Hewitt calls "the great Brâhman conception of a number of subordinate tribes ruled by a very small Aryan minority."

26. The host of proper names in the Rig-Veda must have plunged the first who made them a special study into a state of chaotic bewilderment bordering on desperation. Where was the clue, where the saving thread in this labyrinth? What names were those —of gods, of demons, of men, of nations, of places? This first sorting, with due margin for correcting mistakes, was a gigantic task. And when at last the names of nations and tribes were set apart with tolerable certainty, there still remained the apparently hopeless difficulty of locating them, geographically and ethnologically. Everything that could help in the work was brought together: every indication supplied by internal evidence, by the patient collation of passages, by a minute study of the great epics, by gleaning every crumb of information, however fragmentary, however corrupt, scattered in foreign writings, whether of Greek or Arab. All these rays, some of them very pale and uncertain, gave, when concentrated, a search-light strong enough to dispel the thickest of the gloom that lay on that vast and ancient field, and afford revealing glimpses of most suggestive landmarks. If we trace certain names right through the Rig-Veda, simply writing down each line, or verse, in which they occur, we will be astonished at the amount of information which will result from this mechanical proceeding; and if we repeat it with several names, the feeling of confusion will soon wear away, and make room for a

delightful, increasing sense of order and clearness. Whole leading groups stand out, and of some royal houses we obtain in this way genealogies or dynasties covering several generations—yielding, by the way, additional evidence, if such were needed, of the slow growth of the Rig-Veda in its finished form. Two of these dynasties run parallel from father to son, and are closely connected throughout. They are the royal houses of the TRITSU, whose *purohita* or chaplain was the orthodox Vasishtha, and that of the PURU, their friends and allies. The glory of each of these houses appears to have culminated in a tribal hero: the Tritsu DIVODÂSA, and KUTSA the Puru, or PURUKUTSA. These two peoples, together with three others, the YADU, the TURVASU, and the ANU, are frequently mentioned collectively in the Rig-Veda as "The Five Tribes" or "Five Races."

27. The Tritsu are beyond doubt the chief Aryan nation of early Vedic times—perhaps the original invaders of the Penjâb. If peaceful methods were used, it was not by this tribe; their conquest was all by war, and though they had alliances among the Dasyu nations, many of the latter gradually turned against them and at last formed a confederacy with the object of stopping their too rapid advance eastward, as they took possession of one river after another. Their first great king, Divodâsa, was engaged in a continuous warfare with some fierce mountain tribes of the north, ruled by a chieftain of the name of SHAMBARA, who appears to have constructed a quantity of forts in defence of the many

passes which lead from the highlands into the steeper and wilder Himâlayan fastnesses. These forts, of course, were built of wood, so that the usual mode of attack and destruction in these petty campaigns was by fire. This is why, in the numerous passages in which these exploits of Divodâsa are glorified, both by Vasishtha, the bard of his family, and others, Agni often shared with Indra the credit of the victory. For some reason these forts are always spoken of as being ninety or ninety-nine—probably a way of saying "a great many." "O Lightning-bearer," the poet exclaims in one place, "these are thy deeds that thou destroyedst nine-and-ninety castles in one day, and the hundredst at night."—The Tritsu must have had their hands very full, for, while continually busy in the north, they were fighting a great deal in the southeast; sometimes they pressed onwards, sometimes only held their own against native tribes who strove to prevent their crossing now one river, now another. On the whole they were successful, and victories are recorded, both of Divodâsa and his son—or grandson—SUDÂS, over various nations, especially the Yadu and Turvasu, twin tribes always named together, who appear to have lived south of the Seven Rivers, between the Indus and the Yamunâ. Yet these two tribes were mostly of Aryan stock, and nearly connected with the Âryas of the Indus and Sarasvatî. To make up for this, the Purus, a powerful, originally Dravidian race, who lived in the West and had a standing feud with the horse-breeding GANDHÂRAS of the KABUL valley, were for a long time the

Tritsu's firm allies. Indra and Agni are said to protect both and help them in their wars against their common enemies. In one of the Vasishtha hymns to Agni we read: "From fear of thee the black people fled; they dispersed, leaving behind their goods and chattels, when thou, Agni, blazing for the Puru, didst destroy their forts." (VII., 6, 3.) And in another hymn of the same book (VII., 19), Indra is praised for giving the Tritsu the victory over the Yadu-Turvasu, for helping Kutsa, the Puru king, in his battles, and giving his enemy into his hand. This friendship must have lasted after Divodâsa's death, for one hymn of another book (I., 63. 7), mentions jointly the victories of Purukutsa, as he is often named, and Sudâs, Divodâsa's successor: "Thou, Indra, didst destroy the seven forts, fighting for Purukutsa, O Lord of Lightning; thou didst throw them down, like straw, before Sudâs, and help the Puru out of their straits." True, some scholars give a slightly different reading of this passage, which reverses the sense, thus: "Thou didst throw down Sudâs like straw," and make out Kutsa to have gained a victory *over*, not *with*, Sudâs. Should this reading, which has on its side Roth's and Ludwig's weighty authority, be confirmed, it will only go to show that the great general war, known as "the War of the Ten Kings," from the number of the tribes which formed the confederacy at whose head Purukutsa undoubtedly stood, was preceded by private hostilities between the latter and his former allies, the Tritsu. If so, it might be that the temporary advantage obtained by the Puru prince encouraged the other malcontents to declare themselves and form a confederacy,—some, like the Yadu-Turvasu, from the hope of avenging former injuries, others in self-defence, to check the too rapid advance of that most enterprising of Aryan tribes. The philological point may never be positively settled one way or the other; but the doubt, as will be seen, does not materially affect the general course of things, which is all that really matters to us, students of history. There are a great many similar debatable cases, and it is wise not to make too much of them—unless one is a specialist.

28. The War of the Ten Kings is told in the collections that bear the names of both hostile bards—the Vishvâmitras and the Vasishthas, and the story of the campaign and the decisive battle can be easily reconstructed out of the detached passages and whole hymns which allude to the subject or narrate the chief incidents of the struggle. The Vasishtha hymns are usually addressed to Indra, by later bards, who beseech him to help their people "as he once helped Sudâs and the Tritsu," and it is expressly mentioned in them, as well as in those of the rival house, that the name of Indra and also of Váruna was invoked on both sides—they were, in fact, entreated to "defeat the foes, *whether Aryan or Dâsa*." This is quite a common invocation, and occurs repeatedly in several books, showing, on one hand, that those early conflicts already were in a measure internecine ones, between rival Aryan tribes, on the other that the Aryan gods were already

adopted by many native nations.[1] So the Anu, originally probably of Kolarian stock, are especially mentioned as worshippers of Agni, and we have seen the help given by Indra to the Puru repeatedly mentioned. Nor should it be forgotten that ancient nations were by no means exclusive in their theology, and were quite ready, without in the least betraying their allegiance to their own gods, to do honor, incidentally, to a strange god who had made good his claim to respect by the success and prosperity with which he rewarded his worshippers. Now Indra had become so pre-eminently the ever victorious war-god, that he could very well be praised, and even invoked, by warlike tribes not of Aryan stock or religion.

29. The names of both the enemies and the allies of the Tritsu and their king Sudâs have been preserved for us by the bards of the Rig-Veda. The confederacy, consisting of ten powerful tribes, was headed by the Puru under their hero the great

---

[1] "He whom both battle lines call upon in the fray, both adversaries on this side and on that,—he whom they invoke, standing on chariots,—that, O men, is Indra." (II., 12, 8.)

". . . The warriors who leagued together against us, whether kindred or strange, break their might." (VI., 25, 3.)

"Thou, O Indra, dost strike both foes, the Aryan and the Dasyu." (VI., 33, 3.)

"They (Indra and Agni) strike the foes, both Aryan and Dâsa." (VI., 60, 6.)

"Whatever contemners of the gods, be they Dâsa, be they Ârya, O glorious Indra, do battle against us, give us an easy victory over them, thy foes." (X., 38, 3.)

"Thou (Agni) didst take the goods of mount and plain, and didst strike the foes, both Âryas and Dasyus." (X., 69, 6.)

Etc., etc.

Kutsa, and by the Bhâratas who, already converted by Vishvâmitra, were to become so thoroughly Aryanized, and to take such a prominent position that, in after days, "the Land of the Bhâratas" was to become a synonym for "Aryan India." The names of several other famous chieftains are mentioned as having perished in the decisive battle. Neither were the Tritsu unprovided with allies, and in the array of the latter we are startled to find two very familiar names—those of the Parthians and the Persians—PRITHU and PARSU, though there is really nothing so very wonderful in the fact that chips of the two chief Eranian tribes should have, like others, wandered south of the Himâlaya. A people named VISHANIN, *i. e.* "followers of Vishnu," is also mentioned, almost certainly Aryan sun-worshippers, showing that Vishnuism as a distinctive worship—a sect—had its roots in a remoter past than was hitherto suspected.[1] As though to complete the connection, we find in the list of the Tritsu's allies, the Vishanin bracketed with the SHIVA, which is thought to be a name of the TUGRA, one of the oldest aboriginal Dravidian peoples, whom the Âryas had specially nicknamed "Sons of the Serpent," and who, under the religious designation of Shiva, were very probably the originators of the worship of Shiva under the form or with the attribute of a snake.[2]

[1] Vishnuism is probably originally connected with the transition from the oldest calendar of thirteen lunar months to the reformed solar year of twelve months, presided over by the twelve Âdityas.—See Mr. Hewitt's *Early History of Northern India.*

[2] *Ib.*, ii., pp. 232, 233 (*J. Roy. As. Soc.*, xxi., new series). In the Russian epic cycle there is an evil champion demigod, the constant

That all these peoples had even then already become much mixed, partly with Aryan elements, is more than likely. At all events it takes one's breath away to find the three component elements of modern Hinduism: Brahmanism, Vishnuism, Shivaism, arrayed before us in the Rig-Veda in precisely the same juxtaposition: Tritsu, Vishanin, Shiva!

30. The confederacy had planned the campaign well and was sure of success. Nor does the Tritsu bard underrate the danger, but plainly states that Sudâs "was surrounded" and cried out for help to Indra, who cut a way for him through the enemies, in consideration of the prayers sent up by his friends, the white-robed Vasishtha priests. The confederates' plan was simply to surprise the Tritsu, whose settlement had advanced as far as the Sarasvatî, while they themselves were drawn up in battle array on the northern side of the Purushnî (modern Ravî).[1] The two hosts, therefore, were separated by two intervening rivers—the Vipash (modern Bias) and the Shatadrû or Shutudrî (modern Sutlej). These the confederates intended to cross, as we are very explicitly informed by a hymn of the Vishvâmitra collection. As this historical document is also one of the few faultless poetical gems in the Rig-Veda, we shall try to give an idea of it, as far as a meagre prose version can do so. It is most finished in form, and—a rare merit in these old songs—consistent

---

enemy of the heroes or *bogatyrs*, who goes by the name of "Tugàrin the Serpent." Our folk-lorists have been greatly puzzled to account for the name and where it came from: might the key be found here?

[1] Mr. Hewitt draws attention to this river's name as suggestive of the Purus' original home having been on its banks.

throughout, without an anticlimax or a digression. The form is that of a dialogue between the Rishi and the rivers, arranged in couplets of two verses each, the one being spoken by the poet, while in the other the rivers reply; the introduction is in the narrative form.

"1. Down from the mountains, in merry race, like two mares let loose, or two comely mother-kine at play, Vipash and Shatadrû run along, carrying their milk-like waters.

"2. Spurred on by Indra, like swift charioteers, ye hasten to the mighty mass of waters; with swelling waves ye beautiful ones run close to one another.

"3. I went down to the most motherly of streams, to Vipash, the wide, the fair,—to the two that, like a pair of mother-kine fondling their calves, wander along to meet in one broad bosom.

"4. 'Swelling with sweet waters, travelling along towards the god-created bosom, nought can stem our swift current: what is the wish of the bard, that he calls to us rivers?'

"5. Hark to my devout song, and stay your course for a brief rest, ye holy ones; to you rivers calls my heart's loud prayer; with longing I call out to you—I, the son of Kushika.

"6. 'He whose arm bears the lightning, Indra, broke the way for us, killing Vritra, who shut in the waters; the beauteous Savitar, the god, guides us on; following his lead, we spread our waters wide.'

"7. This heroic deed be praised for evermore, that Indra did when he cut the Serpent in pieces. With his lightning he struck the robbers; the waters sped away whither they longed to go.

"8. 'Forget never, O bard, this word of thine; let the latest generations hearken to it; give us a loving word in thy songs, O poet, let us not be forgotten of men, and honor shall be paid to thee.'

"9. Hear then, sisters, what the poet says: I came to you from far with loaded wagons. Now bend ye low, give me an easy ford; let not your waves touch my axle-tree, O Rivers.

331 29.—THE SHATADRÛ OR SHUTUDRÎ (SUTLEJ).

"10. 'We will heed thy word, O Rishi, that cam'st to us from far with loaded wagons; I bend low before thee as a willing slave, as to her lord submits the bride.'

"11. But when the Bhâratas' host, animated by Indra and full of ardor, has quickly forded thee, then let the current shoot up again with arrow's fleetness; this is the boon I beg of you, ye holy ones.

"12. The Bhâratas, filled with the ardor of battle, have crossed; the bard did win the rivers' favor. Now swell, now grow rapidly, to end the work, and hasten onwards, with well-filled beds." (III., 33.)

31. The bard in this last verse, with truly poetic licence, describes as an accomplished fact that which he only wished to happen, but which did not really happen. For in reality, the event was exactly reversed: the Tritsu took the initiative and it was they who crossed the Vipash and Shatadrû (the fording of which Indra made easy to Sudâs), astonishing the enemy by appearing unexpectedly, in battle array, on the southern bank of the Purushnî. Then there was a veritable scramble; one after another the confederate tribes with their leaders jumped into the river, "thinking, fools that they were, to cross as easily as on dry land." The horses and the chariots were badly handled by the current, and those who did cross, came out on the other side like stampeding cattle without a herdsman. Many chiefs were drowned; the slaughter was terrible: over six thousand warriors fell "by Indra's might"; the booty "given into Sudâs' hands" was immense, and the survivors had to pay heavy tribute. The Tritsu victory was complete, and there was nothing to hinder their further advance eastward to the Yamunâ (Rig-Veda, VII., 18). The fate of the Puru hero Kutsa is not ex-

pressly mentioned, but there is a curious incidental allusion which would almost make us believe that he was taken prisoner. In that one verse Kutsa's tribulations are obscurely hinted at, and the birth of TRÂSADASYU, son of his daughter PURUKUTSÎ, seems to be considered as a consolation or compensation sent him by the gods.

32. Trâsadasyu became a very powerful sovereign, the first of Indian princes to bear the highest royal title, "king of kings" (*samraj*). A solid peace must have followed the disastrous battle on the Purushnî, for Trâsadasyu invariably appears as the Âryas' firm friend and ally; his successors, through several generations, are frequently mentioned, not only in the great epics, but in the Rig-Veda itself. But his people gradually changed its name, and became known as the Kurus, who take such a prominent position in the country as depicted in the great epics. This change of the name is explained, as usual, by a genealogical fiction: Kuru, we are told, was a great-grandson of Kutsa, and was so great a king that his entire people was thenceforth named after him. In the same manner the Tritsu disappear; but we are expressly told that they continued to acquire lands and the Yamunâ is—rather abruptly—mentioned in connection with them. But if their name disappears, that of the Vasishthas and their bigoted orthodox school does not, and it turns out, from this and other indications, that the land which the Tritsu finally occupied, became that stronghold of fanatical Brahmanism, caste, and absolute priestly rule, which is designated in the most perfect of Brahmanic

codes, that of Manu, as the BRAHMÂ-VARTA, the only country in which it is lawful for a really orthodox Brâhman to reside. This is the text:

"That land, created by the gods, which lies between the two divine rivers, Sarasvatî and Drishadvatî, the sages call Brahmâvarta.

"The custom handed down in regular succession among the castes and the mixed races of that country is called the conduct of virtuous men.

"*From a Brâhman born in that country let all men on earth learn their several usages.*"

This as distinguished from the entire country between the Himâlaya and the Vindhya and between the eastern and western oceans, which is called ÂRYÂVARTA, and is good to live in, but not preeminently holy as that small chosen tract. The twice-born should strive not to live outside of Âryâvarta, for the rest of the continent is the country of the Mlekkhas (barbarians) where it is lawful for the Shûdra to reside, but which the twice-born should avoid.

APPENDIX TO CHAPTER VIII.

THE STORY OF THE FLOOD IN INDIA (THE MATSYA AVATÂR).[1]

1. THE story of the Flood exists in Hindu literature in several versions, always as an incident of some more or less bulky work or collection, except one, which forms the subject of a short separate narrative or Purâna—the MATSYA (*i. e.* "Fish") PURÂNA. It is also given in very abridged form in another of the lesser Purânas, the AGNI-PURÂNA; but the two fullest and most elaborate versions are those in the BHÂGAVATA PURÂNA, one of the most important of these writings, consecrated to the glorification of Vishnu, and in the great epic itself, the Mahâbhârata, where it occurs among many legends told on various occasions by this or that learned Brâhman, for the entertainment or instruction of this or that royal hero. These versions have been known to Sanskrit scholars for half a century and more, but being found imbedded in such a late, and in some cases almost modern body of literature, representing Hinduism even more than classical Brahmanism, those who had detected the foreign ring of the story were naturally led to attribute it to late Semitic importation, directly connecting it with the Biblical account in Genesis. The surprise was therefore great when a version came to light in one of the great Brâhmanas, the SHATAPATHA ("Brâh-

[1] In connection with these pages it is absolutely necessary to read over carefully Chapter VII. of the *Story of Chaldea*, more especially the incident of the Deluge, pp. 314–317.

mana of A Hundred Paths"), suddenly removing the legend into an age closely bordering on the Vedic, in which we find it presented, in a monument of distinctly Vedic literature, as an ancient legend accounting for the origin of the present human race. The point of view was shifted at once in a way which necessitated entirely new adaptations, and some peculiar details in the later versions, which will be seen mutually to complete one another, only now won their proper recognition and interpretation.

2. Professor Max Müller published the first translation of the then newly discovered Shatapatha version.[1] We here give the latest and most authoritative one, edited and indorsed by the same veteran scholar[2]:

"1. In the morning they brought to Manu water for washing, just as now also they are wont to bring water for washing the hands. When he was washing himself, a fish came into his hands.

"2. It spake to him the words: 'Rear me; I will save thee.'—'Wherefrom wilt thou save me?'—'A flood will carry away all these creatures; from that I will save thee.'—'How am I to rear thee?'

"3. It said: 'As long as we are small, there is great destruction for us: fish devours fish. Thou wilt first keep me in a jar. When I outgrow that, thou wilt dig a pit and keep me in it. When I outgrow that, thou wilt take me down to the sea, for then I shall be beyond destruction.'

"4. It soon became a large fish. Thereupon it said: '*In such and such a year that flood will come.* Thou shalt then attend to me and prepare a ship, and when the flood has risen thou shalt enter into the ship and I will save thee from it.'

"5. After he had reared it in this way, he took it down to the sea.

---

[1] *History of Ancient Sanskrit Literature*, p. 425 *ff.* (1859).

[2] In the Shatapatha Brâhmana, translated by Julius Eggeling; *Sacred Books of the East*, vol. xii., 1882.

And in the same year which the fish had indicated to him, he attended to his advice by preparing a ship; and when the flood had risen, he entered into the ship. The fish then swam up to him, and to its horn he tied the rope of the ship, and by that means he passed swiftly up to yonder northern mountain (Himâlaya).

"6. It then said: 'I have saved thee. Fasten the ship to a tree, but let not the water cut thee off whilst thou art on the mountain. As the water subsides, thou mayest gradually descend.' Accordingly he gradually descended, and hence that slope of the northern mountain is called 'Manu's descent.' The flood then swept away all these creatures and Manu alone remained here.

"7. Being desirous of offspring, he engaged in worshipping and in austerities. . . ."

Manu offered much milk-curds and clarified butter (*ghee*), and in the course of a year, lo! his accumulated prayers and sacrifices took a visible body and stood before him in the shape of a beautiful woman, the divine IDÂ. He lived with her as his wife, and they became the progenitors of a new race—"this race of Manu," as the Aryan Hindus call themselves.

3. This oldest and simplest version presents only the most general outlines of the familiar story, and if it stood alone it would not warrant any very definite conclusions. We are not even told who the fish was, and can only conjecture that it was a divine being or a heavenly messenger. The version of the Mahâbhârata comes next in point of time, it is far more complete, and contains some suggestive particulars. To begin with, we are not left in doubt as to the person of the hero, who is introduced with his usual patronymic, which shows him to be the brother of Yama, as known to us from other sources.

"There was a great Rishi, Manu, son of Vivasvat . . . (who, through a great many years, gave himself up to the practice of the most fervid religious austerities. . . .).

"Once a fish came to him on the banks of the Chîrinî, and spake: 'Lord, I am a small fish; I dread the stronger ones, and from them you must save me. For the strong fish devour the weaker; this has been immemorially ordained as our means of subsistence. Deliver me from this flood of apprehension, and I will requite the deed.'

"Hearing this, Manu, filled with compassion, took the fish in his hand, and threw him into a jar bright as a moonbeam. In it the fish, being excellently well tended, grew; for Manu treated him like a son. After a long time, he became very large and could not be contained in the jar. Then, seeing Manu, he said again: 'In order that I may thrive, remove me elsewhere.'

"Manu then took him out of the jar, brought him to a large pond, and threw him in. There he continued to grow for very many years. Although the pond was two *yojanas* long and one broad, the lotus-eyed fish found in it no room to move; and again said to Manu: 'Take me to Gangâ, the dear queen of the ocean-monarch; in her I shall dwell.'

"Manu accordingly took the fish and threw him into the river Gangâ. There he waxed for some time, when he again said to Manu: 'From my great bulk I cannot move in the Gangâ; be gracious and remove me quickly to the ocean.' Manu took him out of the Gangâ and cast him into the sea.

"When he had been thrown into the ocean, he said to Manu: 'Great lord, thou hast in every way preserved me: now hear from me what thou must do when the time arrives. Soon shall all these terrestrial objects, both moving and fixed, be dissolved. *The time for the purification of the worlds has now arrived.* I therefore inform thee what is for thy greatest good.

"'The period dreadful for the universe, moving and fixed, has come. Make for thyself a strong ship, with a cable attached; *embark in it with the seven Rishis and stow in it*, carefully preserved and assorted, *all the seeds* which have been described of old by Brâhmans. When embarked in the ship, look out for me: I shall come recognizable by my horn. So shalt thou do. I greet thee and depart. These great waters cannot be crossed over without me. Distrust not my word.'—Manu replied: 'I shall do as thou hast said.'

"After taking mutual leave, they departed each on his own way. Manu then, as enjoined, taking with him the seeds, floated on the billowy ocean in the beautiful ship. He then thought on the fish, which, knowing his desire, arrived with all speed, distinguished by a horn. When Manu saw the horned leviathan, lofty as a mountain, he fastened the ship's cable to the horn. Being thus attached, the fish dragged the ship with great rapidity, transporting it across the briny ocean, which seemed to dance with its waves and thunder with its waters. Tossed by the tempests, the ship whirled like a reeling and intoxicated woman. Neither the earth, nor the quarters of the world appeared; there was nothing but air, water, and sky.

"In the world thus confounded, the seven Rishis, Manu and the fish were beheld. So, for very many years, the fish, unwearied, drew the ship over the waters, and brought it at length to the highest peak of Himâvat. He then, smiling gently, said to the Rishis: 'Bind the ship without delay to this peak.' They did so accordingly. And that highest peak of Himâvat is still known by the name of NAUBANDHANA ('the Binding of the Ship').

"The friendly fish then said to the Rishis: 'I am the PRAJÂPATI BRAHMÂ, than whom nothing higher can be reached. In the form of a fish I have delivered you from this great danger. Manu shall create all living beings—gods, asuras, men, with all worlds and all things, moving and fixed. By my favor and through severe austere fervor, he shall attain perfect insight into his creative work and shall not become bewildered.'

"Having thus spoken, the fish in an instant disappeared. Manu, desirous to call creatures into existence, performed a great act of austere fervor, and then began visibly to create all living things. . . ."

In this version (not to dwell on its amplification and remarkable literary perfection), three important features are added, which all greatly enhance its intrinsic connection with the Chaldean and Biblical original: 1st. The Flood is said to be sent because the time has arrived for the purification of the world—or for its punishment, as it amounts to the same thing[1]; 2d, Manu is not saved alone, but is allowed to take a few human beings (not his friends or family, but the seven holy sages of Hindu legend) and "the seeds"[2]; 3d, the mysterious fish reveals himself to Manu and his companions as Brahmâ the One Supreme Deity, and speaks to them and bids Manu repeople the world[3]; only, with the bombastic exaggeration which has grown on the race since the time of the comparatively sober Veda, he does not limit his command to earth and the human race, but orders him to *create*, besides men, gods, and asuras, and all the worlds.

4. This exuberant imaginative element is still more developed in the version given in the Matsya (or Fish) Purâna, one important feature of which is

Chaldean Deluge Tablet.	*Genesis VII.–IX.*
[1] . . . The God Êa spoke to me his servant: "Men have rebelled against me, and I will do judgment against them . . . the heavens will rain destruction . . . *the appointed time has come.*	. . . And God looked upon the earth, and behold, it was corrupt. . . . And God said unto Noah . . . I do bring a flood of water upon the earth, . . . and everything that is in the earth shall die. . . .
[2] . . . I brought together and stowed into the ship . . . *the seed of life of every kind*, my family, my men servants and my women servants . . . and also my nearest friends. . . .	. . . Thou shalt come into the ark, thou, and thy sons, and thy wife, and thy sons' wives with thee. And of every living thing of all flesh . . . shalt thou bring in the ark . . . to keep them alive.
[3] (Hâsisadra is not given any mission or task, but simply translated with his wife into immortal life.) See *Story of Chaldea*, pp. 314–317.	And God blessed Noah and his sons, and said unto them, Be fruitful, and multiply, and replenish the earth.

that the divine preserver is revealed not as Brahmâ, but Vishnu, a change which could have taken place only after the schism which divided Brahmanism into several sects. One of these had adopted the rather insignificant solar god of the Rig-Veda and invested him with supremacy, as the ever watchful preserver and savior of all creation.

The Matsya Purâna introduces Manu as "a heroic king," the patient son of the Sun, who had attained so high a degree of holiness that he abdicated in favor of his son (name not given), in order to devote himself wholly to ascetic practices, which he kept up with intense fervor during a million years (!) "*in a certain region of Malaya*" (Malabar). Once, as Manu was offering an oblation to the Pitris in his hermitage, a small fish fell on his hands along with some water. Then follows the incident we are already familiar with: the fish is successively transferred into a jar, into a large pitcher, into a well, into a lake, into the Ganges, and lastly is thrown into the ocean.

"When he filled the entire ocean, Manu said, in terror: 'Thou art some god, or thou art VÂSUDEVA. [1] How can any one else be like this? Reverence be to thee, lord of the world.' Thus addressed, the divine JANÂRDANA, [1] in the form of a fish, replied: 'Thou hast well spoken and hast rightly known me. In a short time the earth, with its mountains, groves, and forests, shall be submerged in the waters. This ship has been constructed by the company of all the gods for the preservation of the vast host of living creatures. Embarking in it all living creatures, both those engendered from moisture and from eggs, as well as the viviparous, and plants, preserve them from calamity. When, driven by the blasts at the end of the *yuga*, the ship is swept along, thou shalt bind it to this horn of mine.

[1] Two of Vishnu's "thousand names."

Then, at the close of the dissolution, thou shalt be the PRAJÂPATI ('lord of creatures,' in this case 'creator') of this world, fixed and moving."

By "all living things" are certainly meant specimens of each kind, as no ship could have been imagined large enough to contain all individual living things existing, just as "plants" undoubtedly also signifies specimens, or rather the seeds of plants. As for human beings, only one holy Rishi is named by Vishnu as Manu's companion. On being questioned more closely, the god explains that the great deluge will be preceded by a universal conflagration which, following on a hundred years of drought and famine, shall consume the world so the earth shall become as ashes and the æther itself shall be scorched with heat. Even the gods and the planets shall be destroyed. Of the former only Brahmâ is to be preserved, of the latter the sun and moon. The Vedas also are to be saved in the ship. An important point on which the story of the Matsya Purâna differs from the Chaldean original is that the great cataclysm is not sent in punishment, but occurs as the ending of one *yuga* or age of the world, ushering in the beginning of another, every such change of period, in the Brahmanic belief, being marked by the destruction and resurrection of the universe. The narrative ends rather abruptly:

"When the time announced by Vâsudeva had arrived, the deluge took place in that very manner. Then the god appeared in the shape of a horned fish; the serpent ANANTA[1] came to Manu in the shape of a rope. . . . He then attached the ship to the fish's horn by the serpent rope, as he stood upon the ship. . . ."

5. This same absence of moral point distinguishes

[1] Ananta—"the Endless"; the symbol of eternity.

the elaborate and dramatic relation in the Bhâgavata Purâna.[1] There also occurs at the end of one of the great ages "an occasional dissolution of the universe," during which the world is submerged in the ocean. But another and, if possible, greater disaster befalls gods and men: the Vedas are stolen and carried away by "the strong HAYAGRÎVA," a demon of the race of the giant DAITYAS, who are forever warring against the gods and marring their good works, and it is on discovering this deed that Vishnu takes the form of a fish. The human hero of the deluge-incident is not Manu, but "a certain great royal Rishi," called SATYAVRATA, the righteous *King of Dravida*, a devoted worshipper of Vishnu, given to the usual austere practices, and who, in the then following new era, is born again as Manu, son of Vivasvat.

"Once, as in the river Kritamâlâ *(a river of the country of Dravida, or Malabar)*, he was offering the oblation of water to the Pitris, a fish came with the water in the hollow of his hands."

Here follows the request for protection, the transfer of the growing fish from one receptacle to another, and the recognition of him by Manu as the disguised god Vishnu. To the enquiry why he had assumed this disguise, the god replies:

"*On the seventh day after this* the three worlds shall sink beneath the ocean of the dissolution.[2] When the universe is dissolved in that

---

[1] Bhâgavata—"the Blessed One"; one of the most sacred names of Vishnu. This Purâna is specially devoted to the glorification of the god and his various incarnations or Avatârs.

[2] Compare Genesis vii., 4: "*For yet seven days, and I will cause it to rain upon the earth* . . . and every living substance that I have made will I destroy. . . . 10. *And it came to pass after seven days that the waters of the flood were upon the earth.* . . ."

ocean, a large ship, sent by me, shall come to thee. Taking with thee the plants and various seeds, surrounded by the seven Rishis, and attended by all existences, thou shalt embark on the great ship and shalt, without alarm, move over the dark ocean. When the ship shall be vehemently shaken by the tempestuous wind, fasten it by the great serpent to my horn, for I shall be near."

Everything happens as predicted, and when "the dissolution" is over, Vishnu slays Hayagrîva and recovers the Veda, while "King Satyavrata, master of all knowledge, sacred and profane, became, by favor of Vishnu, the son of Vivasvat, the Manu of this era."

This is the so-called MATSYA-AVATÂR, or Fish-Incarnation of Vishnu—one of ten disguises assumed on different critical occasions by the Preserver, to save the world from some great danger, and one of which is yet to come, at the end of the present *yuga*, or era. The Agni-Purâna's story, though somewhat more concisely told, is so exactly the same, with no detail added or altered, as not to require quotation.

6. The great French Sanskritist, Eugène Burnouf, who edited and translated the Bhâgavata-Purâna, was familiar with all these versions, excepting only the oldest, that of the Shatapatha-Brâhmana, which was not known in his time as yet, and he is very positive about the kernel of the story having been imported from Babylon. His only mistake lies in assigning this importation to late historical times, while there is so much, both in the subject-matter and in sundry particulars, that points to an infinitely earlier intercourse, in pre-Aryan times, between the kindred people of Dravidian India and archaïc or

THE MATSYA-AVATÂR, OR FIRST INCARNATION OF VISHNU IN THE FORM OF A FISH TO RECOVER THE SACRED BOOKS LOST DURING THE DELUGE.

Chaldean Babylon. The identity between Manu's divine preserver and Êa, the preserver of Hâsisadra, is more than accidentally indicated by the fish-disguise of the former, which is also the symbolic form of the latter, as abundantly shown by the monuments, and even appended to the god's name in one of his most momentous incarnations, that of ÊA-HAN (Oannes), the Fish-god, the civilizer of Chaldea.[1] Nor are such details to be overlooked as that the Manu of the Indian books, whose righteousness and piety make him so exact a counterpart of the patriarchs Hâsisadra and Noah, is said to be a king *of Dravida*, and is shown performing his devotions on the banks of a river of the land of Malabar, for they conclusively point to the way by which the most notable legend of the old poem of Erech travelled into India long before the future Aryan lords of the country were heard of. That it should have been part of the large mass of native lore incorporated centuries later in the religious literature of the then ruling race, was but natural—it certainly deserves the honor.

7. It is scarcely necessary to point out the identity of the final incident—the stopping of the ship on a high mountain top ("Mountain of the land of Nizir," Mount Ararat, Himâvat), followed by the dialogue between the preserved patriarch and his divine preserver, the sacrifices he offers, and the mission given him of repeopling the earth. But it may be not uninteresting to recall a bit of modern folk-lore, familiar to us from infancy, yet which it might not occur to

[1] See *Story of Chaldea*, pp. 84, 85.

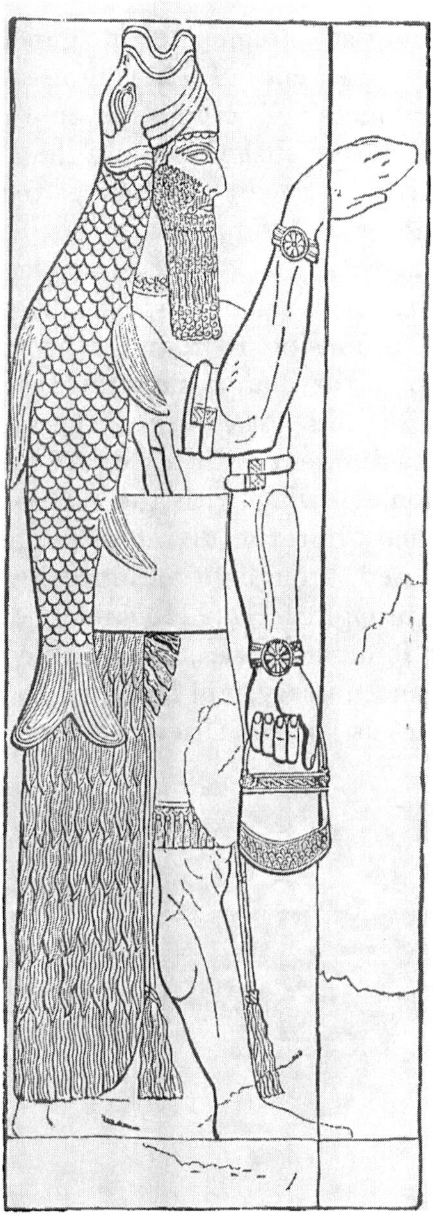

OANNES.

THE GOD ÊA.

one person in a hundred to remember in connection with the venerable old legend, of which, however, it probably is an infinitesimal crumb or chip: the North-German tale of the Fisherman and the Little Fish, so charmingly told in dialect—as heard from the people—by the great Grimm. The beginning, at least, is identical with that of the Manu legend. The fisherman catches a small fish, who begs for life and freedom, promising to requite the merciful deed, whereupon the compassionate fisherman throws him back into his native sea. The sequel, of course, is entirely different: it is a story of human greed and ambition, growing with the indulgence, and finally punished; but the divine character of the Fish is maintained throughout and most vividly, even majestically, brought forth. How many of our favorite and most familiar stories, the humble comforters of cottage and nursery, will be found to have wandered down to us by such devious and long-obliterated roads!

CHAPTER IX.

THE RIG-VEDA: EARLY CULTURE.

1. NO one who has read at all attentively the many Rig-Veda hymns and passages quoted in the preceding chapters but will have formed a more or less distinct picture of the civilization and culture of those early times, of the intellectual and moral attainments of those who could think and sing thus. Out of things said or implied, mentioned directly or in the form of similes, the picture, stroke by stroke, must have grown into a goodly general sketch, conjuring up before us much the same phases of existence as now go to make up human life: same in substance, different in garb; same in kind, different in degree. Princes and warriors and priests,—battles and rural peace,—things of the farm, the field, and the forest, and the various crafts of men,—all contribute their quota to that sketch. We must now attempt to fill it in with more life-like details, more finished lights and shades—still from the same exhaustless mine, the Aryan book of books—the Rig-Veda.

2. Philosophers of a gloomy turn have often said that the most important act of life is death, as it is

what we came into the world for. Certain it is that one of the first things we want to know about a race or nation is—what views it held upon that ever absorbing, because ever mysterious, subject, and that our judgment of that race or nation greatly depends on what we learn of those views and of the honors it paid to its dead, its treatment of their remains and the ceremonies observed in connection therewith. This being the case, we shall not have to be ashamed of our early Aryan ancestors. For not many funeral rituals can vie in beauty and significance with that which we can reconstruct from their sacred books. The tenth book of the Rig-Veda contains several hymns which could have served no other purpose, and though it is avowedly a late book, the ground matter of such parts as this must be of necessity very ancient, for the conceptions about death and future life are always among a race's oldest. From the merest perusal of the so-called funeral hymns, we see that the Âryas of the Sapta Sindhavah (and of course their later descendants), though they had a wholesome love of life and earnestly prayed that their dear ones and themselves might be spared to the full natural span of "a hundred winters," yet had no morbid terror of death, and, while keeping the departed in honor and loving remembrance, certainly did not mourn as those without hope. Their hope was that those who had gone before would lead a happy and glorified existence with the ancient Fathers of the race and their own ancestors down to the immediately preceding generation, happily waiting to be joined by their own descendants, "feasting with the gods," in the realm of good King Yama. Thither their spirits were conveyed on the fiery pinions of the Messenger Agni, whose consuming touch had power only over the grosser, earth-born parts. This is the later form of funeral, which has endured among Brahmanic Hindus to this day, and the texts which accompany it we have no trouble in distinguishing from others, that could have fitted only a rite of burial, not of cremation. These are contained in the famous hymn X., 18, one of the most beautiful of its kind in any time or country. It is evident that burial was the earlier form. The words are so suggestive of the acts performed that it is easy to imagine, from them alone, the sacred action as it proceeds. The dead is laid on the ground, on a consecrated spot. His bow is in his hand; his widow sits by him, near the head. Relatives and friends stand in a wide circle. The officiating priest places a stone at some distance from the body, within the circle; it is the dividing bourne, beyond which the living may not pass, and which MRITYU, Death, is invited to respect. As he does this the priest speaks:

"1. Depart, O Death, go thy way—the path which is thine own, far removed from that of the gods. To thee I speak, that hast eyes, hast ears: harm not our children, not our men."

Then turning to the assembled mourners:

"2. Ye who came hither in Death's footsteps, yourselves possessed of life, increasing in wealth of treasure and of progeny, be ye in spirit pure and holy!—3. Divided are the living from the dead. Propitious was our sacrifice this day, and we shall hence depart to dance and to be merry, for still is life our own.—4. This bourne I set, that of the living none may haste to yonder goal; theirs be the full-prest measure of a hundred autumns, and may this rock keep Death away from them.—5. As days on days still follow in succession, and season closely follows season, nor comes the later before the earlier, so shape their lives, Creator.—6. Fulfil your term of years, and live to a ripe old age, as many as are here, running your race in turn, and may Tvashtar, the skilful Maker, give you length of days."

Only after this blessing on the living has been pronounced, do the rites really begin. The women enter the consecrated precinct and pour oils and butter on the corpse, to the following text.

"7. These women here, not widows, wives of noble husbands, and mothers, let them first approach with unguents and with clarified butter; tearless, not sorrowing, festally attired, let them go up to the dwelling (of the dead)."

Here the brother of the deceased, as his representative, or, in default of a brother, an adopted son, a pupil, or an old servant, takes the widow by the hand, saying:

"8. Arise, O woman, to the world of life. His breath is gone, by whom thou liest,—who took thy hand once and espoused thee; thy wedlock with him now is ended." [1]

Then the same person takes the bow out of the lifeless hand, with the words:

---

[1] It is these two verses—7 and 8—which have acquired such great celebrity and importance, as affording conclusive proof that the Vedas do not yield any precedent and authority for widow-burning, but quite and expressly the contrary. The sense of verse 7 has been perverted by the change of *two letters in one word*, and some slighter discrepancies in the interpretation of another word. But those two letters really have to answer for the horrors of the suttee.

"9. His bow I take from the hand of the dead, that it may be to us for help, and strength, and fame. Stay thou yonder; we here, as doughty men, will, in battle, smite the foe."

Now the actual interment begins; the body is laid in the ground, the earth is shovelled over it, and a mound erected, the "house of death." As the different acts are performed, the priest speaks the accompanying words:

10. Hie thee to Earth, the Mother; to the wide-spread, blessed Earth; to the pious man she is a maiden soft as wool; may she guard thee from evil.—11. Open wide, O Earth, oppress him not. Be gracious unto him; shelter him kindly, cover him, Earth, even as a mother covers her infant with her garment.—12. Now let the house of clay stand firm and steadfast, borne on a thousand pillars; may it ever be sprinkled with clarified butter, and be a shelter unto him for aye.—13. I have heaped up the earth around thee, and may this clod not hurt thee as I place it over thee. May the Fathers guard this house, and Yama prepare thee a dwelling in the world beyond."

3. The stern and sober spirit of this valediction, so healthily remote from idle sentiment and lament, yet not loveless withal, and breathing a simple faith, unmixed as yet with speculation, would alone point to the extreme antiquity of the rite it accompanies. When cremation was introduced, it became necessary to modify the ritual and adapt it to new texts. These are all contained in Book X., and are so suggestive as to require no commentary. Yet the hymn X., 18, was too old and sacred ever to be discarded; it was only broken up into parts, some being recited during—or before—the cremation, and the others from verse 10 on, being reserved for the ceremony

of collecting and interring the bones. The following is this later ritual as it stands in the Domestic Laws (Grîhya-Sûtras) of Âshvalâyana. This code

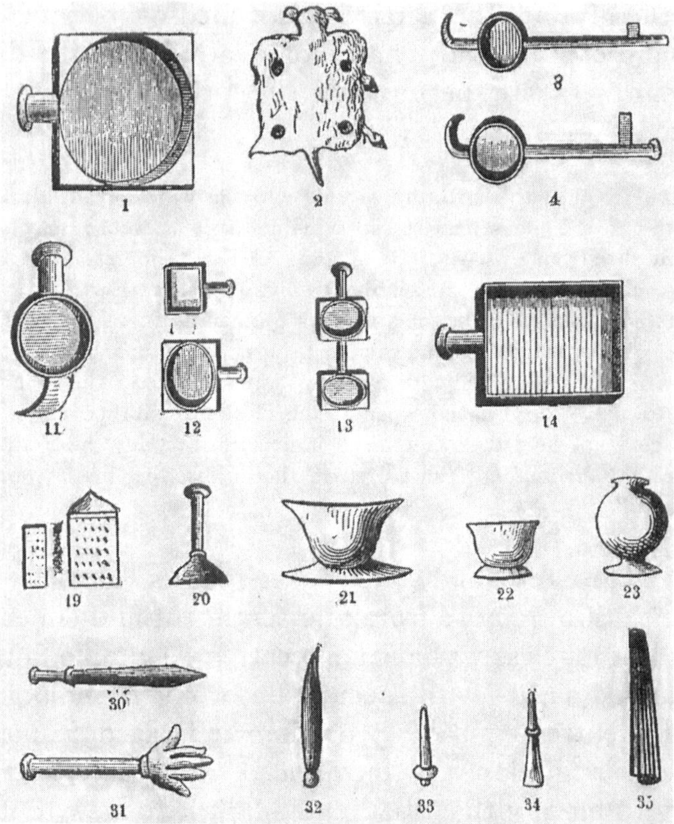

32.—SACRIFICIAL IMPLEMENTS: PANS, DISHES, SPOONS, BOWLS, CHOPPER, POKER (IN THE SHAPE OF A HAND), KNIFE, SCRAPER, ETC.

being a portion of the Vedic literature, and the funeral ritual it prescribes so exactly adapted to the texts in the Rig-Veda, we can hardly doubt its having been in use already among the late Vedic Âryas, at all events when they had reached the valleys of the Gangâ and Yamunâ, where the transition from purely Vedic to Brahmanic culture must have been finally elaborated.

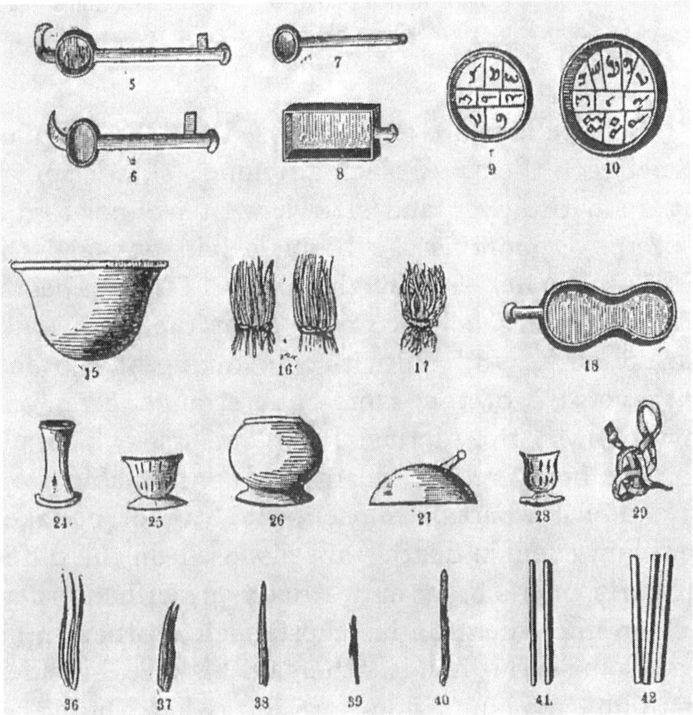

33.—MORE DISHES: BOWLS, SPOONS, LADLE FOR THE *GHEE* (MELTED BUTTER), SACRIFICIAL GRASS, KINDLING WOOD, BURNING WOOD, ETC.

4. After a spot, at a distance from dwellings, has been selected, in accordance with certain strictly prescribed requirements, the relatives of the dead man carry thither his sacred fires and the sacrificial implements he used in life, leading an animal—usu-

ally a black goat. When the procession arrives at the chosen spot, the priests walk round it thrice from right to left, sprinkling it with holy water and repeating the verse which drives away evil spirits:

> "Go hence; withdraw; depart from here. The Pitris (Fathers) have already prepared for him a place of bliss. Yama holds ready for him an abode of rest, where blessings flow as rivers night and day." (X., 14, 9.)

The three fires are then disposed and fuel is piled up between them. A black antelope's skin is spread out upon the pyre and strewn with sacrificial grass (*kusha*). Upon this the body is laid out and the widow takes her seat by the head. The rite begins with her being helped down from the pyre (with verse 8 of X., 18), and with the taking of the bow (with verse 9 of the same). A strange ceremony now follows; the sacrificial implements—which, unlike the bow, are the dead man's inalienable property, almost a part of himself, that cannot be taken from him even in death—are disposed on the different parts of his body in a strictly prescribed order; such an implement on his chest, such another on his head, some in his hands, others on his face, his sides, his thighs, etc., until none are left, when those that are hollow (ladles, dishes, spoons, etc.), are filled with melted butter. The goat, meanwhile, has been slain and flayed, and is stretched on the body, so as to fit it exactly, limb for limb, as a protection from the flames; the whole is then covered with the hide. One of the texts recited in the course of this tedious operation is verse 10 of X., 14:

"Go thy straight way, past the two dogs, the sons of Saramâ, the spotted and four-eyed; go where the Fathers, lavish of gifts, live in joy with Yama."

After several oblations have been offered on the body itself, the priest gives the word: "Light the fires together!" Omens are drawn for the future state of the deceased from the greater or lesser rapidity with which the fires reach the pyre and the body; nor is it a matter of indifference which fire reaches it first. If all three touch the body at the same time, this is said to portend the highest luck. While the process of cremation is actually going on, the priest recites numerous hymns, or parts of hymns—the appropriate verses only, most of them very beautiful. The following (X., 14) is one of the finest:

"1. Him who crossed the great mountains and spied out the road for many, King Yama Vaivasvata, the gatherer of men, honor with an oblation. Yama was the first who found the way to that home which cannot be taken from us. Those who are now born go by their own paths to the place whither our ancient fathers have departed. . . ." (*The deceased is addressed*): "Go forth, follow the ancient paths on which our Fathers went. The two kings shalt thou behold, Váruna and Yama, where they revel in bliss. There join Yama and the Fathers, where every wish is granted in the highest heaven; free from blemishes enter thy home there, with a new and shining body clothing thyself. . . . (*To Yama*): Let the two dogs, thy watchers, the four-eyed, the guardians of the road, protect this man; make him prosperous, deliver him from suffering and disease. Yama's two messengers, brown, broad of nostril, and insatiable, wander about among men, taking away their lives: may they long let us behold the sun, and give this man renewed and happy life."

Agni is then prayed to deal gently with his charge (X., 16):

"Scorch him not, consume him not, O Agni; rend not his skin or his limbs. When thou hast matured him, convey him to the Fathers. . . ." (*The deceased is addressed*): "Let thine eye go to the sun" (Sûrya), thy breath to the wind (Vâyu); to earth or to the sky go with thy several parts, into the waters or into the plants, as best beseems. The goat is thine, O Agni; her kindle with thy heat, consume with thy flames. But this man's unborn part convey, assuming thy most auspicious forms, to the abode of the righteous. . . ."

The *unborn part!* Was ever the very essence of "the soul" more felicitously expressed?—A special guide is provided, in the person of Pûshan, the protector of wayfarers. (X., 17.)

"May Pûshan guide thee hence, the wise, the universal shepherd. . . . Pûshan knows all the abodes; he guides us safely, carefully. . . . Pûshan is born on both the paths, that of heaven and that of earth, and goes back and forth between both, knowing the way to the happiest abodes." [1]

"He who is burnt by one who knows all this goes to the heaven-world (*svarga-loka*) with the smoke. This is certain." Thus the author of the Sûtra, setting the seal of comforting assurance on the directions just given for the performance of one of the most solemn and sacred of rites.

5. Before the body is quite consumed, the officiating priest recites verse 3 of X., 18 (see above), whereupon all leave the place without turning to look back.

[1] The context of this makes plain the highest (mystical) meaning of Pûshan's title "Lord of the Path," the naturalistic meaning of which presents little difficulty. (See pp. 235, 236.) The "path," the "road," which he is asked to "lay out," is that from this world to the other; the "wayfarers," whose guide and protector he is, are the dead, on their way to "the happiest abodes." He shares with Agni the office of *Psychopompos*.

On their way they bathe in pure water and, after donning clean clothes, sit where they are till night descends, when they go home and re-enter their dwellings as the stars appear, or while part of the sun-disk is still visible. The relatives of the dead lead a quiet and secluded life until the half consumed bones are collected and interred. This ceremony takes place about ten days later, on a certain, prescribed, auspicious day; it is followed by that of heaping up the earth and placing a tombstone on the spot; the verses 10–13 of X., 18, are recited as the different acts are performed. On returning home, after bathing, the relatives perform the first *shraddhâ*—rite with oblations to the deceased, who is now formally placed among the Pitris and entitled to the honors and worship which belong to that reverend company.[1]

6. The question so often asked, "Did the Vedic Âryas believe in a future life?" becomes idle indeed in view of all this. But when we would inquire more particularly into their conception of the forms which that life was to assume, we find nothing definite. We are at first inclined to feel disappointed, but soon arrive to a perception that in this reticence lie a great beauty and charm. The hope, the faith, are very firm and definite. Death, though named "the Ender," ends only what had a beginning here, in this lower world. There is in man a part that was "not born" and therefore cannot die. That

[1] "The proper meaning of *shraddhâ* is "faith." A rite performed in honor of the departed is an act of faith, for it is *believed* that it will be mutually beneficial.

part, freed by the purifying flames from the earthly dross that clings to it, is "restored" to its home to lead a happy and immortal life, reunited to the friends that have "gone before." That is all. *What* is this life? What are its conditions, its occupations? Vague imaginings only give answer. The blessed dead are admitted to contemplate the glory of "the two Kings," Váruna and Yama, where they sit under (or on?) "the tree of beautiful foliage, feasting and drinking,"(X., 135) (soma of course)—aye, and to share in the feast, for are not the Fathers called "the soma-loving"? an accepted manner of speech, to say that they (like the Ribhus) have received the gift of immortality. But all this is vague; the one belief of a materialistic character which is positively expressed and insisted on is that in a resurrection in the flesh, even while the body is supposed to be disintegrated and resolved into its elementary component parts. In the same breath with which the priest addresses the departed, saying, "Let thine eye go to the sun," etc., he also bids him enter his heavenly home "clothed in a new and shining body," "free from blemishes," and immediately goes on:

> "Give up again, Agni, to the Fathers, him who comes offered to thee with oblations . . . *let him meet his body*. Whatever part of thee any blackbird, or ant, or serpent, or beast of prey has bitten, may Agni heal all that, and Soma, who has entered into the Brâhmans."

One thing appears certain: that the "new body" with which the departed was to "clothe himself," must have been imagined as a glorified, probably an unsubstantial one. Was this a foreshadowing of the "astral body" of modern esoterism? Why not? Almost everything in India can be traced to the Veda. The most definite impression we receive, however, is that of a floating, a hovering, in infinite space, in a flood, a sea of light. This impression is given and renewed by a number of passages all through the Rig:

"Sûrya follows Ushas, the radiant, as a lover follows a maiden, where the god-fearing live from age to age and go from bliss to bliss." (I., 115.)

"In the midmost heaven, they lead a life of bliss." (X., 15.)

"O might I enter Vishnu's blessed abôde, where the god-fearing dwell in joy; for they are the friendly host of the mighty strider, and the source of sweetness is in Vishnu's highest place . . . resplendent with light is the supernal abode." (I., 154.)

And that most beautiful song of longing, of hope, of adoration, IX., 113 ("Where there is eternal light," etc.—see p. 180), is all bathed in and pervaded with the light that never was on land or sea.

7. So much for "the god-fearing." And what of the others? Was there a hereafter for *them*, and how did the Âryas of early Vedic times picture it? If they did, it was in even more indefinite and misty guise. In conformity with Aryan dualism, if the good live in eternal light, the wicked must be consigned to darkness everlasting, and that is about all. Váruna and the other Âdityas especially are the avengers of wrong, as we have seen, and they cast the unrepentant into a "pit," which is as greatly dreaded as their famous "nooses" or "fetters"—darkness, disease, and death.

"The keeper of Rita is not to be deceived. Full of wisdom, he surveys all beings. Those that are displeasing to him, the ungodly, he casts down into "the pit. . . ." (II., 26, 8.)

"Remove your nooses, O gods [the Âdityas]; remove my sin; seize me not as a bird in the nest. Be with us this day, O worshipful ones; I will tremblingly nestle against your heart; protect us, ye gods, from the devouring wolf and from falling into the pit." (II., 29, 6.)

"Indra holds no kinship with those who press no soma; he is neither friend nor brother to them; he casts the unfriendly into the depths." (IV., 25, 6.)

"Cast down our enemies into the nethermost darkness," a Rishi prays to Indra.

8. It was not unnecessary to dwell thus long on the vagueness, the indefiniteness—we might say the spirituality—of the Aryan conception of a future life as we find it expressed in the Rig-Veda, because it differs so exceedingly from what we are familiar with in later, Brahmanic, times. And the change soon comes. In the Atharva-Veda already we are confronted by a thoroughly materialistic paradise and hell. We are informed exactly of the pleasures which wait on the blessed dead, and the torments which the wicked dead suffer. The few delicate touches, which show us the Fathers "revelling in bliss" with Yama and Váruna under "the tree of beautiful foliage," which is the sky with its stars, are spread and flattened out into a broad description of prosaic delights: every pious inmate is approached by beautiful, luminous, gentle cows, who never kick and are always ready to be milked; mild breezes and soft showers cool the air; there are ponds of clarified butter, streams of honey, and rivers of milk and curds. No one is rich or poor, powerful or oppressed.

The beautiful verse of IX., 113—"Where there is happiness and delight, where joy and pleasure reside, where the desires of our desire are attained"—is interpreted in the sense of the most earthly delights, —with the assistance of the fascinating Apsáras, the *Houris* of Indian mythology. In short we have before us Islam's paradise in its completeness. On the other hand the pit of nethermost darkness has become a hell—a "hell of hells"[1]—where great criminals sit in a pool of blood and eat hair for food, while the tears of the wronged and the water in which the dead are washed are their only drink. Yama, too, the luminous, the gentle king of happy spirits, who was dreaded and terrible only because Death *is* terrible after all, even at his mildest, changes fast into the grim ruler of the various hell-worlds (*tâla*, *nâraka*), the ruthless judge and torture-master, tricked out in all the cheap horrors of the later popular devil. It is not yet so in the Artharva-Veda, to be sure, but there already the son of Vivasvat wears a forbidding aspect as the impersonation of Death itself—"Yama-Mrityu."

9. There are various kinds of Pitris: the Fathers of individual families, those of tribes, and the Fathers of the race. It is a general way nations have, this of making tutelary spirits of their remote ancestors, to whom they then look for aid and protection. They generally go the further length of making those ancestors god-descended, thus not only keeping up the dear and sacred family bond through all ages past and to come, but also asserting their own con-

---

[1] *Talatala*, the original form of the Greek *tartaros*.

nection with a heavenly home, their own originally divine descent. This is but a way of expressing the dimly perceived higher and better self, the consciousness of the presence in us of a something divine, self-acting and independent of our will. Other nations have raised to this dignity their ancient heroes, the fighters and lawgivers, the founders of their states and royal houses. But the Âryas of India, true to the early developed sacerdotal bent of their race, claimed descent from their ancient sacrificers and priestly poets (Rishis)—their saints—and, through them, kinship with the gods. Thus arose the sacred hosts of heaven—the Angiras, singers of hymns, the Bhrigus, whose name connects them with the sacrificial fire,[1] and many others, generally in troops or groups; also the numerous single saints or holy patriarchs, severally honored as the progenitors of sacred priestly families or of the human race itself, such as Vasishtha, Vishvâmitra, Kashyapa, and numbers of others, later ones, not to be found in the Rig-Veda. To all these are ascribed not only extensive power, together with the constant desire to interfere in and direct the affairs of men, but the highest cosmical functions, even to active participation in the work of creation and that of preserving the worlds. This we find clearly indicated already in the Rig, foreign as it is to

---

[1] "Bhrigu" comes from a root, BHRIJ—"to burn, roast," and must have been an old name of "flame," of Lightning itself. It survives in Greek *phlégô*, Latin *flagrare*, *fulgere* (to blaze, to *fl*ame, *fl*are, *fl*ash, be resplendent), with all their derivatives, chief of which is the Latin *fulgur*, "lightning bolt," not to speak of their numerous posterity in our modern tongues.

the exuberant extravagances of later Brahmanism. What else but such cosmic work—expressed in conventional Vedic phrase—are the Angiras doing, when they "help Indra break open the stable and let out the cows"? or the Fathers (Pitris generally), when they are said to have adorned the black horse with pearls (to light the stars in the sky), and to have placed darkness in the night and light in the day or to have spread out heaven and earth in concert with Soma? (VIII., 48, 13), or when they are called "warders of the Sun" (X., 154, 5), and said to have "brought the great light"? It should be remembered, though, that they do all this, not in the naturalistic order of things, but through the spiritual power conferred by the faultless performance of rites and sacrifices. It is as impersonations of ritualistically perfect prayer that the Angiras "break open the stable," because such prayer has compelling force over nature, and brings rain, sunlight, keeps the world in place, etc. It is as the representatives of this same spiritual power that the Pitris have so much to do with ordering or producing natural phenomena. Nevertheless the path of the Fathers is distinct from that of the gods, for it is that of death (see X., 18, 1, and 88, 15), by which all men are to follow. It is meet therefore that the oblations offered to both should also be different. So, while the Fathers are soma-lovers and soma-drinkers and have a general invitation to come and partake of it at sacrifices with the gods, special offerings are reserved for them at their own particular commemorative festivals—the *shraddhâs*—principally a kind of wheat cake or dumpling called *pinda*, one of which is provided for every Pitar invited.[1] For there were different kinds of *shraddhâs*, on different occasions and anniversaries. Some were sacred to the memory of one departed relative, some to that of the family dead generally, and some to that of all the pious and glorified dead—a sort of All Saints' Day. The great hymn, X., 15, would seem to have been fitted for a solemnity of the latter kind; but the last verse shows it to have been used at funerals. Of course that particular verse may have been added specially for such occasions and omitted at other times.

"1. Let the Fathers arise, the upper, the lower, and the middle,[2] the offerers of soma, they the kindly ones, versed in sacrificial lore, who have entered spirit-life—let them be gracious to our invocations.—2. We will pay reverence to-day to the Fathers who departed in early times, and to those who followed later; to those who reside in the earth's aërial space and those that are with the races of the beautiful dwellings.[3] . . . 4. Ye Fathers, who sit on the sacrificial grass, come to us with help; these oblations we have prepared for you: partake of them; bring us health and blessings unmixed.—5. We invite the soma-loving Fathers to partake of the food they love, placed for them on the grass; may they come and hear us, help us and bless us.—6.[4] . . . Do us no injury, O Fathers, on account of any offence which we, after the manner of men, may have

---

[1] Hence the name: *pinda-pitriyajna*—"cake oblation to the Fathers."

[2] The three worlds, the three birthplaces of Agni.

[3] This has been understood by some as meaning the races of men, while others interpret "the races of gods." More probably the latter.

[4] This is approximative. One translator has "intercede for us," another "speak graciously to us," etc. But there is no doubt about the help and blessing sued for.

committed against you.—7. Sitting in the lap of the dawns, give wealth to the pious mortal, to your sons, O Fathers, grant them plenty and prosperity.—8. May Yama, rejoicing with our ancient Fathers, the best, the gracious, who have come to our soma-oblations, drink his fill, eager, with the eager Vasishthas.—9. Come, O Agni, with those who are longing and athirst, sitting with the gods, versed in sacrifice, praised in hymns by Rishis, with the benevolent Fathers, the true, the wise, who dwell in light.—10. Come, O Agni, with the thousands of ancient and later Fathers, eaters and drinkers of oblations, who are reunited with Indra and the gods, who praise the gods in light.—11.—Come hither, ye Fathers that have been tasted by fire (cremated). . . . 13. The Fathers who are here, and those who are not here; those we know and those we do not know; thou, O Agni, who knowest all beings (*Jâtavedas*), knowest how many they are. . . . 14. Along with those Fathers who were burned and those who were not burned by fire,[1] and who are gladdened by our oblation in the middlemost heaven,—with these, O Self-resplendent, convey this body to the spirit-world and shape it according to our desire."

10. If a people's ideas on future life and their treatment of their dead yield a good standard by which to judge of their spirituality, their ideas on domestic life on earth and their treatment of their women form an even more decisive test of the degree of ethical culture they have attained. Here, again, and on the same showing—that of the Rig-Veda,—we have no reason to be ashamed of our early Aryan ancestors. The direct evidence it affords is scant, if we count by pages, being contained almost entirely in the great wedding hymn, X., 85; but it is quite sufficient to show that the position held by the Aryan woman in Vedic Penjâb was a most honorable, nay, exalted one, which later influences and

[1] In allusion to the two rites of cremation and burial.

developments changed by no means for the better, but rather, and very much, for the worse. Nor is only the later dire doom of widows meant by this—unknown, as we have seen, to the early Âryas,—but also, and even chiefly, the woman's home life, as wife and mother. She appears to have been on a footing of perfect equality with her husband, subject absolutely to no one in his house, not even to his parents, let alone his brothers and sisters. What is more, she was a *willing* bride; and, though it was customary to make the official demand through third persons, it is more than probable that her consent was made sure of first, and indeed that she was frequently awarded the privilege of choosing out of many suitors. This fine old Aryan custom endured far into the classical Brahmanic period, and the epics frequently show us noble maidens holding solemn levees on such occasions—the so-called *Svayamváras*—a custom abundantly vouched for by the traditions of other nations of Aryan stock—Greeks, Teutons, Celts. In her father's house the Aryan maiden enjoyed the usual shelter and cherishing, and her brothers were her born champions and protectors. For we find passages in the Rig-Veda where the fate of the brotherless orphan maiden is deplored because she has to look out for a husband herself, and those who wrong such a maiden are said to be "born for that fathomless place"—the nameless pit of darkness into which Váruna casts evildoers.

11. The sacredness of the marriage tie and the marriage rite is impressed on men in truly Vedic guise by a description of a marriage in heaven, which

forms the introduction to the wedding hymn. This marriage of Sûryâ, the Sun-maiden, with Soma, is evidently presented as the prototype of all earthly marriages, and as attesting the divine origin of the institution. That in this case, as always, their heaven was only a reflection of their earth, never occurred to the pious performers of the rite, for of *that* no people is ever conscious,—not the masses, anyhow. Sûryâ is the daughter of Savitar, who gives her, "consenting in her heart," to Soma. The Ashvins are the bridegroom's best men (who made the demand), and Agni is the bride's escort (who rides before her and brings her to her husband). The naturalistic interpretation of the myth presents no great difficulty. The Sun-maiden (only another form of the Dawn), can very well wed with Soma in any of his capacities. Perhaps, though, his sacerdotal aspect, as king of sacrifice, is the most appropriate, not merely because of the Dawn's connection with holy rites, but chiefly because the development of the simple myth-nucleus shows Sûryâ to have undergone the same spiritually ritualistic transformation as so many originally naturalistic myth-persons, into an impersonation of Prayer. The enumeration of her bridal paraphernalia is wholly symbolical: "Beautiful in sooth were Sûryâ's bridal robes": they were made of different sacred metres. Heaven and earth were the frame of her chariot, that chariot itself "her heart's thought," hymns were the beams that supported it, "the two ears" the wheels, "knowledge" was her cushion, "seership" her jewelry; sacred songs were the diadem on h r brow and ornaments in her hair; the Rig and the Sâman were the steers who drew her chariot "along the easy path of heaven." We have here all the pomp and circumstance of Vedic sacrifice, and the symbolical description ends with this remarkable verse: "Two wheels of thy chariot, O Sûryâ, the Brâhmans know, according to truth; but the third, the hidden one, is known only to the deep-inquiring." The allusion is here to "the two worlds," visible and known to all, and to that third world, mysterious, invisible, which is the very sanctuary where the origin of things (of the gods) is forever hidden from mortal sight, and towards which the searching thought of the seers is ever drawn. Yet in the face of all this, the popular impression seems to have been that the marriage of Sûryâ and Soma is that of the Sun (feminine, as in Germany) and the Moon. Two verses (18 and 19) of the hymn admit of no other interpretation: "These two children wander one after the other by their wonderful power; they go dancing round the place of sacrifice.[1] The one beholds all existing things; the other, ordaining the times, is born again and again." The harmonious cöoperation of the two rulers of the heavens is presented as the model of an harmonious wedded life.

12. The rest of the hymn is really a collection of wedding formulas and sayings, loosely strung together, unlike the great funeral hymn, X., 18, which presents such a beautifully sequenced, harmonious whole. But the action is as clearly discernible

---

[1] "Through aërial space" says Zimmer.

through the accompanying text. So we can easily imagine the bride's parents giving her their final blessing and formally releasing her from her duty to her own home and family, to transfer it to the new, as they recite these verses:

"Straight and thornless be the path by which our friends go to their wedding. May Aryaman and Bhaga conduct us all; easy to manage be the household. . . . I release thee *here*, but not *there*. There I bind thee with auspicious bonds, that these twain, O gracious Indra, may be rich in sons and rich in substance.—May Pûshan lead thee hence, taking thee by the hand; may the two Ashvins drive thee on their chariot. Hie thee to the house which thou art to rule."

Some blessings follow the bride on her way, one of which is a most remarkable and direct assumption of "heredity" as a lurking danger:

"*The diseases which follow the brilliant bridal procession from her own clan, let the venerable gods drive them back to whence they came.* Let not waylayers molest the wedded couple; may they pass safely through all dangers on well laid out paths; may all fly far away who bring evil.—Beautifully is the bride adorned; come, all—contemplate her; then, after wishing her happiness, depart to your homes."

The actual marriage rite consisted in the bridegroom's taking the bride's right hand and leading her three times around the household fire, from left to right, and in the sacred formula he recited in so doing:

"By thy right hand for happiness I take thee, that thou mayest reach old age with me, thy husband. Aryaman, Bhaga, Savitar, Puramdhi (?), gave thee to me, to rule our house together."

"To thee, O Agni, was Sûryâ first presented with her wedding escort; so now give thou this bride to her husband, and offspring besides."

It is not clear who recites this last verse. Scarcely the husband. At her arrival at her new home the bride is welcomed with these verses:

"Here may delight be thine through wealth and progeny. Give this house thy watchful care. Live with thy husband, and in old age may you still rule your household.

"Here now remain, nor ever part; enjoy the full measure of your years; with sons and grandsons sporting, be glad in heart within your house."

It is the husband who pronounces the final benediction. These verses are the most important and significant, as determining the position of the future housewife:

"Children and children's children may Prajâpati give us; may Aryaman bless us with wealth unto old age. Enter, not evil-bringing, thy husband's homestead. Within the home may man and beast increase and thrive.[1] Free from the evil eye, not lacking wedded love, bring good luck even to the beasts; *gentle of mind, bright of countenance, bearing heroes, honoring the gods, dispensing joy.*[2] . . . This bride, O gracious Indra, make rich in sons and in happiness. Grant her ten children, and spare her husband as the eleventh. —Rule then and govern over thy husband's father and mother, over his sisters and his brothers.—May all the gods unite our hearts. . . ."

How absolute the wife's and mother's supremacy, as here proclaimed and consecrated by the husband! And what a terrible falling off from this high standard is presented by the condition of women, as modified in later Brahmanism, and especially Hinduism, by all sorts of foreign deteriorating influences

[1] The text has "the two-footed and the four-footed."

[2] Might not the passage in italics be labelled for all times, "The Whole Duty of Woman"?

and of speculative lucubrations, the condition which endures to this day and makes of the bulk of Hindu women one of the most deeply oppressed, pitiable fractions of humanity. Even the popular life of modern nations—especially the Slavs and Germans, where the son's bride enters her husband's family in an avowedly subordinate capacity, and becomes almost the bond slave of his parents, his sisters' servant and scapegoat—falls far short of the ideal of domestic life set up by our so-called "barbarous" early ancestors. That such an ideal implies monogamy is self-evident.[1]

13. Of course the entire marriage ritual did not consist of only hymn X., 85, any more than the entire funeral service consisted of hymn X., 18. Both are completed and supplemented by verses from other hymns, from the Rig-Veda and the Atharva-Veda, the latter being little more than amplifications of the Rig texts, and mostly lacking their concise directness, their simplicity. On the subject of love and marriage customs much more may be gathered from scattered passages, mostly illustrative similes and illusions—as when a poet says to Indra and Agni, inciting them to liberality, "I have heard that ye are more lavish in gifts than a son-in-law or a bride's brother," and others. Some spells, too—

[1] The texts which have been adduced as evidences of polygamy prove at most the existence of harem-life, not that of polygamy as a legal institution, under which several or many wives have equal conjugal rights. Besides, it is always the rich and the powerful who are alluded to in such passages—and thëse have at all times allowed themselves (and been able to afford) exceptional latitude in their domestic arrangements.

of very rare occurrence in the Rig-Veda,—are preserved; one by which a girl lays the household asleep—from her old grandfather to the watchdog—in expectation of her lover's visit; one for the defeat and destruction of a rival. The Atharvan abounds in such passages and incantations, but our object at present is to reconstruct Aryan life in its more unalloyed form, as presented on the internal evidence of the purer Rig.

14. There are a few so-called hymns which are really nothing but short poems, descriptive of this or that particular feature of contemporary life, good or evil—what the Germans would call *Culturbilder*,—and have nothing to do with religion; and if they have been incorporated in the collection, contrary to the rule that every hymn shall be addressed to some god or gods, it must have been because their great literary merit and cultural importance was early recognized, and the framers of the sacred canon saw no better way of preserving them. Some of them greatly confirm us in the impression that the Aryan moral code, as mirrored in the Rig-Veda, bore, on the whole, a singularly pure and elevated character. So nothing can be more nobly beautiful, in feeling and wording, than the following, on almsgiving, or rather on the duty of giving, of helping, generally (X., 117):

"1. The gods have not ordained hunger to be our destruction. Even those who are full-fed are overtaken by various forms of death. He who gives, becomes not poorer for it, but the miser finds no comfort.—2. He who, himself well provided, repulses the poor man, whom he knew in better times, when he asks for food and drink, such a man also finds no comforter.[1]—3. He is the bountiful man who gives to the lean beggar who comes to him craving food. Success attends that man in the sacrifice and he secures for himself a friend in the future.[2]—4. That is no friend who will not share with a friend who comes to him seeking for sustenance. Let every one depart from such a man—his house is no place to stay at—and seek for some one else, who is liberal, though he be a stranger.—5. Let them who can do so, help those in need; let them look down the long path (of futurity): for oh, riches revolve like the wheels of a chariot; they come now to one, now to another.[3]—6. In vain the fool obtains food: I tell the truth,—it becomes his destruction. No friend will be his, nor companion; he who has his food to himself has his sin to himself."

15. The leading vices of the Aryan race have always been drinking and gambling. The Rig-Veda bears ample witness to both. The materialistic symbolism of the Soma-worship greatly helped to confirm, almost inculcate, the former, by the stress it laid on the supposed divine (fiery) element in the sacred intoxicant.[4] Gambling—in the form of dice—is also frequently alluded to.[5] But we would scarcely expect, at so early a date, a portrayal of a gambler's career, so modern, we may say, so alive with actuality, as that given in the so-called hymn

---

[1] Roth's translation is followed in this verse.

[2] Muir's rendering. Grassmann has: "He meets the same treatment when he asks for assistance," and Roth: "He willingly meets the cry for help."

[3] We must remember that the wheel simile was probably not trite three thousand years ago. And yet—it *may* have been even then: it is used so glibly! and occurs repeatedly.

[4] We have seen that against the abuse thus fostered an important part of Zarathushtra's reform was directed.—See *Story of Media*, etc., p. 118 *f.*

[5] See hymn to Váruna, p. 223; to Ushas, I., 92, 10, p. 223.

X., 34. It is the gambler who speaks in his own person, and no *habitué* of Monte Carlo could lay bare more remorseful and helpless self-condemnation in the ruthless grip of the enthralling passion, or depict more graphically its disastrous effects on home and family.

"1. The tumbling, exciting dice delight me as they roll on the board; they are to me like a draught of the soma-plant growing on Mount Mûjavant.—2. My wife never quarrelled with me or irritated me. She was kind to me and to my friends. But I, for the sake of the hazardous dice, have spurned my devoted spouse.—3. My mother-in-law detests me; my wife rejects me; the gambler finds no comforter. Nor can I see what a gambler is good for, any more than a valuable horse worn out with age.—4. Others pay court to the wife of the man whose wealth is coveted by the impetuous dice. Father, mother, brothers, cry out: 'Who is the man? Take him away bound!'[1]—5. Resolve as I may, 'I will play no more, for all my friends desert me,' the moment I hear the rattle of the brown ones [dice], I hasten to the tryst, as a woman to her lover.—6. The gambler goes to the assembly [of gamblers] full of confidence: 'to-day I win.' But the dice inflame his desire by making over his winnings to his opponent.—7. They are like fish-hooks that pierce the flesh; deceivers, that burn and torture. After a brief run of luck, they ruin the winner; yet are they to the gambler sweet as honey.—8. Their troop of fifty-three [in allusion probably to the points] disports itself after rules as fixed as Savitar's ordinances. They bow not to the wrath even of the fiercest—the king himself makes obeisance to them.—9. They roll downward; they bound upward;—having no hands, they overcome those who have. These celestial coals, when thrown on the dice-board, scorch the heart, though cold themselves.—10. Forsaken mourns the gamester's wife, the mother for the son who roams she knows not where. It vexes him to see his own wife and then to observe the wives and happy

---

[1] He probably having staked his own liberty and lost—the depth of disgrace.

homes of others.—11. In debt, anxious, eager for money, he goes to other people's house at night.[1] In the morning he yokes the brown horses [the dice]; by the time the fire goes out, he breaks down miserably.—12. To him who is the leader of your great host, the king of your whole band, I will not begrudge gifts—I swear it with outstretched fingers.—13. 'Let the dice alone; tend thy farm; rejoice in thy goods and be content. Here, gamester, is thy cattle; here thy wife.' This word spake to me the adorable Savitar.—14. Make peace then and take pity on me, nor entice me any longer with your dire witchery, O dice! Let your wrath, your enmity, abate. Let another pine, a bondsman to the brown ones!"

16. That the vice of gambling should breed the worse vice of cheating at play stands to reason. Accordingly we find it mentioned in the Rig-Veda with a frequency and familiarity which shows the practice to have been a common one, though accounted very heinous.[2] It even would seem to have been a favorite accusation to hurl, out of malice, at an enemy, on a par and jointly with that of the still more abhorred practice of witchcraft. Such, at least, is the suggestion which appears to be offered by a very curious passage in the long so-called "cursing hymn" of Vasishtha (VII., 104). The fanatical, irascible old Rishi was a vigorous and comprehensive curser, and, while he was about it, anathematizing the foes of his people and of his gods, he gave a "raking" to his own personal enemies, vehemently repudiating certain aspersions on his character:

---

[1] To beg, or to steal?

[2] It is evidently alluded to in the verse quoted on p. 223 (I., 92, 10): Ushas *cheats* men out of their lives, as the "clever gambler" his associates out of the stakes.

"He who attacks me with lying, angry words when I go my ways, thinking no evil, let him, O Indra, come to nothing, as water that is taken up in the hollow of the hand. . . . If, O Agni, I *were* a cheating gamester,—if I *did* honor the gods hypocritically! But why art thou wroth with me? Cast the slanderers into misery.—Let me die this day if I ever practised witchcraft, or ever destroyed any man's vital power by spells: may he, therefore, lose his friends who falsely called me wizard.—Him who said to me, the pure, 'A wizard art thou,' who, himself a fiend, boasted 'I am holy'—him may Indra slay with his great weapon, may he fall into the nethermost depth."

17. The first part of this effusion is the most energetic piece of cursing in the whole Rig-Veda, and speaks volumes for the Vedic Âryas' capacity for wholesome, whole-hearted hatred of their native foes or religious antagonists. Indra and Soma are jointly implored to deal with them:

"Indra and Soma, burn the devils, destroy them, throw them down, ye two Bulls, the people that grow in darkness! Hew down the madmen, suffocate, kill them; hurl them away and slay the voracious.—Indra and Soma, up together against the cursing demon! May he burn and hiss like an oblation in the fire! Put your everlasting hatred upon the villain who hates the Brâhman, who eats flesh, and whose look is abominable.[1]—Indra and Soma, hurl the evildoer into the pit, even into unfathomable darkness! May your strength be full of wrath to hold out, that not one may come out again."[2]

The third part consists of a string of curses on a variety of evil spirits and goblins that lurk in the night—some invisible, some in all sorts of uncanny

[1] "Brâhman" here has the meaning "he who prays rightly," and may apply to the priests as a *class*, not yet as a *caste*, except as there may be said to be "caste feeling," or strong dislike and aloofness, on the part of the Âryas against the natives—Dasyus.

[2] Max Müller's rendering.

forms—dog, owl, cuckoo, hawk, birds that whirr through the darkness, defiling sacrifices—and ends with a prayer to Indra, for protection against "the fury of the wizards" and the wiles of witches, and for the destruction of both them and "the idols with the crooked necks."[1] On the whole it seems as though Vasishtha and his particular people—*i. e.*, the tribe whose *purohita* he was, for whom he prayed and sacrificed—were molested and beset in this manner to an unusual extent. Which may not appear strange if we remember that Vasishtha was the uncompromising foe of the native races, the fierce champion of Aryan exclusiveness, the founder of Brahmanic orthodoxy and priestcraft in their more offensive forms. It is no wonder that those whose enlightenment he opposed, whom he despised, abominated, and cursed, should have retaliated in all direst ways known to them. (See pp. 320 *ff.*)

18. The few instances we find in the Rig-Veda of the active use of spells may certainly be classed under the head of "white"—or harmless—magic, since they consist almost entirely of the gathering and handling of herbs, apparently not even accompanied by conjuring—except in the case of a woman, who digs up a plant to make a love potion of, for the routing of a rival in her husband's affections (X., 145). She appears to have been successful, for there is a song of triumph and exultation at having got rid of all intruders and secured her proper place as sole ruler of her household. But the general and approved

---

[1] Grassmann.

uses of herbs and plants were evidently for healing purposes, as shown in the so-called "Song of the Physician"—really an herb-healer, who wanders about the country with his box of ashvattha-wood. The good man makes no secret of the fact that his chief object is a livelihood. This charming *Culturbild* abounds in little homely touches which throw just the side-lights we are so eager for on the manners and ways of those otherwise unattainable times. The healer begins by formally announcing that he will sing the praise of "the herbs, the verdant" which are among the oldest of things.

". . . Hundred-fold are your ways, thousand-fold your growth, endowed with hundred various powers: make me this sick man well. . . . Give me victory as to a prize-winning mare. . . . For I must have cattle, horses, and clothes. . . . You will be worth much to me, if you make my sick man well. He in whose hands herbs are gathered as numerous as nobles [or princes, *râjans*] in the assembly, he is accounted a skilful healer, a tamer of fiends and diseases.—The watery, the milky, the nourishing, the strengthening, —here they all are together, to heal what is wrong with him.—The herbs' fragrance escapes [from the box] as a herd from the stable, to earn a good price for me—and thy life for thee, good man. . . . No let or hindrance keeps them back; they are as the thief who breaks through fences. . . . When I, O ye simples, grasp you sternly in my hands, sickness flees away, as a criminal who fears the grip of the law. In your progress from limb to limb, and from one articulation to another, ye drive sickness before you, as surely as a severe judge's sentence.—Flee then, sickness, flee away—with magpies and with hawks; flee on the pinions of the winds, nay of the whirlwinds."[1]

19. That our herb-healer was no exception with his "eye to business," is most graphically shown by

[1] Roth's translation is here followed.

the following short and humoristic piece, which, besides, is of importance as bearing witness to the absence of caste divisions in the thorough confusion of pursuits which it describes:

> "We men have all our various fancies and designs. The carpenter seeks something that is broken, the doctor a patient, the priest somebody who will sacrifice.—The smith, with well-dried wood, with anvil and with feather fan, to activate the flame, seeks after a man with plenty of gold.—I am a poet, my father is a doctor, my mother a grinder of corn. With our different views, seeking for gain, we run (after our respective objects) as after cattle."

20. It is, of course, possible to extract from the hymns infinitely more material—mostly fragmentary—than we could attempt here for the reconstruction of Vedic life. This has been done exhaustively by H. Zimmer, in his unique and most valuable work, *Altindisches Leben*, to which we refer the more inquiring of our readers; with the remark, however, that he takes his material from all the four *Samhitâs*, and therefore presents probably a somewhat later picture of Aryan culture than that which we have, in this chapter, striven to evolve almost entirely from the Rig-Veda alone.

CHAPTER X.

THE RIG-VEDA: SACRIFICE.

1. IT seems at first sight as though a chapter on Vedic culture must be wofully incomplete if it does not include a picture of the status of the priests in the social and moral order of those early Aryan communities, and a description of their ministrations, which may all be comprised under the one head of YAJNA—Sacrifice. But it is just because of the immense extent of the subject, and its immense import not merely in the actual life, outer and inner, but in the evolution of the religious and philosophical thought of one of the world's great races, that it cannot possibly be disposed of among other matters, but imperatively demands—when it cannot have a book —a chapter to itself.

2. The priests who confront us in the Rig-Veda, though already forming a distinct class (not caste), are simpler in attitude and in organization than their successors, the Brâhmans. Instead of the large array of priests of various rank, specialists in numberless details of ritual, there is the priest generally—*hotar*, and the tribal or family priest—*purohita*. That the ritual, however, was already complicated and exceed-

ingly precise, is shown very clearly through all the Rig texts. The priests' services were appreciated and rewarded accordingly. There is a whole class of texts—usually verses appended or interpolated—known under the name of *dânastutis.* They consist of lists of the presents received from wealthy chieftains and royal patrons, intermingled with praises and blessings, and frequently mentioning the occasion which prompted the largess —*dakshinâ* is the technical word. Historically these are, of course, among the most valuable texts, from the glimpses of contemporary life and manners which they afford. We meet there, too, familiar names—of tribes known to us from the historical portions; of famous kings belonging to the more powerful dynasties. Thus Divodâsa, king of the Tritsu, is one of three kings who are named as having given a large bounty out of the booty gained in a successful expedition against Shambara, the mountain chieftain: 10 steeds, 10 baskets full of raiment and other articles, 10 lumps of gold, 100 head of cattle. Another time Sudâs, Divodâsa's son, is one of the givers. Then it is a king of the Turvasu who presents two illustrious priestly families with 60,000 head of cattle, while a king of the Yadu rewards the Kanvas for a victory over the Parsu (a Persian tribe) which is attributed to the efficacy of their prayers, with a *dakshinâ* of 300 horses, 10,000 cattle, many double teams of oxen. Again Trâsadasyu, grandson of the powerful Puru king Kutsa, sends the Kanvas 50 women slaves. Handsome chariots and harness are highly prized; the horses are frequently said to be "richly adorned with pearls."[1] One Kanva priest exults in advance over an expected *dakshinâ* in cattle, which he has reason to think will be so abundant that people will say Vala, the cave-demon, has given up his kine. Of course, the more generous the givers the higher the praise. The Kanvas appear to have come in for more good things than any of the others. It is still one of their family who boasts of having received from a king with the significant name of "Wolf to the Dasyu" (*Dasyavevrika*), on occasion of a great victory over black native tribes, a *dakshinâ* of 100 white cattle as shining as the stars of heaven, 100 bamboo reeds, 100 dogs, 100 tanned hides, 100 mats of a certain grass, 400 bay mares. A certain king Tchitra must have shown unheard of liberality, to judge from the praise bestowed on him: "Only Indra gives as much, or wealth-dispensing Sarasvatî," exclaims the priest (again a Kanva); "Tchitra is a real king [*râjan*], all the others are wretched little kinglets [*râjaka*], those that live along the Sarasvatî. But he—he is like a thundering rain-cloud, and gives a thousand myriads." (Of what? not specified.)

3. Sometimes approval is expressed in a cool, almost condescending tone: "Not the most carping mortal, ye warriors, can find fault with you." But when a priest is dissatisfied, he is not slow in expressing his displeasure, usually in the form of sneers and sarcasm. A Prithu (Parthian) king, who gave

---

[1] This must have been a customary way of ornamenting harness and bridles; hence the simile of the starry night-sky as a black horse adorned with pearls.

only two horses and twenty cows for a victory, is taunted with being hard to get anything from, while another is likened to a Pani chief, and dismissed with the ironical remark: "That is why our loyal singers [priests] have so much to say in praise of Bribu, that most liberal of princes. The *maghavans* [princes] give out of ostentation." This ill-natured remark from a Vasishtha sounds like the grim old Rishi himself. But no modern diatribe could surpass in scathing irony two *dânastutis*, evidently composed with the intent of securing to the givers immortality of the undesirable kind:

"O friends," the first begins, "get up your enthusiasm: how are we to give due praise to Shara, the generous, the liberal giver?—Many of the singers [priests] who spread the sacrificial grass will praise thee as is meet, O Shara, if thou dost present them with a calf apiece, as thou didst us.—The noble son of Shuradeva, the wealthy lord, brought us three each a calf, leading it by the ear, as one does a goat, that she may stand and let her young nurse her."

Another is indignant at having received, for some elaborate hymns to the Ashvins, of his composing, only a chariot without team or harness. He makes fun of it, holding the divine Twins responsible for his disappointment.

"From the Ashvins, the rich in horses, I received a teamless chariot; it pleased me much in sooth.—It will have to push on somehow with me to the place where men drink soma, the handsome wagon.—Let me have nought to do with dreams or with wealthy misers: they are equally unsubstantial." [1]

[1] For chapter and verse to all this, see Ludwig *Rig-Veda*, vol. iii., pp. 273–277, where he gives a list of all the *dânastutis*, which may then be looked up in the hymns.

4. It is evidently of set purpose that these—we may well call them mercenary—effusions were incorporated in the sacred *samhitá*, embalmed in it as flies in amber, for the edification of all coming generations. They were to inculcate, by precept and example, by praise and withering scorn, the paramount duty, not merely of honouring and supporting the priesthood, but lavishing, heaping gifts on them. Though, when we read of all these tens and sixties of thousands of horses and cattle, these untold "myriads" of unknown things, we cannot rid ourselves of a suspicion that these wonderful lists were sometimes deliberately swelled, the better to enhance the priests' merits and claims. There still, however, remains enough, even with this margin, to astonish and puzzle—the rewards are so out of all proportion to what seems to us the simple ministration of conducting religious services—unless there was more in them than meets the eye at first sight. Which, indeed, was the case. For the priests were not thought merely to assist and lead the devotions of their people, in praying and rendering thanks for happy events, such as a victory gained, a successful expedition, for the prospering of crops and cattle, for increase in offspring and wealth. No, these results were directly attributed to and thought to depend on, the praying (*brahma*) of the priests, their text-reciting, the sacrificial rites performed by them; they would not have taken place if the priests had not done these things or had not done them in the right way. This is perfectly illustrated by a very effective passage in one of the historical Vasishtha hymns:

"Irresistibly smiting, O Indra and Varuna, ye stood by Sudâs; ye heard the *brahma* that cried aloud to you: successful was the sacrifice of the Tritsu *purohitas*.—Both hosts called on you in the battle, for victory and booty, when ye helped Sudâs and the Tritsu, when they were encompassed around by the Ten Kings.—The ten confederate kings who do not sacrifice could not conquer Sudâs. Efficient was the prayer of the partakers of the sacrifice [the priests], the gods came to their sacrifices.—To Sudâs, hard pressed in the Battle of the Ten Kings, ye gave help, O Indra and Varuna, when the Tritsu, white-robed and with braided hair, humbly prayed to you."[1]

Now the "ten kings," as we have seen, were not all Dasyu, or wholly Dasyu, and if they invoked the Aryan gods in battle, they must have sacrificed to them. But they (*i. e.*, their priests for them) must have blundered, for sacrifice, when rightly performed, *compels* the result. What bounds, then, should a king set to his liberality in gratitude for a victory which he *owes* to his *purohita* and assisting priests?[2]

5. This notion of obtaining certain exceptional boons through the force of prayer and sacrifice, is not as foreign to our mode of thinking as that which ascribes to them, as produced by them, the regular

---

[1] Meaning the Tritsu priests, this being the priestly garb.

[2] Not all priests were wealthy, though. We meet here and there curiously suggestive plaints like that of a priest who laments that rivals crowd him on all sides, till he is ready to faint with want and exhaustion and care gnaws him as a mouse gnaws its own tail, "me," he adds pathetically, "me, thy singer, O Indra, mighty one!" (x. 33, 2–3). We have seen in the satirical song ix. 112, that the priest's "seeking for someone who will offer libations" was a social fact as universally admitted as that of the carpenter looking for a job or the doctor for a patient. (See p. 381.) We may be sure that such poor bread-winners did not belong to illustrious and ancient priestly families, like those of the Vasishthas, Kanvas, Bhasadvâjas, and the like.

recurrence of the beneficent phenomena of nature—rain and light, the alternation of night and day, the coming of the dawn and the sun, of the moon and the stars. Nor is there anything unlogical in this: once it is admitted that the gods do their work in response to sacrifice, the converse proposition is by no means far-fetched, namely that they will *not* do it *unless* so solicited. It remains for us to find out wherein lay this compelling power of the *brahma* (ritualistically correct prayer), and the *yajna* (ritualistically perfect sacrifice). This is equivalent to the question: What was the essence and nature of Aryan sacrifice?

6. Abel Bergaigne, of all Vedic scholars, has treated this question most thoroughly, has gone deepest and nearest to the root of it. The conclusions to which his investigations lead him can be summed up as follows: Sacrifice is an imitation of the chief phenomena of the sky and the atmosphere. Now it is a notion as old as the race, that a thing ardently wished for may be made to come to pass in reality, by performing or reproducing that thing in effigy. This strange aberration was one of those that died hardest, for we find it very much alive down to the later Middle-Ages, in the form of that spell of the Black Art which consisted in making a wax effigy of an enemy, then melting it over a slow fire or sticking a pin into the place where the heart should be, in the expectation that the person treated thus in effigy would waste away with consumption or heartbreak. The custom of executing criminals, of burning or hanging obnoxious persons in effigy,

when they are out of reach, is clearly based on the same primitive idea. And if efficient for evil, why should not the same spell be efficient for good also? Sacrifice, looked at from this point of view, would be, then, a sort of beneficent conjuring, in accordance with the bright and genial Aryan spirit, while the dark and lowering Turanian nature revels in spells and incantations for malicious, injurious purposes.[1]

7. Two things are needful: light and rain—Fire and Water—Agni and Soma. They are produced in two of the three worlds—the Sky and the Atmosphere. The Devas (powers of nature) are always producing them. Agni is always being "found" in the waters: as Lightning in the cloud-sea (*samudra*), as the Sun in the golden waters of the sea of light. The Cows are always being found and brought back to be milked: the cloud-kine with their rain-laden udders; the light-kine with their golden milk—the Dawns and their rays. This is the gods' allotted work, and they do it unremittingly, following "the broad path of Rita" (the Law). Only they need sustenance, to invigorate them and keep them ever living, ever young; this sustenance they receive by partaking of the "drink of immortality"—the *amrita*—the heavenly Soma which they distil ("press"), out of the watery elements somewhere in the highest heaven, the hidden world, the Sanctuary of the Universe. All this work, this everlasting keeping of

[1] Bergaigne mentions a custom which he was told of as still existing on the Isle of Ceylon, and which consists in placing near a growing fruit a pasteboard effigy, of the size which it is desired that the real fruit should attain.

the world-machinery going, has an object: to benefit the race of men that dwells on earth (of course the righteous, well-thinking men, *i. e.*, the Âryas, and such of the others as they approve of). It is but meet, therefore, that men should try to please the gods, keep on good terms with them,—not merely out of gratitude, but also because, should they be displeased, they might sulk and "strike," and then where would this earth and its denizens be? Thanks can be expressed in words and gifts, and the gods shall have both, unstinted. Only, the bulk of men can feel, but not always express; are willing to give, but do not always know what and how to give, and the consequences of giving offence might be serious. So men will do wisely to leave these things to their poet-priests, as their mouth-pieces and dispensers—those superior, mysteriously gifted individuals, human, yet more than human "into whom the divine Vâch has entered" (see p. 270), and who, therefore, can commune with the gods without fear or diffidence, with ever-flowing, river-like, musical speech, who are on intimate terms with those bright, beneficent, but awful Powers, understand their nature, their likes and dislikes, and know exactly what offerings must please them, and how to make such offering acceptable. But it is no more than human nature, in returning thanks for favors received, to request the continuance,—if possible, an increase—of them. The thanksgiving then becomes a prayer, the thank-offering a bribe. The whole transaction degenerates into a bargain. The gods are praised and entreated, *encouraged* to do their work and bestow boons, and it is *expected* they will. For even mere mortals—let alone higher beings, noble and mighty—would scorn to accept and not give. Here again the priests, as specialists in matters of etiquette and intercourse between "the two worlds," (which are said to be as nearly connected as two neighboring villages), are the natural go-betweens and masters of ceremonies. These matters are all-important, for the very existence of the universe, and, therefore, of men, is at stake, and, to attend to them properly, the priest must devote to them all his time, his undivided study, and attention. It is only right therefore—on the principle of division of labor—that he should be exempted from other duties, and only just that he should be supported in dignified comfort and remunerated on special occasions, when his ministrations have proved particularly and palpably successful. This is the conception of sacrifice and priesthood we are familiar with from our study of the religions of antiquity. But the specifically Aryan sacrifice, which has been developed by Indian Brahmanism to its uttermost possibilities, and endures, to a great extent, to this day, goes a step further, the step indicated by Bergaigne.

8. It is understood that the Devas are beneficent and well-disposed, as willing as they are able, to bestow benefits and—what is more important still—to "keep the world going." [1] Still, it were very desir-

[1] It may be remarked incidentally, that this is the original and literal meaning of "Rita." The root RI means "to flow," and we find it in the Greek *rheô* and again in our own *river*. The Supreme Law, the Cosmic Order, is the even flow of natural phenomena—the natural sequence of things; "*Es ist der Lauf der Welt.*"

able to be able to *coerce* them—of course by fair means—into doing what we want: that would make things absolutely safe for men. Here comes in that old, old notion—of producing a thing by an imitation of it. On the "finding" of the heavenly Agni and the heavenly Soma, in obedience to the "fixed ordinances" of Rita, the preservation, the continuance of the world hangs as on a hinge. Let Agni and Soma, then, be "found" (produced) here on earth, strictly according to the "fixed ordinances" of sacrificial Law and Order—the *rite*, the *ritual*.[1] The sacred act on earth shall be the companion piece to that in the sky and the atmosphere; the counterpart shall be as exact as inventive ingenuity, aided by poetical imagination, can make it. The terrestrial Agni is "found," "hidden" in the plants—the wood of the *aranî*, and in the terrestrial Soma, the plant that gives the fiery drink which warms and invigorates, exhilarates and inspires, till men cry out: "We have drunk the Soma, we have become immortal, we have known the gods"; in the waters, too, for it is in water that the bruised and broken stems are laid, to start the fermenting process which evolves the fiery element of the beverage. This water is the counterpart of the heavenly Waters, the Mothers of Agni, and the large kettle or vat into which the Soma is pressed is called the *samudra*. The other ingredient is milk—the milk of the earthly cow, the counterpart of the heavenly and atmospheric Kine of Light and Rain. Agni and Soma were

[1] Really the same word as "Rita";—it is more than an identity of root.

both "brought from afar," the former "from Vivasvat," the latter from "the house of Tvashtar"—*i. e.*, from the sky, luminous and frowning; therefore the consecrated spot on which the sacrifice takes place, becomes "the seat of Vivasvat." The *vedî*, (the place spread with sacred *kusha* grass), is "the seat of the gods." Thunder is the voice, the speech, the song of the gods—the divine VÂCH. This Vâch has "entered into the Rishis," and they sent her forth as the sacred word—the well-worded prayer, the beautifully fashioned hymn. Thunder also is the crashing of the grinding stones, and rain the Soma that drops through the sieve or the woollen filter and flows and runs, noisily, abundantly, into the vats—as the rain which drops, and flows from the sky, amid thunder and lightning, is Soma, *amrita*. The counterpart is complete. The sacrificial rite—the earthly Rita—reaches out and across, as a bridge between "the two worlds," till it joins and is merged into the heavenly Rita, and both together form "the broad and ancient path which leads to the one goal"—the path along which Saramâ took Indra and the singing Angiras,[1] and another "broad path" appears—the broad path of the heavenly *dakshinâ*—the rich gifts (light, rain, and all the regularly recurring beneficent phenomena) with which the "liberality" of the Devas rewards the sacrificing of men, as the earthly *dakshinâ* is the reward conferred on the officiating priests by the "liberality" of their patrons, whether royal or private.

9. That such compelling power is really ascribed

---

[1] See pp. 256–261.

to the ritualistically perfect sacrifice, is proved by texts so explicit and numerous, that the only difficulty is that of selection. Within our limits, two or three must do. They do not leave room for much doubt. The first is taken from an elaborate rain-hymn (X., 98), by a Rishi of the name of Devâpi. He begins by invoking Brihaspati, the "Lord of Prayer," and imploring him to inspire him and "place in his mouth" "a strong unfailing hymn, to procure rain" for Shantanu, his patron. Brihaspati personally responds to the appeal:

> "The honeyed drops shall fall from heaven; Indra, bring us a thousand wagon loads. Devâpi, officiate as *hotar;* sacrifice at the right time and honor the gods with an oblation."

Now for the result:

> "The Rishi Devâpi, son of Rishtishena, having undertaken the office of *hotar*, found favor before the gods: he poured the heavenly waters from the upper sea down into the lower. The waters were detained by the gods in that upper sea; they flowed down, let loose by Devâpi. . . . Brihaspati gave the efficient rain-prayer to the Rishi."

In I., 88, the Maruts are entreated to come on their "lightning-laden, shining chariots," drawn by steeds fleet as birds, and making the earth resound with the noise of their wheels. "Through many days" the Rishi then says, "the anxious ones repeated this prayer addressed to you and plied the rain-compelling sacrifice; by their prayers, by their hymns, the Gotamas upset the water-vat, to drink." A bold figure, but perfectly intelligible and thoroughly Vedic. We find it again, slightly altered and developed, in another rain-hymn, X., 101. The vat or barrel has become a well:

"Prepare the buckets, pull the thongs [used as ropes, to lower and raise the buckets]; let us empty the water-abounding, exhaustless well![1] The well with well-made thongs and buckets, the water-abounding, exhaustless, I now am emptying."

Of course knowledge, great and varied, is required to make the prayer and sacrifice efficient.[2] The least omission or error would be fatal. For, sacrifice being an imitation or reproduction of the celestial drama, it must run as smoothly, be as free from blemish. A hitch or blunder in the sacrificial *rita* must produce a corresponding disturbance in the heavenly Rita or even course of the Cosmic Order, and the safety of the universe is endangered. This is what is meant by the constant allusions to "knowledge," the great value of "knowledge," to "the wise," those "who know," by "the right path," on which the gods (especially Agni and Soma, the two "Kings of Sacrifice") are entreated to maintain their worshippers. Hence also the great danger for laymen of meddling with such things. It is said: "The ignorant has enquired of him who knows; being instructed by him who knows, he acts. And this is the good of instruction: he obtains [literally 'finds'] the flow of

[1] Slightly contradictory. But Vedic metaphor must not be held quite to modern rhetorical standards.

[2] Prayer and sacrifice always go together: *yajna* and *brahma;* and when sacrifice alone is mentioned, prayer is implied. "Sacrifice without prayer (*abrahmâ yajnah*) is said not to be pleasing to the gods; even Soma pressed without prayers (*abrahmâno*) leaves Indra indifferent. (VII., 26, 1.)

the rushing ones [the Waters]."[1] All these premises being accepted, we shall scarcely be inclined to dispute the assertion, that only *that* king rules prosperously in his own country, obeyed by his subjects, and irresistibly wins his enemies' treasures *and also those of his own people* (characteristic, this!), before whom walks a *purohita*.

10. We see now why the ancient Fathers, the first sacrificers—*i. e.*, the inventors of sacrifice—are held in such high honor, rank as nearly, if not quite, the equals of the gods, are credited with so many cosmic functions,—nay, are said to have actively assisted in the work of creation itself. (See pp. 364–365). Sacrifice was their work of art, the richly patterned web, the endless chain or warp,—one end of which they hold, in their high place in the abodes of eternal light, while the other descends unbroken down to earth, held firmly by "those who know," and add, thread by thread, to the woof. Each *mantra* recited, each *sâman* sung, each sacrificial rite accomplished, is such a thread. And still the tissue grows, and still the pattern spreads, resplendent and many-colored, and the sacrificial shuttle is never still.

11. If the terrestrial sacrifice is a reproduction of the celestial phenomena on which hinges the existence of the world,—in mythical phrase the "finding of Agni and Soma"—and thereby influences them and helps produce them, the question quite logically presents itself: "And what produces them up there?" and it is no less good logic (mythical logic) to reply: "Celestial sacrifice of course." Somebody

[1] A. Bergaigne's rendering, *La Religion Vedique*, i., p. 137.

sacrifices in heaven, to accomplish the same results that we strive for—and attain—by sacrificing here on earth. Forthwith the mental process is reversed. The entire universe becomes a huge place of sacrifice and every act of the great heavenly and atmospheric drama is strained so as to make it the parallel of a corresponding act in the sacrificial drama on earth. Agni, as the Sun, is the offspring of the golden *aranî* manipulated by the Ashvins; Agni's blazing log burns brightly in the sky; the sea of light out of which he rises in the East is the *ghee* (clarified butter) made of the golden milk of the dawn-cows, which feeds the flame on the altar and makes it leap and soar; the pillars of light that rise straight out of the darkness at daybreak are the sacrificial posts; the slanting rays, so visible before the sun is yet in full splendor, are the sacrificial grass with which is strewn the *vedî*, the seat of the gods, which is the great orient East itself. As Lightning, Agni is found in the celestial ocean, is drawn from the motherly waters by "the ten fingers" of heavenly sacrificers; is struck out of the rock (the black thundercloud). The storm-drama can easily be converted into a celestial Soma-sacrifice, simply by reversing the symbolism of the terrestrial Soma-sacrifice. This is done all through Book IX. of the Rig-Veda (the Soma book) till at times one is puzzled to know whether one is in the sky or on earth. Soma is the divine race-horse sent out "to win the prize"; the "sisters" or "maidens" are the waters which fondle him as the ten fingers the stem of the plant; the voices of the storm—thunder and the singing of the Maruts or

Angiras—are the hymns and the noise of the grinding-stones; the sky is the filter or sieve; the *samudra* is the kettle where the divine drink is mixed; earth is the receiving vat; the atmosphere is the space between the sieve and the vat; the heavenly cows whose lordly Bull Soma is, are the added draughts of milk. And Agni (as Lightning) is the *hotar*, the officiating priest, the wise conductor of the sacrifice. In a word, as has been well and pithily said—"the whole ritual of sacrifice, with all its offerings and appurtenances, its priests and offerings, is bodily translated from the sphere of human action to the world of the gods."[1]

12. The next question in our mythical Catechism is "Who are the celestial Sacrificers?" One answer is so obvious as to suggest itself: The ancient Fathers, the sainted Pitris—the progenitors of the illustrious priestly races, and, as tradition often has it, of the human (or at least Aryan) race generally. This suits admirably with their semi-divine nature: inventors or "finders" of Sacrifice "up there," who transmitted their knowledge and power, like a precious milch-cow, to their descendants on earth. Of the many texts which convey this conception the most uncompromisingly decisive is the short hymn X., 181, which

"tells not only that Vasishtha, Bharadvâja, a troop of ancient sacrificers, who are not named, brought or received from the sky, from the Sun, from the Creator's luminous abode, from Savitar, from Vishnu, this or that oblation, this or that particular prayer, but that they 'found the supreme essence of sacrifice which at first was out of

[1] H. W. Wallis, *The Cosmology of the Rig-Veda*, p. 79.

their reach and hidden' (verse 2), that they 'found by prayer the *fallen* sacrifice, the first sacrifice which went to the gods.' That is the word: *fallen*. Like fire, sacrifice has fallen, dropped down from heaven, and men only send it back there, as fire is sent back to heaven."[1]

Celestial sacrifice, then, is the model, terrestrial sacrifice the copy. There is more than imitation; there is absolute identity, since the two chief elements are the same—Agni and Soma, in their terrestrial forms. That is why the power, the effects are the same. Here is a fine text in point: "As thou, O Agni, didst perform the office of *hotar* on earth; as thou, O Jâtavedas, didst perform the office of *hotar* in heaven,—so, with this oblation, honor the gods,—make our sacrifice successful this day as thou didst make that of Manu." (We know that Manu's sacrifice after the Flood resulted in re-peopling the earth. See pp. 337, 339.)

13. But, as we go through the Rig-Veda, picking out and sorting the texts that bear on Celestial Sacrifice, we find that it is not only the ancient Fathers who are actors in it, but quite as often *the gods themselves*. The result is always the same, of course; they "find" Agni and immediately institute him their *hotar* and *purohita*, (themselves becoming the rich patrons—*yajamânâh*—for whose benefit the sacrifice is performed), whether in his atmospheric form as Lightning, or in his heavenly form as Sun,—for Sûrya is expressly called the *purohita* of the gods (VIII., 90, 19). "Mitra and Váruna," one poet tells us, "and all the Maruts, O mighty Agni, sang a

[1] A. Bergaigne, vol. i., pp. 107 *f*.

hymn to thee, when thou didst rise, O Sûrya, above the races of men."[1] This is clear; scarcely less so is the following: "Three thousand three hundred and thirty-nine gods did homage to Agni; they fed him on *ghee*, they spread out for him the sacred grass, and instituted him *hotar*." Another result of the god's sacrificing is *the sending of Agni down to earth* for at the same time that they make him their priest, they also make him "their messenger" (another form of the "Descent of Fire"). There is a hymn (X., 88) which describes in most of its verses the sacrifice performed by the gods. "The world was hidden, swallowed in darkness." The gods sacrificed, and Agni was born; there was joy in heaven and on earth, as he covered with his splendor the two worlds and the atmosphere. Into "this Agni" (the fire lit in heaven) the wise, holy gods poured libations, singing hymns—then they divided him into three parts or forms, and placed one as Sun in the sky—to "travel forever inextinguishable and shine day by day." The hymn is long and elaborately mystical; but this is the substance of it.

14. But to whom is the celestial sacrifice offered? That is a question which does not seem easy to answer. As regards the Fathers, the matter is simple enough: they sacrifice to the gods, of course. But to whom can the gods sacrifice? Two texts (both late) contain the answer. One is worded in general terms, the other is explicit. The former (X., 90, 16) says that "the Devas having, by sacrifice, earned their right to sacrifice, attained to the highest heaven,

[1] III., 14, 4. Bergaigne's rendering, vol. i., p. 115.

where the ancient gods are." The second text (X., 151, 3) occurs in the hymn to Shraddhâ (Faith):—"As the Devas worshipped with faith the mighty Asuras . . ." The "gods," therefore—the Devas—sacrifice to the "ancient gods"—the Asuras—Dyâus, and Vàruna, and probably Rudra, Tvashtar, Parjanya; the younger, Indo-Aryan gods to the mighty primeval-Aryan deities, whose rule is supreme, whose abode is the highest, and whom, in the end, they supplant—or nearly so.[1]

15. Transcendental symbolism could take only one step more—and took it. There is a certain number of hymns addressed, not to one particular deity, but to many, or to all, collectively (*vishvedevâh*). Of these X., 65 is particularly fine, because it invokes all the great nature-gods by name, with a brief mention of their attributes and functions. It is a masterly epitome of Vedic mythology. It has the following astonishing verse:

> "Drinking with Agni's tongue, heavenly, pure in mind, they sit by the centre of the sanctuary. They powerfully supported the heavens, they poured down the waters. Having invented [literally 'begotten'] the sacrifice, *they offered it to themselves*."

Other texts might be adduced, pointing to the

---

[1] Bergaigne suggests that this may have had something to do with the transformation which the meaning of the word "Asura" underwent. A subtle feeling of hostility crept into and pervaded the attitude of the followers of the second, Indo-Aryan, towards the few grand and particularly awful deities of the first, Proto-Aryan, dispensation, and by the usual process, that feeling was transferred to those deities, and a certain unfriendliness, even malignity, ascribed to them. The Greek theogony presents a parallel case.

same conception,[1] but they are not considered very clear and readings vary somewhat. This one, however, does not seem to be doubtful. We are so used to the idea of sacrifice being an offering tendered to higher beings in thanksgiving or supplication, that our mind at first refuses to grasp what seems so utter an absurdity as these same higher beings sacrificing *to themselves.* A bit of etymology may help us. If we take the word "sacrifice" in its literal Latin sense—that of "sacred action," not "offering" in particular, "oblation" being the proper word for that—the strange paradox will assume a somewhat different aspect. Celestial sacrifice, as a "sacred action," performed by the gods to "delight themselves," presents nothing absurd or incomprehensible. This is about as far, however, as mythical metaphysics *can* go,—and, having got so far, perhaps we too have found the "supreme essence" of Aryan sacrifice "in the highest heaven."

16. After the spirit, the letter; which means in this case the actual forms and rites of the terrestrial sacrifice. On this all-important feature of Aryan India, which Brahmanism developed to such unheard-of proportions, we can gather but little technical information in the Rig-Veda; for that we must go to the Brâhmanas and the Sûtras. The pressing of the Soma, indeed, is abundantly described and illustrated in the Rig. But the great Soma-sacrifice of the classical and epic period, though not more holy in essence, was, in practice, a very different affair: requiring preparations on an immense scale, taking up

---

[1] VI., 11, 2; X., 81; X., 7, 6.

many days with introductory rites and attendant ceremonies, and giving occupation to numbers of priests going into the hundreds, all of whom expected—and received—ample *dakshinâ;* so costly, in fact, as to be beyond the means of private devotion, and reserved for the most imposing public occasions, such as (and especially) the inauguration of a King or the celebration of a great victory. On such occasions it was very frequently preceded by the Horse-sacrifice (*ashvamedha*), the distinctively royal sacrifice, which could be performed also by itself, usually by kings desirous of offspring. Epic poetry will, in due time, furnish us with gorgeous and most detailed descriptions of this gigantic pageant. For the present we must be content with such information as we can find in the Rig-Samhitâ. And that in truth is unexpectedly complete, once again bringing before us a stage of ritualism and symbolism strangely at variance with the long-alleged "simplicity" of religious conception and worship in the Rig-Veda. This information is contained in two hymns (I., 162 and 163) which celebrate the sacrificial Horse, now describing with almost repulsive realism the actual slaughter and burning of the victim, now divinizing him in mystic strains which leave one in doubt whether it is an animal that is spoken of, or himself, Soma the King.—This assimilation, one might almost say identification, is certainly intentional, carrying out the idea of the reproduction of heavenly things on earth. For Agni (both as Lightning and as Sun) and Soma are, as we have seen, the heavenly coursers, and the horse on earth is their representative, their symbol, and when specially devoted to them, becomes one with them—"goes to them" in death. Indeed he is of their race—*devajâta.* Therefore he is said to have "three forms," his

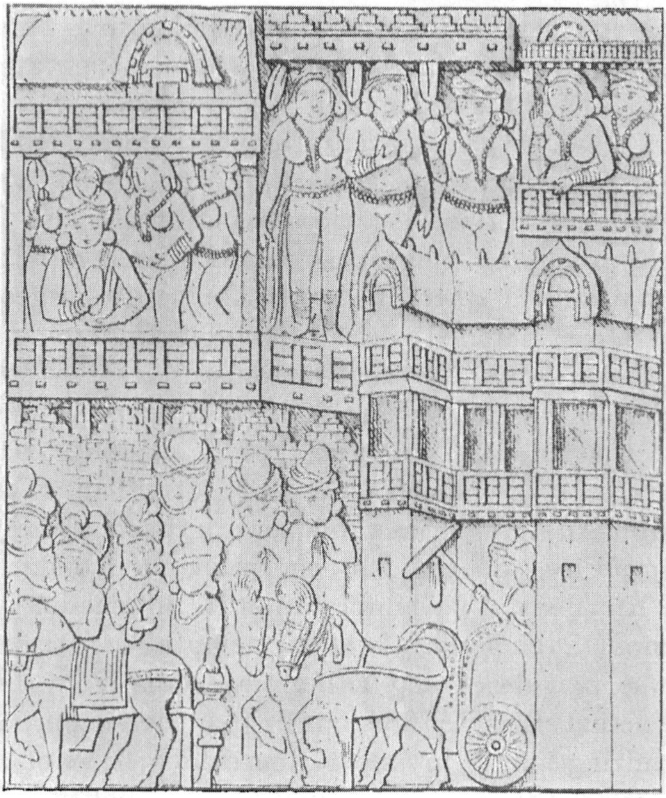

34.—PART OF A HORSE-SACRIFICE PROCESSION (LATE WALL SCULPTURE).

"highest birthplace" is with Váruna, his winged head "speeds snorting along the easy, dustless paths of heaven." Winged is his body, his spirit pervading as the wind. And immediately after this:

"The fleet courser is proceeding towards the place of slaughter, his spirit intently fixed on the gods. The goat precedes him, the wise singers follow. The courser is proceeding towards the most glorious of abodes, to the Father and the Mother" (probably Dyâus-Heaven and Aditi, for he is once called an Âditya); "for even this day will he go to the gods, most welcome to them. . . ."

The description of the actual sacrifice is given with such completeness in I., 162, that it will serve our purpose almost without any commentary:

". . . When they lead by the bridle the richly adorned courser, the omniform goat [*vishvarûpa*] is led, bleating, before him. . . . Pûshan's allotted share; he will be welcomed by all the gods. . . . Tvashtar will conduct him to high honors. When men lead the horse, according to custom, three times around [the place of sacrifice], the goat goes before [and is killed first] to announce the sacrifice to the gods.[1] The priest, the assistant, the carver [who is to divide the carcass], he who lights the fire, he who works the pressing-stones, and the inspired singer of hymns—will all fill their bellies with the flesh of this well-prepared offering. Those who fashion the post [to which the victim is to be bound], and those who bring it, and those who fashion the knob on top of it, and those who bring together the cooking vessels—may their friendly help also not be wanting. The sleek courser is now proceeding—my prayer goes with him—to the abodes of the gods, followed by the joyful songs of the priests; this banquet makes him one with the gods."

Here follows a sort of litany, long and tedious, but very curious, in which all that is the horse's own, even to the particles of his flesh that may adhere to the post, or the axe, or the nails of the sacrificing

[1] The goat is always Pûshan's "allotted share" at sacrifices; the same at funerals. (A funeral is a sort of a sacrifice, for the dead man is "offered" to Agni and by him conveyed to the gods, like any other offering). This is why a goat is harnessed to Pûshan's chariot, quite as much as on account of his rustic functions and character.

priest, and the fat that may drop from the pieces of flesh, roasting on the spit—is bid follow him and be "his own among the gods"; the same with anything that has ever been used by him or for him—his halter and blanket, his trappings and accoutrements; all the grass he ever ate, or stepped or lay or rolled on; all the vessels and implements and dishes that are going to be used to dress and cook and serve his flesh. This consecration is accompanied with the rather idle wish that nothing that will be done to him may cause him pain—neither the fire, nor the smoke, nor the seething pot; and the hymn ends as mystically as it began:

> "May not thy breath of life oppress thee when thou goest to the gods; [*i. e.*, 'may thy death-struggle be brief and easy']; may not the axe injure thy bodies;[1] may not a hasty, unskilled carver, blundering in his work, cleave thy limbs wrongly. Forsooth, thou diest not here, nor dost thou suffer any injury; no, thou goest to the gods along fair, easy paths; the two *harits* [Indra's] and the dappled deer [the Maruts'] will be thy comrades. . . ."

17. One verse (8) of I., 163, evidently describes the sacrificial procession. "After thee, O Horse, comes the chariot; after thee, *the man;* after thee the hosts of the girls. . . ." As the verse ends with the statement that all the world is anxious to win the Horse's favor and that the gods themselves recognize his "heroic might" (if not even his superiority in heroic might), it has generally been taken mythically, all of it; while it is very proba-

[1] Bergaigne positively reads "bodies" in the plural, and interprets it as a mystical allusion to the threefold form of the Agni-and-Soma-horse, with which the sacrificial horse was identified, as seen above.

ble that we have here another of those mixtures of myth and reality which are so confusing and misleading. In the Horse-sacrifice as originally instituted, and practised too, "the man" was indeed led after the horse, as the goat was led before him, and for the same purpose—to be sacrificed. For there can be no doubt whatever that human sacrifices were part of ancient Aryan worship. As shown elsewhere,[1] certain premises being accepted, nothing could be more logical, necessary, even juster; it merely meant going the whole length, and it is hardly probable that any race missed this stage of cruel logic, when sentiment is not yet sufficiently developed to stay the hand armed by what is mistaken for reason. The Indo-Âryas outdid all others in plain-speaking consistency. They openly classed man among animals, counting him as the noblest and first, but still as one of them, *primus inter pares*, as has been felicitously remarked. Sacrifice was of two kinds: bloody and bloodless. Five "animals" are declared fit victims for the former: man, the horse, the steer, the sheep, and the goat. At a solemn sacrifice all five victims are to be immolated. Vedic rituals of undoubted authenticity—Shrauta-Sûtras and texts in the Yajur Veda, all Shrutî "revealed"—give the most detailed instructions as to the occasions of such sacrifices and the manner of them. One of these occasions was the building of city walls, when the bodies of the five victims were to be laid in the water used to mix the clay for the bricks, to which their blood was supposed to give the necessary firm-

[1] See *Story of Assyria*, ch. iv., especially pp. 118–129.

ness—and probably, consecration. Another was the Horse-sacrifice, *ashvamedha*. Then there was the out-and-out human sacrifice—*purushamedha*—which ranks still higher, and for which the victim must be a Brâhman or a Kshatriya, to be bought for a thousand cows and a hundred horses. An intensified form of *purushamedha* is that in which a large number of victims—166 or even 184—men of all sorts and conditions—are immolated. The Shatapatha-Brâhmana itself, the most important of all, describes this wholesale slaughter-ceremony. But the ritual suddenly breaks off and drops into narrative, giving us the following legend: "Then, when the fire had already been carried around the victims (all bound to the several sacrificial posts) and they were just about to be killed, a voice was heard to speak: 'O man, do not accomplish it! If thou didst accomplish it, one man would eat the other.'" To understand this, we must remember that the flesh of victims was partaken of by the sacrificers. It is therefore probably—and nothing could be more natural—the horror of cannibalism which caused the frightful practice to be abandoned, at the cost of logical inconsistency. Substitutes were used at one time, such as golden human heads. Yet the custom of associating a human victim with the horse and goat in the *ashvamedha*, seems to have persisted for a while. Only it is prescribed to buy for the purpose an old, decrepit, infirm leper, for whom, "going to the gods" could be only a most happy release. But even this wretched wreck must belong to one of the holiest and most illustrious Rishi families. However, the dislike of spilling blood and taking life (unless in war) which became so conspicuous and beautiful a feature of later Brahmanism, was already growing on the Indo-Âryas, and the same Brâhmana—the Shatapatha—formally declares bloodless offerings to be more acceptable and fully as efficient, as usual, in the form of a legend or parable:

"The gods at first took man as victim [literally 'sacrificial animal.'] Then the sacrificial virtue [*medha*] left him and went into the horse. They took the horse, but the *medha* went out of him also and into the steer. Soon it went from the steer into the sheep, from the sheep into the goat, from the goat into the earth. Then they dug the earth up, seeking for the *medha* and found it in rice and barley. Therefore, as much virtue as there was in all those five animals, so much there now is in this sacrificial cake [*havis* made of rice and barley], *i. e.*, for him who knows this. The ground grains answer to the hair, the water [with which the meal is mixed] to the skin, the mixing and stirring to the flesh, the hardened cake [in the baking] to the bones, the *ghee* with which it is anointed to the marrow. So the five component parts of the animal are contained in the *havis*.

18. Human sacrifice is not mentioned in so many words in the Rig-Veda; but it is alluded to, transparently, to use the Vedic phrase, "for those who know." Not only in verse 8 of the Horse hymn, quoted above, but more undoubtedly in two texts which allude to the rescue of one SHUNAHSHEPHA, an adopted son of the Rishi Vishvâmitra:

"Bound Shunahshepha thou, O Agni, didst deliver from a thousand posts because he prayed fervently to thee; so deliver us, too, O shining *hotar*, from our bonds.—(V., 27.)

"Váruna the king will deliver us, he whom the captive Shunahshepha invoked once on a time. For Shunahshepha, being trebly bound to the post, called out to the Âditya.—(I., 24, 12, 13.)

An allusion to the same old story is certainly contained in verse 21 of the following hymn, I., 25: "That I may live, take from me the upper rope, loose the middle, and remove the lowest." Indeed, tradition was so positive on the point that it ascribed both these hymns to Shunahshepha himself. This would show that Váruna's "threefold fetters or nooses" are not *always* the allegorical ones of darkness, sickness, and death, but like most of the Rig-Veda's mysticism, have an underlying realistic meaning to them—very realistic in this case. The story itself we find in one of the great Brâhmanas, possibly the oldest, the AITAREYA, which belongs to the Rig-Veda, and therefore was bound to explain such obscure passages and allusions. This is convincing evidence of the fact that though the Brâhmanas are necessarily later, they may and often do contain matter older than the Rig itself. For what is alluded to in a work as generally known, must have existed before that work did. The following is the story condensed.[1]

19. There was a powerful king, HARISHCHANDRA, who had a hundred wives, but no son. By the advice of a great sage who lived in his house, he went to Váruna the King and said: "May a son be born to me, and I shall sacrifice him to thee!" Váruna said "Yes," and a boy was born to the king who named him ROHITA. Váruna soon claimed the child. But the father succeeded in obtaining respite after respite, until Rohita grew to young manhood, and

[1] It is also told in the Râmâyana and some Purânas, with unessential variations.

was girt with his armor. Then Váruna would wait no longer, and the king could find no more excuses. So he said to his son: "Child, he gave thee to me, that I sacrifice thee to him." The son said "No," took his bow, and went to the forest, where he lived for a year. Then Váruna vented his anger on the king, whom he afflicted with dropsy. Rohita, meanwhile, met a Brâhman on his wanderings, who advised him to travel. It was Indra in human form. "The fortune of a man who sits," he said, "sits also. It rises when he rises, sleeps when he sleeps, and moves when he moves. Travel! A traveller finds honey, a traveller finds sweet figs. Look at the happiness of the sun, who, travelling, never tires. Travel!" Rohita travelled six years, at the end of which he met in the forest a starving Rishi, of the holy Angiras race, who had three sons. Rohita said to him: "Rishi, I give thee a hundred cows; I ransom myself with one of these thy sons." The father embraced the eldest and said: "Not him!" The mother embraced the youngest and said: "Not him!" So they agreed to sell Shunahshepha, the middle son. And Rohita took him to the king, who offered him to Váruna in exchange for his son. Váruna said: "Yes; for a Brâhman is better than a Kshatriya," and ordered the king to prepare a great royal sacrifice. Shunahshepha was to be the victim for the day when the Soma is offered to the gods. Vishvâmitra was the *hotar* on this occasion. But when Shunahshepha was prepared, they could get nobody to bind him to the sacrificial post. His own father, who had sold him, did it for a hundred more cows. But no one could be found to kill him. His father declared himself willing to do that also for still a hundred more, and approached his son, whetting his knife. Shunahshepha thought: "They will really kill me, as if I were not a man.[1] I shall pray to the gods." He prayed to them all in succession, one sending him on to another. Ushas came last. While he prayed to her his fetters were loosed and dropped off him, and the king's dropsy left him, so he was well again, and the victim that was to have been was requested, instead, to perform the sacrifice of the day. The Rishi now claimed his son and wanted to take him back with him. But Shunahshepha absolutely refused to follow him, appealing for protection to Vishvâmitra, who supported him, saying: "Dreadful was he as he stood with his knife ready to kill. Be not his son. Come and be my son." Shunahshepha said: "Tell us thyself, O son of a king, how I, who am an Ângîrasa, shall become thy son."[2] Vishvâmitra replied: "Thou shalt be the eldest of my sons, thy offspring shall be the first; thou shalt receive the heritage which the gods have given me." On this understanding the adoption took place. Vishvâmitra had a hundred sons, fifty of whom (the elder half) rebelled at having a

[1] On such occasions, explains the commentator, it was customary to release the man and the larger animals at the last moment, after their purification by carrying the fire around them (see above, the legend from the Shatapatha), and only the sheep and the goat were killed. Thus was sacrifice commuted into consecration. (See *Story of Assyria*, pp. 121, 124.)

[2] Vishvâmitra, though a Brâhman in dignity and a Rishi, was, as we know, a Râjana by birth.

stranger placed over them. Their father cursed them, and they went forth as outcasts, they and their descendants becoming the worst of Dasyus. The other fifty cheerfully submitted, and, receiving their father's blessing, lived happy and prosperous.[1]

20. It is very easy to disentangle the kernel of this story from the Brahmanic additions and flourishes, which, however, for once do not mar it. Disapproval shows from every line, and we are allowed to infer that already at a very early period this most awful of all sacred rites was only simulated in the performance, instead of being carried out to the bitter end. But that very disapproval is manifestly a protest against something that really existed, and we cannot exonerate our Aryan ancestors from the blot which appears to rest on all races—that of having, at some time, practised the abomination of human sacrifices.

---

[1] See Max Müller, *Ancient Sanskrit Literature*, pp. 408–419.

CHAPTER XI.

THE RIG-VEDA: COSMOGONY.—PHILOSOPHY.—RETROSPECT.

1. OF the many fleeting moods which waft a fragrance of true poetry from the too often barren, or —worse still—weed-ridden garden-beds of the Rig-Veda, there is undoubtedly none that interests us and appeals to us more than the questioning mood, which now and then, quite rarely, breaks out in unexpected places—the bud of choicest promise on the tender yet already vigorous plant of earnest human thought, as distinguished from mere imaginative speculation, great as is the charm of the latter. When those old Rishis (who, personally, may not have been old when they thought and sang!), when they pause in the midst of an invocation, a hymn of praise, to ask wonderingly, sincerely, "Where is the sun by night?" "Where go the stars by day?" "Why does the sun, being neither supported nor fastened to anything, not fall down?" "Of the two —Night and Day—which is the elder, which the younger?" "Whence comes the wind and whither goes it?" and "how is it that it raises no dust on the paths of heaven? nor the chariot of the sun

either?"—we are overcome by a feeling as of awe, tender and pathetic, as when we hear the first earnest questions (very much the same, too!) from the lips of our children in the midst of their amusing prattle, and mark the widely opening eyes with the first sharp gleam of the spirit life in them, as each in turn reaches out feeble but longing hands, instinctively groping for the fruit of the tree of knowledge, with no dimmest perception of either its sweetness or its bitterness, its blessings or dangers. For the spirit that has once queried so is awake and will never be laid to sleep again; it has started out of the repose of latent into the activity of conscious life, and has grappled the universal problem it is to wrestle with to the end and do its share to solve: the separation of that which may become known from that which never can be.

2. It is peculiar that the direct question is never asked: "*Who* made the world"—or worlds—but only *how* it was made: how "they" made it, or—in the latest stage, when philosophical abstraction has reached the conception of one creator (a *dhâtar*, a *prajâpati*, a *vishvakarman*)—how *he* made it,—and *out of what*. This particular question fully thought out and adequately worded, we encounter in two speculative hymns, of Book X., addressed one to "all the gods" (*vishvedevâh*), and again to Vishvakarman, "the artificer, or fashioner, of the universe."

"What indeed was the wood, what the tree, out of which they fashioned [after the manner of carpenters] the heaven and the earth? these two stand fast and grow not old forever, while many days and mornings pass away." (X., 31, 7.)

"What was the standing-place, what the stable support, the position, and how was it, from which Vishvakarman, the all-seeing, produced the earth and disclosed the heaven by his might? . . . What indeed was the wood, what the tree out of which they fashioned the earth and the heaven? Inquire, ye wise ones, with your minds, what it was on which he took his stand when he made fast the world." (X., 81, 2 and 4.)

These verses are found in the Yajur-Veda also, and one of its commentaries, the Taittiriya-Brâhmana answers the question thus:

"Brahma [neuter] was the wood, Brahma was that tree out of which they fashioned the heaven and the earth. Wise ones, with my mind I declare unto you, he took his stand on Brahma when he made fast the world."

Perhaps as good an answer as the subject will admit, at this transition stage from Vedic naturalism to the spiritualism and pantheism of the Upanishads, —the stage when the Brahma is already felt as the universally present, latent life and force, which, manifested, becomes both matter in its tangible form and spirit in its active working, but not yet as the One, self-existing Soul of the All and Creator of the Worlds.

3. Like all the phases of thought recorded in the Rig-Veda, the ideas on the making of the world pass before our eyes through several progressive stages, the first and simplest of which is well represented by this statement in one of the Vasishtha hymns: "Vàruna stemmed asunder the wide firmaments; he lifted on high the bright and glorious heaven; he stretched out apart the starry sky and the earth" (VII., 86, 1). The same things are said of other gods also. But

when it comes to details, three distinct conceptions crystallize out of hundreds of texts bearing on the subject: (1) the gods *built* the world, carpenter-fashion, as the Âryas built their houses; (2) the gods—this or that couple, especially Heaven and Earth or the gods generally—*gave birth* to the world, after the manner of living beings; (3) the world was created through Sacrifice, as by Sacrifice it is kept going. The first of these conceptions may be classed almost entirely under poetical imagery; the second, in great part, with an evident but rather clumsy flight into symbolism; while the third, purely theological, soars into almost unattainable regions of abstruse mysticism.[1] Although the progression from simple to complicated is manifest, and such a progression implies progress and evolution, implying in their turn a vast period of time, it does not follow that the transition from step to step can be followed, much less chronologically classified. There is no method in the presentation of the three conceptions; they are expressed promiscuously, often two, sometimes all three, in one and the same hymn, though the mystic vein is decidedly predominant in those which otherwise show internal evidence of lateness, and of which the greatest number (not by any means the totality) is collected in Book X. This shows that all three stages of thought had already been passed when the canon of the Rig-Veda was finally established, yielding still additional proof of the prodigi-

[1] This is the conception so amply developed in the preceding chapter, and the final consecration of which will be given a few pages further on.

ous antiquity of the subject-matter of the collection, which was to save it from oblivion and further corruption for a generation who had gone far greater lengths on the two opposite ways—the freedom of soaring thought and the bondage of priest-ridden ritualism.

4. We have seen the sun described as a tree with its top down and its roots up (see p. 144), and are familiar with the thoroughly worked out image of the heavens as the tree of the wonderful foliage; this quite easily led to the question: "What was the wood, what the tree?" etc. And as to the birth theory, we are well used to such expressions as "the Bright-one is born of the Dark-one" (Day of Night), "Heaven and Earth whose children are the Devas," and the like. This is one form, and a very favorite one, of the so-called "mythic riddles," with which the Rig-Veda teems. The sacrifice-theory we went into at great length in the preceding chapter; but we have now to examine a most important hymn in which it finds its crowning expression—the widely famous, mystic PURUSHA-SÛKTA (X., 90), to which allusion has already been made as belonging to the very latest stage of the Rig-Veda—if not already to the period succeeding it—and savoring more of the Ganges than the Indus, since it contains the only formal mention of caste in the collection (see p. 280), and of the original three Vedas, perhaps even the Atharva Veda. In a way this hymn supplements and completes the most mystical of the verses addressed to Vishvakarman, the "Artificer of the Universe": "The highest, the lowest

and the middle stations that are thine, teach to thy friends at the sacrifice; do thou sacrifice to thyself, delighting thyself,"—or that to Agni (X., 7, 6): "In Heaven sacrifice, O Deva, to the Devas . . . and in the same manner sacrifice to thyself, O thou of the beautiful birth." For these passages do not inform us *what* or *whom* the gods are to sacrifice—or rather sacrificed—as a means of creation. Indeed we saw that in this very vagueness lay the best answer, by leaving us to imagine the heavenly phenomena of light and storm as a "sacred action performed by the gods for their own delight, in accordance with an eternal law." But such majestic, comprehensive vagueness did not suit the subtilized and de-poetized brains of the later theologians. Everything had to be explained and told all about, leaving no room for dreaming and imaginings. So we are given, in the Purusha-Sûkta, the story of Creation in the guise of a Divine Sacrifice with a precision and fulness of detail which make of it a complete Cosmogony,—one, too, which left its trace on that of other kindred races.[1] The peculiar theme was most probably suggested by human sacrifices, when the institution—avowedly a very ancient one, as we shall presently see—was still in active force; the fact that the Purusha-hymn is particularly mentioned as having been sung actually *at* human sacrifices *(purusha-medha)* favors this hypothesis.

5. Purusha—more correctly *the* Purusha, the Pri-

---

[1] Compare the Scandinavian Cosmogonic legend (in the Edda) of the making of the world out of the different members of the primeval giant Ymer's body.—For the meaning of the word "Cosmogony" see *Story of Chaldea*, pp. 259 *ff*.

meval Giant or Male Principle, THE MAN—is the victim whom the gods offer up and the dissection of whose body—which is simply *the material to work with*, the whole of pre-existing MATTER, with its latent possibilities for generating life—produces the various parts of the universe with their denizens, of course with special reference to our habitable earth, as far as known to the Âryas of India. With these few hints and the insight we have been gaining all along into the mythical metaphysics of Brahmanic theology, the Purusha-Sûkta will need but little comment to be intelligible.

1. Purusha of the thousand heads, the thousand eyes, the thousand feet, covered the earth in all directions and extended ten finger breadths beyond.—2. Purusha is this whole universe, whatever has been, and whatever shall be, and a possessor of the immortality which groweth great by food (offered in sacrifice ?).—3. So great is Purusha, yea, greater still. One quarter of him is all that hath been made, three quarters of him are the immortals in heaven.—4. With three feet Purusha mounted up, with one foot he remained here; then he spread out on all sides and became that which eateth and that which eateth not.[1]—5. From him the *Virâj* was born, and from the *Virâj* again Purusha.[2] As soon as he was born he reached out beyond the earth at both ends.—6. When the gods prepared the sacrifice with Purusha as the offering, the spring was the sacrificial butter, the summer was the fuel,

[1] "One foot" and "three feet" is literal; and so A. Bergaigne renders it. Other scholars translate "one quarter" and "three quarters," and this version is retained in v. 3, because there the other would be *too* grotesque. We shall see presently what the mystic "foot" means.

[2] The *Virâj* is a ponderous and solemn sacred metre, said to consist of *forty syllables*. That metre is born of sacrifice and sacrifice of metre is a familiar mystical conception. This is the explanation given by the Shatapatha-Brâhmana; it commends itself by its simplicity and its conformity to Vedic modes of thought and speech.

the autumn was the (accompanying) oblation.—7. On the sacrificial grass they anointed the victim, that Purusha who was born in the beginning; him the gods sacrificed, whose favor is to be sought, and the Rishis.—8. When the sacrifice was completed, they collected the fat dripping from it; it formed the creatures of air, and the animals that live in forests, and those that live in villages (wild and domestic).—9. From this sacrifice when completed were born the Rig-hymns, and the Sâma-hymns, and the incantations (probably the future Atharvan); and the Yajus was born from it.—10. From it were born the horses and all the cattle that have two rows of teeth; the kine were born from it; from it the goats and sheep were born.[1]—11. When they divided Purusha, into how many parts did they cut him up? What was his mouth? What were his arms? What are his thighs and his feet called?—12. The Brâhman was his mouth; the Râjanya was made from his arms; the Vaishya he was his thighs; the Shûdra sprang from his feet.—13. The moon was born from his mind; the sun from his eye; Indra and Agni from his mouth; from his breath the wind was born.—14. From his navel came the air; from his head sprang the sky, from his feet the earth, from his ear the regions; thus they formed the worlds.—15. When the gods bound Purusha as victim, preparing the sacrifice, seven enclosing bars of wood were placed for him, thrice seven layers of fuel were piled for him.—16. So the gods through sacrifice earned a right to sacrifice; *these were the first ordinances.* Those mighty ones attained to the highest heaven, where the ancient gods abide, whose favor is to be sought."

6. It is a common saying that any one fool can ask questions which it takes seven wise men to answer. The case is sometimes reversed. It takes genius and soul to ask certain questions, and minds which are not master minds take on themselves to answer them. This is the case with most questions in the Rig-Veda. What heights and depths of thought, of reverent longing for the truth—the absolute truth—

[1] It will be noticed that these are the very four animals who, with man (Purusha) at their head, are declared fit for sacrifice (see pp. 406-409).

are revealed by such questions as these: "Who has seen the First-Born, when he that had no bones (*i.e.*, form) bore him that has bones? Where is the life, the blood, the Self of the universe? Who went to ask of any who knew?" (I., 4, 164). The word which philosophical scholars have rendered "the Self" is *âtman*, literally "breath" or "spirit" (which is the same thing), and derived from the same root, AS, "to breathe," which has given one form of the verb "to be" in Sanskrit and several other Aryan languages.[1] With every desire to penetrate into the very abstract inness of things, the human mind, being unable ever quite to cut itself adrift from the realities of material existence, was compelled to hold fast this slight thread of materialism; but then, of material things, what could be *less* material, more unsubstantial? A breath—a thing which is not seen, yet is life itself, for when it stops, life ceases! Who or what, then, is the breath, the life, the *âtman* of the universe,—its essence, real, yet invisible? Surely, more spirituality is required to be the first to ask these questions, than for all the writers of the Upanishads to answer them. For these are some of the themes of those grand Brahmanic treatises which embrace all that the ancient Greeks used to understand under the name of "philosophy," and which included investigations and theories concerning creation, the nature of things, the study of the world and what it holds. In this sense all the cosmological and metaphysical portions of the Rig-Veda may already be entitled Upanishads, as they certainly

[1] Sskr. *asmi*, Slav. *esmi*, Lat. *sum*, etc., etc., "I am."

form the transition to the Upanishad period and literature. The Purusha-Sûkta has been so called; so we may call a short cosmogonic piece (X., 190), wonderfully concise and comprehensive both, and quite intelligible when we have the key to this class of speculations with its peculiar form of speech:

"From kindled heat (*tápas*) Right and Law were born (*sátya* and *rita*, the Cosmic Order,) and Night, then the watery flood.—And from the watery flood the coursing year was born, disposing Day and Night, the ruler of all that close the eyes.—And in their order the Creator formed the sun and moon, and heaven and earth, the regions of the air and light."

This might truly be called a Vedic genesis-chapter, but it is by no means the only one. Many are the passages—not all in the late portions either—where the Origin of Things is set forth in the same pregnant, but obscurely mythical form. One of the finest is a passage in the second hymn to Vishvakarman (X., 82, 5–6), which, in the guise of one question and answer, contains in substance the main fact of the later Brahmanic cosmogony. The waters, it is there said, received the first—or primordial—germ containing all the gods,—the germ which rested alone on the lap of the Unborn—AJA—the One in whom all existing things abide. Who does not see how easily this "first germ" could become the World-Egg (more commonly known as the Mundane Egg) floating for ages unnumbered—"from the beginning"—on the primeval waters of Chaos, until the Principle of Universal Life, the Brahma (neuter) which rested therein, latent and inactive, sprang out as Brahmâ (masculine), the active creative principle—the Maker of all the worlds?

7. The "Unborn,"—frequently also called "the One," EKAM—means that which has always existed without being born of anything, the Eternally-Preexisting, of which all things are born, when the desire of manifesting Itself awakes in It. Sometimes the One is named AJA EKAPÂD, literally "the One-footed Unborn"—a seemingly grotesque appellation, which has given rise to as grotesque interpretations, but which is really only one of those attempts at expressing the inexpressible in some kind of tangible form in which the Aryan thinkers of India have always dealt, regardless of extravagance in the wording. For in the Rig-Veda, the "foot" may stand for the world in which the foot's owner abides. So Vishnu is said to know his own highest abode,—the third, while only two are known to men—and the source of light is said to be "at his feet;" and his "three strides" also mean nothing else than that he has his feet in the three worlds,—the two visible ones and the third, highest, invisible one (see p. 240). Again, the Purusha has one foot on the earth, and three in the heavenly worlds of the immortals, *i. e.*, in the two other worlds *and* the fourth—the highest, invisible one (see p. 420). For there is always one world more than the known number. If "the two worlds" are spoken of—Heaven and Earth—there is a third; if "the three worlds"—Earth, Atmosphere, and Heaven—there is a fourth; this third, this fourth world is the hidden, the unreachable, unknowable one, which is also sometimes called the Sanctuary of the Universe, and the Navel, *i. e.*, the Parent, the Centre, of all Origins. Sometimes, by a peculiarly

Vedic play on numbers, each world is again divided into three, and we have, instead of "the two worlds," "the six worlds": then there is the seventh.[1] This supernumerary hidden world is the only one in which the One Unborn abides, equally mysterious and unconceivable, yet firmly *felt* to exist,—*believed* in though not seen; it is, in Vedic riddle-phrase, the only world in which he has his foot,—hence Aja Ekapâd, "the One-footed Unborn." The verse quoted a few pages back: "Who has seen the First-born?" etc. (I., 164, 5) is followed up by these eager questionings:

> "Not knowing, I go to ask of those who know, that I may know, I who do not know: he who stretched apart and established the six worlds, in the form of the Unborn, did he also establish the seventh? Let him speak here who knows the hidden place of the beautiful Bird."

The admission of ignorance (and it occurs over and over through the Samhitâ), so simple, so sincere, is deeply touching. They will "go ask," but they hardly hope to be answered. The poet who describes Vishvakarman as the "First-born of the

---

[1] So the chariot of Sûryâ, like that of the Ashvins has three wheels; two the Brâhmans know, "but the third, the hidden one, is known only to the deep-enquiring" (see p. 370). And the mystic World-Bull in IV., 58, 2–3 (one of the many hymns that treats of Sacrifice in mystic guise) has two heads, three feet, four horns, seven hands, because he is present in all the worlds: the two, the three, the four, and the six—with always the hidden world added. The seven bars of wood and the thrice seven layers of fuel, laid for Purusha (see p. 421) belong to the same order of ideas: they symbolize the six worlds, plus the one hidden world (see A. Bergaigne, *Religion Védique*, vol. ii., pp. 20–25).

Waters," as "our father, our creator, our maker" (see p. 264) concludes reverently and sadly: "Ye never will behold him who gave birth to these things; something else it is that appears among you. Wrapped in darkness, and stammering, wander through life the singers of hymns." So that those ancient fathers of our race's greatest thinkers, of the men for whom thought became a fine art, the occupation and the end of life, had already found the wisdom which concedes that some questions are answered best when left unanswered; had, in all humility, learned the lesson which comes so hard to our overbearing modern Science, when she too—for with all her imperfections she is honest—is forced to bend her haughty head, and break her proud lips to utter the words most galling to her self-confidence: "I do not know."

8. In their efforts to pierce the gloom of things before time was, "before (or beyond ?) the earth, the heaven and the Asura-gods," the Vedic thinkers achieved a conception of primeval chaos, unquickened as yet by the first fiat of Creative Will, yet brooded over by the Divine Presence, which their great poetic gift enabled them to clothe in such words as, to use Max Müller's enthusiastic expression, "language blushes at, but her blush is a blush of triumph." It is the famous cosmogonic hymn X., 129, the great Vedic Upanishad, which contains more than in germ the substance of those later Brahmanic philosophical treatises, which received the name of VEDÂNTA-UPANISHADS, *i. e.*, "the end or final goal of the Veda." One of the great

beauties of this matchless piece is that, while reaching the uttermost bounds of philosophical abstraction, it is never obscure, unless to the absolutely uninitiated.

"1. Nor Aught nor Naught existed then; not the aërial space, nor heaven's bright woof above. What covered all? Where rested all? Was it water, the profound abyss?

"2. Death was not then, nor immortality; there was no difference of day and night.[1] That One breathed breathless in Itself [*i. e.*, existed, but without exerting or manifesting itself]; and there was nothing other than It.

"3. In the beginning there was darkness in darkness enfolded,[2] all was undistinguishable water. That One, which lay in the empty space, wrapped in nothingness, was developed by the power of heat.[3]

"4. Desire first arose in It—that was the primal germ of mind, which poets, searching with their intellects, discovered in their hearts to be the bond between Being and Not-Being.[4]

---

[1] *I.e.*, "time was not yet," because time is known only by the alternation of day and night. Therefore, in Genesis I., the first work of creation is to "divide the light from the darkness."

[2] Compare all this to Genesis I., 2: "And darkness was on the face of the deep, and the spirit of God was moving (or brooding) on the face of the waters."

[3] *Tápasas*, "by heat" or "out of heat." Attention has been drawn to an important difference in the reading given in the Taittiriya Brâhmana—*támasas*—which would mean "out of darkness." It is suggested that this might have been the older reading.

[4] Desire (to manifest itself) the first stirring of sentient will, which must itself precede action. The word is *káma*. It became (from obvious association) the word for "love" and the name of the love-god. The Greek language and mythology presents an exactly parallel case: Eros, the name of the love-god, originally means "desire." And by the light of this marvellous effort of Vedic thought, the main features of the Cosmogonic fragment in Hesiod's Theogony acquire a new and startling significance: "Sing the sacred race of immortals who sprang from Earth and starry Heaven and murky Night, whom the briny deep bore [in X., 190—see above, the 'watery flood' is born from Night]. . . . Foremost sprang

"5. The ray of light which stretched across these worlds, did it come from below or from above? Then seeds were sown and mighty forces arose, Nature beneath and Power and Will above.

"6. Who indeed knows? Who proclaimed it here,—whence, whence this creation was produced? The gods were later than its production—who then knows whence it sprang?

"He from whom this creation sprang, whether he made it or not, the All-Seer in the highest heaven, he knows it—or he does not."[1]

Startling indeed are the last lines—most startling the last words. The despondency, the hopelessness of them, is like the sudden relaxing of a superhuman tension. It also seems to foreshadow the cloud which was to fall on the spiritual life of the Âryas of India, after altered conditions of life, and especially the physically enervating climatic influences of their new abodes, had changed the joyous, somewhat belligerent, nature-worship, utterly untrammelled with laming self-consciousness, of the first settlers of the Sapta-Sindhavah into the introspective brooding, so destructive to action and single-hearted enjoyment, of the dwellers on the Ganges. That cloud was their incapacity to make their religion a comfort to themselves. True, they did not seek for happiness, but for Absolute Truth. So when their powerful intellects led them to a perception of The One, there was no joy in the finding, unless it were the cold joy of the enquiring mind—the gleam of the beacon that lights but warms not,—

Chaos, and next broad-bosomed Earth [*prithivî*], . . . and Eros, most beautiful of immortals. . . ." This Eros is the Cosmogonic Kâma—Desire—of our hymn—the prompter of the act of creation.

[1] See especially Max Müller's *Ancient Sanskrit Literature*, pp. 559–564.

for there had not been love in the seeking. And THE ONE was to them IT—remote, impersonal, therefore as good as non-existent. Yet, if they had not looked for happiness, they missed it all the same; they missed it so, that life, with its miseries unrelieved by trust or hope, became worthless—existence a burden, deliverance from which was the one thing devoutly to be wished for. But this is trespassing on a decidedly post-vedic field, on things which are, as just shown, only foreshadowed in the Rig.

9. This question of monotheism in the Rig-Veda has been all along an exceedingly vexed one. In the first place, can the Vedic Âryas be said to have achieved monotheism at all? Strange question to ask of so rampantly polytheistic a religion! Yet the perception of The One Unborn existing before time and beyond space, to which they struggled by sheer force of reasoning, is very near it; it is, at all events, the nearest even their descendants, those champion thinkers of the world, ever came to it. They came near it, but still they missed it—in what manner we have just seen—at least as we understand the word.[1] The earlier Vedic poets perhaps came nearest of all to *that*, when they prayed to Váruna, the punisher and *forgiver* of sins, when they bade men "fear him who holds the four dice before He throws them down," and assured them that "his path is easy and without thorns who does what is right" (I., 41), before subtle arguing had killed intuition

[1] Not so the Eranians. The Avestan Ahura-Mazda, as Zarathushtra saw and heard Him, is not a principle or *a* god, but God.

and warmth of feeling. Yes, they *almost* hit the mark then, but glanced off somehow.

10. There is another tendency which runs through the entire Rig-Veda and which, at first sight, looks like a reaching out towards monotheism. It assumes two forms. The first, which we have had repeated occasions to notice, is that of extolling the particular deity invoked at the time above all the others and ascribing to it the same actions and functions which, in other hymns, are named as especially belonging to this or that god. This is the stage which will retain the name improvised for it by Max Müller: HENOTHEISM or KATHENOTHEISM; *i. e.*, the worship, not of one god only, but "of one god at a time." This peculiarity is accounted for by the worshipper's wish to ingratiate himself with the god he addresses and of course asks favors from; and the explanation is good—so far as it goes. But it is superficial. There is far more to the practice than a mere point of courtesy or etiquette, as is shown by another way the Vedic poets have, and which will be found, on examination, to come from the same deeper source: that is their inveterate passion for identifying one god with another, or with several other gods, or several gods—or all—together. Profound scholars have seen in this only a puerile trick, a juggling with names and ideas resulting in nothing but puzzlement and confusion. But a closer study soon convinces that there is much method in the madness. The seemingly mechanical process of looking up and stringing together texts bearing on the matter, proves, in this case as in others, most helpful and

light-bringing. The easiest of such identifications to interpret is that of such late abstractions as Vishvakarman, Prajâpati, with several of the earlier great gods—Indra, Váruna, Tvashtar, Savitar, etc., simply because those names, as already pointed out, were originally mere epithets—"All-Maker," "Lord of Creatures." When Vishvakarman is described as the First-Born of the Unborn (for the phrase "the First-Born resting on the lap—literally the *navel*—of the Unborn," can have no other meaning)[1] we have another and covert identification, far more difficult to unravel, but on the same line of thought. Before we attempt to do so, we must study the First-Born under still another name, that of HIRANYAGARBHA, the "Golden Germ," or "Golden Embryo," which Professor Max Müller has felicitously rendered "the Golden Child" in his translation of the most beautiful hymn, X., 121, in which the greatness and the works of the Creator, here named Hiranyagarbha, are celebrated in poetry which will stand comparison with that of the Book of Job. Very remarkable is the burden at the end of each verse which we must imagine as being taken up in chorus. The poet who sings of the glory of The One, feels the inconsistency, and asks, "Who is the god to whom we shall offer our sacrifice," *i. e.*, "*which* of all the many gods to whom we address our prayers, is this One, to whom we are here to sacrifice this day?" Here is the entire hymn:

[1] Identical in meaning, if differently worded, with X., 129: the First-Born is the active creative principle which develops out of the One Unborn, the quiescent, unmanifested principle of life.

"1. In the beginning there arose the Golden Child. He was the one born lord of all that is. He established the earth and this sky:—Who is the god to whom we shall offer our sacrifice?

"2. He who gives breath [*i. e.*, life], He who gives strength; whose command all the gods revere; whose shadow is immortality, whose shadow is death:—Who is the god, etc.

"3. He who through his greatness is the one king of the breathing and awakening world; He who governs man and beast:—Who, etc.

"4. He whose greatness the Himâvat, the *samudra*, the Rasâ proclaim[1]; He whose these regions are, as it were his two arms:—Who, etc.

"5. He through whom the sky is bright and the earth firm; He through whom the heaven was established,—nay the highest heaven; He who measured out the aërial space:—Who, etc.

"6. He to whom the two battle-hosts, sustained by his support, look up trembling in spirit, there where the risen sun shines:—Who, etc.

"7. When the mighty waters pervaded the universe, holding the germ and begetting fire, thence He arose, who is the sole life of gods:—Who, etc.

"8. He who by His might looked even over the waters which gave strength and lit the sacrifice;—He who alone is god above all the gods:—Who, etc.

"9. May He not harm us, the Creator of this earth; who, ruling by fixed ordinances, created the heaven; who also created the bright and mighty waters:—Who, etc."

11. The writers of the Brâhmanas make it a business to answer all the questions left open by the more truly inspired Rishis—and we often wish they did n't. In this case, however, it might have been worse. We read in the Shatapatha, "*Who* [*i. e.*, the Unknown God whom the Rishi sought] is Prajâpati:

[1] Prof. Max Müller renders (and so do most translators): "these snowy mountains, the sea and the distant river." But the original Vedic names convey a special, very marked flavor, and as they have repeatedly occurred and been discussed in the preceding chapters there was no objection to giving them.

to him let us offer our sacrifice." And some conscientious theologian forthwith embodies the answer in a verse which he tacks on to the beautiful poem, the flattest anticlimax that ever was devised: "O Prajâpati, no other than thou hath embraced all these created things; may what we desired when we called upon thee be granted to us; may we be lords of riches." Prajâpati—Lord of creatures, or "of created things"—being a descriptive name given to many of the great gods in their *rôle* of creators, is a satisfactory answer, as far as it goes. But it does not go far or deep enough. We have at last arrived at the point where we cannot be satisfied with less than an entire solution of the riddle which we call the Rig-Veda; where we must lift the veil of the very sanctuary itself and see what is the real essence of that One whom "wise poets make manifold by words." For that is to what, in the end, amounts all that shifting and merging of divine personalities into one another, those multitudinous identifications.

12. If we collect, then carefully con these texts, we shall be led to the conclusion that there is one divine person who attracts and absorbs the others somewhat as a larger globule of quicksilver does any number of smaller ones. And as that globule, at the slightest jolt, breaks up again into an elusive bevy of small ones, so that divine entity, just when we think we are fairly grasping it, suddenly vanishes, and the polytheistic host confronts us in full array. That divine person or entity is Agni, he of the "three abodes" and the "three bodies"—as Sun, Lightning, and Fire. We see the often fanciful identifi-

cations tending that way, vaguely, obscurely, till now and then the poets are surprised into a definite statement which leaves no room for doubt. There is an entire hymn of many verses (II., 1) in which the poeṭ, after rehearsing the various births of Agni —from the Waters, from the cloud-rock, from the trees, from the herbs—proceeds, systematically, to identify him with nearly every god in the pantheon. Agni, he tells us, is Váruna, Mitra, and the other Âdityas; he is Indra and Vishnu, Tvashtar and Rudra, and the Maruts; Pûshan and Savitar, even the Ribhus, and others. More convincing, because briefer and simpler, is verse 46 of that long and mystical hymn I., 64, out of which some striking passages have already been quoted:[1]

"They call him Indra, Mitra, Váruna, Agni; then he is the beautiful-winged heavenly Bird. That which is One the wise call it by divers names: they call it Agni, Yama, Mâtarishvan."

Or this (quoted in part already): "Wise poets make the beautiful-winged, though he is One, manifold by words." The circle narrows, and we read: "O Agni, many names are given thee, O god, immortal ruler."

[1] Hillebrandt calls this hymn the "riddle-hymn." It is still considered obscure in many portions; but as general comprehension of the Rig-Veda, both as to spirit and form, increases, it becomes more intelligible. Some of the riddles are most ingenious and quite easy. Such is the description of the Year as the "twelve-spoked wheel of Rita which circles round the heavens without the axle ever getting heated or the wood rotten, while 720 twin brothers keep climbing up on it" (360 days and as many nights). The riddles in which the inevitable Cow and Calf are turned loose are among the hardest, because these symbolical animals have come to mean anything and everything.

At last it closes, and it is announced: "AGNI IS ALL THE GODS." Herewith we have the sought-for clue.

For the Âryas of the Rig-Veda were—Fire-Worshippers.[1]

After the stupendous collection has been subjected to every known process of analysis and disintegration, this is the residue left in the crucible. So much will plainly appear even from the limited but carefully picked selection of hymns and detached passages in the present volume.

13. From these it must have become clear long ago that the whole naturalism of the Rig-Veda, its entire conception of the universe and its working, hinges on two sets of natural phenomena: those of Light (Heat is included, though not specially mentioned till late), and of Moisture, embodied in Agni and Soma. And we cannot perceive or comprehend Agni's real nature so long as we persist in narrowing it down to the conception of Fire—one form of him only, and not the most divine. Agni is Light—the light which fills and pervades Space—which has its highest abode in that eternal, mysterious world above the heavens, beyond space itself, where are the hidden sources of all things—the Sanctuary, the Navel of the Universe, where Day and Night themselves, the unequal, ever separated sisters, meet and kiss (I., 185, 5). From this supernal world Agni

---

[1] And probably the Indo-Eranian Âryas also. Not so the Zoroastrians, to this day so mis-named. The very essence of Zarathushtra's reform consisted in transforming Fire- and Soma-worship into a symbolical act.

descends and manifests himself. He is "born" or "found" in the heavens as the Sun, in the atmosphere as Lightning, on earth as Fire. These are his three visible Bodies or "forms." But he invisibly pervades, lies hidden in, all things. In the plants—or how could he be brought forth out of them? In the Waters,—for out of the heavenly ocean the lightning flashes, and with the rain he descends into the earth, thence mounts into the trees and herbs as sap, and lies concealed in them until brought forth by design or accident. In animals and men—for what but his divine presence accounts for the warmth in their bodies? and that warmth is Life, for when it leaves the body, life goes. Soma himself is only Agni's other self, the liquid form of him, the hidden principle of life which makes of the moisture that pervades all nature, the invigorating *amrita*, the Drink of Immortality, which keeps her forces living and ever young. As to the earthly Soma, the fermented and intoxicating sacrificial beverage, Agni's divine presence is trebly manifested in it: by the flame which the alcoholic liquid emits and feeds; by the heat it diffuses through the veins of the partakers; by the exhilaration, the fervid enthusiasm, nay the inspiration, which seizes on those who have tasted it, and makes them feel in direct communion with the god, makes them say that the god has entered into them and they have become as gods. In the form of Soma, it is Agni whom the worshipper receives into himself, for the two are One.[1] It is Soma who,

[1] See pp. 173–175: "Soma who has entered into the Brâhmans" (X., 14).

from his bright bowl, the Moon, dispenses the gentle dews that feed the plants, but hidden in the dews —as in the rain, as in the clouds—Agni descends, for he is the Child of the Waters. Thus the ancient Âryas not only preceded the early Greek schools of philosophy in constructing a theory of the world, but greatly surpassed them in wisdom; since, while some of the Greeks declared Water to be the elementary principle of the world, and others Fire, the Vedic Âryas, by a marvel of intuition, had, ages before, reached the perception that only in the union of both—of Heat and Moisture—lies the universal life-giving principle.

14. All the Devas having to do with light, lightning, fire, or rain, it is clear that, taking the stand just developed, it is quite possible to drive them to bay and expose them, as so many Vedic thinkers have done, as mere names—endowed with a fictitious individuality—to find the *nomen* (name) behind the *numen* (deity), to use a phrase of Professor Max Müller, which was a revelation in its day; then we behold in them only so many Persons of Agni, in the word's original meaning of—Masks.[1] No wonder that a riper age discarded them all as MÂYÂ—"illusion" and sought the One behind them. Only the stage of naturalism had then been passed, and the One was no longer Agni.

15. The mysticism of the Rig-Veda has its source:

---

[1] See M. Müller's *Biographies of Words*, III., "PERSONA." Originally "mask," then the aspect one presents, the face one puts on, the character one enacts. The "persons" of a deity may be defined as its different manifestations.

1st, in the connection of Agni—as Brihaspati or Brahmanaspati—with the two great acts of worship, prayer and sacrifice; 2d, in the belief in a supernal, hidden world, the source of light, and the "highest abode" of all divine beings; 3d, in the kinship men claim with Agni, and owing to which that world is their "home, which cannot be taken from them (X., 14), to which they are "restored" when they leave this world by "the path of death" by which the Ancient Fathers preceded them, whom they go to join in that Abode of Light. And who more meet to carry them thither "by the easiest paths" than Agni himself in his fiery form, the Messenger, the Priest?[1] This fully accounts for the substitution of cremation for the earlier rite of burial.[2]

16. As religious mysticism develops into philosophical speculation, the same principle of Light-and-Heat in union with Moisture (the Waters) as the factor of Creation and the Supporter of the Worlds still holds good: the First-Born, the "first germ, containing all the gods," (powers of nature), from its resting-place on the lap of the Unborn, is received by the Waters (X., 82, 5–6), and it is heat (*tápas*) that quickens it with the first stirrings of desire (*kâma*) (X., 129, 3–4).

[1] ". . . This man's unborn part convey to the abode of the blessed. . . . Give up again, Agni, to the Fathers him who comes offered to thee with oblations. . . ." (X., 14.)

[2] That this was actually the idea, is proved by a notice in the Aitareya-Brâhmana, which informs us that "formerly," at sacrifices, the *yûpa* or sacrificial post to which the victim had been bound used to be thrown into the fire after it, *because it represented the sacrificer*, and thus placed him in communion with the gods—"sent him to the gods."

Agni, then—Light-and-Heat—is the Divine pre-existing and self-existing One, who (when manifested) fills and pervades the worlds, abides in and contains all things.

In this way, in this sense, were the Âryas of India Fire-Worshippers. In this way, after repeatedly reaching out for Monotheism, they missed it at last and found instead Pantheism, which they held fast.

And thus the transition from pure nature-worship to the transcendental metaphysical mysticism of Brahmanism is effected gradually, smoothly, within the Rig-Veda itself, and when we take up the story where the Rig-Veda drops it, we shall find in it no break, no abrupt turn from the "easy paths," along which we have been led so far.

THE END.

PRINCIPAL WORKS READ OR CONSULTED IN THE PREPARATION OF THE PRESENT VOLUME.

BARTH, A. THE RELIGIONS OF INDIA. Translated from the French by Rev. J. Wood. London, 1882. 1 vol.

BERGAIGNE, Abel. LA RELIGION VÉDIQUE, d'après les hymnes du Rig-Veda. Paris, 1878–1883. 3 vol.

BÜHLER, G. DIE INDISCHEN INSCHRIFTEN UND DAS ALTER DER INDISCHEN KUNTSPOESIE. (Sitzungsberich der Kais. Akad. der Wissensch. in Wien, XI.) Wien, 1890.

———THE LAWS OF MANU, translated, with extracts from seven Commentaries. (Vol. XXV. of the "Sacred Books of the East" Series.) Oxford, 1886. 1 vol.

CHANTEPIE DE LA SAUSSAYE, P. D. LEHRBUCH DER RELIGIONS GESCHICHTE, Erster Band, Freiburg, J. B. 1887. (Popular.)

DE GUBERNATIS, Angelo. LETTURE SOPRA LA MITOLOGIA VEDICA. Firenze, 1874. 1 vol.

———LA MYTHOLOGIE DES PLANTES; ou, Légendes du Règne Végétal. Paris, 1878–1882. 2 vol.

———ZOÖLOGICAL MYTHOLOGY, or the Legends of Animals. London, 1872. 2 vol.

DONNER, Dr. O. PINDAPITRYAJNA, das Manenopfer mit Klössen bei den Indern. Abhandlung aus dem Vedischen Ritual. Berlin, 1870. 36 pp.

DOWSON, John. A CLASSICAL DICTIONARY OF HINDU MYTHOLOGY AND RELIGION, Geography, History, and Literature. London, Trübner's "Oriental Series," 1879. 1 vol.

DUNCKER, Max. Geschichte des Alterthums, vol. III.: DIE ARIER AM INDUS UND GANGES. Leipzig, 1879.

EGGELING, Julius. THE ŚATAPATHA-BRÂHMANA, according to the text of the Mâdhyandina School. Part I., Books I. and II. (Vol. XII. of the "Sacred Books of the East" Series.) Oxford, 1882. 1 vol.

GELDNER, Karl, und KAEGI, Adolf. SIEBENZIG LIEDER DES RIG-VEDA, übersetzt von; mit Beiträgen von R. Roth. Tubingen, 1875.

GELDNER UND PISCHEL. VEDISCHE STUDIEN, I. and II.

GRASSMANN, Hermann. RIG-VEDA, übersetzt. Leipzig, 1876–1877. 2 vol.

HAUG, Martin. THE AITAREYA BRAHMANAM OF THE RIG-VEDA, edited, translated, and explained. Bombay, 1863. 2 vol.

HEWITT, J. F. NOTES ON THE EARLY HISTORY OF NORTHERN INDIA, *Journal of the Royal Asiatic Society*, 1888 and 1889.

HILLEBRANDT, Alfred. UEBER DIE GÖTTIN ADITI (vorwiegend im Rig-Veda). Breslau, 1876. 51 pp.

———VARUNA UND MITRA, ein Beitrag Zur Exegese des Veda. Breslau, 1877. 159 pp.

———VEDISCHE MYTHOLOGIE. Erster Band. Breslau, 1891.

HUNTER, W. W. THE INDIAN EMPIRE: Its people, history, and products. Second edition. London, 1886. 1 vol.

JONES, Sir William. INSTITUTES OF HINDU LAW; or, THE ORDINANCES OF MENU. Edition of 1869, London. 1 vol.

KAEGI, Adolf. THE RIG-VEDA, the Oldest Literature of the Indians. (Translated by R. ARROWSMITH, with additions to the Notes.) Boston, 1886. 1 vol.

KUHN, Adalbert. MYTHOLOGISCHE STUDIEN. First vol.: DIE HERABKUNFT DES FEUERS UND DES GÖTTERTRANKES. Gütersloh, 1886. (Second edition.)

LASSEN, Christian. INDISCHE ALTERTHUMSKUNDE. London, 1866–1874. 2 vol. (Second edition.)

LEFMANN, Dr. S. GESCHICHTE DES ALTEN INDIENS. (Oncken's Series "Allgemeine Geschichte in Einzeldarstellungen.") Berlin, 1880.

LUDWIG, Alfred. DIE NACHRICHTEN DES RIG- UND ATHARVA-VEDA ÜBER GEOGRAPHIE, GESCHICHTE, VERFASSUNG DES ALTEN INDIENS. (Abhandlungen der kön.-böhmisch. Gesellsch. der Wissensch. VI. Folge, 8 Band.) Prag, 1875. 58 pp.

———DIE PHILOSOPHISCHEN UND RELIGIÖSEN ANSCHAUUNGEN DES VEDA in ihrer Entwickelung. Prag, 1875. 58 pp.

——DER RIGVEDA, oder die heiligen Hymnen der Brâhmana. Prag, 1878. 5 vol.

MUIR, J. ORIGINAL SANSKRIT TEXTS on the Origin and History of the People of India, their Religion and Institutions. Second edition. Paris, 1872–1884. 5 vol.

MÜLLER, F. Max. ANCIENT SANSKRIT LITERATURE, A History of. London, 1859. 1 vol.

——SCIENCE OF RELIGION, Introduction to the. London, 1873. 1 vol.

——SCIENCE OF LANGUAGE, Lectures on the. New York, 1875. (From the second London edition, revised.) 2 vol.

——CHIPS FROM A GERMAN WORKSHOP, vol. I. and II. New York edition, 1876.

——ORIGIN AND GROWTH OF RELIGION, Lectures on the; as illustrated by the Religions of India. (Hibbert Lectures for 1878.) 1 vol.

——BIOGRAPHIES OF WORDS AND THE HOME OF THE ÂRYAS. London, 1888. 1 vol.

——INDIA, WHAT CAN IT TEACH US? New edition. London, 1892. 1 vol.

MYRIANTHEUS, Dr. L. DIE AÇVINS, oder Arischen Dioskuren. München, 1876. 185 pp.

OLDENBERG, Hermann. The GRIHYA-SÛTRAS, Rules of Vedic Domestic Ceremonies, Part I. ("Sacred Books of the East" Series, vol. XXIX.) Oxford, 1887. 1 vol.

PERRY, Edward Delavan (of Columbia College). INDRA IN THE RIG-VEDA. (*Journ. of the Amer. Or. Soc.*, 1880.) 92 pp.

ROTH, Rudolph. ZUR LITTERATUR UND GESCHICHTE DES WEDA. Stuttgart, 1846. 148 pp.

SCHERMAN, Dr. Lucian. PHILOSOPHISCHE HYMNEN AUS DER RIG- UND ATHARVA-VEDA-SANHITÂ verglichen mit den Philosophemen der älteren Upanishads. Strassburg and London, 1887. 96 pages.

SCHROEDER, Dr. Leopold v. INDIENS LITERATUR UND KULTUR in historischer Entwicklung. Leipzig, 1887. 1 vol. (Popular.)

ST. MARTIN, Vivien de. ÉTUDE SUR LA GÉOGRAPHIE DU VÉDA. Paris, 1860. 1 vol.

WALLIS, H. W. THE COSMOGONY OF THE RIG-VEDA. London, 1887. 1 vol.

WEBER, Albrecht. HISTORY OF INDIAN LITERATURE. London, 1878. 1 vol.

——INDISCHE SKIZZEN. Vier bisher in Zeitschriften Zerstreute Vorträge und Abhandlungen. Berlin, 1857.

——INDISCHE STREIFEN; Kritisch-Bibliographische, auf dem Gebiete der Indischen Philologie, seit dem Jahre 1849.

WESTERGAARD, N. L. UEBER DEN ÄLTESTEN ZEITRAUM DER INDISCHEN GESCHICHTE, mit Rücksicht auf die Litteratur. Breslau, 1862. 93 pp.

WILLIAMS, Monier. RELIGIOUS THOUGHT AND LIFE IN INDIA. London, 1883.

——INDIAN WISDOM. 1 vol. Third edition. London, 1876.

WILSON, Horace Hayman. SELECT SPECIMENS OF THE THEATRE OF THE HINDUS. London, 1871. 2 vol.

WURM, Paul, GESCHICHTE DER INDISCHEN RELIGION, im Umriss dargestelt. Basel, 1874. 1 vol. (Popular.)

ZIMMER, Heinrich. ALTINDISCHES LEBEN; die Cultur der Vedischen Arier nach den Saṃhitâ dargestellt. Berlin, 1879. 1 vol.

Numerous pamphlets and essays in the *Zeitschrift der Deutschen Morgenländischen Gesellschaft*, the *Journal of the Royal Asiatic Society*, the *Proceedings* and *Journal* of the *American Oriental Society*, the *Victoria Institute*, and other special periodicals, and the *Encyclopædia Britannica*. Also works and papers bearing on the subject more or less remotely, and such as would not be of much use to students. The works and sources which, though consulted, are to be used specially in connection with the next following volume on Brahmanic India, are not mentioned here.

Oldenberg's new book, *Die Religion des Veda*, Berlin, 1894, was not received in New York in time to be utilized in the present volume.

Z. A. R.

INDEX.

B

N

P

S

The Story of the Nations.

MESSRS. G. P. PUTNAM'S SONS take pleasure in announcing that they have in course of publication, in co-operation with Mr. T. Fisher Unwin, of London, a series of historical studies, intended to present in a graphic manner the stories of the different nations that have attained prominence in history.

In the story form the current of each national life is distinctly indicated, and its picturesque and noteworthy periods and episodes are presented for the reader in their philosophical relation to each other as well as to universal history.

It is the plan of the writers of the different volumes to enter into the real life of the peoples, and to bring them before the reader as they actually lived, labored, and struggled—as they studied and wrote, and as they amused themselves. In carrying out this plan, the myths, with which the history of all lands begins, will not be overlooked, though these will be carefully distinguished from the actual history, so far as the labors of the accepted historical authorities have resulted in definite conclusions.

The subjects of the different volumes have been planned to cover connecting and, as far as possible, consecutive epochs or periods, so that the set when completed will present in a comprehensive narrative the chief events in the great STORY OF THE NATIONS; but it is, of course, not always practicable to issue the several volumes in their chronological order.

Heroes of the Nations.

EDITED BY

EVELYN ABBOTT, M.A.,

FELLOW OF BALLIOL COLLEGE, OXFORD.

A SERIES of biographical studies of the lives and work of a number of representative historical characters about whom have gathered the great traditions of the Nations to which they belonged, and who have been accepted, in many instances, as types of the several National ideals. With the life of each typical character will be presented a picture of the National conditions surrounding him during his career.

The narratives are the work of writers who are recognized authorities on their several subjects, and, while thoroughly trustworthy as history, will present picturesque and dramatic "stories" of the Men and of the events connected with them.

To the Life of each "Hero" will be given one duodecimo volume, handsomely printed in large type, provided with maps and adequately illustrated according to the special requirements of the several subjects. The volumes will be sold separately as follows:

Large 12°, cloth extra	$1 50
Half morocco, uncut edges, gilt top . . .	1 75

HEROES OF THE NATIONS.

Nelson, and the Naval Supremacy of England. By W. CLARK RUSSELL, author of "The Wreck of the Grosvenor," etc.

Gustavus Adolphus, and the Struggle of Protestantism for Existence. By C. R. L. FLETCHER, M.A., late Fellow of All Souls' College.

Pericles, and the Golden Age of Athens. By EVELYN ABBOTT, M.A.

Theodoric the Goth, the Barbarian Champion of Civilisation. By THOMAS HODGKIN, author of "Italy and Her Invaders," etc.

Sir Philip Sidney, and the Chivalry of England. By H. R. FOX-BOURNE, author of "The Life of John Locke," etc.

Julius Cæsar, and the Organisation of the Roman Empire. By W. WARD FOWLER, M.A., Fellow of Lincoln College, Oxford.

John Wyclif, Last of the Schoolmen, and First of the English Reformers. By LEWIS SERGEANT, author of "New Greece," etc.

Napoleon, Warrior and Ruler, and the Military Supremacy of Revolutionary France. By W. O'CONNOR MORRIS.

Henry of Navarre, and the Huguenots of France. By P. F. WILLERT, M.A., Fellow of Exeter College, Oxford.

Cicero, and the Fall of the Roman Republic. By J. L. STRACHAN-DAVIDSON, M.A., Fellow of Balliol College, Oxford.

Abraham Lincoln, and the Downfall of American Slavery. By NOAH BROOKS.

Prince Henry (of Portugal) the Navigator, and the Age of Discovery. By C. R. BEAZLEY, Fellow of Merton College, Oxford.

Julian the Philosopher, and the Last Struggle of Paganism against Christianity. By ALICE GARDNER.

Louis XIV., and the Zenith of the French Monarchy. By ARTHUR HASSALL, M.A., Senior Student of Christ Church College, Oxford.

Charles XII., and the Collapse of the Swedish Empire, 1682-1719. By R. NISBET BAIN.

Lorenzo de' Medici, and Florence in the 15th Century. By EDWARD ARMSTRONG, M.A., Fellow of Queen's College, Oxford.

Jeanne d'Arc. Her Life and Death. By Mrs. OLIPHANT.

Christopher Columbus. His Life and Voyages. By WASHINGTON IRVING.

Robert the Bruce, and the Struggle for Scottish Independence. By Sir HERBERT MAXWELL, M.P.

Hannibal, Soldier, Statesman, Patriot; and the Crisis of the Struggle between Carthage and Rome. By W. O'CONNOR MORRIS, Sometime Scholar of Oriel College, Oxford.

Ulysses S. Grant, and the Period of National Preservation and Reconstruction, 1822-1885. By Lieut.-Col. WILLIAM CONANT CHURCH.

Robert E. Lee, and the Southern Confederacy, 1807-1870. By Prof. HENRY ALEXANDER WHITE, of the Washington and Lee University.

The Cid Campeador, and the Waning of the Crescent in the West. By H. BUTLER CLARKE, Fellow of St. John's College, Oxford.

Saladin, and the Fall of the Kingdom of Jerusalem. By STANLEY LANE-POOLE author of "The Moors in Spain," etc.

Bismarck, and the New German Empire. How it Arose and What it Displaced. By W. J. HEADLAM, M.A., Fellow of King's College.

To be followed by:

Moltke, and the Military Supremacy of Germany. By SPENCER WILKINSON, London University.

Judas Maccabæus, the Conflict between Hellenism and Hebraism. By ISRAEL ABRAHAMS, author of "The Jews of the Middle Ages."
